偉龍夜冷百貨
偉龍工程
信昌
水喉五金
DAIKIN
ESSO

wanchai
coastline

新昌工業大廈
TL 1389

灝 東
LD 3766
MM 5692

BZ 33

雪梨汁 19 番茄汁 19
石榴汁 19 特飲系列
木瓜汁 19
火龍果汁 19
甘蔗汁 19
益力多系列
瘦身系列
蘋果益力多
SALE
$ 23
任何果汁配
Papaya

投票站 入口
請前往 三多里

維修工程進行中
Works In Progress
維修工程進行中
Works In Progress
JUDICIARY
終審法院
JACKSON ROAD
PUBLIC ENTRANCE
YOU ARE HERE

HSBC

Applied Research & Design Publishing

Curb-scale

Sony Devabhaktuni

Hong Kong

Infrastructures of the street

[SAR]

CURB-SCALE
HONG KONG

CONTENTS

Acknowledgments 17
Introduction 19

Narratives of Infrastructure 27

5 HONG KONG STREETS
Queen's Road West 51
Queen's Road Central 61
Queen's Road East 71
Castle Peak Road 81
Pound Lane 103

Infrastructures of Protest 113

INDEX 137

Street Drawing 189

Abbreviations 208
Works Cited 209
Colophon 215

ACKNOWLEDGMENTS

Work on this project involved many hands. Most recently, Fan Xinkai and Soo Kwan Yau April went over the drawings a final time for the preparation of the book. Sze-To Wai Lam Linda also helped with this work. There is never a right moment to stop, as each layer of additional information, and each trip back to the street, reveals what has been missed, changed, or removed. In finalizing the work, I hope the drawings suggest the possibility of their own continuing. And also that the gap between them (as descriptions) and the world, is experienced not as a distance, but as a thickness that occludes and makes uncertain one mirrored reality from another.

Before thinking about a book, I worked with a number of research assistants who tested ways to film, photograph, and draw the streets, and ways to order and organize what became the index. Their work was invaluable: Chan Shu Man Amanda, Chen Chieh-Hsuan Jasmy, Cheung Hoi Ching Minia, Choi Chung Hei Vincent, Lai Shu Fun Kevin, Li Xuechen Sigo, Ng Tsing Yin Provides, and Zhu Jiqi Tod were all part of this effort.

Leung Sin Tone Cynthia assisted early on to prepare materials for the symposium and exhibition “Urban Inventories: Documentation as Design Project,” organized by Carole Lévesque and Thomas-Bernard Kenniff at the Université du Québec à Montreal in March 2019.

The Department of Architecture at the University of Hong Kong provided financial support for research assistants. The department’s fund for design research publications helped to cover a printing subvention. My thanks also to Gordon Goff and Jake Anderson at Applied Research and Design, who supported the project through its long, sometimes uncertain, development.

Manuela Dechamps Otamendi worked on the graphic design of the book. It is our third collaboration, and I am grateful for the attention and thought she brings to her work (and for her patience and fierce commitment). My colleagues at HKU, Cole Roskam and Eunice Seng, encouraged and supported the work in everyday ways. Joanna Mansbridge pointed me in directions I would otherwise not have turned; our conversations about Hong Kong and our writing collaborations have been central to my life here. Min Kyung Lee is one of the first and last people I spoke to about the curb-scale. She has been an influence on the project in important ways. For all of their contributions, the book’s omissions and miscues are my own.

I'd like to thank my parents for their support.
Guillaume and Raffaella for their friendship.
And my students in Hong Kong for sharing small parts of their lives with me.

INTRODUCTION

This is a book about the streets of Hong Kong, a claim might give pause as the street is vast as a subject, as is Hong Kong. For this reason, I'd like to start by saying what the book is not. This book about Hong Kong's streets is not a physical guidebook. It won't help you get around the city. It is not a history of Hong Kong's physical development; nor does it offer an accounting of the communities that are at home here. Some books tell these stories well, describing Hong Kong's contradictions in ways that have been important to my own approach. By approach, I mean arrival and the way one only just begins to be a part of a place: a turning toward that is part of beginning from outside. [1] What this book also is not, is a manual for urban design. In more or less direct ways, architects and urbanists have offered thoughts on how to make cities better and make better streets. Some of their concerns are my own, but I am skeptical of those kinds of lessons.

What this book does, is use drawing and writing to put together an idea about the street as an infrastructure. Hong Kong brought on questions that shaped this idea and was the ground for its development. The kind of infrastructure that I am interested in is made legible through the "curb-scale." This scale of looking makes it possible to consider the street and infrastructure in a different way. This difference counters architectural descriptions of Hong Kong that arise from arguments about a global, postmodern space: as flattened, depthless, continuous, and smooth. This reading was seductive in its totalizing and exotic characterization of changes wrought by consumption, congestion, and capital markets—Hong Kong being an exemplar. Yet it is also unsatisfying: viscerally, experientially, and conceptually. While discourses of globalization that posit an end to history or a flattened world have lost credibility, architecture continues to traffic in their corollary imaginations. They are a-hard-to-scrub residue, a hangover that stays into the night after the night before: an architecture of introverted, conditioned, groundless spaces and abstracted individuals whose dreams register in multiple languages all spelled in the symbols of currency. What has become difficult to distinguish is if that spatial malaise was a description of architecture and cities

1 Two books I return to are Ackbar Abbas's *Hong Kong: Culture and Politics of Disappearance* and Dung Kai-cheung's *Atlas: The Archaeology of an Imaginary City*. These works remain relevant to changes taking place in Hong Kong despite having been written 25 and 20 years ago, respectively. That both allude in different ways to a city that is no longer there, speaks to concerns for Hong Kong's future.

as they are, as they would undoubtedly continue to become (with our complicit resignation), or as we hoped them to be.

But the long 20th century is finally coming to an end, with authoritarian creep and the paroxysms of pandemic and climate making obliviousness untenable. The ironic sheen of a hands-off, distant, matter-of-fact coolness has little appeal faced with civilizational crisis. But the closing of the 20th century has not arrived "pointing towards" somewhere. [2] Instead, it deflated with the emptying of easy oppositions: local and global, rural and urban, home and work—ways of ordering the world and thinking about cities and architecture that no longer hold up.

What remained of such oppositions along with imaginations of the global city and its accessorial architectural tropes fell apart in those weeks confined in corners of rooms housing home offices. Covid emptied out places of encounter: sites where we meet and go to each other. It reflected back empty spaces on the mirrored surfaces of clipped-on cladding and vacated cities with an air of exhaustion (even if for moments that air was crystal clear). The misfortune of being alone in such spaces hollows out sense where there should be *anything*, calling into question the architectural production of these past decades. Rather than a *pointing towards*, the cultural theorist Lauren Berlant argued that we are in a period of transition that she calls "the long middle of change." This recognition comes first from acknowledging the "brokenness" of the current situation, and in engaging in an unlearning that provides "figures and propositional means" to muddle through what is an unfamiliar interval of uncertainty: more uncharted somehow than the "planes of transcendental consistency or revolutionary breaks that promise new beginnings." [3] What is most difficult then, is to accept that what comes after is not something, but this thing, and the struggles to see anew the sites, people, and cities around us that constitute our homes and our public home.

It is in this context that this book—about Hong Kong, about the street, and about earlier ways of thinking (imagining) that seemed to get in the way—came to be. Those lingering visions of 20th-century urban space bracket subjectivity with the expectation of certain ways of being:

2 Roberto Mangabeira Unger's interventions at architectural forums in the early 1990s, when he was dean of the Harvard Law School, led to the articulation of a social program for architecture that included this notion of a "pointing towards." See Roberto Mangabeira Unger, "The Better Futures of Architecture," in *Anyone*, ed. Cynthia Davidson (New York: Rizzoli, 1991), 28–37.

3 See Lauren Berlant, "Sex in the Event of Happiness," Feminist Theory Workshop, Duke University, March 22–23, 2019, https://youtu.be/h7X6j0af7Bo.

as listlessly conditioned as the air. This forecloses the possibility of the political and diminishes the uncertain, contingent, and yet-to-come nature of the future. [4] Upholding this uncertainty and openness becomes, in the context of transition to something that is yet to be, the only productive and bearable attitude.

Curb-scale Hong Kong makes place for another imagination of the city. This imagination asserts the relevance of the street as a site of affective charge where the political is possible. It does this by thinking of the street as an infrastructure, and by thinking of infrastructure differently. The spatial and political turmoil of Hong Kong's recent past subverted spatial qualities that are familiar to us through postmodern readings of the city: interiorization, privatization, and the continuity of linked circulations. These spatial qualities were figured in relation to the city's presumed role as a global conduit for capital flows. But at the same time, these events also suggested that such a reading failed in its capacity to account for the ways in which the street and the ground itself became a contested site. In order to recognize this ground, a different way of thinking about the street as an infrastructure can help to realign our imaginations of the urban space of Hong Kong. This, in turn, points the city toward the possibility of lives and futures that are open. I am not proposing that the forces of commercialization and spatial homogenization are negligible, nor that they did not play a role in recent contestation. Only that they are not all. And that to treat them as all is to fail to recognize the multiple and contradictory natures of a city where a financialized economy that orients the articulation of space was thwarted by a ground that perdures. The street lasts as a trace of the long and recent past, undone and reassembled in ways that assert a yet-to-come.

The curb-scale counters descriptions of the street that reduce its physical reality to topology or network. Tools of calculation and representation oriented in that sense slip easily between domains of engineering and traffic science. They rehearse the objectivity, distance, and an abstracted analytical frame of a quasi-scientific regard, while exhausting the possibility that there could be other ways to describe the street's material reality. Architecture has been left largely at a loss between latching on to such descriptions or finding alternative engagements with the street: through readings of its social, informal, or programmatic happenings.

The curb-scale describes the street's physical

4 On keeping the future open, see Doreen B. Massey, *For Space* (London: Sage, 2005).

reality as an overlap of elements. These elements come apart and are put back together in a constant instantiation, informed by political, economic, social, and material considerations; by people who clean, maintain, repair, modify, and alter the street instructed by chains of command and pages-long .pdfs of drawing standards and guidance notes. By elements, I mean: the drain that catches the work glove or the smooth stick of wood; the curb that swerves to make place for the access hatch; the unloosened railing. These things comprise a curb-scale of infrastructure that not only conducts, channels, and prescribes the movement of information and energy that make the city possible, but also are part of a larger field of affective registers that constitute the city as an ambivalent site of attention.

The book describes these infrastructures through drawings and text. Where practices of mapping make visible economic, social, temporal, and material forces that undergird the functioning of ecosystems, cities, regions, or territories, the drawings of the curb-scale make visible what is already present at hand in the street at our feet. The street's elements appear in the drawings as constellations of decision, error, and contradiction that function in ad hoc and planned movements aligned with administration, maintenance, and policy. In this making visible of what is always and already before us, there is also an attending-to that opens up larger questions about the logics that make things how they are and the decisions that comprise the public realm as it is: multiple, overlapping, incoherent, and irreconcilable agencies, affects, and allegiances. By attending to them, we can begin to touch upon the affective pull that a city has—of the drain and curb and guardrail. This tug also founds the possibility of the city acting as a world between others, and the political engagement that this necessarily entails. This imagination builds on contemporary discourses that question what infrastructure is: the kind of life it sustains. And the ways we act reciprocally to care for the processes that it makes possible. This counts as well for design, where an understanding of the curb-scale becomes a requisite knowledge for attending to the networks of infrastructural relations that any intervention becomes a part of.

The book is divided into sections that are graphically distinct, but interwoven in ways that allow for readings forward or backward. Longer-form essays situate the shorter texts and drawings in between. The essays stake out a conceptual terrain for the curb-scale while the

drawings and short texts act as demonstrations. Part one looks at the stories we tell about infrastructures. I argue that infrastructural narratives have been powerful in their influence over Hong Kong's political economy, and in the way some contemporary architectural and urban discourse describes its urban spaces. The second part looks at the way the 2019 protests arrested infrastructural movement and asserted the street as a ground of contestation. [5] Those events reinforce the curb-scale as a way of conceiving infrastructure and describing the street, both literally through drawing and in terms of the stakes it sets out for city life together.

I take up this issue of drawing in part three by looking more closely at the way streets are drawn. Typical sections, standard drawings, circulation diagrams, and street manuals reflect a rationalization and codification of the street as a discrete object of technical management. I look specifically at Pierre Patte's celebrated section and the lesser-known plan that accompanies it. These drawings comprise—already three centuries ago—two alternatives for thinking about the street either as a reproducible technical instant or a ground of simultaneous and entangled relations. In contrast to well-known publications on the street from the last fifty years that comprise largely European examples, I turn as well to recent projects of drawing the public realm in Hong Kong to consider their different attitudes toward the street. These different examples situate drawing at the curb-scale, foregrounding the way it describes the street as an infrastructure (of infrastructures) and renders legible a relational ground. Finally, I argue that the curb-scale functions in a relationship to abstraction that views its power not only as a capacity to leave things out, and to isolate, distance, and objectify, but also to render the liveliness and mess of things as they are through an effort of drawing everything. The value of drawing things "as they are" lies exactly in its very impossibility and the choices, deliberation, and care that goes into such a process.

The drawings comprise five continuous stretches of Hong Kong streets and an index of their elements. Both sets of drawings are accompanied by texts that do their own kind of work. The index names, identifies, and separates, while describing how each element is a coming together

5 The Anti-Extradition Law Amendment Bill Movement began in March of 2019, and continued into 2020, despite the amendment's withdrawal in September 2019. I refer to the protests as the "2019 protests" throughout.

of rules, administrations, processes, protocols, and errors that are themselves inscribed by social, political, economic, and material relations. These forces flow through the elements of the street under our feet, giving them a charge that ultimately provides the pull of the city. The task was not to synthesize that complexity but instead to question whether it was possible at all to begin to touch upon it immediately without losing the messiness of city-ness.

The texts that open each street try to describe what was made sensible in the world that was drawn: what the curb-scale made legible as a reading or potential. What became accessible through the *attending-to* that drawing demands; and perhaps also, in a more inchoate and unformed way, becomes legible to the reader who partakes in them. I was influenced by George Simmel's essay "Bridge and Door" about the relation between connection and separation, about the simultaneous movement that makes connecting and separating possible in human cognition, at the same time that the physical world proscribes their union. [6] Simmel's essay ultimately is about the nature of relationality and how we make sense of our encounter with the world, and the things that comprise it. We could describe this also as the "thrown togetherness" of a place, the pushing and pulling of things coming and going (into being) that each have their own gravitational charge, at once holding elements together while allowing their free articulation. [7]

I'd like here also to speak about beginnings and endings that were important: beginnings that led to the material gathered together, and endings that open toward questions I hope the curb-scale makes possible. I began looking at Hong Kong's streets four years ago, in the spring of 2018. My colleague in the department of architecture at the University of Hong Kong, Wang Weijen, invited me to join a study he was leading on the redevelopment of the Cheung Sha Wan neighborhood in northern Kowloon. I told Weijen that I wanted to make drawings of the street, and he immediately supported this perhaps odd intuition. Vernon Chang and Alana Tam worked with me that summer to draw Castle Peak Road and Cheung Shun Street, and they also prepared a catalog of elements.

6 Georg Simmel, "Bridge and Door," *Theory, Culture & Society* 11, no. 1 (1994), https://doi.org/10.1177/026327694011001002, https://journals.sagepub.com/doi/abs/10.1177/026327694011001002.

7 Massey, *For Space*, 141.

In the intervening years, the work moved from this intuition about the ground to a somewhat more systematic work. With research assistants who joined for shorter and longer periods, we mapped out administrative responsibilities in the government, looked at street design manuals from around the world, classified the city's streets, and completed drawings for eleven streets on Hong Kong Island and in Kowloon. The five streets that made their way into the book each tell a story and exemplify the curb-scale as a method of drawing and looking. I don't, however, claim that they are representative of Hong Kong or that they comprise a scientific sampling of more than 2,000 km of roadway. The diversity of Hong Kong's roads extends from new town enclaves in the New Territories, to island-village footpaths, to highway overpasses cut between and through buildings, among others. Drawing any one of these different types of street would reveal something else about Hong Kong and about the way the curb-scale functions as an infrastructure of infrastructures, conditioning life in this city.

If the curb-scale makes it difficult to look at (and think about) the street again in the same way, then so what? What does that change? I described earlier how the pandemic, climate peril, and creeping authoritarianism have brought an end to the expectation of marked ruptures or revolutionary beginnings. Each of these events has also suggested ways in which the street is perhaps the most critical space of the public realm: we could argue this in some cities both in terms of the square meters that streets occupy and their function as a place for meeting and going to others. Writing in 1974, the geographer Ronald J. Horvath described how the spread of "machine space" in the form of "streets, alleys, parking spaces, driveways, garages, gasoline stations, car washes, automobile supply stores," disoriented priorities for human settlements and redirected resources needed by people—including "people space"—toward the automobile, while at the same time leading to a "territorial alienation." [8]

Ruptures opened by Covid, protest movements taking over streets, and the ongoing, simultaneous breakdowns caused by overbuilding in the face of human-caused shifts in climate intensities, have created positive and negative urgencies to reclaim the street as a "people space." The curb-scale, I think, can be critical in terms of foregrounding the sets of priorities, decisions, and protocols that are oriented around the propagation of machine space as well

8 Ronald J. Horvath, "Machine Space," *Geographical Review* 64, no. 2 (April 1974): 167–88.

as the countervailing pull and push that the street has on our lives. These tendencies are perhaps nowhere more explicit than in Hong Kong, where machine space reveals stark inequalities, ecological mismanagement, and a prioritization of cars over people.

The curb-scale does away with a diagrammatic reduction of the street into dedicated zones for cars or for people, instead describing adjacencies, overlaps, and articulations that index negotiations between design, legislation, administration, and maintenance. The curb-scale can help us attend to this complexity and act upon it as a contested ground. The curb-scale introduces an idea of simultaneity into drawing that makes possible an engagement with time. As a site of multiple overlapping infrastructures, the street is always undergoing interventions that allow for the functioning of the city. These interventions are unfigured in our representations of street life.

The drawings acknowledge efforts that are being reproduced every day to keep the city running. These efforts are well or poorly managed, and involve labor that is structured in ways that are more or less equitable or exploitative. This way of looking at the street and the city, situating the temporal and the contingent within representation, offers possibilities for how drawing functions to design places of life and how we design them. It contributes to trans-scalar, temporally unloosened, and materially charged approaches such as mapping, climatic analysis, and narrative whose basis lies in a continual questioning of drawing as thinking about sites, cities, territories, and architecture.

I hope the book provokes other thoughts about what the curb-scale could offer. I leave the drawings uncommented, hoping that they carry with them a potential to sustain, on each page, a time and attention of looking: and more than this, that they can change a way of seeing that opens the imagination to a different sense of what the street is, both here in Hong Kong, and elsewhere.

Narratives of Infrastructure

NARRATIVES OF INFRASTRUCTURE

> *There are real reasons to be attentive to thought's imagination.*
> —Doreen Massey, *For Space*

The curb-scale loosens infrastructure from abstractions of systems and expectations of scale. It makes the street legible as a configuration of elements ordered by rules and decisions: underfoot, overhead, at our fingertips. This ordering is enacted in policy supported by technical consultations and executed through chains of command linked by protocols. The curb-scale is a relation between matter and life, between lives. It performs the street—conditioning some ways of moving, orienting, and assembling while prohibiting others. It has a command over how we occupy the city. It figures subjectivity through this address. The curb-scale is a way of imagining the street as an infrastructure of infrastructures. The drawings in this book support these claims. In the texts, I look to others who set themselves the task of grasping infrastructure's ontology: as a spatial agent, as life-sustaining movement, as the city; or as a concept whose stabilization has yet to be enforced, still up in the air.

BELOW AND AFTERWARDS

The *Oxford English Dictionary* traces "infrastructure" to late-19th-century France. "*Infra-*," meaning below, describes a spatial underneath that makes possible what comes afterwards. The word appears at least twenty times in 1875 in the *Journal Officiel de la République Française,* the daily record of government proceedings. The word's very utterance is at first excused in the halls of government as an uncouth borrowing from engineers, but recurs in discussions about funding for France's growing rail system. [1] In the National Assembly on December 3, the government's representative Paul Léon Acloque describes infrastructure as "*la partie aléatoire*" of rail construction: work that has some inherent uncertainty, including "the purchasing of land, engineering and earthworks." [2] "Infrastructure" makes terrains viable for later private investments that are "easy to evaluate": this easy

1. Assemblée Nationale, "Seance du jeudi 2 décembre 1875," *Journal officiel de la République française* (Paris), December 3, 1875, 9959, https://gallica.bnf.fr/ark:/12148/bpt6k62103230.

2. Assemblée Nationale, "Seance du vendredi 3 décembre 1875," *Journal officiel de la République française* (Paris), December 4, 1875, 9984, https://gallica.bnf.fr/ark:/12148/bpt6k6210324d. The complete text reads: « En 1842, le Gouvernement avait compris qu'il devait venir en aide aux compagnies et prendre à sa charge la partie aléatoire des chemins de fer, c'est-à-dire — et ici je me vois forcé de me servir

d'un terme que l'honorable M. Clapier qualifiait de barbare,—l'infrastructure, comprenant l'acquisition des terrains, les terrassements et les travaux d'art, laissant aux compagnies les dépenses faciles à évaluer, d'après des devis certains, telles que la pose de la voie et les constructions. » [In 1842, the government understood that it had to come to the aid of [rail] companies and take on the incidental costs of rail construction, meaning—and here I find myself using a term that the honorable Mr. Clapier qualified as uncouth—infrastructure, comprising the purchasing of land, earth, and engineering works, that leave the rail companies, costs that are easy to evaluate with estimates that are more or less certain, such as the installation of the tracks and buildings.]

3. Annalisa Meyboom, "Infrastructure as Practice," *Journal of Architectural Education* 62, no. 4 (2009): 72, http://www.jstor.org/stable/40481065.

to evaluate "superstructure," includes the tracks themselves and adjacent buildings of rail companies.

Superstructure—the private investment made possible by the government's infrastructural work—is therefore contingent on the state's "acquisition of lands," speaking to the imbrication of private finance and public authority in infrastructure's earliest articulation. That this rail network served an important military function pulls tight this knotted relation: capital, land, bureaucracy, and material leveraged to prioritize and allot the movement of resources.

An understanding of infrastructure as a "below," a kind of structuring underneath, makes its way through the engineering disciplines, remaining largely unchanged from the word's earliest use. While the literal sense of underneath would disappear so that infrastructure could be all around, what remained was a sense of infrastructure as something that supports, subtends, and makes other things possible. In *infra-* there is also a "further below on the page" that points to a temporal relation of *afterwards*. This suggests the way infrastructure comes first, and makes things possible in the future. Despite these relatively stable meanings, architecture's infrastructural turn is marked by questions about what exactly infrastructure *is*.

In her 2009 essay, "Infrastructure as Practice," Annalisa Meyboom first looks to a *Merriam-Webster* dictionary definition to find an answer: "Infrastructure can generally be defined as an underlying foundation or basic framework of a system." [3] As a "foundation," infrastructure is engineered, fabricated, and situated in the earth. As a "basic framework," it is abstracted into "a system" and conceived as a topology liberated from any specific material emplacement. This state—between built material emplacement and abstracted system—informs our imagination. We understand that infrastructure is often both things at once, holding both qualities in place. Often, it is that double quality of system and emplacement that generates a slight tug of feeling when we confront an infrastructural element in the world; an awe that relates to knowing that what is visible to us—a pylon, a rail bridge, train tracks—is one part of a larger network that extends into and across the earth. Meyboom concludes from her reading of the definition that infrastructure is "essentially that which supports and facilitates human activity." [4] The nature of these activities has become more complex with increased mobility, advances in technology, and the development of cities. As abstract systems become interdependent and virtualized, their infrastructural emplacements are at once increasingly sequestered and ever-present. As mobilities implicate greater distances and speeds, their spatial impact on living together becomes more predominant. Infrastructure no longer brings to mind an out-of-sight underneath, but rather the immediate and pervasive facilitation of collective life that expands to encompass and connect.

Infrastructure's role in determining the physical scale of projects, the impact of these projects on wider regions and communities, and the need for closer collaboration with technical professions has meant that it has moved to the center of architectural concerns. Narratives that foreground connection, mobility, landscape, and territory have reoriented architecture's purview and impact. Works like *The MESH Book: Landscape/Infrastructure* and *The Landscape of Contemporary Infrastructure* sought in different ways to situate this turn. [5] The former contends that infrastructure brings different built environment disciplines into relation in ways that pose new challenges and call for more robust theory. The latter tackles architectural bigness with an approach to ordering and identifying strategies that drive design. Brian Hayes's *Infrastructure: A Field Guide to the Industrial Landscape* brought infrastructure into the popular imagination with photographs that made networks, systems, and processes *visible*: seeing what was already there. [6] In these works, infrastructure is linked to engineered and technical competence; it undergirds the movements necessary for human settlements and is a medium that supports exchanges.

In his essay "Landscape as Infrastructure," also from 2009, Pierre Bélanger expanded architectural understandings of infrastructure to include the role that the biophysical landscape plays in sustaining human activities.

4. Ibid.
5. Julian Raxworthy and Jessica Blood, *The MESH Book: landscape/infrastructure* (Melbourne: RMIT Publications, 2004); Kelly Shannon and Marcel Smets, *The Landscape of Contemporary Infrastructure* (Rotterdam: nai010, 2010).
6. Brian Hayes, *Infrastructure: A Field Guide to the Industrial Landscape* (New York: W. W. Norton, 2005).

7. Pierre Bélanger, "Landscape as Infrastructure," *Landscape Journal* 28, no. 1 (2009), 80.

8. Ibid., 83.

Bélanger's essay opened imaginations of infrastructure from "singular, specialized or technocratic disciplines such as civil engineering or urban planning" toward a "decentralized" conception of infrastructural operations. [7] This switched out readings of infrastructure as an autonomous, monofunctional system, with an understanding of intertwined processes. Importantly, these processes linked human and nonhuman actors, and the underneath-ness of "infra" supported ecologies. The impact of infrastructure on these ecologies may be planned and controlled, or entirely accidental; this impact can be more or less exploitative and extractive, but nevertheless transfers life-forces for human ends. This change in thinking transforms landscape itself into a vital, sustaining ground that is in a constant process of change. Importantly for practices of design, Bélanger foregrounds how "clandestine, accidental, temporary field-operations such as excavation, demolition, de-engineering, dredging, backhauling, backfilling and storage" interact with ecological processes and systems —either by design or through an opening toward the unexpected. [8] It is this opening which also begins to suggest that infrastructure is not simply a stable ground passively facilitating life, but a medium transformed by the very processes it supports. This way of thinking about infrastructure—as itself in movement—transforms it from a fixed, nominative term linked to a stable underneath, toward a more open concept whose very putting together and deployment is the start of a work that can be done.

MATTERS, CONDITIONS, AND FORMS

Midway through Leos Carax's *Les Amants du Pont-Neuf* (1991), the two protagonists of the film wake from a drunken evening to find themselves reduced to the size of rats. The Parisian bridge of the movie's title is hardly recognizable: instead, the curb towers above and the cobblestones are a vast, mineral *plage* that rises to form a horizon. At the time of its production, *Les Amants du Pont-Neuf* was the most expensive French film ever made. Carax reconstructed the bridge and its surroundings in southern France after permissions to film in central Paris expired.

One critic, writing shortly after the film's release, described the scene in the gutter as a surreal expressionism, with Paris turned into a plaything: "a gigantic whirling and humming toy, mysterious and luminous." [9] The film is full of infrastructural wonder. The Metro, the Seine, streets, and *passages* become a *parcours* of the main characters' desperation and love—the sheer depravity of their affection for each other matched only by their extreme attachments to the city. The two characters are in an emotional push and pull with the urban environment, appropriating these spaces inappropriately—running, screaming, kicking, in joyous and raucous visceralizations of a city space that is coded, ruled, and ordered.

In the moment they find themselves scaled down, the curb, gutter, sidewalk, and carriageway become the enclosure of the city itself. Their joy and insouciance suggest a new world to explore and terrorize. As rats in the gutter, their bodies slip into the possibility of seeing things anew. There is both a sense of looking again at the city, of reentering into a relation with its spaces, places, and things, and of breaking apart the codes that habitually hold them in place. When they wake up amongst the detritus of the gutter, there is a world.

The scene recalls the opening of Jane Bennett's book *Vibrant Matter*—a study of our relationship to *things*—where the author describes debris caught in a storm drain in Baltimore. This moment for Bennet is the beginning of a new awareness and the start of what would become an intellectual project to consider and attend to the thing-world. What she sees are:

> one large men's black plastic work glove
> one dense mat of oak pollen
> one unblemished dead rat
> one white plastic bottle cap
> one smooth stick of wood [10]

Bennett argues for a vitality of things. This vitality begins with matter, and the way this matter pulls affectively and calls to attention by the force of interpellation. Things, in her reckoning, have tendencies and potentials—to act toward each other, toward us, or toward the nonhuman—that are liberated from our centeredness or intention. They are a life-world that is inextricably caught up in our own, such that the thought

9. Jonathan Rosenbaum, "The Problem with Poetry: Leos Carax," *Film Comment* 30, no. 3 (May 1994): 16.

10. Jane Bennett, *Vibrant Matter: A Political Ecology of Things* (Durham: Duke University Press, 2010), 4.

experiment of closing one's eyes to imagine a dividing line separating the nonliving from the living becomes implausible. While Bennett is struck by the affective charge of the array of nonhuman things in the drain at the side of the road, we could consider as well their *enframing* in an infrastructure that conveyed and bracketed this bringing together. A particularly wicked storm, a surcharge of water—objects and bodies prevented by the drain's design from entering the city's tunnels.

Infrastructure brought together this tableau, while at the same time being part of that very thing-world. The anthropologist Brian Larkin proposes it this way: "Infrastructures are matter that enable the movement of other matter." [11] We can think of infrastructure as an abstracted diagram of forces, operations, and processes, but also experience it as things of and in the world. Larkin goes further to argue that infrastructures are entangled in ways that make their operations dependent on certain movements while supporting others: for example, his computer, the electricity it relies on, and the measurement it gathers to control that energy.

What do these entanglements do for and to life? Hannah Arendt's distinction between labor, work, and action in *The Human Condition* begins to answer the first part of the question. [12] As a support for "labor," infrastructure makes possible those essential functions that are immediately consumed and critical to sustaining our existence: washing, drinking, eating, brushing one's teeth. Arendt describes labor as a kind of toil that "always moves in the same circle... prescribed by the biological process of the living organism" whose end comes "only with...death." [13] Infrastructure replaces that circle of toil by allowing humans to move on to other forms of engagement, no longer bound to tracing "the same circle." For Arendt, those new engagements are what constitute the "rectilinear course of [human life's] movement" and "cut through the circular movement of biological life" making distinction possible. [14] This straight line, with beginning and end, is the diagram of mortality that informs the human condition; it is a telos that distinguishes this existence from the circular processes that dominate

11. Brian Larkin, "The Politics and Poetics of Infrastructure," *Annual Review of Anthropology* 42, no. 1 (2013): 329, doi.org/10.1146/annurev-anthro-092412-155522.
12. Hannah Arendt, *The Human Condition* (Chicago: University of Chicago Press, 1958).
13. Ibid., 97.
14. Ibid., 19.

other forms of life. For Arendt, "the mark of all laboring [is] that it leaves nothing behind, ...the result of its effort is almost as quickly consumed as the effort is spent." [15] Infrastructure supplants mark-less effort with a thing-world that reduces the time and energy that we each spend to fulfill those essential labors. Through this supplanting, human activity turns toward leaving behind more enduring traces: marks that escape consumption through work and action.

Work, the activity of hands, leaves behind a durable world of things that constitute the human artifice. This world has a potential for multiplication that contrasts with labor's cyclical repetition. [16] The work of the hands thus makes possible the accretion of a durable infrastructural world that supports human activity in its move out from the toil of labor toward other ways of being. Work can leave behind tangible reifications of thought in poetry and painting. In action people are able to engage in speculative forms of sociality that imagine new ways of being together. For action to take place in the world, the public realm must be constituted as a space of disclosure that supports the precarity of political engagement. Arendt writes that the "uncertainty not only of all political matters, but of all affairs that go on between men directly, without the intermediary, stabilizing, and solidifying influence of things" would be untenable, as the durable world between us allows for a coming together. [17] Infrastructure, as a product of the work of hands, supports people in their attempt to speak together politically. Infrastructure operates in a double motion, releasing us from the repetitive toil of labor and creating the ground for a space of appearance that is the political. Arendt's accounting of human activity casts infrastructure as both support and facilitator.

In this role, and as part of a world of things that creates conditions for human activity, infrastructure also conditions lives. Arendt argues that "men are conditioned beings because everything they come in contact with turns immediately into a condition of their existence." [18] That contact becomes a "conditioning force" and "the objectivity of the world—its object—or thing—character—and the human condition supplement each other." [19] A human place in the world "would be impossible without things, and things would be a heap of unrelated articles, a non-world, if they were not the conditioners of human existence." [20] In Jane Bennett's enumerated list of the things collected in the storm drain,

15. Ibid., 87.
16. Ibid., 141.
17. Ibid., 182.
18. Ibid., 9.
19. Ibid.
20. Ibid.

21. Larkin, "Politics and Poetics," 336.
22. Larkin turns to Roman Jakobson's description of the poetic as one of six functions present in any speech act. Larkin notes that "what distinguishes the poetic is when a speech act is organized according to the material qualities of the signifier itself rather than to its referential meaning," and proposes that for infrastructure, the "poetic mode means that form is loosened from technical function." "Politics and Poetics," 335.
23. Brian Larkin, "Promising Forms: The Political Aesthetics of Infrastructure," in *The Promise of Infrastructure*, ed. Nikhil Anand, Akhil Gupta, and Hannah Appel (Durham: Duke University Press, 2018): 175–202.
24. Larkin, "Politics and Poetics," 329.

we glimpse into and at this thing-world, the "one"-ness of each counted element, once alive and nonliving. Her enumeration of that commingled world also calls attention to an infrastructure whose conditioning of life is enacted through the movements it sustains. While Bennett is interested in locating the agencies that reside within the material of this thing-world, Arendt's assertion that things condition human existence also opens toward questions about the forms this conditioning takes.

For Larkin, thinking through an aesthetics of infrastructure can help to recognize these forms and the way they call to, or address, our lives. Infrastructures create the "ambient conditions" that subtend experience: whether that is the color of light on the street, the white noise of the nearby autoroute, the voice on the metro. These conditions operate not as representations but through embodied effects: "our sense of temperature, speed, florescence, and the ideas we have associated with those conditions." [21] This ambient experience has a poetic that points to more than its own functioning. [22] The hum of tires on asphalt, the slosh of water through gutters, or the drone of electricity traveling between pylons signals movement, but also calls on memory through the pull of sense to constitute worlds of affect and ideas. These, in turn, figure the way people relate to the city, to the future, and to each other. [23] There is also a political element to infrastructure's significations that works to "address and constitute subjects" through material, technical, administrative, functional, and political constitutions. Highways, dams, and power lines are part of nation-building projects through the protocols they engender and the allegiances, pride, or malfeasance they instantiate in and amongst citizens. A constant shifting between these political and poetic categories of infrastructure's aesthetics constitutes, for Larkin, the larger "promise" that infrastructure holds over individuals, communities, and nations. [24]

RULERS, TERMINALS, AND SOLICITORS

The thing-world of the street has its own forms. To understand them, it is necessary to consider the street as an infrastructure of infrastructures: as made up of elements rather than as an abstracted topology, system, or network. The curb-scale makes this reconsideration possible; it is a scale of close attention that foregrounds the street's political aesthetics. Through the curb-scale, it is possible to identify how the street conditions experience. This conditioning functions through elements we encounter and their forms of address.

The curb-scale's infrastructural rulers mark the ground as a terrain of differential occupation. Rulers make certain types of movement possible, while halting others. For people with reduced mobility, these differences can operate differentially, stopping a trajectory in ways where others may not be impeded. Rulers have political effects by delimiting spaces for some. Rulers are physical materializations within the street that give orders, enact priorities, and reach into subjectivity to enforce or inflict. They become internalized as ways of being in, and being able to move through, the public realm. Rulers figure how we encounter each other as we encounter the city. They function through a logic of measure and inscribe a territory with that logic. Curbs, guardrails, markings on the road, and paving, for example, are determined by this measured logic that apportions, marks off, interdicts, and casts the street into differentially accessible territories. A lamppost is a ruler in the way its cast light is calculated as a function of lumens. The diffuse circumference marks the ground as a space that for some is comfortable passage alone in the night, or that allows cars to speed or slow through streets. Such calculations also determine the thickness of bedroom curtains, or the visibility of the stars.

The curb-scale includes terminals that manifest networks that subtend our lives, making it possible to care for our place in the city. They are the access hatches, hydrants, pipes, and drain covers that act as important nodes of control and entry. They point to the functioning of departments, policies, and maintenance workers, that often invisibly operate and maintain these systems that watch over us. When they are deployed or rupture, the latent functioning of these infrastructures is activated in ways that make legible their affective pull. Breakdowns are troubling in their revelation of the urban realm's fragility. Some writers have argued that it is only through failure that we become aware of infrastructure; others contest such a claim, citing the ways infrastructure always conditions

25. Susan Leigh Star famously argued that infrastructure "becomes visible upon breakdown" in "The Ethnography of Infrastructure," *American Behavioral Scientist* 43, no. 3 (Nov/Dec 1999), 382. Brian Larkin notes that this way of thinking about infrastructure has become "commonplace" and misses how we experience infrastructure's ambient and conditioning effects. Larkin, "Politics and Poetics," 336.

26. Ash Amin and Nigel Thrift, *Seeing Like a City* (Cambridge, UK; Boston, MA: Polity Press, 2017), 3.

our experience. [25] These infrastructural terminals exist in a liminal state of *at-ready-ness*, waiting for their guarded workings to be operated or adjusted.

The curb-scale addresses by soliciting: to touch, press, lean, or sit. This solicitation can be passive and is found in rulers and terminals—railings for support, or a hydrant to prop a foot—but it can also be more active: in buttons, lids, and touch pads. Pressing the pedestrian walk signal enacts an offer to take part in the abstracted systems that regulate the street's functioning. That physical contact provides an illusory charge. That charge comes from a sense that one's needs are being addressed—the button deploys agency, desire, or a more deep-seated need. It doesn't seem to matter that there is also a simultaneous recognition that the solicitation is an empty invitation to take part, that the changing of the light may be timed to only provide the illusion of being connected to that pressing. Sometimes, solicitation happens through the very forms of things. Rounded surfaces, small openings, bright colors, and a responsive give to the pressure of a push all are part of the way curb-scale infrastructures invite our participation. Other infrastructures of solicitation might also function as rulers, such as solar-powered parking meters with digital touch screens counting down minutes and a numerical pad to enter time spent on the street. This coming together of performance, affect, and regulation solicits an engagement at the same time that it acts as a ruler of time and space.

As regulated infrastructures, rulers, terminals, and solicitors order human arrangements with material ones. They move matter in ways that reflects the distribution of written, drawn, and spoken standards through organizational hierarchies of infrastructural design administration. Ash Amin and Nigel Thrift focus on these relationships when they argue that we can understand infrastructure as "arrangements of water, electricity, logistics, communication, circulation and the like" that are "caught up with the moments of standardization, technical compatibility, professional rivalry, bureaucratic imperatives, regulatory competences and general dispositions," which themselves are in relation with practices of maintenance and repair. [26]

The imbricated working of human and nonhuman actors comprises "the 'machinic' quality of infrastructure," and creates a "ground-level hum." [27] As "machinic," the city is an assemblage that entangles people, bureaucracies, and documents that are the realm and progenitor of the city's reproduction. Its "ground-level hum," like the subliminal drone of electrical current passing through wire, is a conditioning force. It functions—like rulers, terminals, and solicitors—to bracket how we move and gather in the street, and how we imagine a city to be a public home.

When Amin and Thrift argue for a "making visible" of the "hidden-in-plain-sight infrastructures" of the city and for "disclosing their force and performativity," this is about recognizing that a "machinic" assemblage involves human and nonhuman actors in the reproduction of the city through its infrastructure. [28] It is a recognition of infrastructure as an overlap and interaction of people, matter, drawing, and ideas in the moving of matter. Not the city as machine, but as this assemblage with its own conditioning ambiance. This recognition also calls for a study of the city that moves out of the specialized, disciplinary silos of techno-bureaucracies or the design and planning disciplines. These closed-off domains are inadequate to the interactions of economy, land, material, and lives that reproduce the city, as they weave through still other domains. This recognition calls as well for a turn to maintenance and repair: a turn to what Susan Leigh Star has called a "study of boring things," that recognizes the "imbrication of infrastructure and human organization." [29] Star argues for ethnographic methods that open toward "a more ecological understanding of workplaces, materiality, and interaction, and underpin...a social justice agenda by valorizing previously neglected people and things." [30] These methods make visible those lives devoted to care for the infrastructures we rely on.

Lauren Berlant asks what repair could mean in a "broken world" where the catastrophes of climate, inequality, and racial injustice stretch thin the supports tasked with maintaining multiple forms of life. She challenges articulations of infrastructure's role in the world by setting herself

27. Ibid., 5.
28. Ibid., 5.
29. Susan Leigh Star, "The Ethnography of Infrastructure," *American Behavioral Scientist* 43, no. 3 (1999): 377–79, https://doi.org/10.1177/00027649921955326. See also Shannon Mattern's writing on "Urban Repair" and her point that contemporary debates about macro-level spending on infrastructure obscure "the phenomenal reality that the world is being fixed around us, every day," in "Maintenance and Care," *Places Journal*, November 2018, https://placesjournal.org/article/maintenance-and-care/?cn-reloaded=1.
30. Ibid., 379.

31. Lauren Berlant, "The commons: Infrastructures for troubling times," *Environment and Planning D: Society and Space* 34, no. 3 (2016): 393, https://doi.org/10.1177/0263775816645989.
32. Ibid.
33. Ibid., 394.
34. Ibid.
35. Ibid., 393.
36. "To attend to the terms of transition is to forge an imaginary for managing the meanwhile within damaged life's perdurance, a meanwhile that is less an end or an ethical scene than a technical political heuristic that allows for ambivalence, distraction, antagonism and inattention not to destroy collective existence." Ibid., 394. For "long middle of change," see Lauren Berlant, "Sex in the Event of Happiness," keynote lecture, 13th Annual Feminist Theory Workshop, Department of Gender, Sexuality & Feminist Studies, Duke University, March 22–23, 2019, 22:50, https://gendersexualityfeminist.duke.edu/13th-annual-feminist-theory-workshop.
37. Berlant, "The commons," 408.

the task of "defining what kind of form of life an infrastructure is." [31] This question leads to a definition of infrastructure as "movement or patterning of social form" that overturns what may appear at a distance to be a "system or structure." [32] Rather than being the spatial stability of a fixed configuration, structure is for Berlant "that which organizes transformation" and acts as "really a convergence of force and value in patterns of movement." [33] Infrastructure relates to these patterns by being "that which binds us to the world in movement and keeps the world practically bound to itself." [34] This image of a double binding transforms the imagination of infrastructure into something closer to the physics of gravity. This binding foregrounds infrastructure's life-sustaining capacity and positions it as a relational set of vectors that link lives on the planet to the rotation of the earth itself.

Berlant's project is to consider infrastructure from within contemporary "brokenness" while looking beyond the urgencies of contemporary crises. [35] She wants to reconsider what could be common in the world not as a solution to the pressing failures of today, but as a condition of what could be imagined further on, beyond the present. She rejects the reassembly of past proximities and instead proposes infrastructure as a way of thinking about the tests, tries, and attempts toward an imagination of distributions, which, in that effort, allow us to make it through this transitional "meanwhile"; or what elsewhere she has called "the long middle of change." [36] Berlant rearticulates infrastructure as a technology in which "all objects are granular and moving toward each other to make new forms of approach from difference and distance." [37] In this imagination, infrastructure becomes the taking on of the challenges of distribution and distributions: of air, water, resources, and social proximities. The curb-scale figures into this task by considering the street as an infrastructure of infrastructures—a configuration of elements that is an organization of transformation such that human lives and nonhuman agencies entangled in a machinic hum produce the street as a site of differential differences that condition our relations to each other.

STORIES, SCRAPS, AND SCALES

Tim Ingold writes that "telling a story is not like weaving a tapestry to *cover up* the world," but rather guides "the attention of listeners or readers *into* it." [38] "Telling," implies a skillful "picking up [of] information in the environment" which, when reassembled, is able to direct an audience along "the same paths as his own." [39] Ingold's covered-up world recalls the Borgesian map that "coincided point for point" with an "Empire" until "the Inclemencies of Sun and Winters" left it in tatters. [40] The futility of Borges's tattered map also brings to mind, as an inversion, Rem Koolhaas's description of junkspace as a "colossal security blanket that covers the earth in a stranglehold of seduction." [41] Like the weighted blankets of more recent times, junkspace interiorizes sound and light with its opaque envelopment. Ingold's understanding of stories eschews the tatters of Borges's 1:1 paper map and the light-sucking enclosure of junkspace. As a tapestry, stories for Ingold do not function as a totality or through an unyielding extension. Their density is not the weight of opacity. Rather, stories function as the picking of threads, the carrying of lines, the exchange of matter and movement in a woven-together field of telling.

Telling stories about the city calls for a mode of collecting information. This picking up and picking at suggests a method that has more in common with the ragpicker than the *flaneur*. Susan Buck-Morss in her writing on Walter Benjamin's materialist philosophy describes the distinction between these two modes. "Note that the figures of the collector, the ragpicker, and the detective wander through the fields of the fossil and ruin, while the fields of action of the prostitute, the gambler and the flaneur are those of wish-images, and of the fetish as their phantasmagoric form." [42] The *flaneur's* scopic relationship with the city foregrounds the emptying of time through a continuous present. The ragpicker treats the city not as a surface to be projected upon, but rather as a material to be taken up and scrutinized:

38. Emphasis in the original. Tim Ingold, "The temporality of the landscape," *World Archaeology* 25, no. 2 (October 1993): 153, https://doi.org/10.1080/00438243.1993.9980235.
39. Ibid.
40. Jorge Luis Borges, "On exactitude in science," in *Collected Fictions*, trans. Andrew Hurley (New York: Viking, 1998).
41. Rem Koolhaas, "Junkspace," *October* 100 (2002): 176.
42. Susan Buck-Morss, *The Dialectics of Seeing: Walter Benjamin and the Arcades Project* (Cambridge, MA: MIT Press, 1989), 212.

43. Ibid., 212.
44. Charles Baudelaire, "Du vin et du haschisch," *Œuvres*, vol. 1, quoted in Walter Benjamin and Rolf Tiedemann, *The Arcades Project* (Cambridge, MA: Belknap Press, 1999), 349.
45. See note 441, in Benjamin, *The Arcades Project*, 981.
46. Benjamin, *The Arcades Project*, 368.
See also from *My City: a hongkong story*: "At this moment, a man who walks like a pair of rusty scissors comes up to a pile of garbage and picks up from amongst the wastepaper a huge, torn piece of newspaper. The members of the cleaning team can see what he is doing, of course, but no one could begrudge him the pleasure of reading a sheet of old newspaper." in Xi Xi, *My City: a hongkong story*, trans. Eva Hung (Hong Kong: Renditions Paperbacks, 1993), 10.
47. Jane Bennett describes this call of things as a tripartite force comprising "slowness," "intercorporeality," and a "strange attraction" of "advenience." See Jane Bennett, "Powers of the Hoard: Further Notes on Material Agency," in *Animal, Vegetable, Mineral: Ethics and Objects*, ed. J. J. Cohen (Santa Barbara: Punctum Books, 2012), 237–70.
48. Buck-Morss, *Dialectics*, 285.
49. Benjamin, *The Arcades Project*, 597.

the ruins of Borges's tattered map provide more knowledge than its point-for-point, 1:1 extension. Buck-Morss writes that for Benjamin, via Baudelaire, "ruins" are "loosened building blocks (both semantic and material) out of which a new order can be constructed." [43] The utility of the refuse that the ragpicker takes up persists in a suspended mode of evaluation. Benjamin cites Baudelaire's enumeration of the ragpicker's task: to be "occupied with rags," to collect and catalog everything, "he collects the garbage that will become objects of utility or pleasure when refurbished." [44] A description of the ragpicker's "jerky gait" is one that Benjamin borrows from Nadar, who used it to describe Baudelaire himself, thus linking the poet's literary activity to the cataloging and picking of material found on the street. [45] To these activities, Benjamin ascribes a kind of "necessary isolation" that makes possible "the interest he takes in the refuse and detritus of the great city." [46] The impulse to "collect and catalog everything" suggests an intimate relationship to the hoarded object, the material agency of its thingness calling out to the ragpicker. [47] Buck-Morss notes that despite this turn to the ragpicker as a methodological description of his own work, Benjamin also recognized the class-bound nature of his experience, and the limitations of the analogy of picking rags on the street. [48] Benjamin writes: "For what do we know of streetcombers, curbstones, the architecture of the pavement, we who have never felt heat, filth, and the edges of the stones beneath our naked soles, and have never scrutinized the uneven placement of the paving stones with an eye toward bedding down on them." [49] His engagement is of a different order and privilege than those for whom the hardness of the street's humid surfaces constitutes a public home.

Telling stories by pulling together threads from the material of the street becomes a way of challenging expectations for how we describe and understand infrastructure. If we think of the street not as a system, but as an infrastructure of infrastructures, then the clues it presents to us are the material configurations that mark its territory. This different scale enforces a proximity of observation and shifts a focus to elements as opposed to system. The street becomes an overlapping of multiple forms of infrastructure —drainage, signage, traffic control, pedestrian management—that makes it less meaningful to consider one such system independent of another.

The curb-scale recalibrates the street as an infrastructure and as an object of inquiry. First, it makes it possible, provisionally, to think of the street through the elements that comprise it, and through the relations between them. This way of looking supplants imaginations of the street as system or as a calibrated surface that lend themselves to calculation and engineered solutions for the regulation and arrest of movement. Second, because the curb-scale enforces a reading of the street as a relation of multiple, contiguous, and overlapping infrastructures, it becomes important to find modes of description that recognize its entanglements. On any given stretch, there are the hatches, levers, gauges, wires, cables, drains, tubes, and ducts each with their own administrative body and technical realm of management. The curb-scale as a mode of drawing the street attends to those overlapping infrastructures, making it possible to thread through the lines of policy, material, and repair that comprise its contingent and lively instability.

The curb-scale reasserts material directness and steers away from the synthetic abstraction that overcomes the street. In his articulation of infrastructure as an "urban apparatus," Reinhold Martin argues that scalar terms like "the global" are often abstracted in ways that prevent an encounter with the "dimensions of the earthly sphere" that are today as material as any other. [50] The global as a material measure challenges more comfortable registers of scale such as the human individual, or "institutions such as the family or the nation, or of bounded spaces such as the town, the city, the territory or the region." [51] Martin argues that these different settled ways of measuring the world produce a dissonance when they enter into conflict with each other. This dissonance makes it necessary to reconsider scale in a way that accepts nonhuman-centered measures of the big and small as having a real, and not abstract, conditioning force on living together on the earth. He argues for a "politics of scale" that refigures space as a "mixture of incommensurable scales" rather than "the arbitrariness of

50. Reinhold Martin, *The Urban Apparatus: Mediapolitics and the City* (Cambridge, MA: MIT Press, 2017), 20, http://site.ebrary.com/id/11275454.
51. Ibid.

52. Ibid., 23.
53. Bruno Latour describes it as "the illusory zoom sliding, without the slightest tremor, from the European continent to the Beaubourg square in Paris, continuously changing scale." He argues that the smooth transition from part to whole, in the map as well as in sociology, leaves little room for politics: a gap that understands relations as not always already determined in advance. If zooming takes us through a sequence of Russian dolls, Latour asks us to "now open all the dolls and plunge them into the plasma," which leaves to be tested, examined, and defined relations between big and small, part and whole. See "Paris, invisible city: The plasma," trans. Liz Carey-Libbrecht, *City, Culture and Society* 3 (2012): 91.
54. Martin, *The Urban Apparatus*, 7.
55. Melissa Cate Christ, "Evidence of Action: Towards an Ecology of Objects," in *Specifics: ECLAS 2013 International Conference Proceedings*, ed. Christiane Sörensen and Karoline Liedtke (Berlin: Jovis Verlag GmBh, 2014): 276–81.
56. See also Alexander J. Felson and Linda Pollak's photographic documentation of the "registration of forces of disturbance, showing effects of stormwater runoff, including erosion, differential settlement of materials, and growth of vegetation" in "Situating Urban Ecological Experiments in Public Space," in *Ecological Urbanism*, ed. Mohsen Mostafavi and Gareth Doherty (Zurich: Lars Müller Publishers, 2010): 352–63.

"mega-, micro-, or sub-, which manufacture a biopolitical, anthropocentric norm as their baseline." [52] He wants us to consider globalization as a scalar effect with material attributes, and not as a way of encountering the world that can be zoomed in and out in a synthesis calculated around the human "I." [53] Martin proposes that we remove the scaling filter of the "I" that coheres incommensurability through human experience. With this renewed vision, when "we gaze down a city street, we see not crowds of individuals or individual crowds but a battlefield and a playing field of relations, of activity, of force, of struggle: this particular universe endlessly going through its motions in this particular way, in every body and everybody, every thing and everything." [54] This gaze at "everybody, every thing and everything" is a look into relational organizations of distribution that make the street an infrastructure of infrastructures. These sets of scalar relations are bound to the street and made legible by looking at the material conditions of its elements.

The curb-scale figures scale in relation to these elements. Their dimensional and material qualities relate to larger narratives imbricated within it. To tell these stories means to act as a ragpicker who collects and catalogs everything, threading between material, social, and affective conditions, looking for evidence as a font of revealing. The curb-scale becomes a politics of scale through the abstraction it resists and the attention it demands. Melissa Cate Christ describes such work in her project to consider "details" of Hong Kong's public realm through "close observation and active engagement." These details come together with "forces such as policy, code, construction, and material practices" to comprise a larger "ecology of objects." [55] The curb-scale pursues this intention and proposes that this revealing also discloses decisions over time by many hands: marks of human judgment. [56] Where design is sometimes conceived as an expertise mediated and carried out through drawings that provide insurance *against* individual initiative, the curb-scale reveals the street to be resistant to such ordering. An ad hoc and negotiated relation to the overlapping and overlaying infrastructures of the street means that the labor of maintaining the public realm is resistant to the ordering prerogative of design.

AESTHETICS AND PARTITIONS

By thinking of the street, the city, or infrastructure in this way, its elements—or objects or things—and the relations that knot through them also comprise an ontology. Bruno Latour, working with the photographer Émilie Hermant, described Paris as an enumeration of standard, everyday objects that order life on the street, arguing that "every one of these humble objects, public toilet or trash bin, tree guard or street sign, phone booth or illuminated screen, contains a certain idea of the Parisian, to whom it sends—through color, form, habit or force—a particular order, summons, authorization, interdiction, promise or permission." [57] These different elements become actors in a larger network that ascribes a flattened agency to the protocols, policies, designs, and drawings that themselves determine how these different objects are fabricated and disposed by the people who situate them in the city. As these objects condition lives, they evince an affective and aesthetic charge that makes them agents within our own experience of the world. Gilbert Simondon argues that technical objects—of the city, of infrastructure, machines—have a beauty that resides in their integration into this world, a world which they extend:

> The telephone call center is beautiful not because of its characteristics as an object, but because it is a key-point in collective and individual life. In the same vein, a traffic light [*sémaphore*] on a train platform is not beautiful in itself, but is beautiful by way of its functioning as a traffic light, which is to say through its power to indicate, to signify a stop or a track to be left free. [58]

57. Bruno Latour and Émilie Hermant, "Paris Ville Invisible," in *Les Annales de la recherche urbaine* ("Paysages en Ville"), no. 85 (1999): 58.

58. Gilbert Simondon, *On the mode of existence of technical objects,* trans. Cécile Malaspina and John Rogove (Minneapolis: University of Minnesota Press, 2016), 194.

59. Keller Easterling, *Extrastatecraft: The Power of Infrastructure Space* (Brooklyn, NY: Verso, 2014), 11.

60. Ibid., 11.

61. Ibid., 21.

To access this aesthetic, it is not sufficient to instrumentalize the technical object, or to use it without thought. Instead, Simondon argues for a kind of empathy with the technical being, an understanding of the diagrammatic schema internal to the functioning of each object. It is with this understanding that we can enter into a relation with that object. This complicity is a recognition that the city or the street is not simply an abstracted space, or even a purely social one, but that it is comprised also of elements that are in relation with each other, and with us. What arises is an injunction to consider these elements and the way they touch upon life.

Telling stories about infrastructure that makes legible its multiple scales, materials, agencies, and actors unloosens earlier ways of thinking about *infra-* as a "below." Keller Easterling argues that infrastructure "typically conjures associations with physical networks for transportation, communication, or utilities...a hidden substrate—the binding medium or current between objects of positive consequence, shape, and law." [59] That infrastructure in this typical imagination is at once "binding" and "hidden" describes the strange magic of its aesthetic. For Easterling, it is not enough to delimit the workings of these distributions within the engineered technical domain of pipes, tunnels, shafts, and electricity. Instead she proposes that we consider "infrastructural space": this is the "shared standards and ideas that control everything from technical objects to management styles," or the "soupy matrix of details and repeatable formulas" that impacts the articulation of the world, from the spaces we move through to the objects we hold in our hands. [60] This matrix is an "active form" that unfolds over time to deal with specific contingencies and circumstances. [61] It comprises not objects, but logics, protocols, and mechanisms that channel the proliferation of material infrastructural emplacements in specific and generic ways across the planet: everything from ISO standards to "managementese" is critical to the objects they (re)produce.

In this telling, there is a parallel "underneath" to the "substrate": it is an "embeddedness" of logics, protocols, and mechanisms that are ruled, governed, and visible only to techno-bureaucratic agents. By recognizing this second parallel underneath, Easterling argues, we can identify how stories about infrastructure mask an organizational "disposition"; the propensity to engage in modes that are either explicit or hidden by layers of institutional protocols and regulations. A disposition is a way of doing things: from making decisions about contract workers to laying pavers on the street. At the same time, these dispositions harden and ossify when narratives become blinders: a kind of "That's how we've always done it," that becomes its own justification. Easterling writes that "these ideological stories have the power to buckle concrete and bend steel, and they can often be difficult to escape." [62]

These stories of infrastructural space also comprise an "operating system" providing "rules of the game" that "makes certain things possible and other things impossible." [63] Understood in this way, infrastructural space comprises an infinite relay of "on" or "off" digital switches that send distributions in one direction or another. [64] Martin puts it another way when he suggests that the "urban apparatus" is a "hardware" whose aesthetic dimension functions by "saying 'yes' to one thing and 'no' " to another. [65] These distributions become an "irreducibly contingent act of differentiation that is repeated over and over again" in an endless articulation of the city. [66] As "operating system" or as "hardware," infrastructure already offers an alternative to smart city discourses by suggesting that what is potentially smart about a city is these choices—the "on" and "off," "yes" and "no" that infrastructure makes possible and enforces—which powerfully inform and perform how subjects (potentially nonhuman subjects as well) are themselves able to make decisions. This "yes" and "no" or "on" and "off" could also be understood as a "stop" and "go" that determines how movements through the city are regulated. On the street, these movements include people, traffic, waste, and water that are constantly being upheld or let go. For people, this halting or moving on becomes a way of conditioning life in the city and relations to others with whom we share the street.

When Larkin argues that this partition has a "political aesthetic," he is interested as well in Jacques Rancière's writings on the distribution of the sensible. Larkin argues that for Rancière, "what links aesthetics and politics...is that...both share an ability to bring into being worlds and to interrupt the distribution of those worlds." [67] This ability to at once engender and disrupt, lies in the way aesthetics and politics are able to "assign objects to a specific place and define who has the ability to speak about them." [68] Rancière is interested in art's political role to rearticulate

62. Ibid., 93.
63. Ibid., 14.
64. Ibid., 75.
65. Martin, *The Urban Apparatus*, 3.
66. Ibid., 3.
67. Larkin, "Promising Forms," 187.
68. Ibid., 187.

these categorizations. Larkin works with this concept to propose that infrastructure operates beyond its technical functioning to "produc[e] sensory experience and through that experience constitut[e] political life." [69] How infrastructures hold promise, comprise ambient experience, and provide affective tugs through their material expressions is told through stories; infrastructure's distributions are political designations of how we live and relate to the city and each other in the world. This is a kind of double and conjoined productivity, that Amin and Thrift identify this way: infrastructures "enable subjects to think, act and feel" and also make possible "collective urban life through their provisions and circulations." [70] This double function of conditioning subjectivity and making urban life possible would seem to suggest a tightly bound knot in which the primary terrain for any contestation of value, sociality, and urban life would be infrastructure itself: that questions over who can do what, where, are infrastructural questions, foreclosed or made possible by stories that regulate those distributions. It requalifies the street not simply as a passive, pregiven surface, but as an actual and active site whose infrastructural functioning takes part in the distributions that qualify life and lives in cities.

69. Ibid., 188.
70. Amin and Thrift, *Seeing*, 17.

5

Hong Kong

Streets

4
1
5
2
3
1. Queen's Road West
2. Queen's Road Central
3. Queen's Road East
4. Castle Peak Road
5. Pound Lane
0 5 10

Queen's

Road

West

This stretch of Queen's Road is cut into rock. What isn't evident in the drawing is its rise, crest, and descent. The curve of the road makes that sequence, played in either direction, even more distinct. There is a kind of double inflection where the top of the hill coincides with the bend. A retaining wall, built over time, holds back the hillside. This hillside, the curve, and the pressure of the earth encased in concrete and stone, create a kind of caesura in movement. Walking from west to east, or east to west, the experience is of two distinct realities. When you reach the top of the hill, expecting to recognize a set of markers, signs, and spaces, there is still a disorientation—from the climb, from the bend in the road, from the retaining wall.

The sidewalk along the southern side of the road hugs the cleaved hillside. This encroachment of the slope into the sidewalk forces an intention that is unusual for moving through the city. Square stumps of concrete that encase retaining rods tying in the earth, jut into the already narrow space left for walking. When you come across someone, or want to overtake them, it is almost impossible to pass. For an instant, the road feels not like walking in a city, but like navigating through a trail worn over time by weary travelers. The choice of whether to take this sidewalk or the opposite one is not simply one of convenience, but of deciding whether to pass through that liminal space.

Where the retaining wall is cast-in-place concrete, weep holes are filled with sediment, some supporting the growth of a wispy system of roots and one or two green shoots. Rats peek out at night from within these tubular dens. The weep holes are marked as well by rust-colored beards that trail along the slope where water streams to the sidewalk. An open gutter leads down the hillside into awaiting drains. Other parts of the retaining wall date from an earlier period and are built in uneven stone blocks. A last segment was finished in shotcrete, to create an undulating, lumpy surface. The engineering of Hong Kong's slopes is overseen by the Geotechnical Engineering Office (GEO) of the Civil Engineering and Development Department; every reinforced slope in the city is tagged and numbered to allow for maintenance and management. Of the 60,000 engineered slopes in the city, the GEO oversees two-thirds, which are government slopes. Private slopes, which comprise the remaining 20,000, are overseen by the Buildings Department.

From the northern sidewalk, the hillside appears as a black-gray carapace. It is possible from this view to recognize how the hill has been cleaved away, then flattened to make a place for the pinched width of the street. The southern sidewalk clings to the base of the cut-back hill, seeming to be almost crushed by a lateral thrust that appears to be imminent rather than arrested. It is possible to make out the top of the hillside, but only barely, as the narrow width of the road and the steepness of the hill means that the angle of view toward the peak is compressed, closing off a real sight of what lies there: the slight grid of a railing and the gable roof of the school that claims the peak. Banyans cling to the top of the different retaining walls. Their roots form a kind of muscled ligature that grasps the stones and concrete. Their canopies project out from the slope into the air above the street. They seem to defy gravity, and form a distant cover, two or three stories high from the road.

The north sidewalk rises, falls, and bends in nearly the same movement as its pair; nevertheless, its larger diameter from some imaginary center point means that the arc that it inscribes as it climbs and descends the hill is less circumscribed, and the view is less foreclosed by the slope. The north sidewalk widens and narrows with projections and entrances to the buildings that run alongside it. At one moment a massive wall enclosing a narrow vacant site projects into the walkway, reducing its width by half.

From the top of the crest of the hill, on the north sidewalk, but not the south, it is possible to see where one has come from and where one is going. To the west, the street descends until it breaks around another corner; to the east, it intersects with Water Street and then reaches a nadir before mounting and disappearing up another slope. In August of 2019, on an evening when protests took place in scattered districts all over the city, a group of demonstrators marched from farther west in Kennedy Town to the China Liaison Office, in Sai Ying Pun. Some protesters faced off with security forces gathered at this intersection—where Water Street meets Queen's Road West. As the night wore on, the forces marched up the hill releasing tear gas that collected at the crest. As the canisters rolled down the hill, demonstrators ran westward with police climbing from the east.

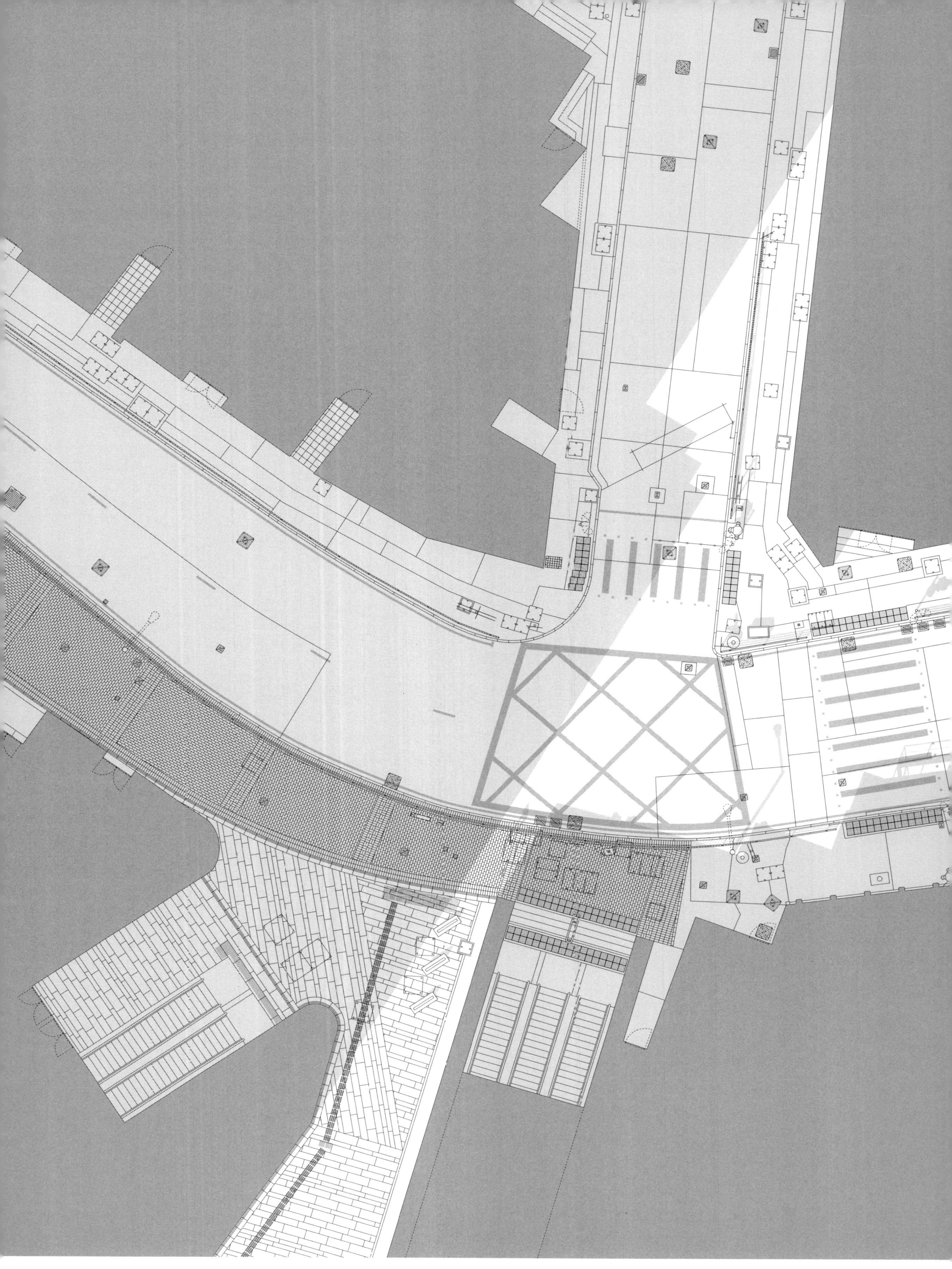

0 5 10

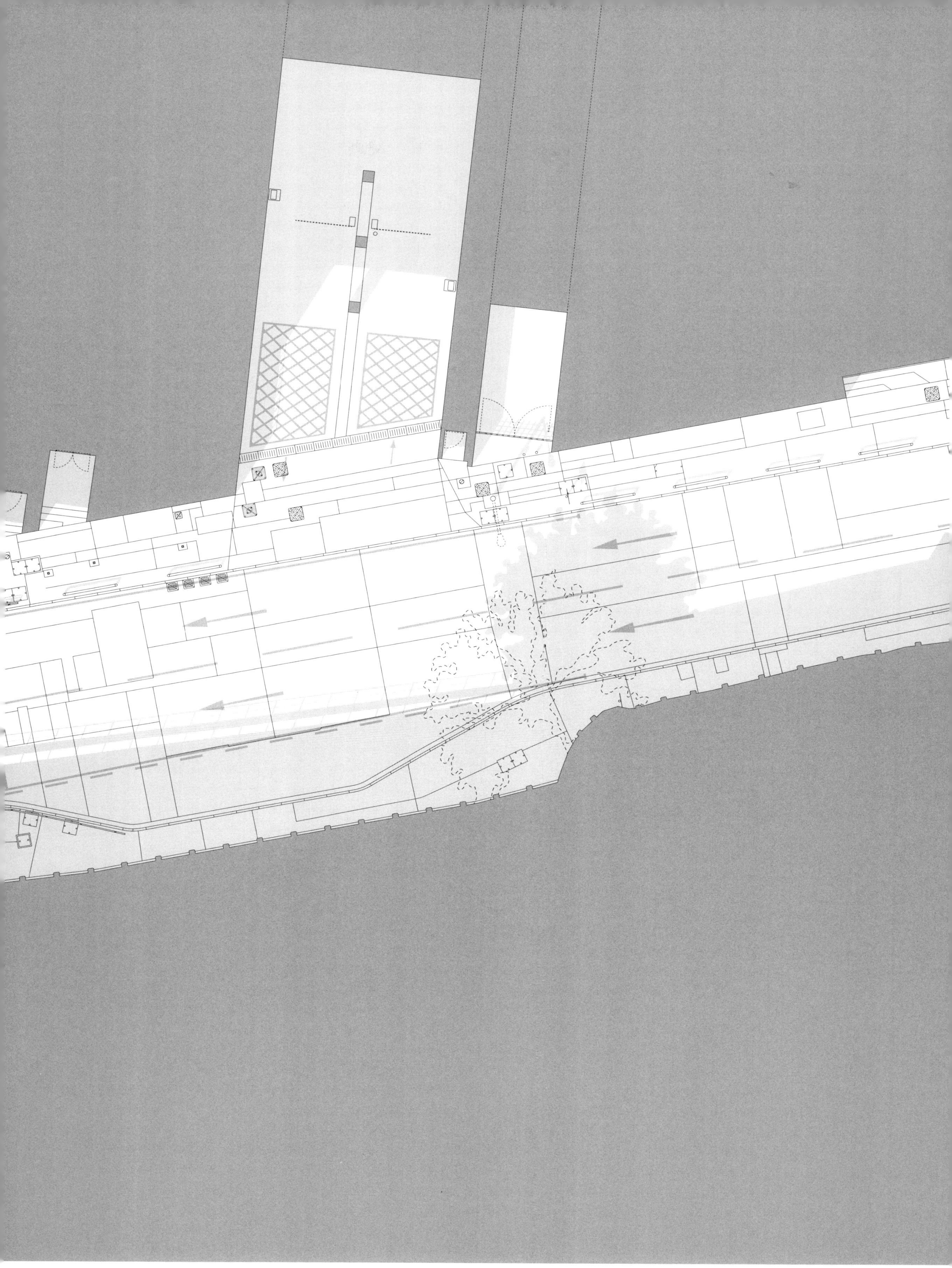

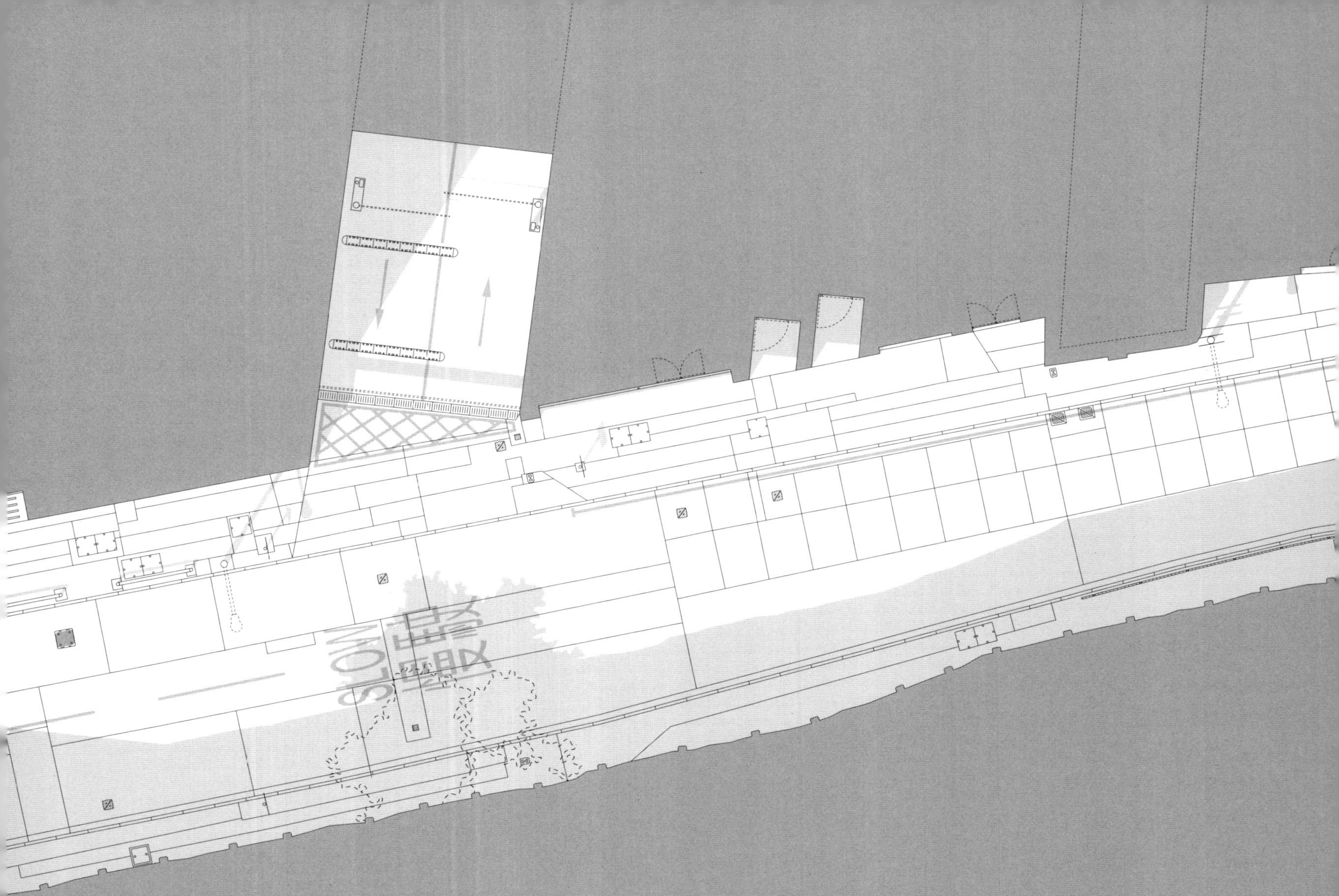

SLOW
慢駛

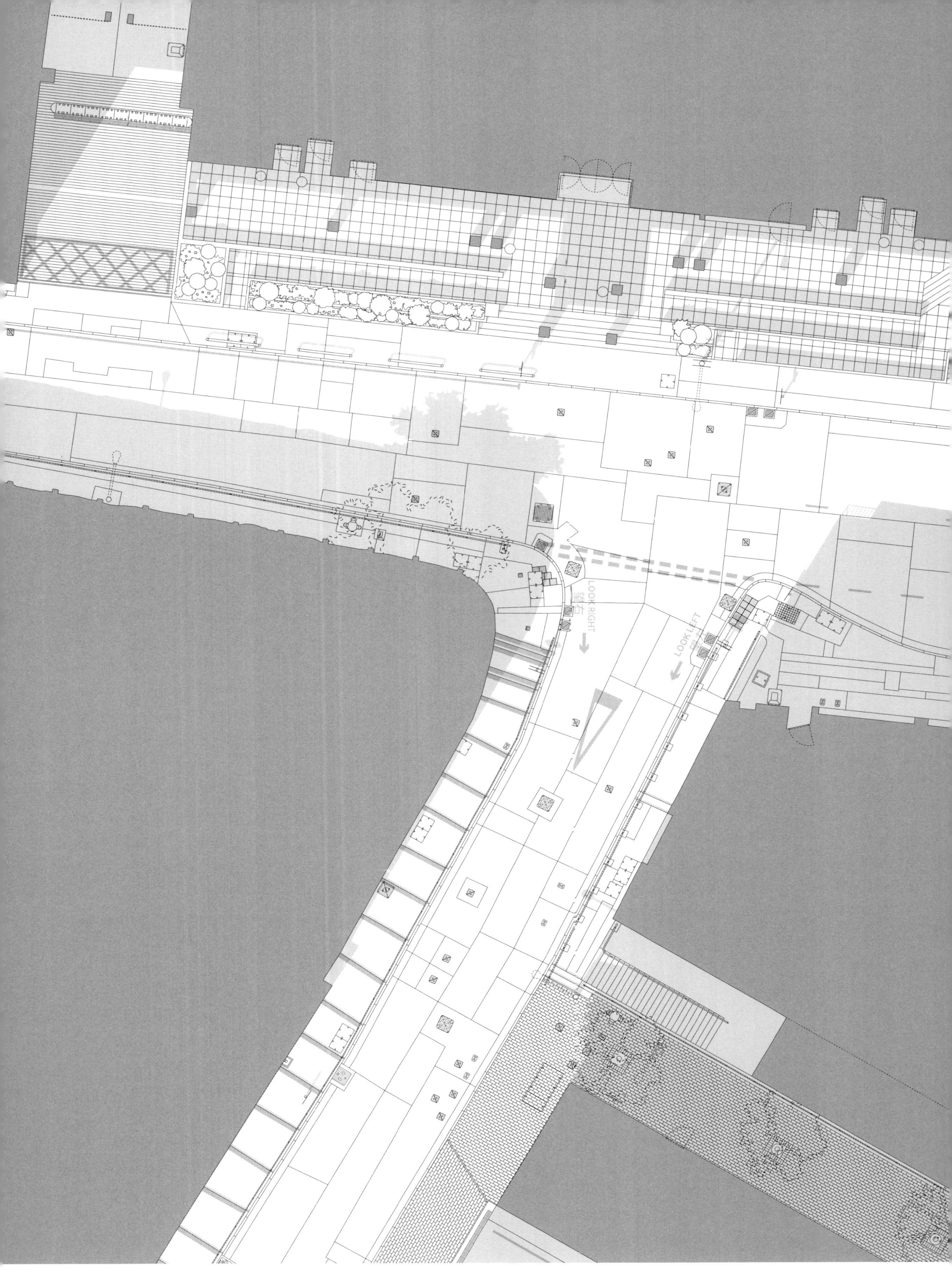
LOOK RIGHT
LOOK LEFT

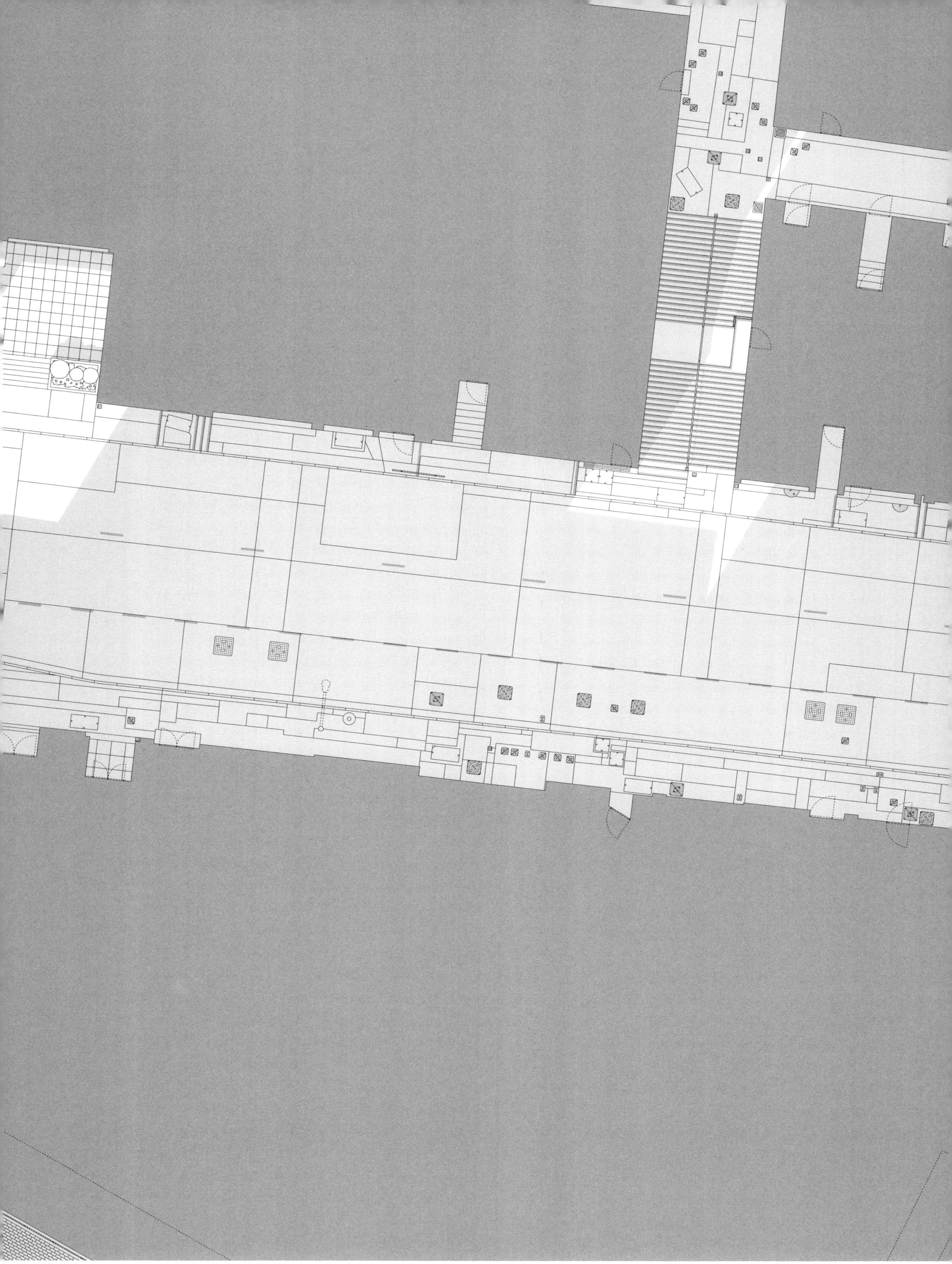

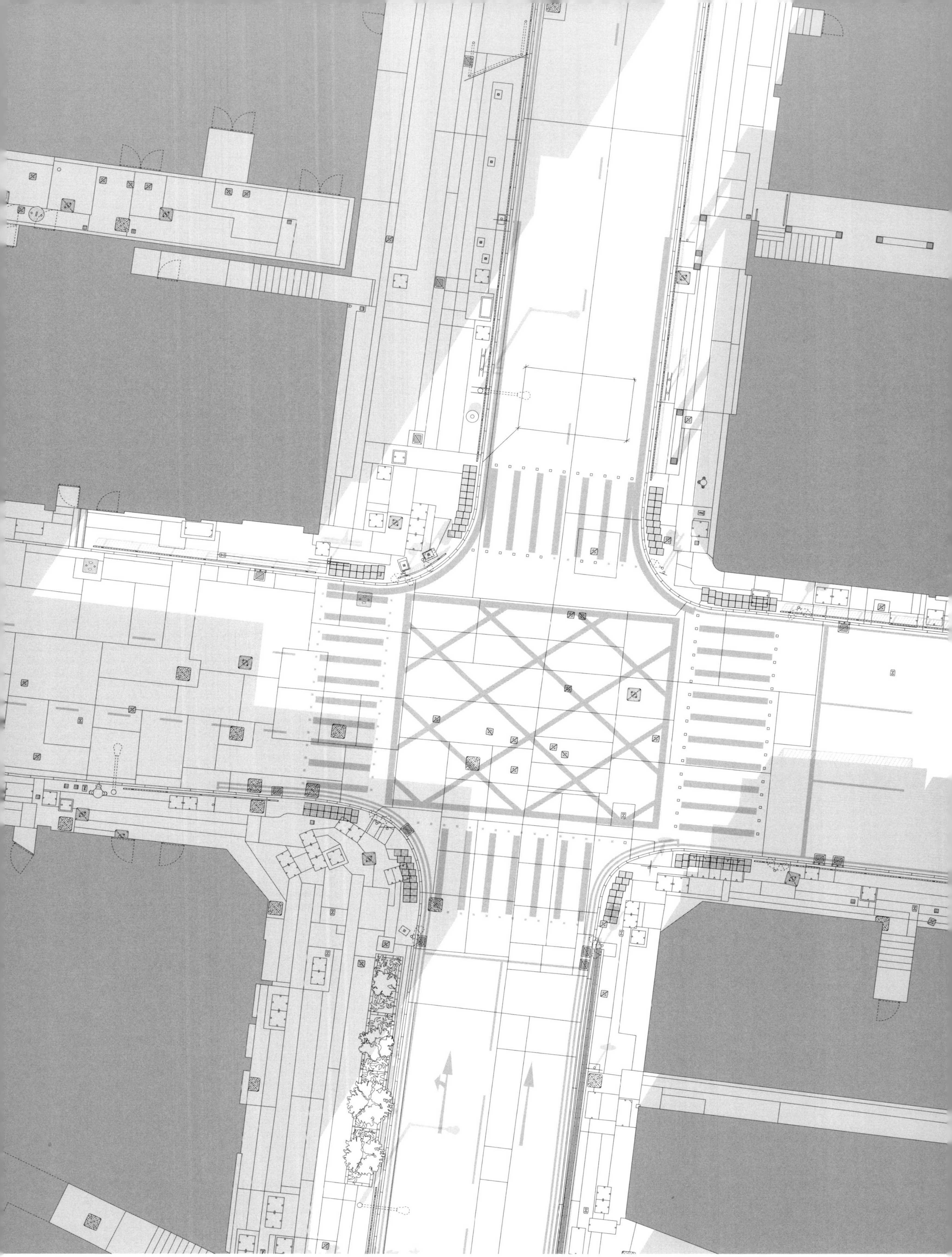

Queen's

Road

Central

Queen's Road Central meets Queen's Road East in a length of street also called Queensway. The stretch in the drawing links the HSBC Main Building with the Bank of China Building, Cheung Kong Center, and the Bank of China Tower. Further to the east, off the drawing, past a site being developed by Henderson Land, is the Lippo Centre. The Henderson Land tower replaces a public parking garage built in 1973. For three years, from 2009 to 2012, the car park was home to a museum run by the Planning Department called the Hong Kong Planning and Infrastructure Exhibition Gallery. The museum is today housed a few blocks closer to the water and called the City Gallery. For more than two decades, the car park also housed the Operations Department of the city's Independent Commission Against Corruption and, for several years in the 1990s, the Hong Kong Government Archives.

In May of 2017, Henderson Land bid HK$23.3 billion for a 999-year lease of the car park site. With 465,000 square feet of approved floor area, the sale amounted to HK$50,064 per square foot of government income. Two weeks after the sale, the government announced that a new land auction, won by Nan Fung Development, had surpassed the car park's total sale price. The Nan Fung parcel was divvied up from the Kai Tak Airport site across the harbor from The Henderson. While some of the saleable Kai Tak land was on a strip of land that jutted into the harbor—the former runway—the Nan Fung parcel is at the edge of the redevelopment next to a new MTR station. It sold for HK$24.6 billion. A per-square-foot cost of HK$12,864, nevertheless, amounted to only one-fifth of the Henderson Land purchase. Snøhetta, the architects of the Nan Fung Project—dubbed Airside—describe a building that "offers visitors access to generous public spaces through a series of exterior plazas and rooftop gardens suited for urban farming, restaurants, events and recreation." [1] In their description of the development for the car-park site—called The Henderson—Zaha Hadid Architects describe how the tower's base is "elevated above the ground to shelter courtyards and gardens cultivated with trees and plants," creating "new civic plazas... enveloped by nature." [2]

Queensway runs along the southern side of The Henderson, separating it from I. M. Pei's Bank of China Tower. The width of the street comprises ten lanes of vehicular traffic, two of which are tramlines. Off-ramps that bracket either side of Queensway bring cars from elevated roads that snake south from the hillside, or lead north toward fast-moving highways that stretch along the harbor. These harbor front, elevated highways and their on and off ramps form a barrier between the city and the water. That barrier is reinforced by large, single-developer parcels that shaped the extension of the city when infill campaigns pushed land into the water.

It is possible to cross Queensway's ten lanes from the Bank of China Tower to The Henderson site by jumping over railings and walking underneath the two overpasses across stranded traffic islands. Otherwise, stairs from either side lead to elevated walkways. The walkways also allow you to continue eastward, joining a network of sky bridges that lead in and out of buildings, avoiding the ground below. There are walkways encircling the site of The Henderson as well. Spiral staircases and ramps supported by massive columns lead to gardens on sites west and south of the new tower. In images produced by the architects, the tops of trees planted in these gardens seem to continue into an impossibly verdant landscape that grows within the tower itself, suggesting that the new development will expand this realm. One of these parks, Chater Garden —like Statue Square nearby to the west—

has historically been the site of protests and gatherings of transnational communities of migrant workers for whom these spaces are a provisional home on their weekly, government-mandated, day off.

The spaces adjacent to, alongside, and underneath the iconic towers that line Queensway are finished by the developers as an extension of the towers themselves. Arrangements of granite planters, benches, and reflecting pools are slotted into the spaces left over from tower footprints. Along Queensway, these spaces are just outside the ground-floor lobbies of secondary entrances. Some workers arrive by cars that enter directly into parking structures occupying massive subterranean spaces. Others come in taxis that swoop to main entrance drop-off areas that are on the southern sides of the buildings. This means that there is little activity on the Queensway side, where one passes on foot. The thinness of the space that is slotted between these entrances and the wide stretch of Queensway is matched in its alienating quality by the ten lanes of traffic that stretch alongside.

In land leases or deeds of dedication, developers negotiate terms by which these spaces generate increased buildable area. These terms—for "areas within private properties dedicated for public use"—note that "public use" means solely "public passage." [3] Other activities can be unauthorized at will. The space underneath the HSBC Building comprises a 3,192-square-meter area that was negotiated under such terms, stipulating that the space would remain open 24 hours a day. [4] Nevertheless, the 2019 protests and the pandemic allowed for discourses of safety and contagion to become quick resources for delimiting the space. The plaza has been periodically taped off, barricaded, and gated shut.

1. Snøhetta, "Airside Hong Kong," https://snohetta.com/projects/525-airside-hong-kong, accessed November 10, 2021.
2. Zaha Hadid Architects, "The Henderson," https://www.zaha-hadid.com/architecture/2-murray-road/, accessed November 10, 2021.
3. Buildings Department, "Public open space," last updated November 25, 2021, https://www.bd.gov.hk/en/resources/codes-and-references/public-open-space/index.html.
4. Buildings Department, "Public open space: Central and Western District," last updated November 25, 2021, https://www.bd.gov.hk/en/resources/codes-and-references/public-open-space/HK/dedicated_areas_HK_CW.html. The plaza also served as an important site for the Occupy Central protests beginning in October of 2011. See: Sonia Lam-Knott, "Carving Enclaves of Alternative Urbanisms in Hong Kong," in Jens Kaae Fisker, et al. (eds.), *Enabling Urban Alternatives: Crises, Contestation, and Cooperation*, Singapore: Springer, 2019: 223–46. https://doi.org/10.1007/978-981-13-1531-2_11.

0 5 10

BUS
LANE

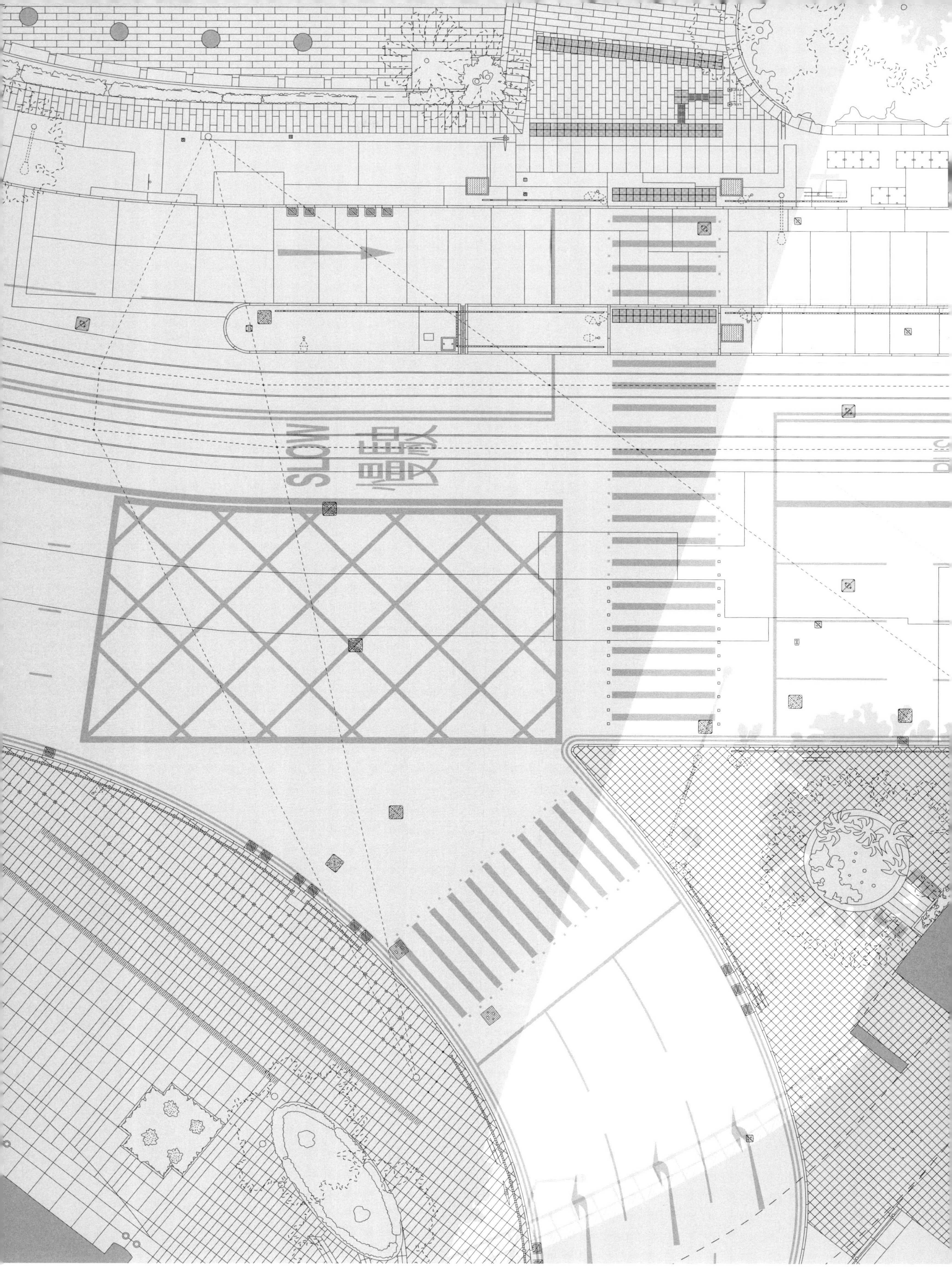
SLOW
慢駛

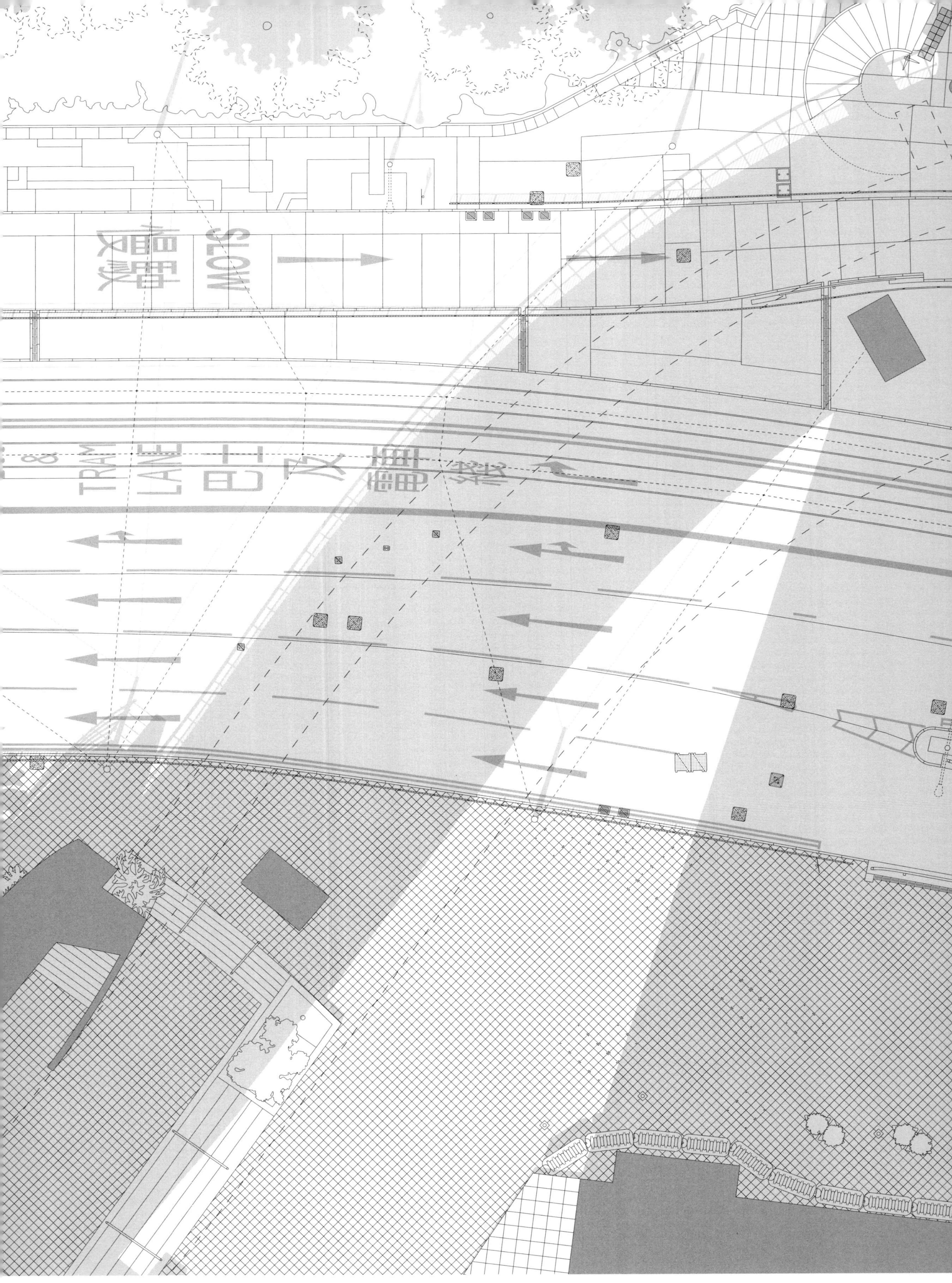
SLOW
& TRAM
LANE

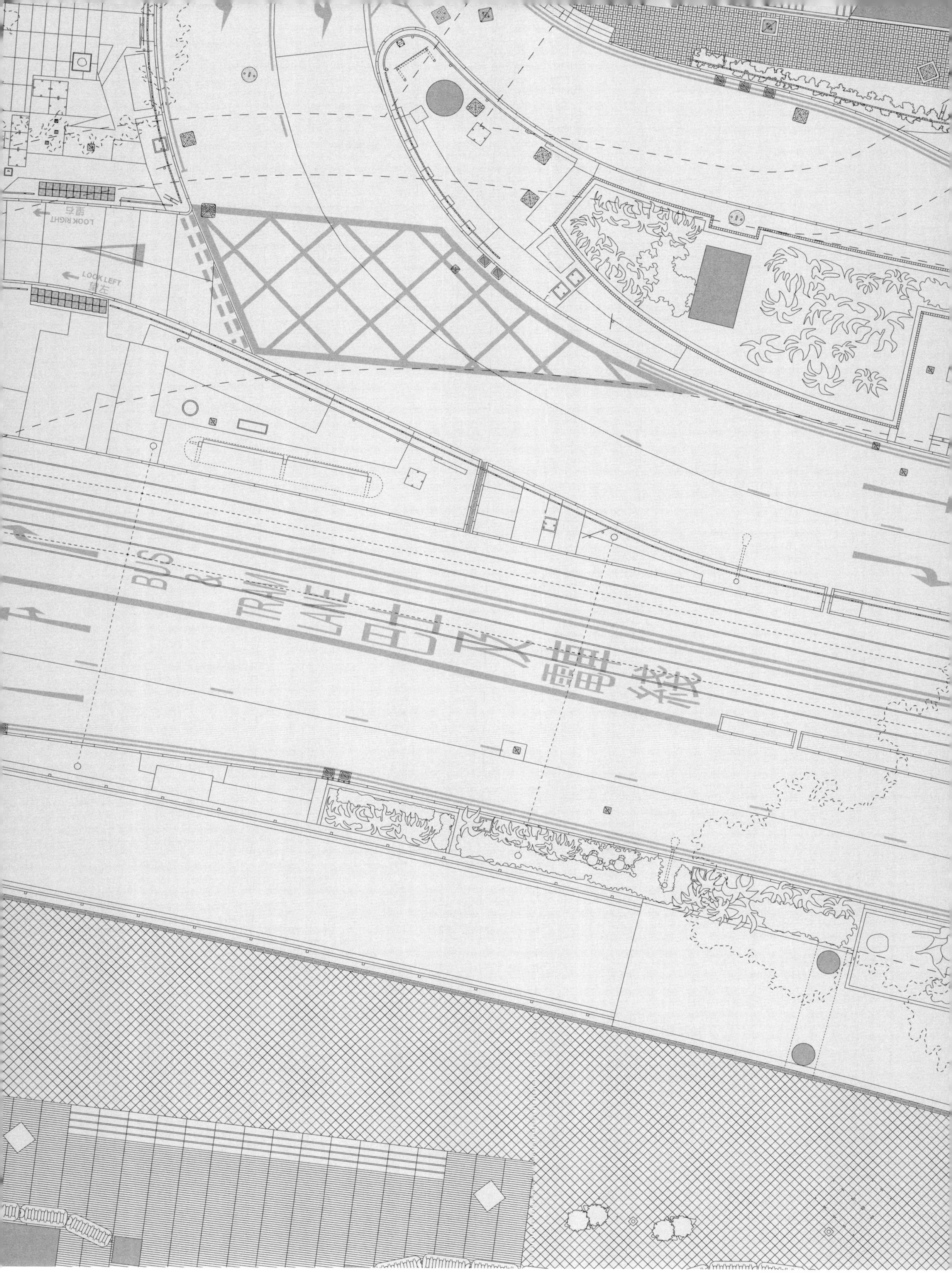
LOOK RIGHT
LOOK LEFT
BUS & TRAM LANE

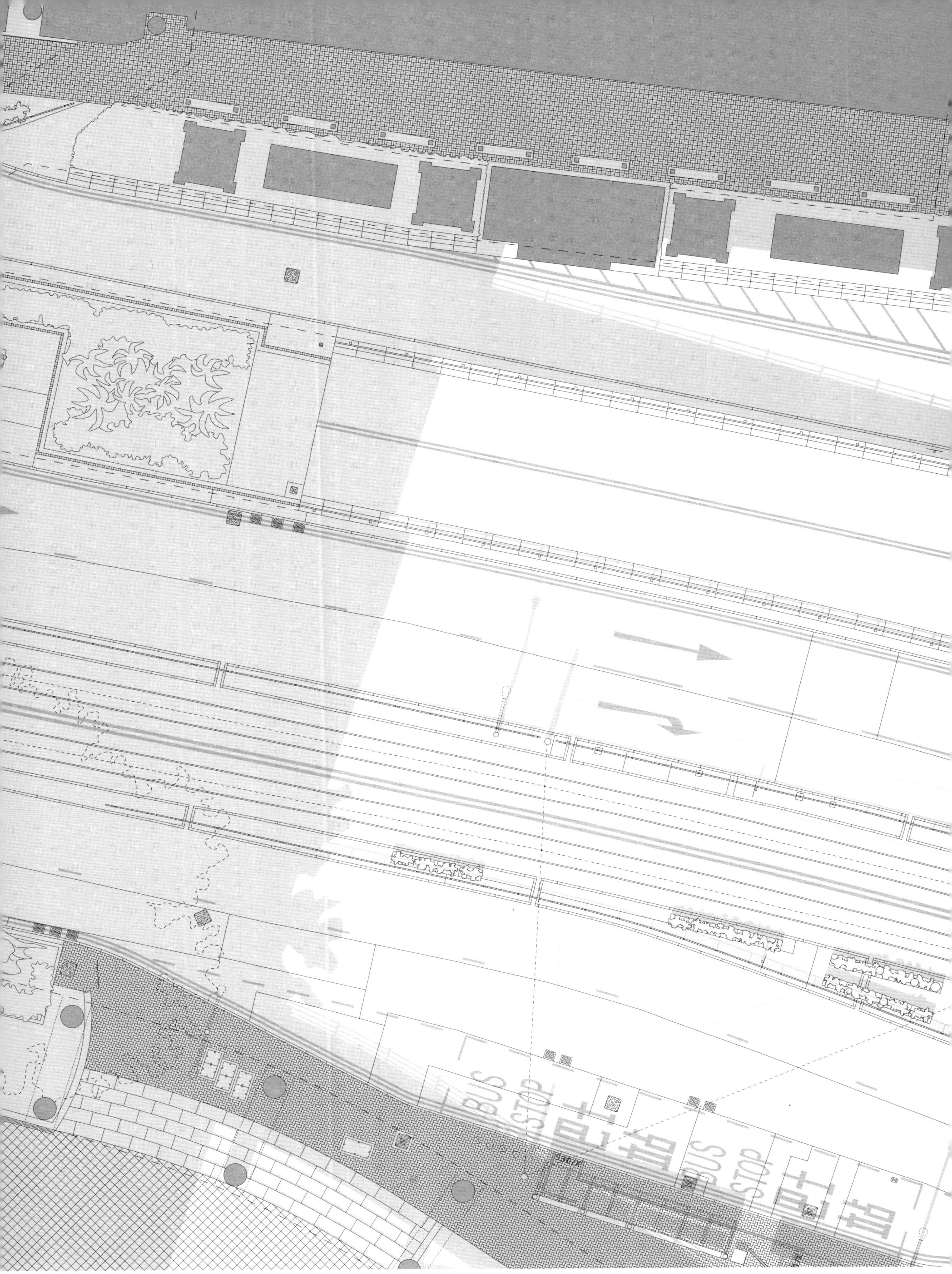
BUS STOP
BUS STOP

Queen's

Road

East

On the southwest corner of Queen's Road East and Monmouth Path is a *Ficus microcarpa* that is classed in the Development Bureau's Tree Register as an "Old and Valuable Tree." The tree is 20 meters tall and has a crown that spreads almost the same dimension across. The register lists the tree's diameter "at breast height"—calculated where a person could encircle a tree with their arms—as 1,880mm, meaning that the tree has a circumference of nearly six meters. The earliest map of Hong Kong to indicate street planting shows several trees near this intersection. [1] It also indicates a stream that descends from the hills alongside a path before disappearing under Queen's Road. Today, the tree occupies a site near one of the only remaining military parcels in the neighborhood. These parcels once comprised the colony's military garrison and were given over to government and private development decade by decade. Today, the People's Liberation Army occupies barracks on what remains of that once important military site.

The tree juts into the sidewalk and is enclosed by a wall that is white brick on three sides and stone on another. Its roots creep over the stone face, covering it like the unknotted ends of a scarf before disappearing into the ground. Pedestrians step onto the street to avoid the tree or navigate up and around on an adjacent plaza, accessible only by steps. The small plaza is finished in green-gray granite tiles and leads to more stairs and an elevator that ascends to an overhead walkway. In one direction, the walkway extends nearly 60 meters over tramlines and two roads, butting into a 43-story tower that serves as the headquarters for the city's police force. In the other direction, a newer pedestrian bridge crosses Monmouth Path and connects to Three Pacific Place, a 33-story tower that occupies 1 Queen's Road East. The green-gray tiles that line the plaza around the Old and Valuable Tree are also used on the sidewalks around this tower. Swire Properties, the developer of the complex, was able to negotiate with the government to redo the sidewalks that ring the small block, including those that front a row of older buildings that remained during the renewal. Stone tiles, custom granite curbs, and public seating create a corporate groundscape that contrasts with the standard red-concrete pavers and patched-up concrete on the opposite sidewalks. Wherever there is new development, walkways, curbs, and other infrastructures of the street are reinstated in ways that depend on the developers' initiative. Sometimes the work goes beyond the government's standards. Other times it only arrives at that minimum.

Swire's improvements to the neighborhood were part of the "Old Wanchai Revitalisation" Public Private Partnership (PPP) that coincided with the development of Three Pacific Place. The campaign sought to "add value to an urban living room of cul-de-sacs, mature trees, and sitting out areas" by leveraging historical and cultural heritage, integrating community input, and improving "street furniture, paving, lighting, railings and signage." [2] Swire's development included the refurbishment of Dominion Garden. The garden is just east of Three Pacific Place and adjacent to a now-displaced burial ground established in 1841 to accommodate the increasing number of British troops who perished while stationed in the outpost. At the back of Dominion Garden is a three-story stone retaining wall with steps integrated into its length. The top of the stairs now give on to a network of streets that replaced the cemetery. Further east, St. Francis Street, named after a church that gave the displaced cemetery its name, is paved with Type-A decorative pavers. These wavy-edged concrete elements are laid in a herringbone pattern at 45 degrees to traffic. The Highways Department has determined this to be the best performing paving and layout for vehicular overruns. That the steep width of St. Francis Street is paved in this way is unusual and was ostensibly part of the effort to "add value" through revitalization.

The Old Wanchai Revitalisation lasted from 2009 to 2012. At the same time that the project promised to better the neighborhood streetscape through the PPP, Swire's Three Pacific Place development also included plans for underground pedestrian tunnels that avoided the street altogether. These would lead to the Admiralty Mass Transit Railway Station (MTR) and to another Swire property: a shopping mall also called Pacific Place. The subterranean link was finished several years after the tower itself and comprised a climate-controlled sequence of stairs, escalators, and moving sidewalks similar to circulation networks throughout the city.

On October 4, 2019, Hong Kong's chief executive invoked the colonial-era Emergency Regulations Ordinance to gazette a law that stipulated that "a person must not use any facial covering that is likely to prevent identification" while at an "unlawful" or "unauthorized" assembly. [3] Protesters covered their faces to avoid being identified and to slow the inhalation of the tear gas that became a frequent implement for crowd control and dispersal. The ordinance was drafted in 1922 to counter a wage strike of Chinese workers that paralyzed the city's port. As originally written it allowed the territory's executive to "make regulations on occasions of emergency or Public danger." [4] The night that the new face covering law was announced, protesters gathered throughout the city. In Wanchai, security forces set up on Queen's Road East at either end of the gathered protesters. They also took up positions on the elevated walkways, including the pedestrian bridge that linked the police headquarters to Three Pacific Place. Protesters used a network of narrow lanes to shift from Queen's Road East to parallel roads to the north, anticipating a back and forth of movements and actions that would stretch into the night.

1. See: "Plan of the City of Victory," Stanford's Geological Establishment London, 1889, https://www.hkmaps.hk/mapviewer.html, in Mathew Robert Pryor, "Street tree planting in Hong Kong in the early colonial period (1842-98)," *Journal of the Royal Asiatic Society Hong Kong Branch*, 55 (2015): 33-56. https://doi.org/10.3316/informit.566986812831499.
2. Oval Partnership, "Revitalizing Old Wanchai," accessed November 10, 2021, https://www.ovalpartnership.com/en/work/project/Revitalizing-Old-Wanchai.
3. Hong Kong e-legislation, "Prohibition on Face Covering Regulation," October, 5, 2019, https://www.elegislation.gov.hk/hk/cap241K.
4. Historical Laws of Hong Kong Online, "Emergency Regulations Ordinance, 1922," accessed November 10, 2021, https://oelawhk.lib.hku.hk/items/show/1570.

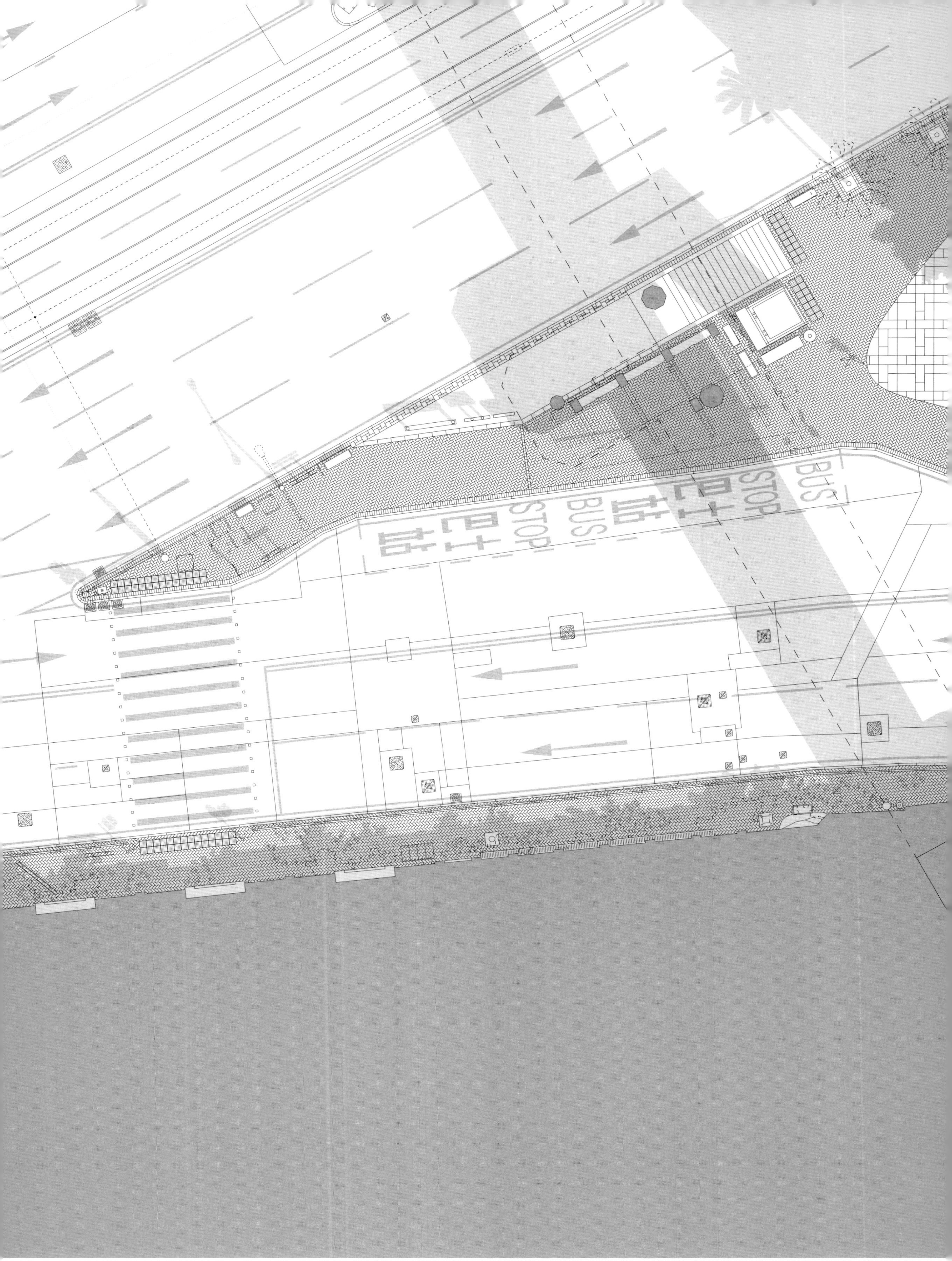

0 5 10

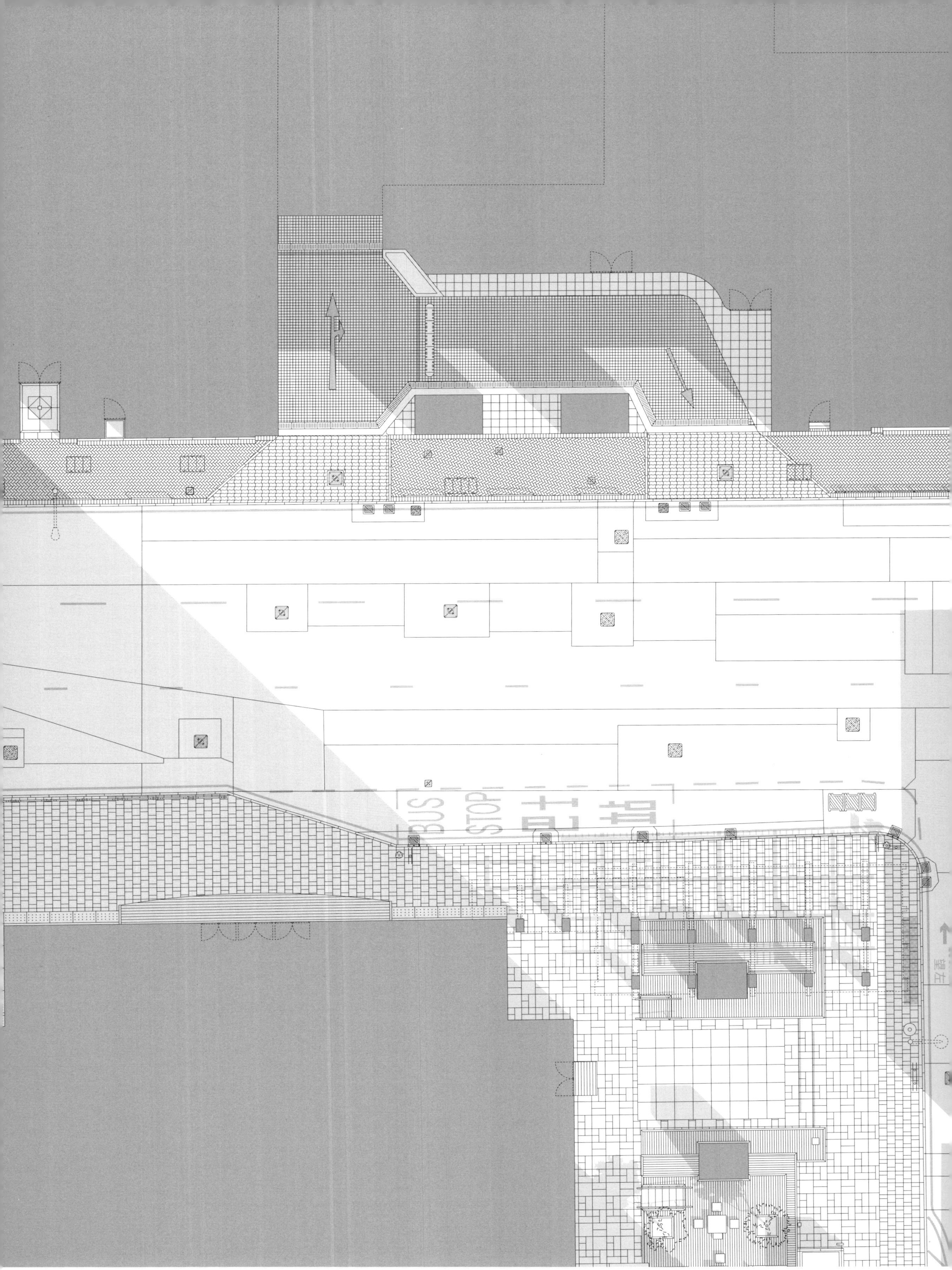
BUS STOP

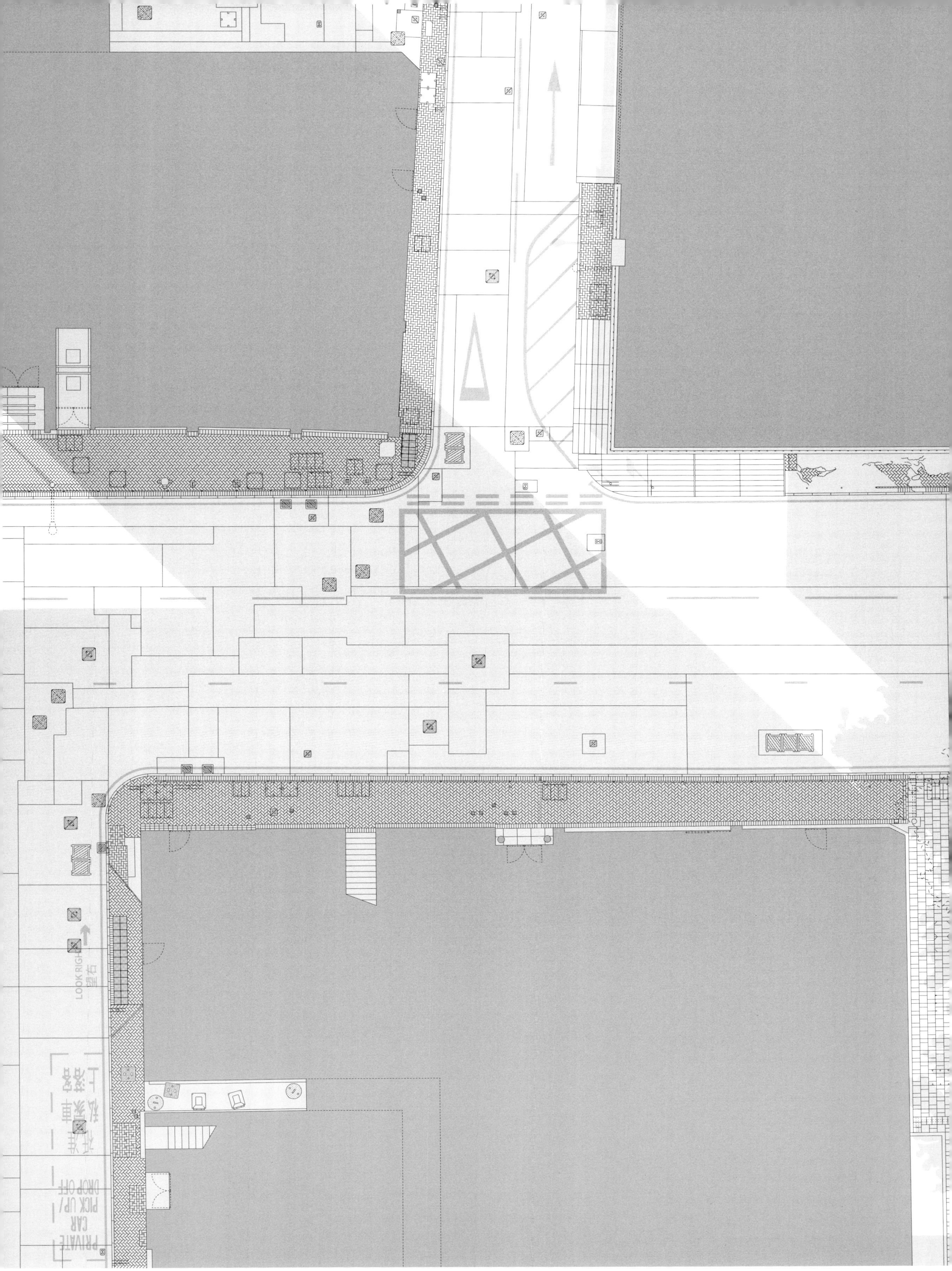
LOOK RIGHT 望右
PRIVATE CAR PICK UP/ DROP OFF
私家車上落客

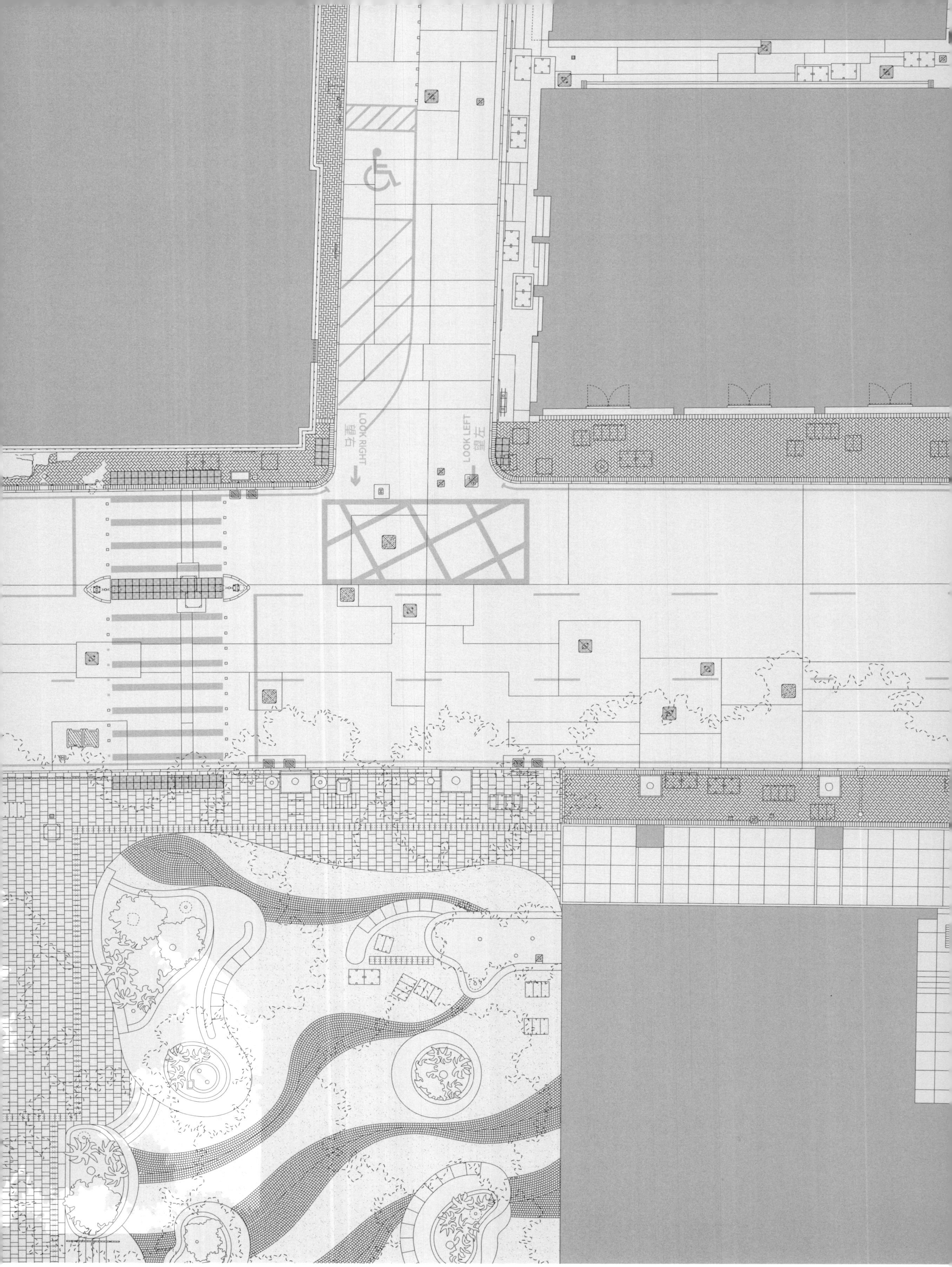

LOOK RIGHT
望右
LOOK LEFT
望左

SLOW

Castle

Peak

Road

Castle Peak Road is the longest thoroughfare in Hong Kong and turns into the Cheung Sha Wan district from the northern reaches of Kowloon Peninsula. It passes in a straight shot through the neighborhood, before slipping between the towering columns of a freeway overpass, circling around a maximum security prison, and arcing northward over hills, along still un-pushed-back coast and into the New Territories. [1] This peregrination was once made in the opposite direction on foot, by refugees from China. There are still stretches flanked by unbuilt land: cut-back slopes cauterized with shotcrete, fallow agricultural terrain, and vacant-looking industrial yards that are logistical way stations for goods arriving into the city's port.

When the road was first marked out at the end of the 19th century, the stretch that figures in the drawing traced an uneven way between steeply rising hills to the north, and the coast immediately to its south. The road was designated by the clearing away, levelling, and compacting of land that had served as a coastal path: maintaining it meant repeatedly responding to storms that washed away earth, and tending plants that encroached its edges. When a path that follows topologies of least resistance coincident with the earth's features becomes fixed with an emplacement of resources, a different sort of time is introduced. A path traces expedient footfalls calculated in the momentary encounter between terrain and intention; a road—noted on maps and marked into the earth—introduces a temporal scale oriented to the future as speculation. A road identifies a direction and suggests a distance to be travelled. It points toward lands open for exploitation, or connects places already settled. By introducing these values, and through the clearing of the road, the surround of the world transforms into a measurable space oriented toward human experience.

Beginning in the 1920s, infill campaigns pushed back the coastline along the road's edge. The newly created land was inscribed with a rectilinear grid. Low-rise industrial blocks predominated in the area until the closing of Kai Tak Airport in 1998 lifted height restrictions, making possible the more recent appearance of towers. Many of the districts in Kowloon comprise such gridded patches, some reflecting a history of infill, others marking out a planned development on what had been agricultural land. During the 2019 protests, this landscape created scenarios of confrontation in which protesters had options for how to direct the course of marches. This was in sharp distinction to Hong Kong Island where the water and hills delimit a corridor of east west movement, with security forces waiting at one or the other end of that axis. [2] Protest events were already markedly different from contestations of the recent past in the way groups would gather in multiple neighborhoods around the city. In Mongkok, Tsim Sha Tsui, and Cheung Sha Wan, these gatherings could disperse more quickly when confronted by security forces, the low horizon of linear streets swallowing up views into the distance.

Experienced for the first time, each moment along Castle Peak Road is actualized as a possibility in the way shopfronts and facades present themselves for discovery. If we had to name this difference—of what happens to a road when it loses its connecting function—perhaps "street" describes this actualization along every moment. In that sense, Castle Peak Road is a "road" only insomuch as that word carries forward the traces of its history. Along this stretch of the street, indentations, projections, and openings disrupt and extend into buildings. Car washes, showrooms, repair shops, and filling stations bring cars across the sidewalk into terrain shared by people and machines. Cavernous garages that stretch the full block of the building, provide place for deliveries, shipments, and running engines, the air inside smelling of exhaust. Unmarked entrances along the street lead to narrow, dark corridors, or wider halls that access elevator banks. Newer developments, set back from the street, are clad in full-height glass, with doors that swing or slide open into air-conditioning.

On the eastern end of this stretch of Castle Peak Road, shops and restaurants spill over from the older residential fabric of Sham Shui Po. In the industrial buildings along the western portion, there are fewer street-front stores. Recesses in blank ground-floor facades enclose doors that open only from the inside. Some of these exits are stepped back from the street, others offer only a slight indentation to signal the outward-opening door. These recesses are used to store push-carts, left overnight, with markings legible to their owner. They also serve as storefronts where sellers set up a small table for shoes, clothes, or other wares, often in an unsorted heap. These exit doors can be two or three in a row. A few vendors in the industrial buildings sell provisions and gifts for relatives who come as visitors to the prison.

1. The prison, called Lai Chi Kok Reception Centre, holds approximately 1,500 male prisoners including pro-democracy activists and protesters arrested under the June 2020 National Security Law.

2. Francis Lee, "Digital Media and Social Movements," April 20, 2021, Architecture, Urbanism and the Humanities Initiative Speaker Series, Department of Architecture, University of Hong Kong, 52:40, https://www.arch.hku.hk/event_/francis-lee-李立峯/?subcat=discussion-lecture-series.

BUS ONLY
LOOK LEFT
LOOK RIGHT
0
5
10

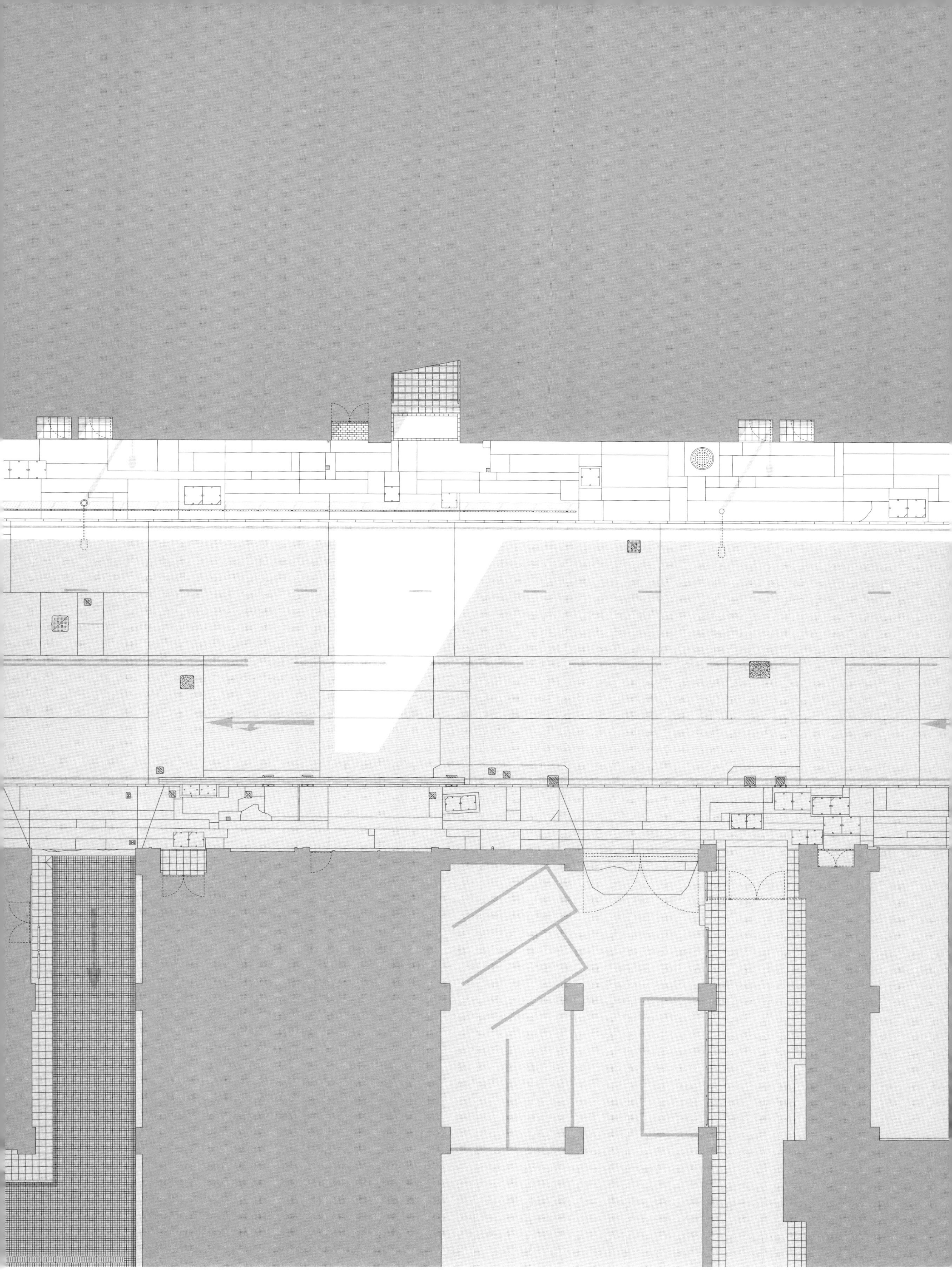

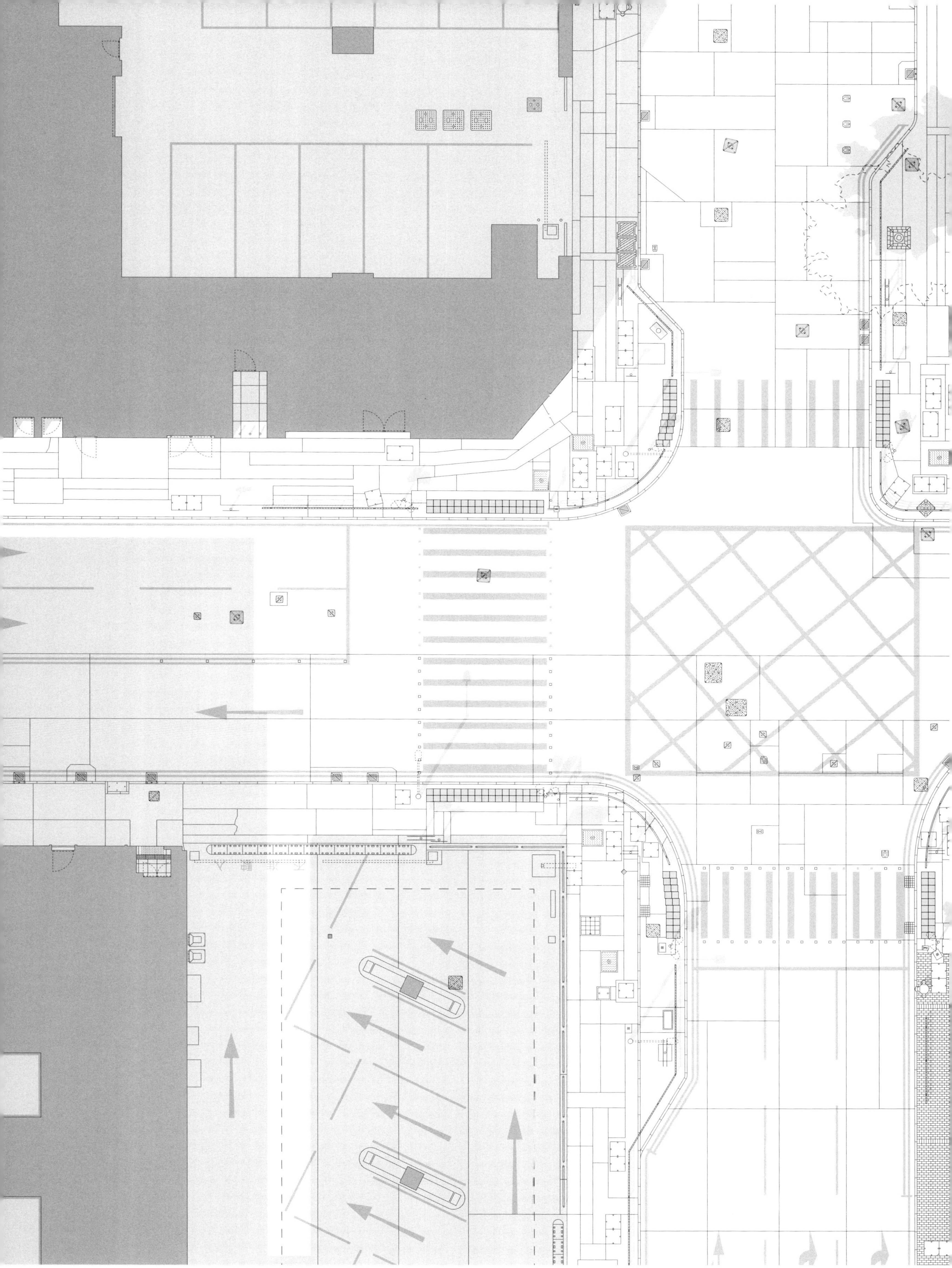

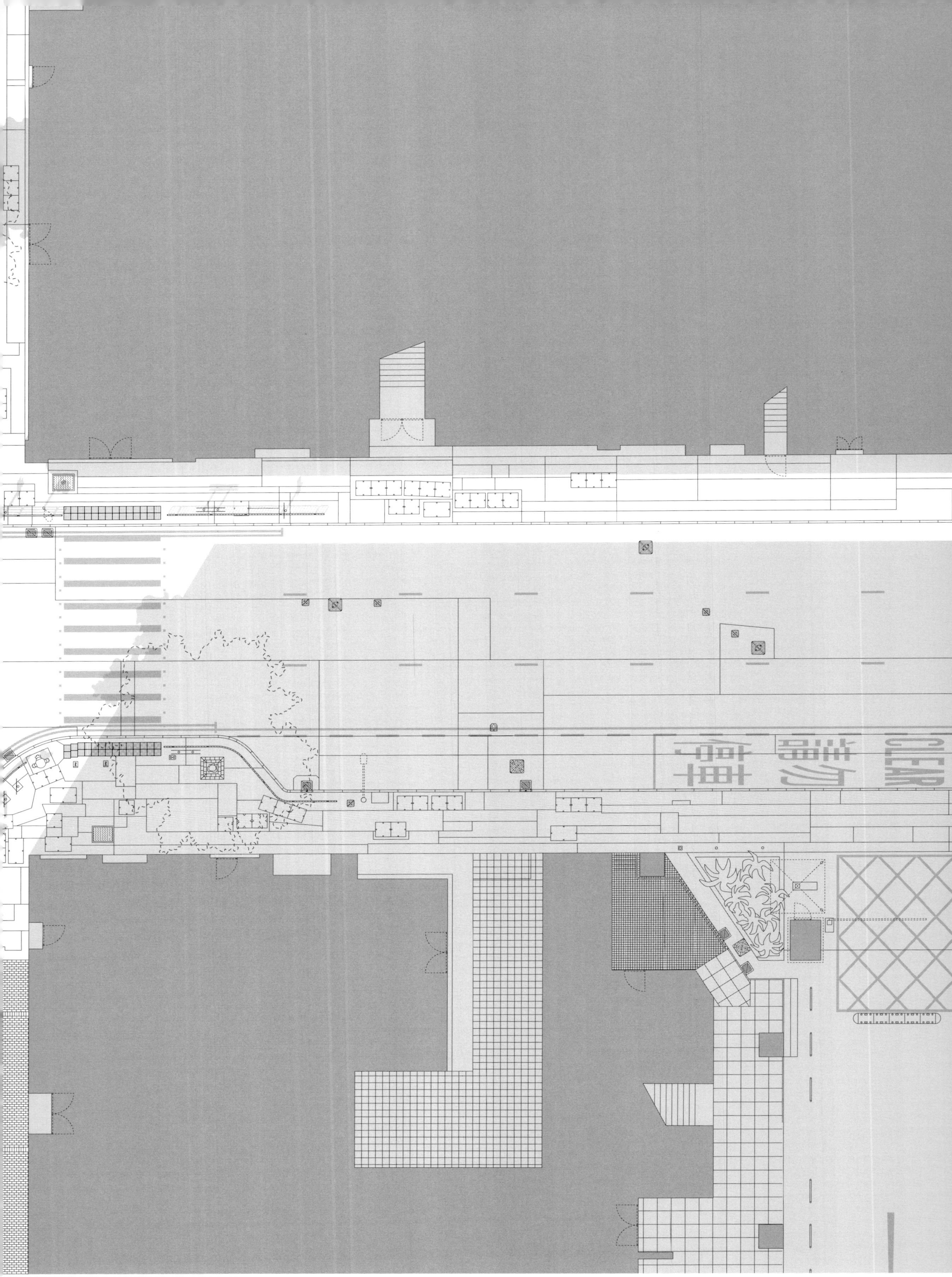
CLEAR

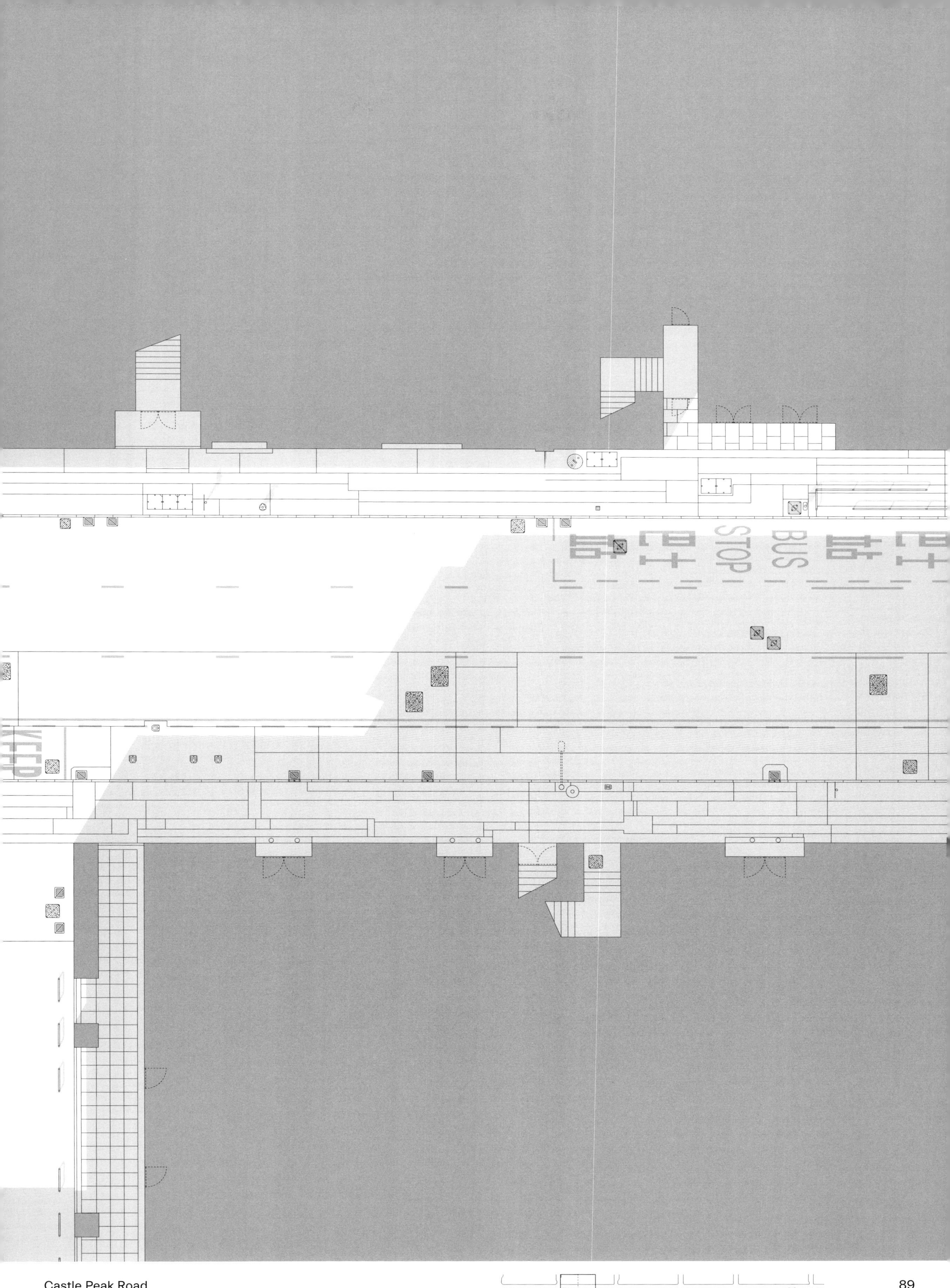

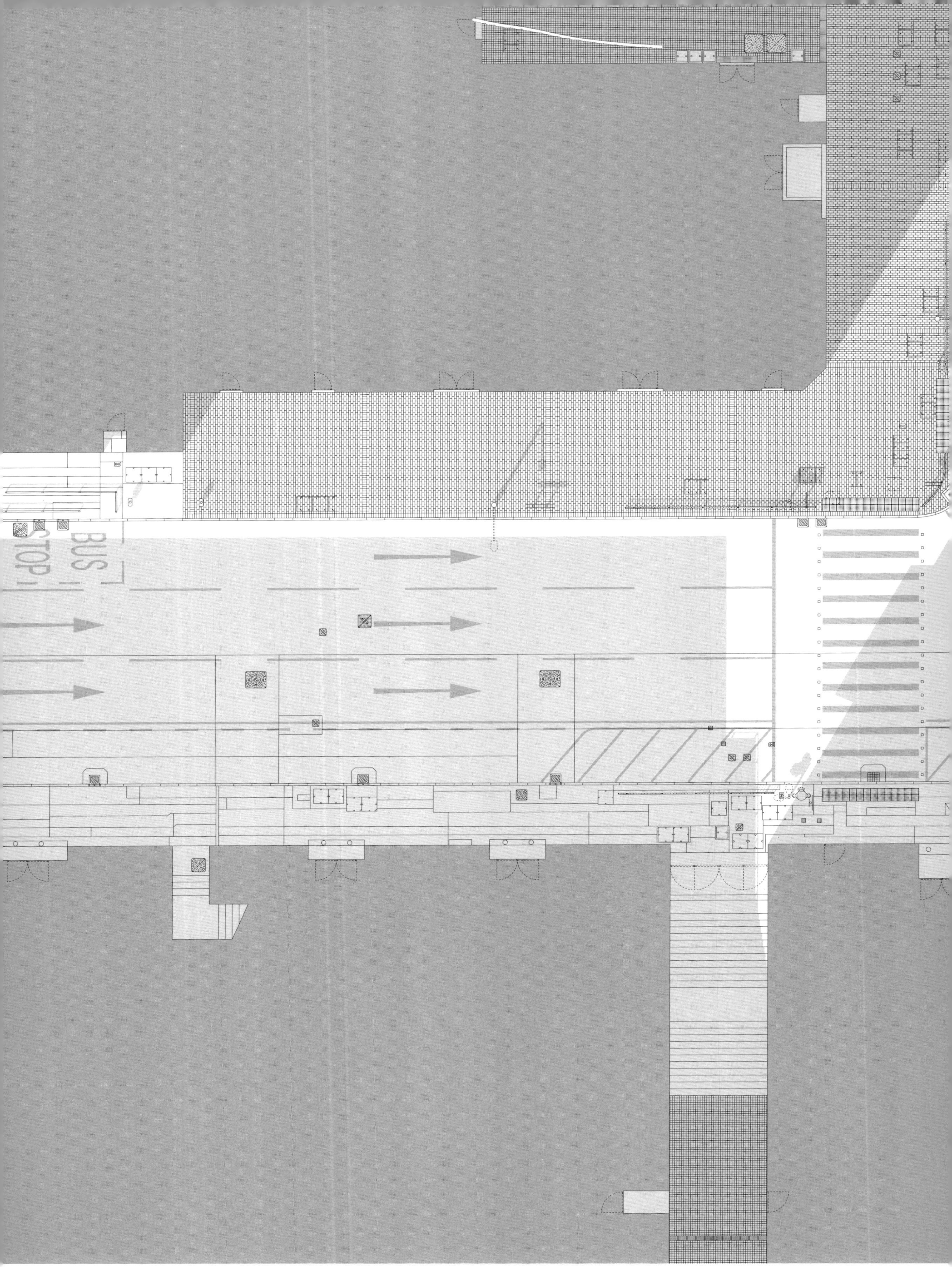
BUS
STOP

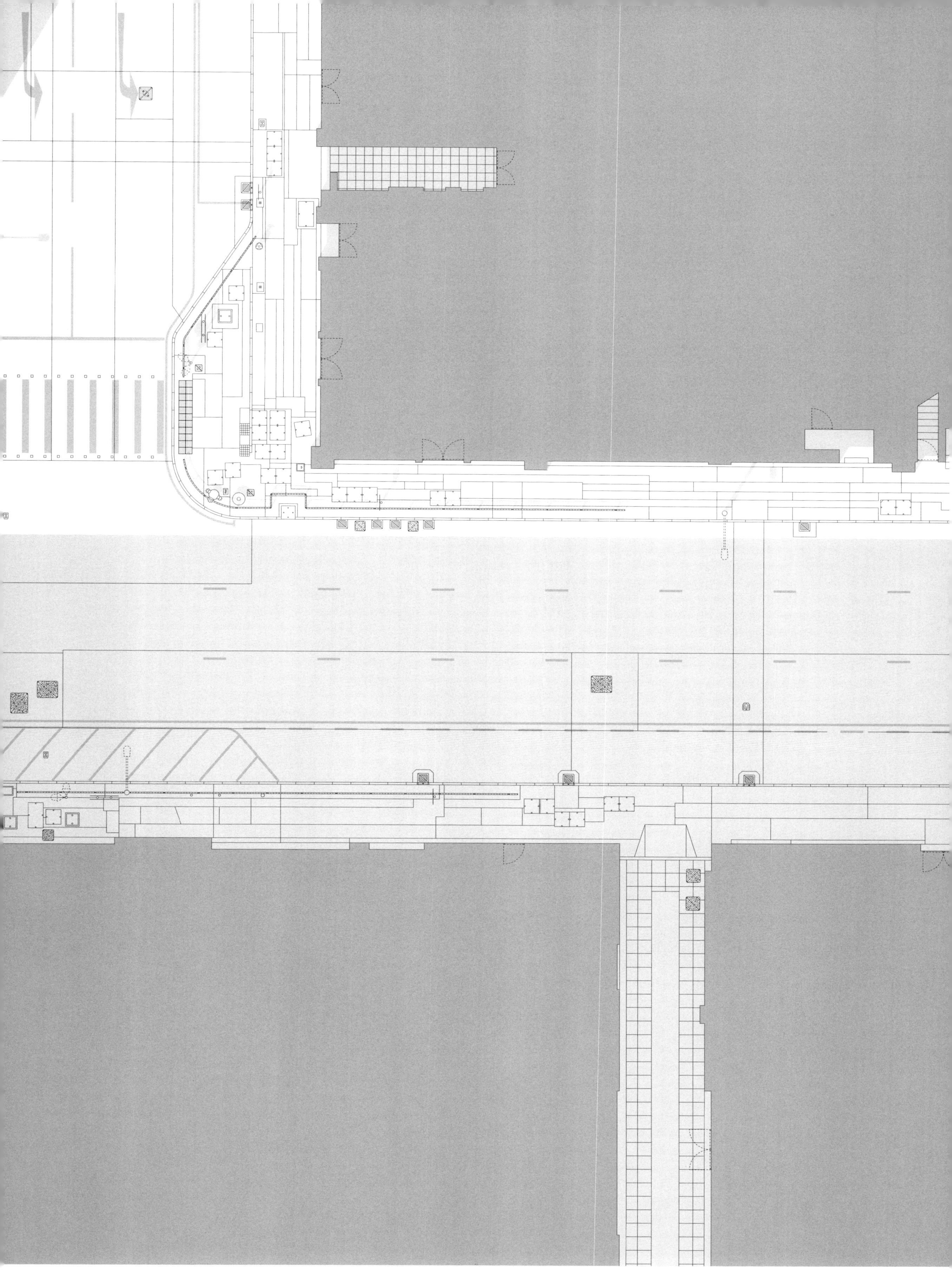

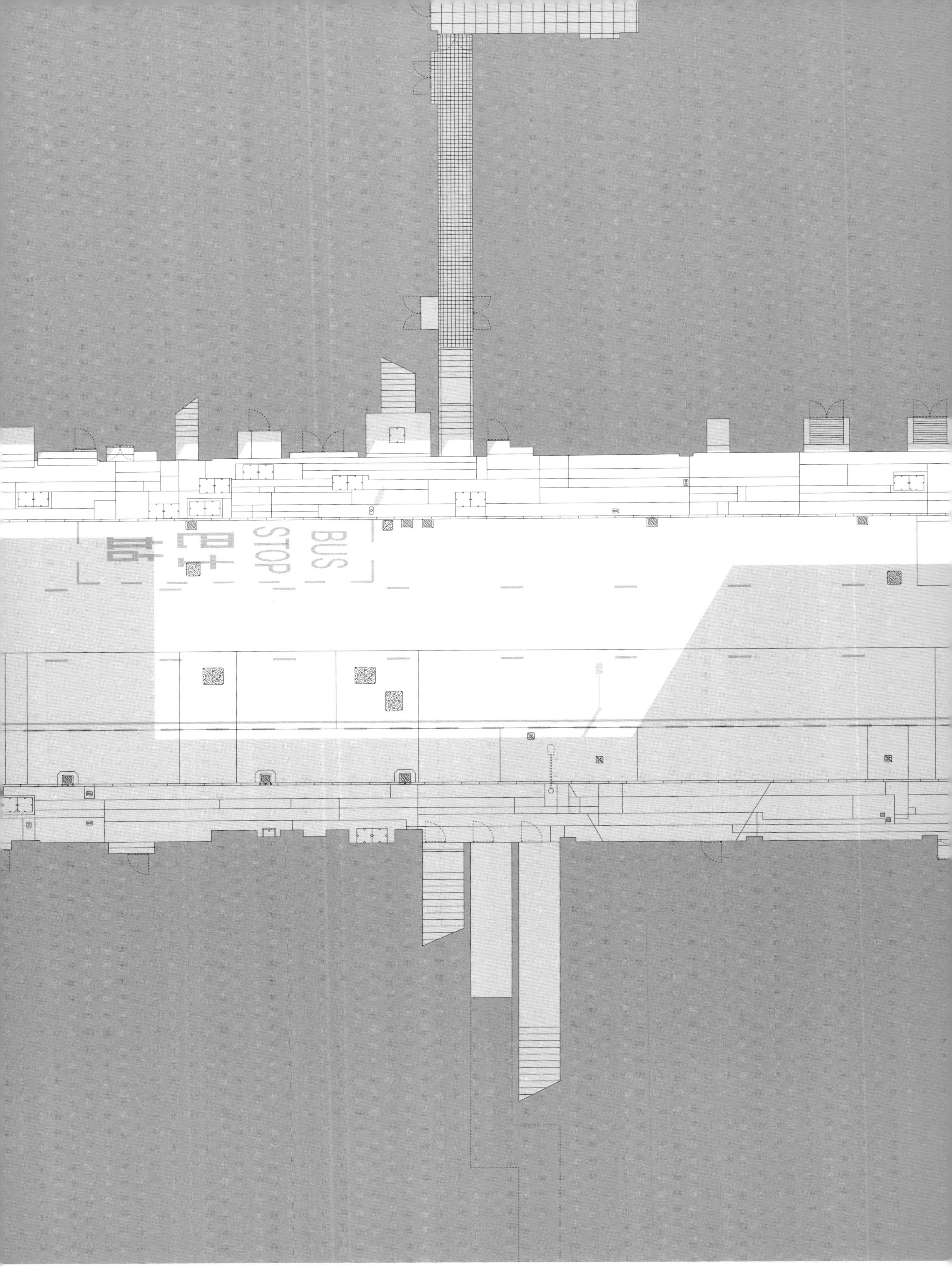
BUS STOP

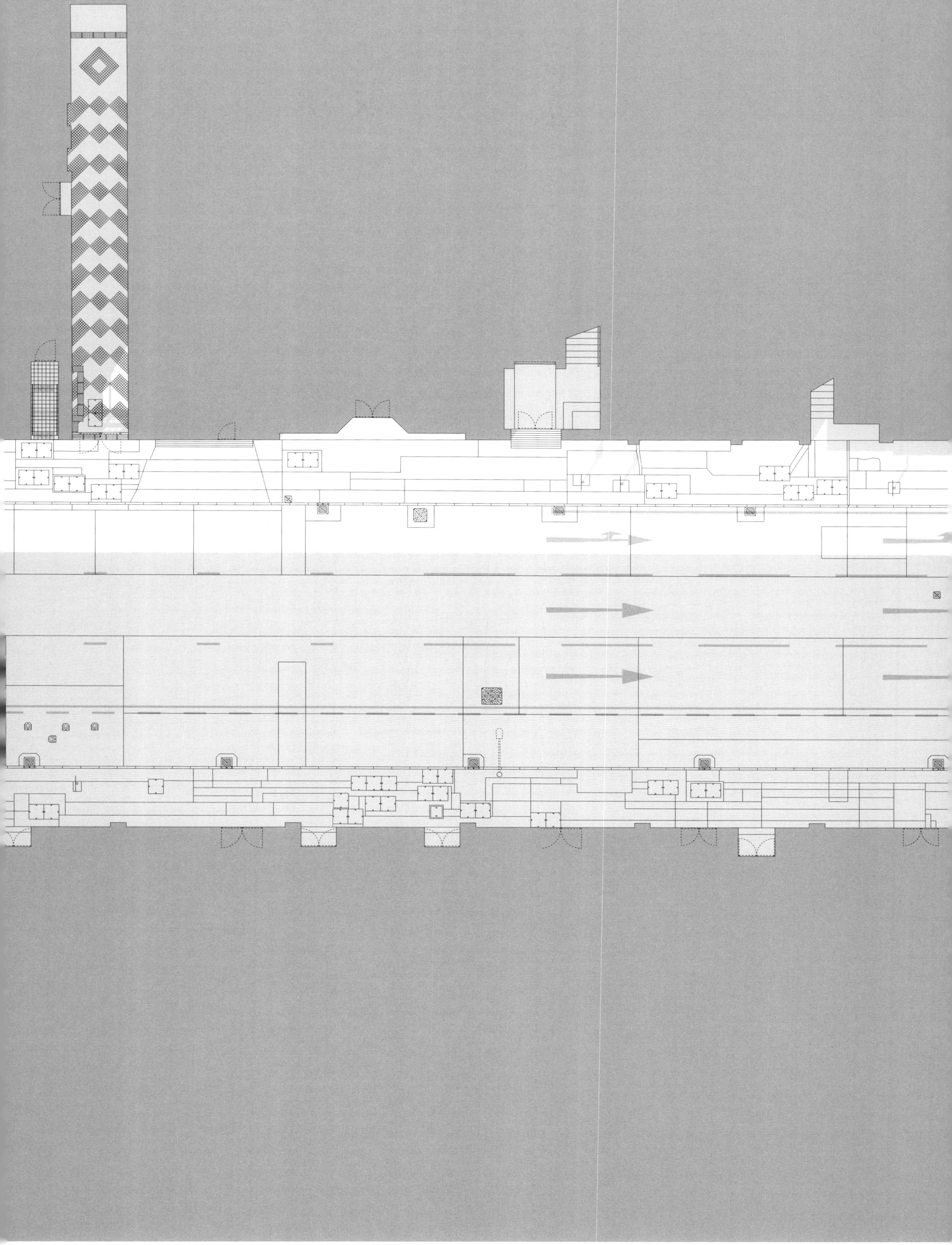

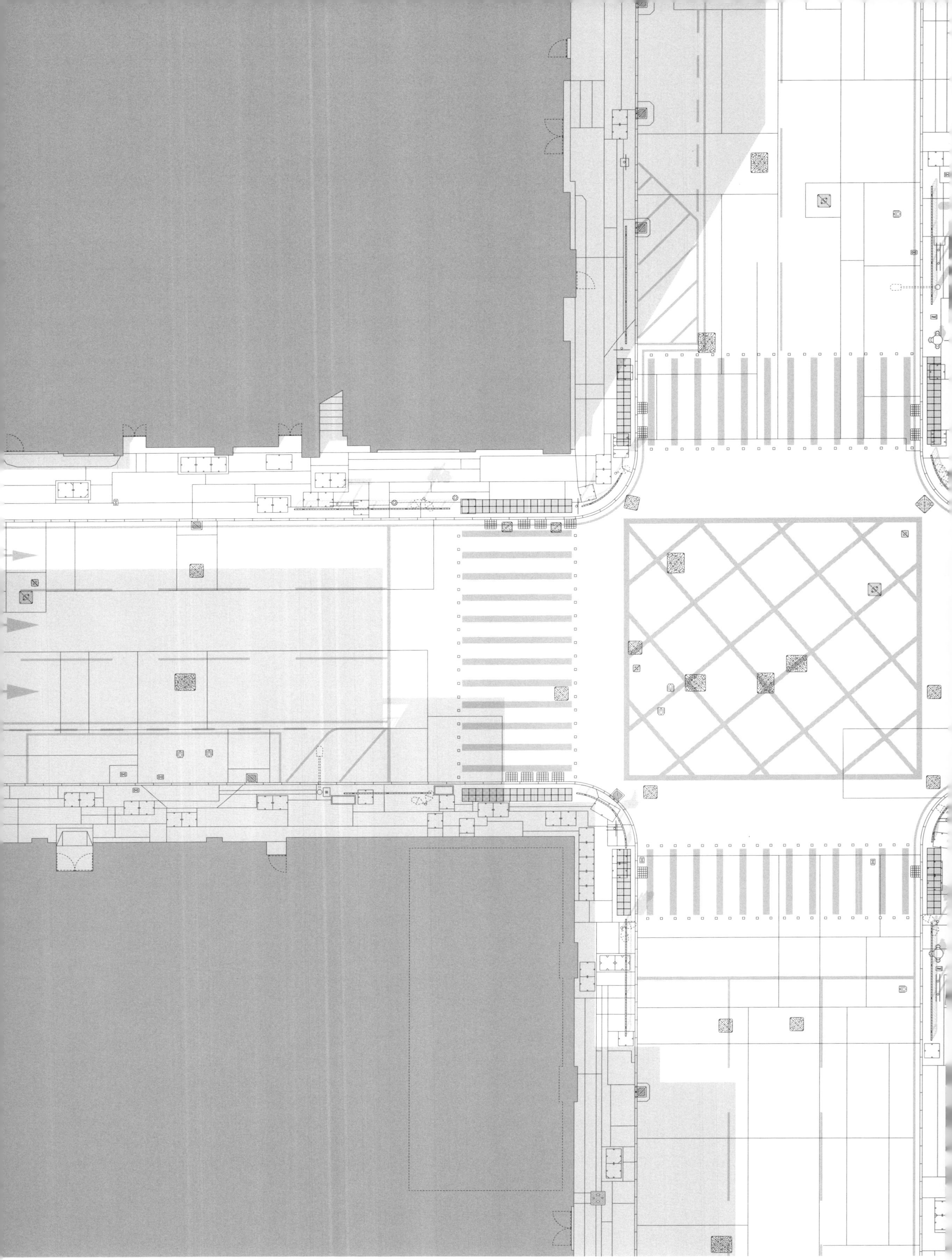

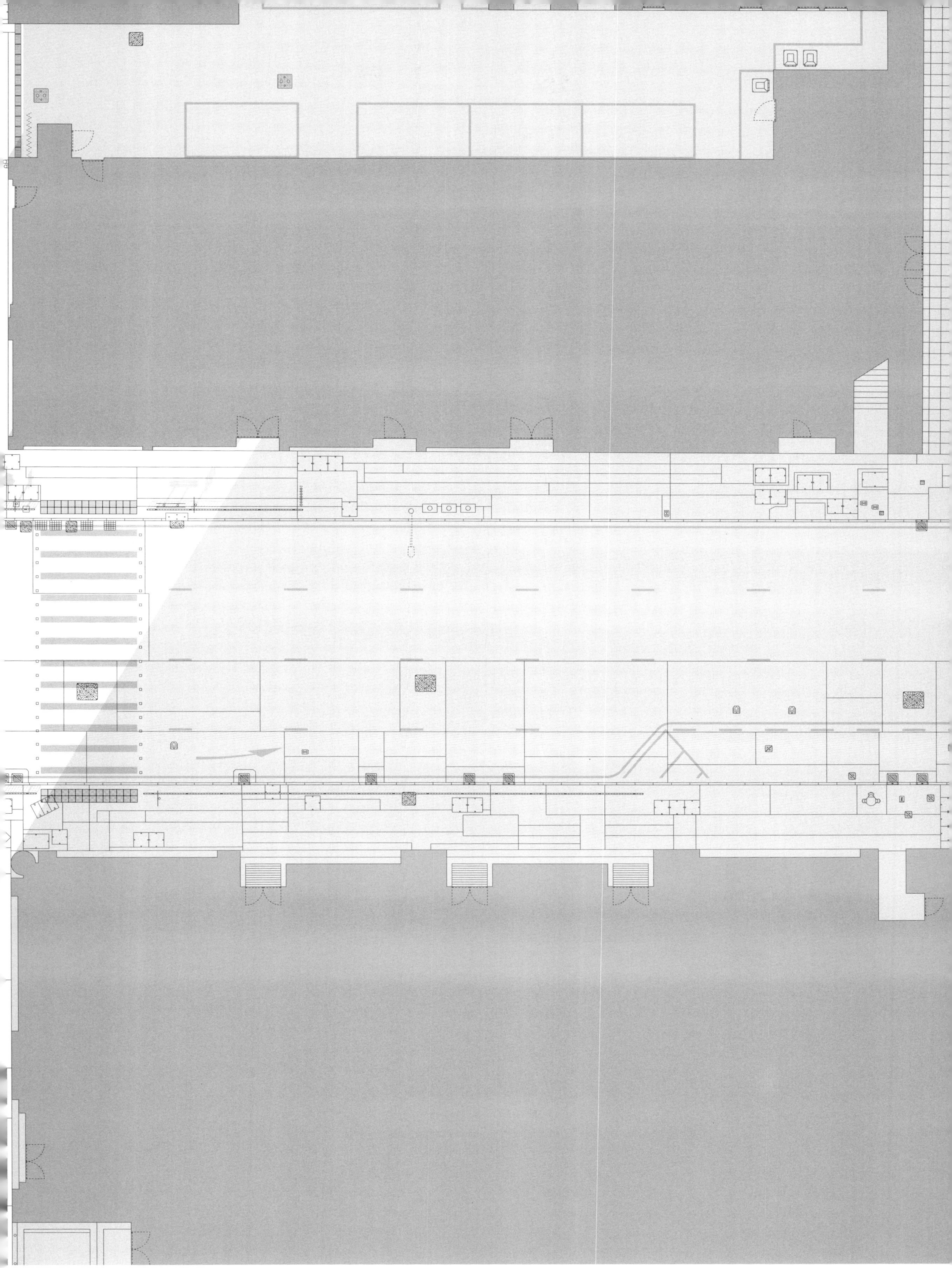

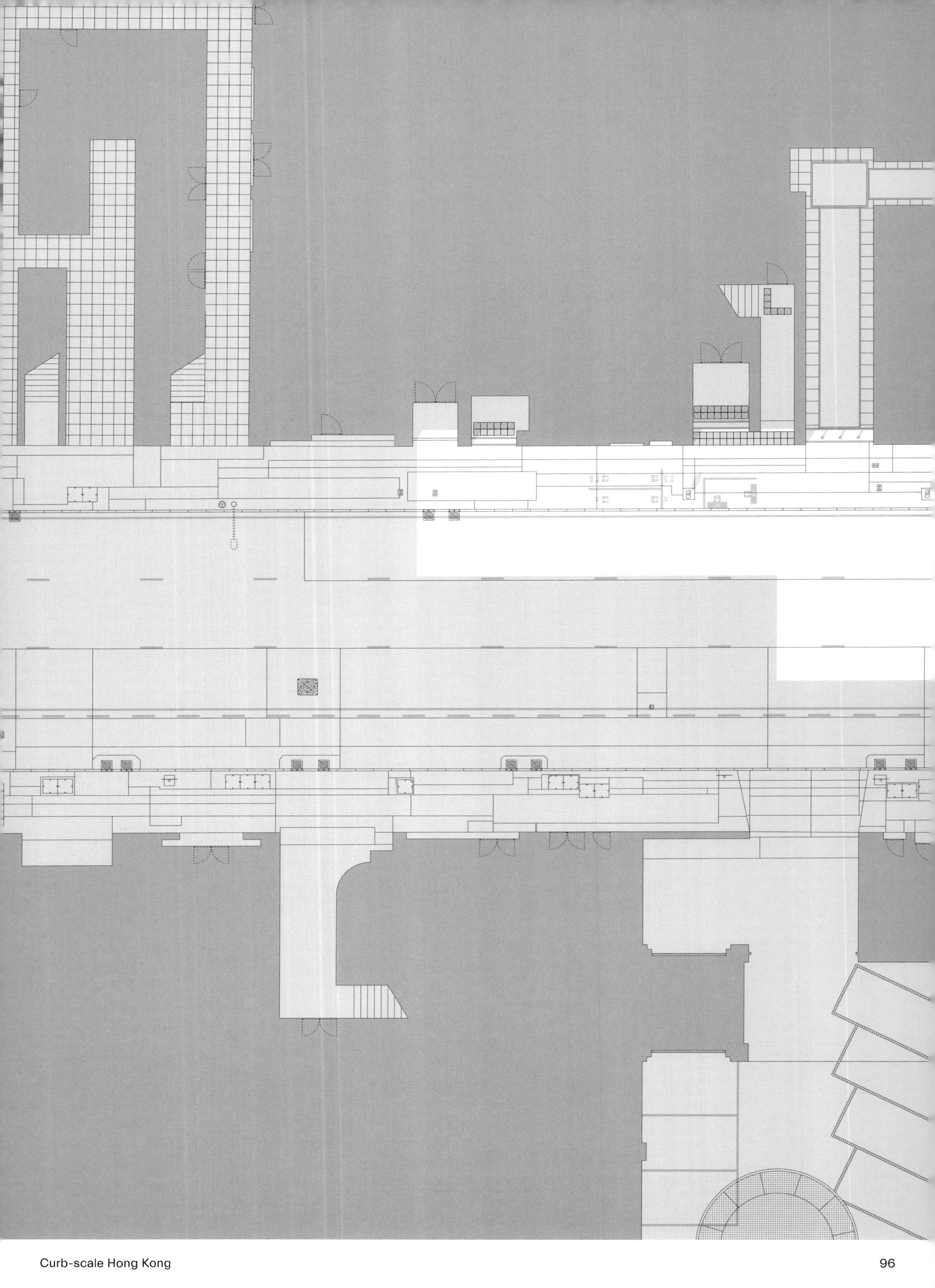

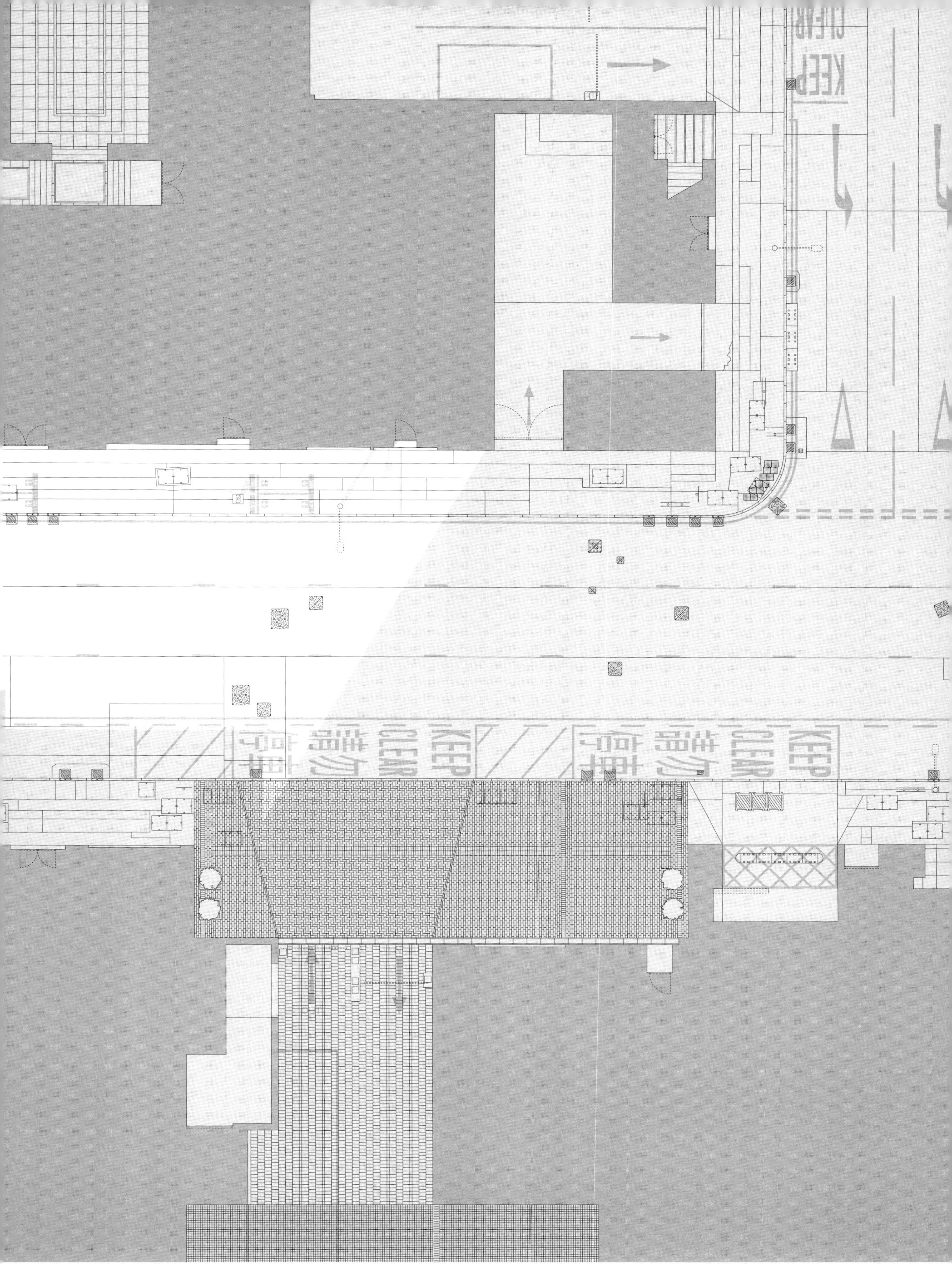
KEEP
CLEAR

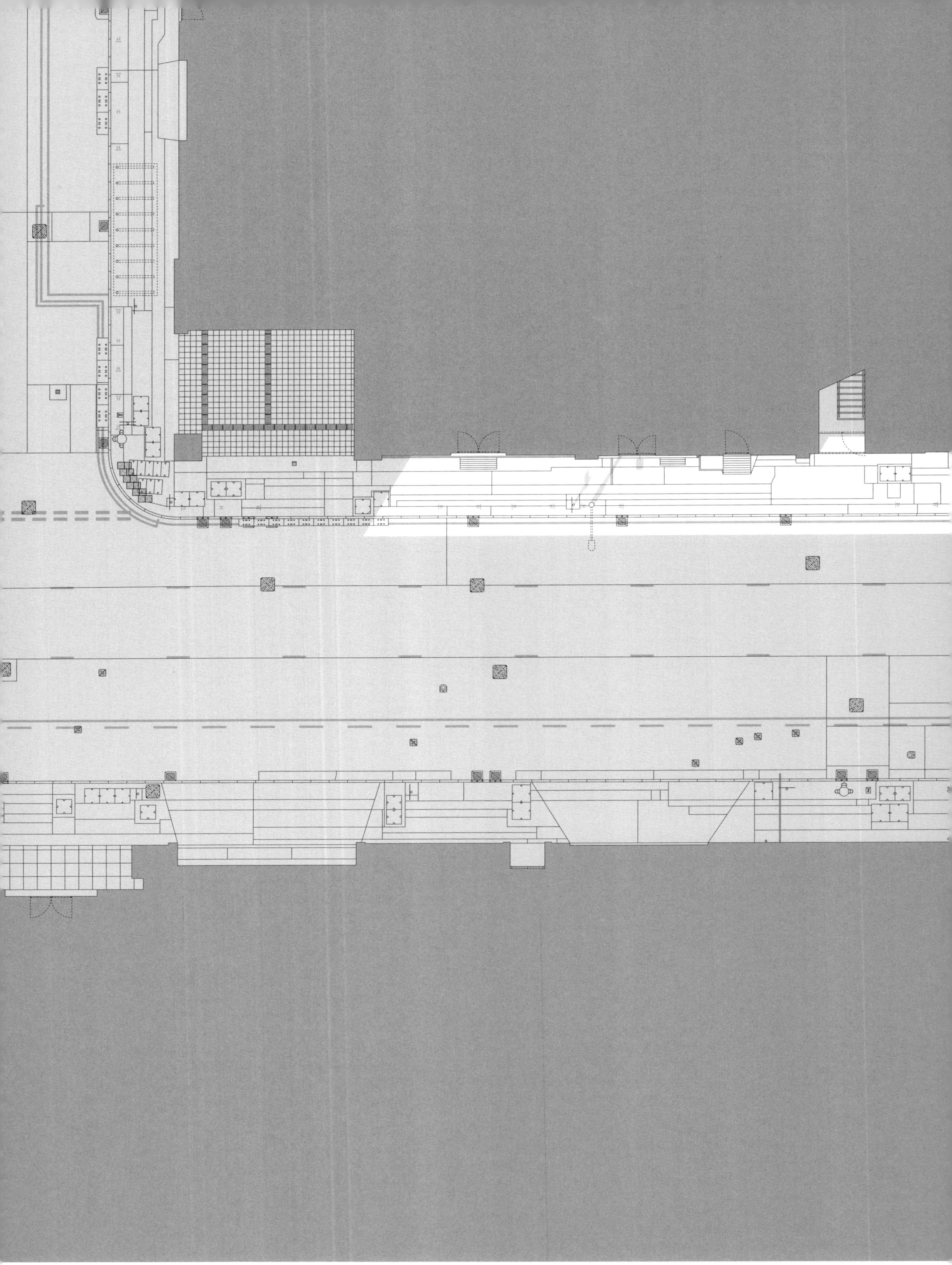

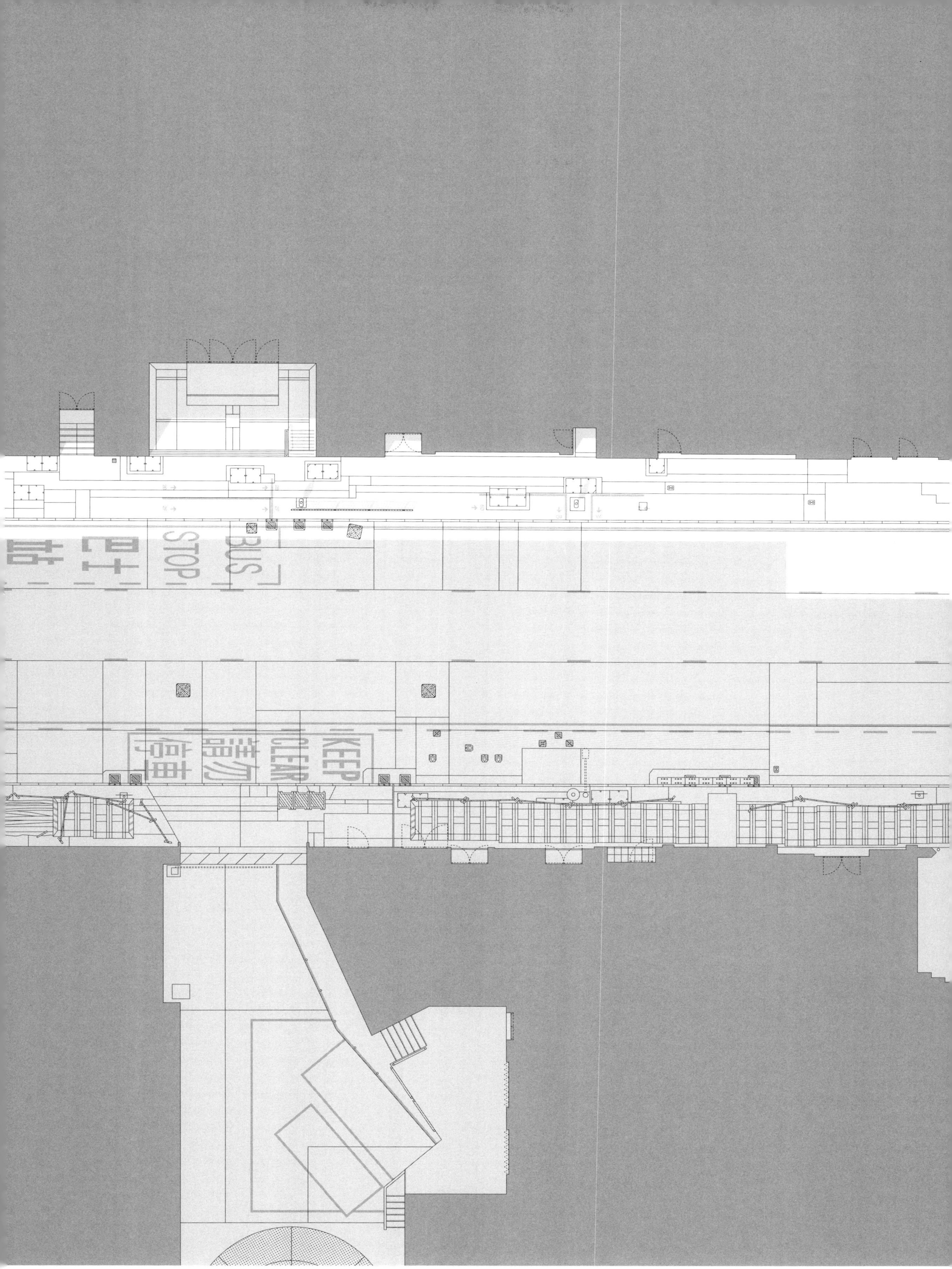
BUS
STOP
KEEP
CLEAR

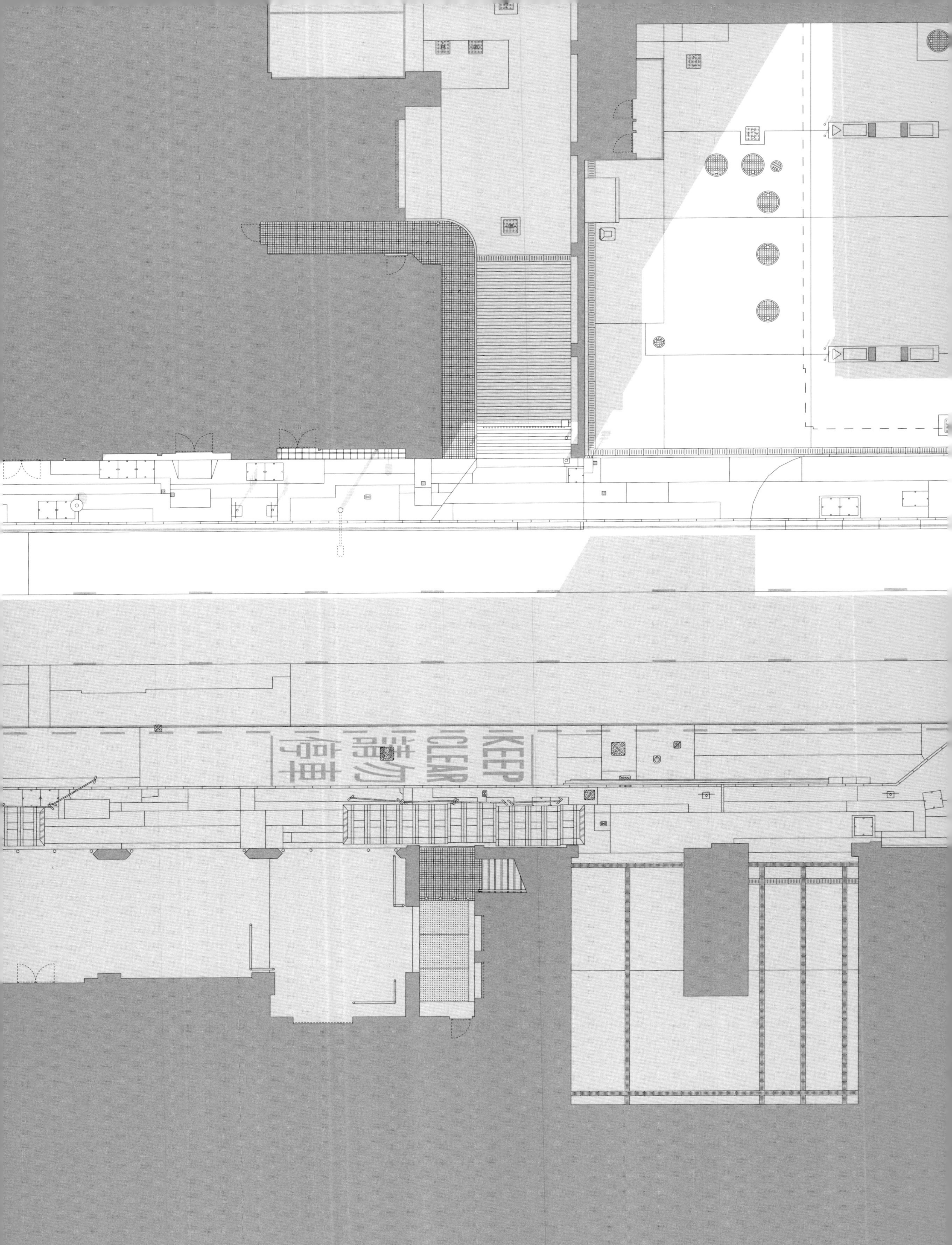
KEEP CLEAR
請勿停車

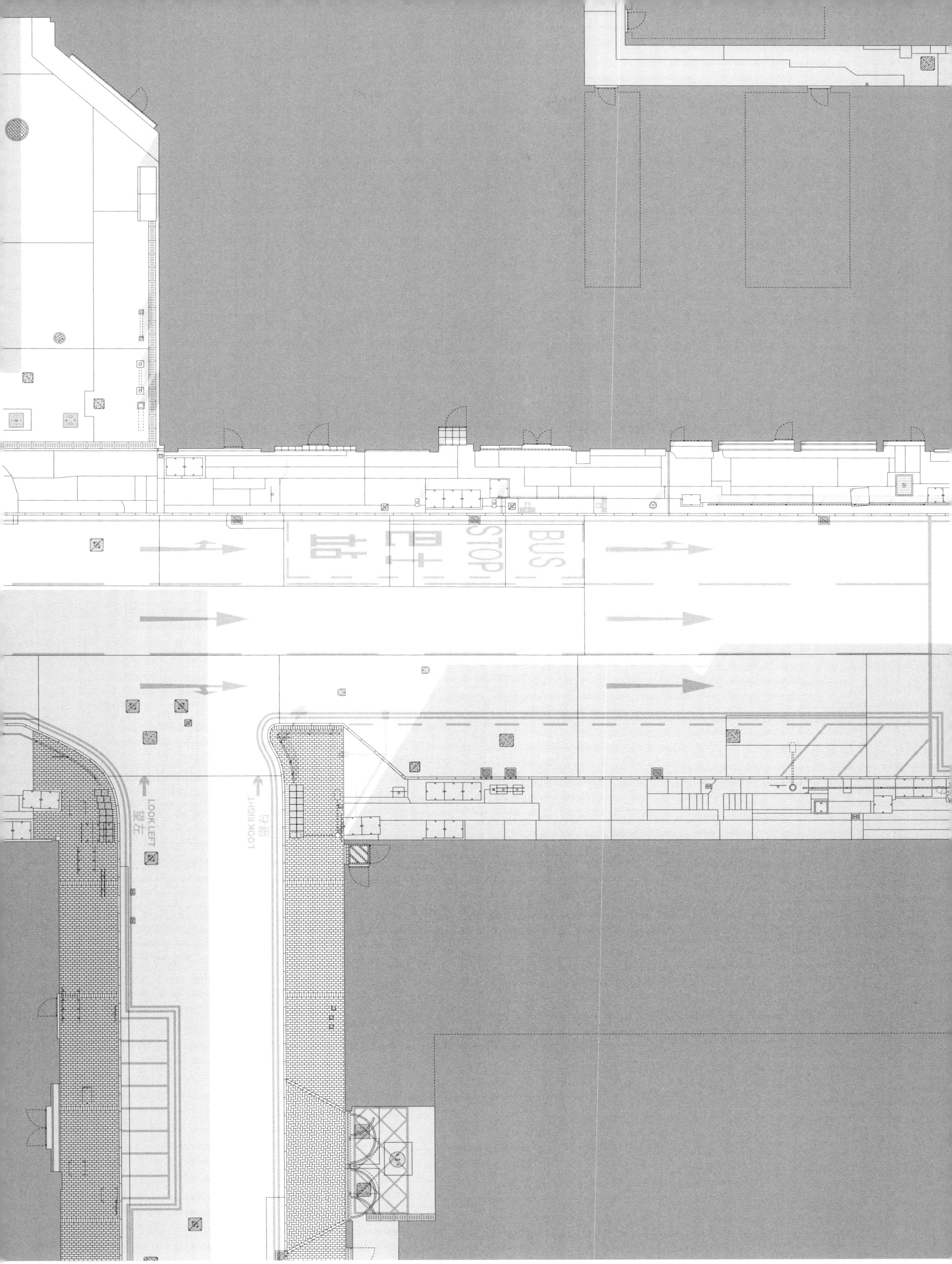
BUS STOP
LOOK LEFT
望左
LOOK RIGHT
望右

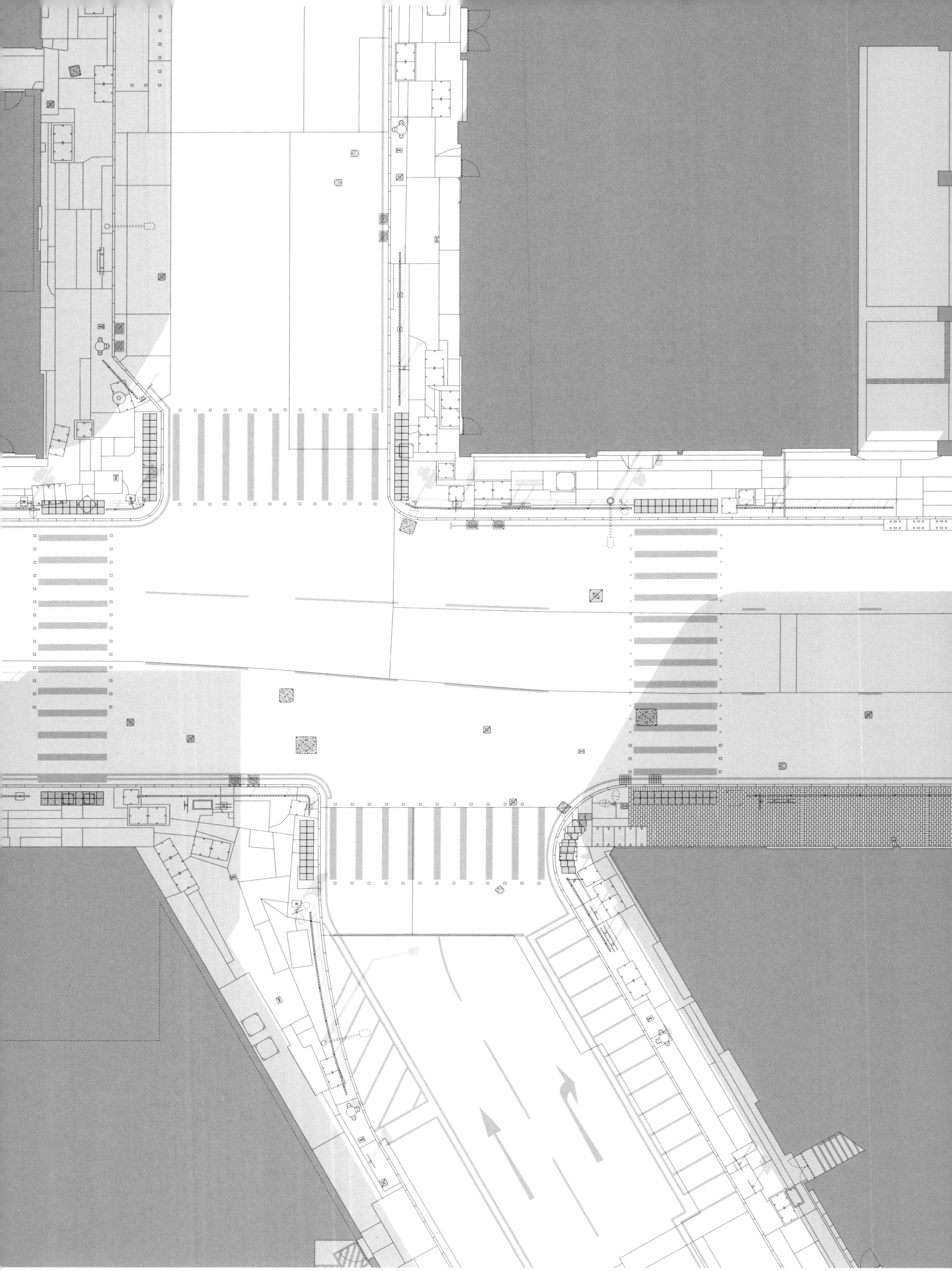

Pound

Lane

Where Po Yee Street intersects with Pound Lane, two shallow steps stretch its full width. Where the steps meet a wall that delimits the street, someone has installed a thin tube of steel. It is bent into a U and fixed upside down so that the upper stroke slopes with the gradient of the descent. The tube is fixed into the ground and reinforced with a mound of cement caked into the angle formed with the wall. The steel has the feel of the handle of a tool, its circumference made perhaps for smaller hands.

This rail is part of a cluster of elements at the intersection. Just a meter away is a red, freshwater, swan-neck hydrant—number 740. Not far from the hydrant, a not-so-tall post with a short lamp arm is turned toward Pound Lane. The lamp faces a semipermanent structure that houses a single-person toilet. The square cabin extends at its base to form a step. The step is sheathed in metal that also reinforces the cabin's corners. A plate on the roof slopes downward toward the back of the cabin and projects over the entrance. Underneath the overhang is a circular light that illuminates the step below. A plane of solar cells is raised off of the structure by a vertical arm that rotates with the sun's movement. Pipes, vents, and doodads bring air and water into the cabin, while waste is stored for disposal.

A sticker on the door announces a telephone number for ISS Environmental Services (HK) Ltd, in case of any issues. According to their website, ISS, is a "a leading workplace experience and facility management company, [that] provides placemaking solutions that contribute to better business performance and make...life easier, more productive and enjoyable—delivered to high standards by people who care." [1] The company provides these solutions in over 30 countries with support for cleaning, catering, back office service, security, and workplace management. The ISS cabin has been placed temporarily during the renovation of the Pound Lane Toilet and Bathhouse whose entrance is a few steps away.

There are more than 800 public toilets in Hong Kong, staffed by 1,030 outsourced attendants who earn an average of HK$11,154 each month. Two mobile cleaning crews, one established in March 2020 with the onset of Covid, ensure "routine cleansing" and additional "deep cleansing services." The government's Food Safety and Environmental Hygiene department, which runs and maintains the toilets, employs 280 people in these two cleaning teams. [2] The bathhouse in the Pound Lane facility is one of 26 spread throughout the territory. Next door to the bathhouse is a temple raised from the street and accessed by a flight of steps. This ancestral hall was built in the mid-19th century as a way station for corpses of early immigrants from China who wished to be repatriated to their villages. It also served as a memorial site for others too impoverished to fund such a trip back.

From its starting point not far from the bathhouse and the temple, Pound Lane rises nearly 50 meters. The street is a stair built into the hillside. It is the spine of a collection of terraces, lanes, and ways with low-rise residential buildings. The construction of each set of stairs differs. Some are independent granite slabs raised from the earth. Others are embedded into the slope or cast in concrete. Pipes run alongside the slope and small, cage-enclosed pumps raised on concrete plinths at landings bring water to the residences. The slope is such that these buildings are built into hollows cut from the earth. You reach their entrances over small bridges that span tall, narrow voids separating retaining walls from windows that look into those shadow-filled gaps.

In 1888 the zone beginning at Pound Lane's uppermost point was set aside "to be preserved in a condition...to render it possible for Europeans to continue to live there in health," and as a bulwark against the "increasing temptation to land-owners to pull down houses adapted for European habitation, and to erect Chinese houses in their place." [3] Not far from the beginning of this reserved zone is an open nullah, engineered into the hillside, that brings water from higher elevations. This drain disappears under the road and into the hill, making its way down the slope until the stormwater is flushed into the harbor. In his book *Atlas*, Dung Kai-cheung includes a chapter on Tai Ping Shan, a small neighborhood of gridded streets that once extended into the area east of Pound Lane. [4] *Atlas* is a fiction that brings together a story of disease and birdsong. It narrates the origins of the garden that replaced a once active district. Pound Lane makes its way through that history.

1. ISS was founded in Denmark in 1901 as a security company providing night watchmen. See ISS, "Reopening Places: It's time to reopen—and rethink—your workplaces," accessed June 1, 2021, https://www.hk.issworld.com/en. Also: Job Daily HK, "ISS Facility Services Limited: Senior Property Officer/Property Officer (Job Ref: ADV/21/277)," accessed June 1, 2021, https://www.jobdailyhk.com/job/issf.
2. Research Office, "Food Safety and Environmental Hygiene: Statistical Highlights," Information Services Division, Legislative Council Secretariat, ISSH07/20-21 (23 November 2020), https://www.legco.gov.hk/research-publications/english/2021issh07-public-toilet-facilities-and-services-20201123-e.pdf.
3. Legislative Council, "Legislative Council, No. 11," Government of HKSAR (27 March, 1888), https://www.legco.gov.hk/1887-88/h880327.pdf. In 1904, a new government ordinance not only regulated the construction of housing but banned Chinese residents from living in elevations "situated above the 788 ft contour" of certain areas of Hong Kong Island. See: Historical Laws of Hong Kong Online, "Peak District Reservation Ordinance, 1904," accessed November 1, 2021, https://oelawhk.lib.hku.hk/items/show/942.
4. Dung Kai-cheung, "The Curse of Tai Ping Shan," in *Atlas: The Archaeology of an Imaginary City*, trans. Dung Kai-cheung, Anders Hansson, and Bonnie S. McDougall (New York: Columbia University Press, 2012), 76–78.

0
5
10

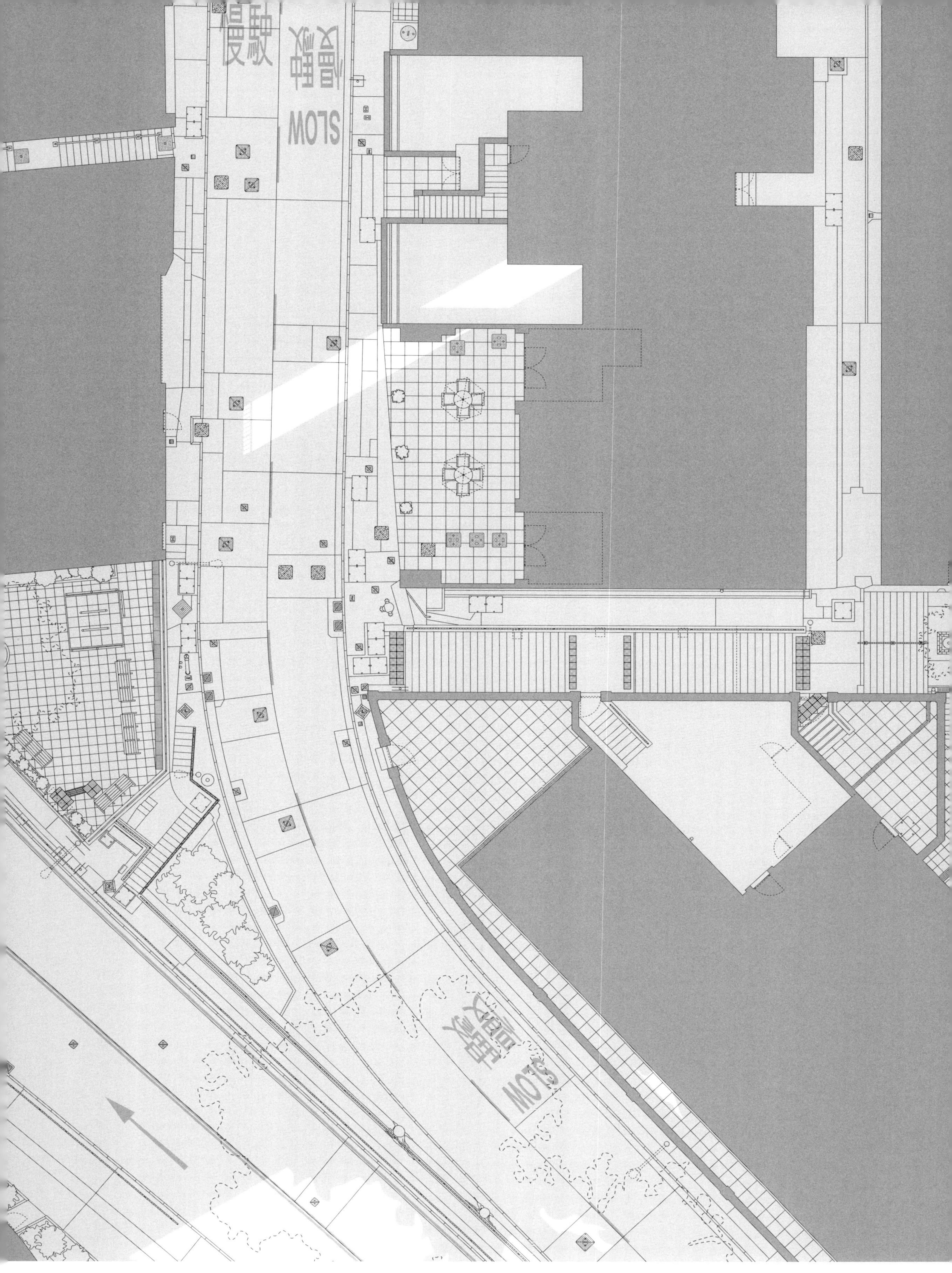
慢駛
SLOW

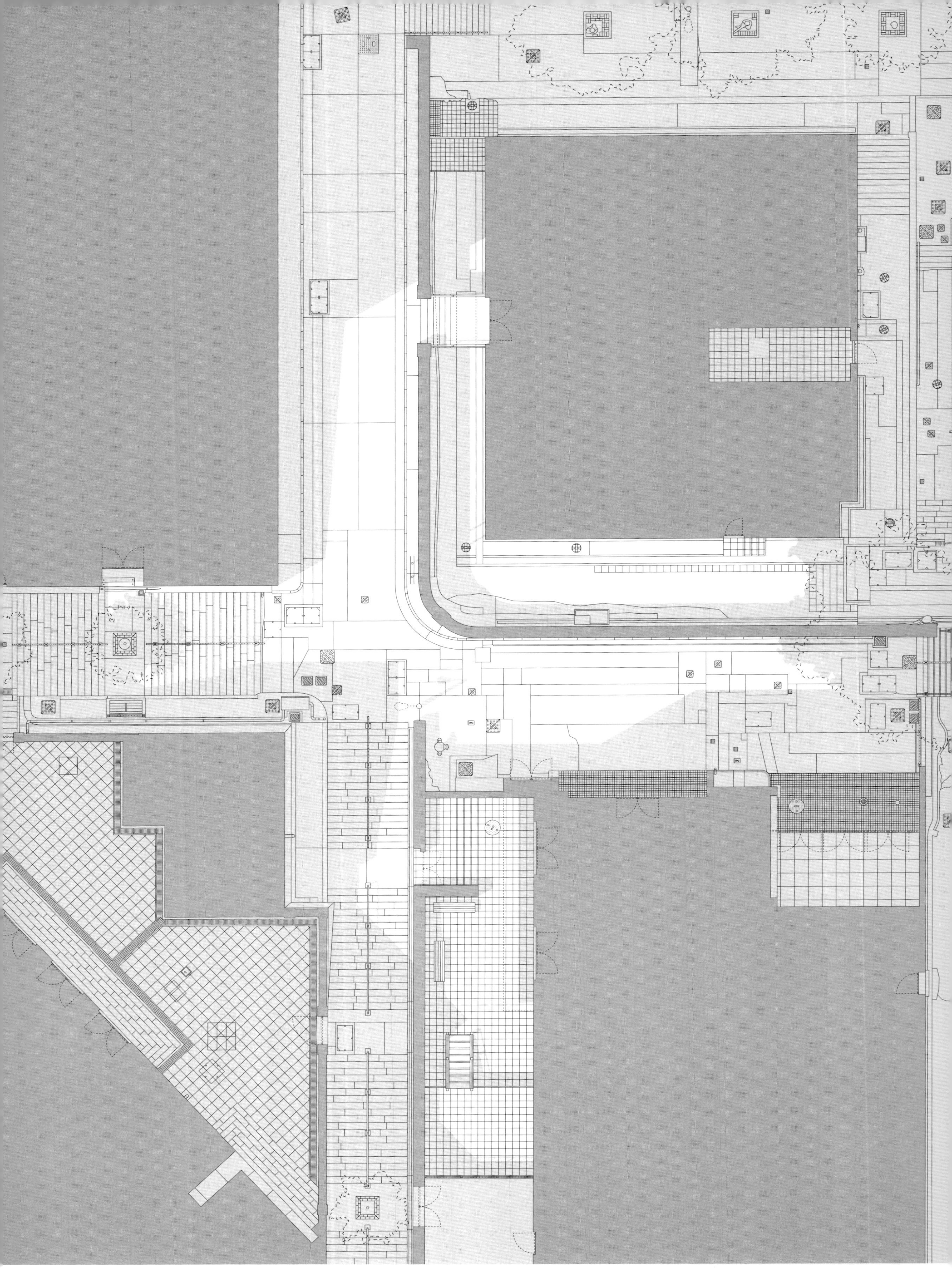

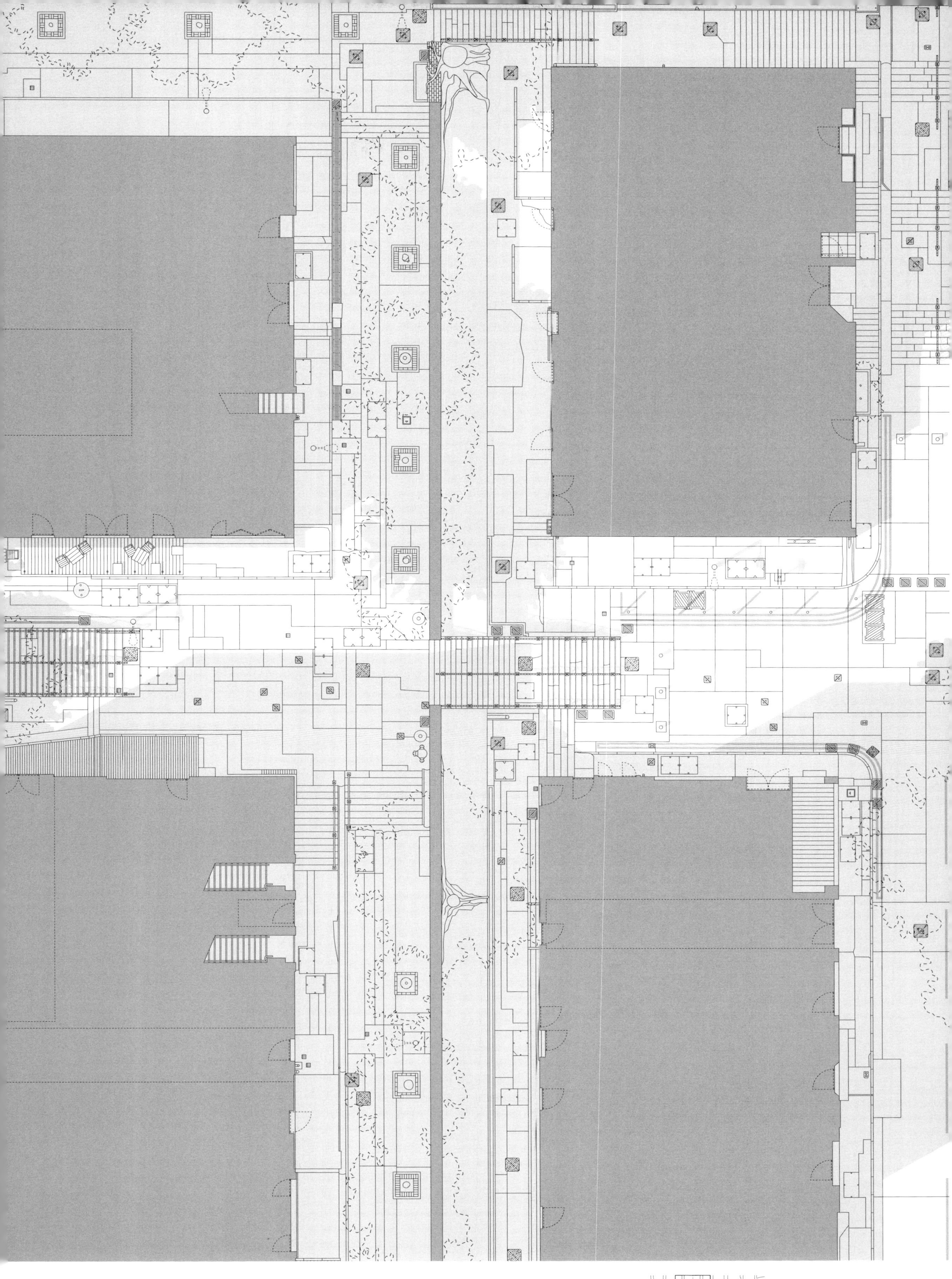

KEEP CLEAR

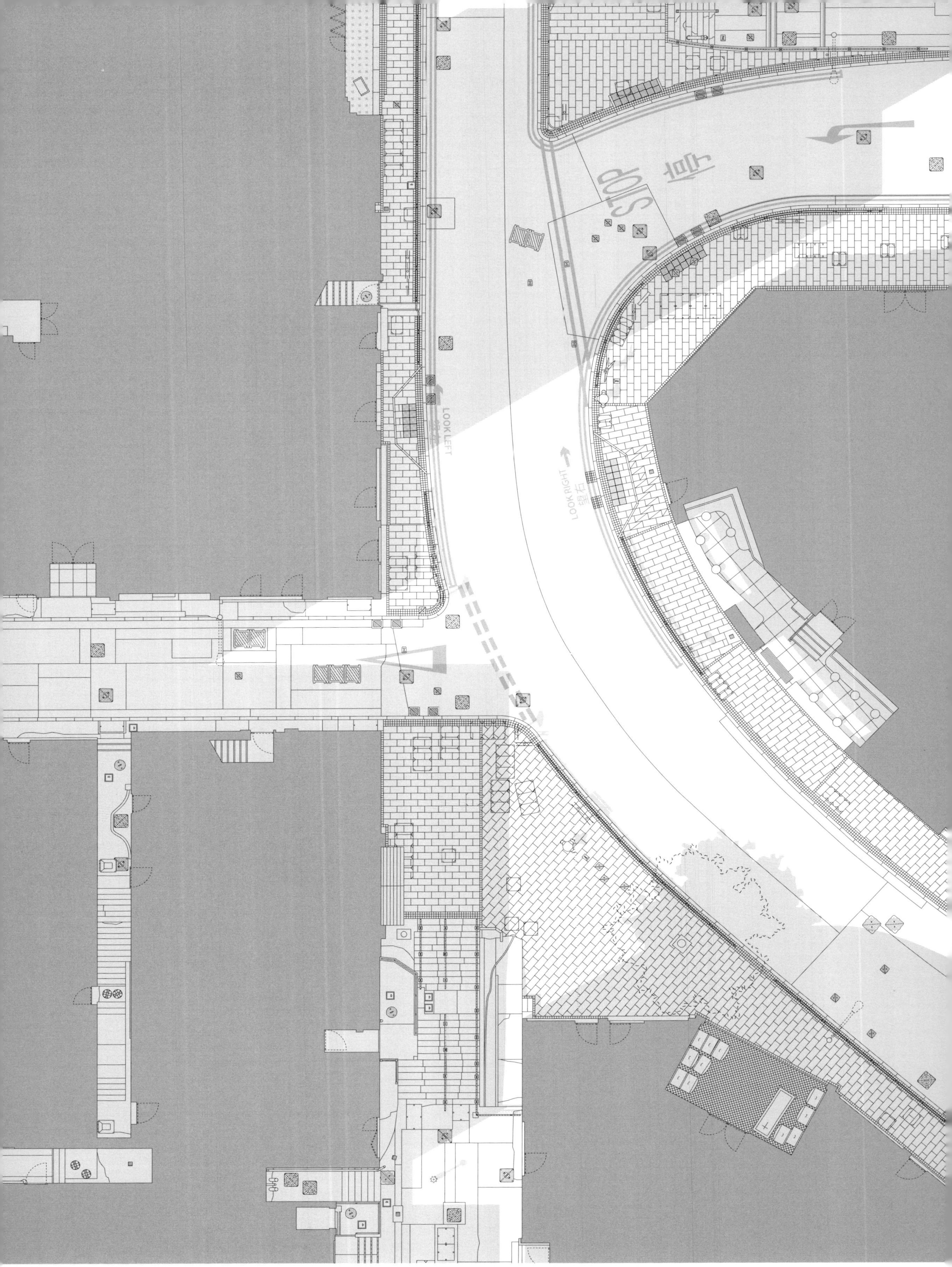
STOP
LOOK LEFT
LOOK RIGHT
望右

Infrastructures

of

Protest

INFRASTRUCTURE, DENSITY, AND PROSPERITY

Infrastructural stories have great power. As Keller Easterling writes, they can "buckle concrete and bend steel" through the force of bureaucratic dispositions that render practices opaque and unyielding. [1] These stories have in the past been heroic tales of engineering and a mastery over nature. [2] They are propagated in photographs, news articles, and popular culture. Dams, bridges, and highways become backdrops for action scenes. Their impending destruction imperils cities and lives. This looming threat of infrastructural failure is often the progenitor of a more generalized social collapse. Brian Larkin's notion of infrastructural "promise" gets at the complexities of these affective registers. Promise entangles "expectation, desire, temporal deferral, sacrifice, and frustration" into practices of administration and politics; this production generates a "realm of discursive meaning" that spins outwards from infrastructure through its "material address." [3] Infrastructure operates on multiple planes of sense: the forces that shape it are bound to how it takes place in our worlds.

Stories of infrastructure in Hong Kong begin with razing, dredging, boring, clearing, pinning: topographic incisions and accretions into an unruly, scraggly peninsula of hills, valleys, and flatlands. [4] On the one hand these stories are heroic tales with physical and territorial connections superimposed in the imagination over virtual and digital links across the globe. They prop up a narrative of Hong Kong as an efficient, world-class city, whose ambitions and free-market influence are outsized in relation to its geographic size and population. This story is nuanced through history: infrastructure as colonial usurpation; as modernizing force; as a driver of trade and commerce (both virtual and real); as a driver of national reunification. In these narratives, infrastructure becomes a world-building exercise that locates

1. Keller Easterling, *Extrastatecraft: The Power of Infrastructure Space* (Brooklyn, NY: Verso, 2014), 93.
2. Annalisa Meyboom, "Infrastructure as Practice," *Journal of Architectural Education* 62, no. 4 (2009): 73, http://www.jstor.org/stable/40481065.
3. Brian Larkin, "Promising Forms: The Political Aesthetics of Infrastructure," in *The Promise of Infrastructure,* eds. Nikhil Anand, Akhil Gupta, and Hannah Appel (Durham: Duke University Press, 2018), 178.
4. There is a pervasive narrative that imagines that Hong Kong's colonial rulers transformed a "barren rock" into a semi-tropical urban garden. See: Robert Peckham, "Hygienic Nature: Afforestation and the greening of colonial Hong Kong," *Modern Asian Studies* 49, no. 4 (2015): 1,177–1,209.

5. Alice Poon's account of years spent working in the offices of Hong Kong's property developers is part of a larger popular discussion on the role of a handful of families that control the availability of real estate. See Alice Poon, *Land and the Ruling Class in Hong Kong*, 2nd ed. (Singapore: Enrich Publishing, 2011).
6. For a comprehensive overview of government land policy, links between land reclamation, government auctions, and Hong Kong's low tax, low regulation regime, see Stephen Brown and Christine Loh, "Hong Kong: The Political Economy of Land," Hong Kong Civic Exchange (June 2002), www.civic-exchange.org/wp-content/uploads/2002/06/21-200206LAND_PoliticalEconomyofLand_en.pdf.
7. On the financialization of Hong Kong's economy since 1996, see Kim Ming Lee, Benny Ho Pong To, and Kar Ming Yu, "Financialization and Economic Inequality in Hong Kong: The Cost of the Finance-Led Growth Regime," in *Hong Kong 20 Years after the Handover*, eds. Brian C. H. Fong and Tai-Lok Lui (London: Palgrave Macmillan, 2018), 127–51, https://doi.org/10.1007/978-3-319-51373-7_6.
8. Wai Han Lo, "Governmentality and Neoliberalism: A Study of Media Discourse on Poverty in Hong Kong," *Journal of Poverty and Social Justice: Research, Policy, Practice* 28, no. 1 (2020): 55–78.

the ambiguous in-between that has characterized Hong Kong's history: as an entrepôt, way station, or virtual portal that provided access for goods and capital to make their way between China and the rest of the world.

In Hong Kong, these stories about infrastructure are told alongside tales of prosperity and density. Together, the three form a rhetorical trope that reinforces and justifies itself, becoming a kind of default response to any issue: inadequate housing, environmentally disastrous ocean-infill schemes, economic inequality, or the razing of neighborhoods for superblock development. Policy decisions and policy inaction are explained or excused with discursive articulations that coordinate the three terms. More recently, challenges to these discourses have weakened their hold on the city, leading to public mistrust of government pronouncements. Popular reporting on "white elephants," widely discussed delays on infrastructure projects, and investigations into outlays have brought scrutiny to the way infrastructural projects channel money to a handful of developers from Hong Kong and mainland China. [5] These projects are linked to government auctions for development rights to land that is released or newly created in coordination with infrastructure. [6] Land auctions provide massive government earnings, making possible a low tax regime for corporations and individuals at all income levels. Auctions benefit from the manufactured scarcity of land and have resulted in the speculative financialization of the economy and increased inequality. [7] Outlays for government services, welfare, and unemployment are minimal, with long-standing, media-driven messaging about the importance of charity and self-help thwarting a more progressive government role. [8] The lack of social security forces senior citizens without family support to continue working in maintenance, security, or street cleaning positions well into old age. Arguments that bring together density, prosperity, and infrastructure serve as alibis for a lack of political will and imagination that sees continued and unceasing development through developer-driven megaprojects as the only possible answer for pressures exacerbated by the territory's seemingly exceptional constraints. [9] Easterling's assertion that ideology can "buckle concrete and bend steel" could be reframed for Hong Kong to describe a political economy oriented toward endless construction—building toward a point of critical failure.

IMAGINATIONS OF FLOW

An imagination of flows is woven through discourses of density, prosperity, and infrastructure. Continuous, uninterrupted movement is understood to engender efficiencies through the smooth distribution of information, bodies, supplies, or goods. Flow counters database structures of point-to-point connection, where discrete bits of information wait to be accessed or operationalized. Databases are an "abstract and homogeneous space of cells and grids" in which dematerialized data is virtually at rest until called upon. [10] As Tiziana Terranova has pointed out, all of these bits of information—and the cells and grids that enclose them—comprise a technical infrastructure of machines in buildings that are themselves in locales and nation-states. Her point is that our imaginations of technological processes are often divorced from their real material impact and consequences. Flow operates in a different but equally pernicious fashion to this "Excel" imagination. Rather than docile and dormant bits waiting to be activated, flow describes information that circulates ceaselessly in a productive and directed displacement that arrives, already at every instant where it is needed. Rather than waiting in a cell to be activated, information circulates at speeds or efficiencies, or through networks, that allow for any movement to be optimized for the singular purpose of its immediate arrival.

9. See, for example, Mee Kam Ng, "Transformative urbanism and reproblematising land scarcity in Hong Kong," *Urban Studies* 57, no. 7 (2020): 1,452–1,468, https://doi.org/10.1177/0042098018800399.
The government's HK$500 billion "Lantau Tomorrow Vision" project, announced in 2018 by Hong Kong's Chief Executive, proposed a 1,700-hectare island infill development in waters between Lantau Island, Hong Kong Island, and the Kowloon peninsula. The Hong Kong civil society leader and environmental policy expert Christine Loh has argued that such land reclamation "must be a last option," but that for the government it comes "much earlier… because the other [options] seem too hard because you have to make policy changes. And policy changes means dealing with difficult people." See: "The Revolution Needed to Achieve Carbon Neutrality 2050," Architecture, Urbanism and Humanities Initiative Speaker Series, Department of Architecture, University of Hong Kong, April 13, 2021, 55:15, https://www.arch.hku.hk/event_/the-revolution-needed-to-achieve-carbon-neutrality-2050/?subcat=auhi.
Such policy changes would implicate powerful village and developer landholding interests in the New Territories.
10. Tiziana Terranova, *Network Culture: Politics for the Information Age* (London: Pluto Press, 2004), 44.

This imagination has come to shape the way we think about capital and people moving through cities: smoothly, incessantly, without friction. Just as virtualized data is divorced in our minds from the physical servers, flow obscures the material emplacements that make any circulation possible. As Doreen Massey argues, "The impetus to motion and mobility, for a space of flows, can be only achieved through the construction of (temporary, provisional) stabilisations." [11] These stabilizations depend on capital investments and material that constitute political choices. Imaginations of flow that naturalize such movement as a contemporary condition fail to recognize the contingent nature of the priorities and logics that uphold it. Massey notes that this "installs an understanding of space, the 'space of flows', which, just like the space of places of modernity, is deployed (when needed) as a legitimation for its own production and which pretends to a universality which anyway in practice it systematically denies." [12] This tension between universality and denial, between the naturalization of flow as a rational functioning and enclosures that keep people out, has become ever more apparent with a pandemic that has rendered unambiguous the way that bodies, air, and viral particulates move through space, shutting down borders and installing distance between bodies.

In the architectural imagination, flow describes a postmodern city in which "junkspace" interiorizes and privatizes civic life into climate-controlled atmospheres of circulation and consumption. Hong Kong came to be understood as an exemplary city of flows, in part due to an extensive network of walkways popularized in the book *Cities Without Ground*. [13] One set of reviewers note that the book reveals Hong Kong to be "a vertical capitalist city, where mobile flow, instead of fixed forms characterize urban life." [14] They propose that the book's drawings "encourage the reader to think of cities as vertical spaces of flows" while also reconceptualizing figure-ground representations and "the notion of 'ground' in contemporary urbanism as a surface, across which daily activities and circulatory networks occur." [15] This last challenge expands an argument of the critic Clancy

11. Doreen Massey, *For Space* (London: Sage, 2005), 94.
12. Ibid., 87.
13. Adam Frampton, Clara Wong, and Jonathan Solomon, *Cities Without Ground: A Hong Kong Guidebook* (San Francisco: ORO Editions, 2012).
14. Bieke Catoor and Chris Perkins, "Re-cartographies of Landscape: New Narratives in Architectural Atlases," *Cartographic Journal* 51, no. 2 (2014): 174.
15. Ibid., 173, 176.

Wilmott, who proposed that Hong Kong was the "perfect backdrop" for this reconceptualization because "as a vertical city of skyscrapers, huddled between steep mountains and reclaimed foreshores, ...'ground' makes no sense physically or culturally." [16] Implicit within these descriptions of a city of groundless topological flow is a reading of the turn-of-the-century city as a globalized node within a larger network of capital. The smooth and seamless system through which Hongkongers circulate coincides with the movement of money, workers, information, and energy promised by a connected city in a flattened world. Flow became the prevailing metaphor for movement at once outside of space and time, yet seamless and continuous.

An ambivalence toward flow resonates through 20th-century aesthetics. Walter Benjamin disavows it altogether as an outdated way of thinking in his notes on early film. He writes that "very characteristic is the opposition, in film, between the downright jerky rhythm of the image sequence, which satisfies the deep-seated need of this generation to see the 'flow' of 'development' disavowed, and the continuous musical accompaniment." [17] Film's "jerky rhythm" modelled time as an irreconcilable disjunction. "Flow," on the other hand, was a falsely projected coherence that sought to smooth out these breaks as a way of taming history. Benjamin continues that, "to root out every trace of 'development' from the image of history and to represent becoming through the dialectical rupture between sensation and tradition as a constellation in being: that is no less the tendency of this project." [18] "Project" here could be the unfinished work that would be collected as *The Arcades Project*, or the effort to establish dialectical materialism as a way to understand history (as a "representation of becoming") through remains that exist as *present* ("between sensation and tradition") in our own day ("as a constellation in being").

Counter to this disavowal of flow is another tendency that idealizes flow when considering the body; Hillel Schwartz describes a striving for fluidity as a defining characteristic of 20th-century movement. He identifies a paradox in which kinesthetic experiences were caught between ideals, or "kinestructs," of a fluid, torso-centered movement, and "kinecepts": actual syncopated and fragmented experiences

16. Clancy Wilmott, "Book review: *Cities Without Ground: A Hong Kong Guidebook*," *Cartographica* 48, no. 3 (2013): 254.
17. Walter Benjamin and Rolf Tiedemann, *The Arcades Project* (Cambridge, MA: Belknap Press, 1999), 845.
18. Ibid.

19. Hillel Schwartz, "Torque: The New Kinaesthetic of the Twentieth Century," in *Incorporations*, eds. Jonathan Crary and Sanford Kwinter (New York: Zone Books, 1992), 71-126.

20. Telma João Santos, "On Turbulence: In between mathematics and performance," *Performance Research* 19, no. 5 (2014): 8, https://doi.org/10.1080/13528165.2014.958347.

21. André Lepecki, *Singularities: Dance in the Age of Performance* (London: Routledge, 2016), 151.

of the world and their representations. Schwartz argues that a modern kinesthetic, striving for the fluidity of kinestructs, influenced the research, development, and instruction of childhood play, public speaking, and dance. Importantly, this fluidity sought to counter the staccato world of the city and the machine. [19] It is this view of flow as counter to the more "jerky" conditions of 20th-century life that would seem to be common to the examples above: for Benjamin, as a negative smoothing over of those conditions, and in Schwartz's examples, as an idealized relief from them. What is interesting is how flow, as an imagination, moves from being *apart* from the staccato mechanics of the world to a veritable description of that very functioning.

Yet, this imagination, in its way of recognizing or abstracting the movements, systems, and transactions that are taking place around them continues an idealization. The mathematician and performance artist Telma João Santos describes this as a misunderstanding of the physics of how things actually move. She notes that physics describes two kinds of flows. One is a turbulent flow that is "disorganized, chaotic and random-in-appearance" and most importantly, "mobilizes three-dimensional space." [20] Turbulent flow describes rubbing, frictions, bumps, and seeming disorganization as the way of movement. The second, "nonturbulent" movement is "laminar flow"; it is an ideal and theoretical description that describes layers of molecules sliding past each other with little disruption. Arguably, when we imagine flow, it is the laminar kind that orients how we think; this perhaps prevents us from actually seeing the disorganized turbulence that characterizes the productive and functioning nature of things taking their place.

This contrast between ideal and real movement plays out in important ways for how we relate to each other and how we imagine movement in space. The dance scholar André Lepecki, building on Santos's work, argues that in the choreographic imagination, the ideal of laminar flow overrides actually existing turbulence to create expectations that the dancer will be "servile and neutral, non-turbulent, an unaffected messenger." [21] At the same time, the ideal of laminar flow also falsely has come to suggest that synchronous, smooth movement expresses "the shared ideals of a community of equals smoothly moving together without breaks, resistances, obstacles." [22] In the relations it inscribes between and amongst choreographically determined bodies, an idealized laminar flow suppresses the role that disruption and incongruity play in the world, while foregrounding an ideal of relations that does not take place. Rem Koolhaas touches on the tension between an idealized understanding of flow and the more complex messiness of movement when he notes that:

> Junkspace is often described as a space of flows, but that is a misnomer; flows depend on disciplined movement, bodies that cohere. Junkspace is a web without a spider; although it is an architecture of the masses, each trajectory is strictly unique. Its anarchy is one of the last tangible ways in which we experience freedom. It is a space of collision, a container of atoms, busy, not dense. ...There is a special way of moving in Junkspace, at the same time aimless and purposeful. It is an acquired culture. [23]

Koolhaas's attempt to set flow straight does little to correct an idealized figuring of movement in spaces of the postmodern imagination. This imagination depends on the "disciplined movement" that Koolhaas disavows and the servile bodies that Lepecki warns against. Where Koolhaas sees junkspace as the last domain of an "anarchy" and "freedom" in which unpredictable, aimless bodies move at their own will, this does little to recognize that the emplacements of junkspace have become increasingly organized around making such wandering ever more difficult: directing, enclosing, and coordinating movement in ways that offer little possibility for a meandering displacement. Koolhaas argues, "Where movement becomes synchronized, it curdles: on escalators, near exits, parking machines, automated tellers." [24] But this curdling only further muddles the terms through which movement, whether disciplined or aimless, continues to be conditioned by spatial emplacements that direct and isolate activity in ways that cut off even the possibility of stepping out from the circulation. The "disciplined

22. Ibid., 152.
23. Rem Koolhaas, "Junkspace," *October* 100 (2002): 179, http://www.jstor.org/stable/779098.
24. Ibid., 180.

25. Zhu Tao, "Power of the Ground," in *The Social Imperative: Architecture and the City in China*, ed. H. Koon Wee (Barcelona: Actar, 2017), 170.

26. Julie Rose, "Hong Kong's Shifting Grounds," *Log* 27 (Winter/Spring 2013): 59.

movement" that Koolhaas refers to is the contemporary choreographic imagination that casts the dancer's body as one of many in a servile synchronicity. Both readings suggest that how we move through the spaces of our cities conditions our agency and our capacity to "experience freedom." While Koolhaas is sanguine about junkspace as an "anarchy" where such freedom is possible, flow's role in structuring the city posits a space that is exhausted of contingency, where small acts of protest find their place only in pockets of leftover space, out of the way of an abiding continuity.

INFRASTRUCTURAL MOVEMENT

Where Koolhaas and the authors of *Cities Without Ground* were cool to the appropriations of these networks, Zhu Tao sees instead a city whose logic is dictated by commercial development and whose spaces are subsumed into ever larger superblocks, such that streets are internalized, commercialized, privatized, and disassociated from what is left of a ground. He notes that the city's interiorization not only ingests and condenses the commercial benefits of the street into the hands of developers, but that this concentration also dismantles the role that the street as a public realm plays as the "spatial foundation" of civic life. [25] Where the street may condition, proscribe, and prescribe ways of being that are nominally figured through a process organized by the government, superblock interiors are designed, regulated, and controlled through a purely profit-driven logic and the behaviors it authorizes. The "spatial foundation" of politics must be coupled with a civic foundation rooted in movement, and with people's capacity to determine their engagement with the city based on how they move in and through it.

In another commentary on *Cities Without Ground*, the reviewer describes Hong Kong's ability to shift large crowds of people through innumerable forms of transportation. She argues that "movement defines the city," and describes "merry hordes traveling on foot" who never need to touch the ground: a fantasy of "untrammelled pedestrian mobility." [26] This reading of Hong Kong's pedestrians contrasts with Zhu Tao's description of "rats" in a maze of tunnels, escalators, and interiors. [27] The ceaseless circulation through privatized spaces of commerce and mobility, into office towers, government buildings, or retail stores, subdues subjects. Similar to how the speed of the automobile has transformed our perception of the city, walking without the ability to stop in Hong Kong's circulatory systems proposes a way of seeing that is different from moving at street level. This foreclosed vision conditions a kind of frantic, single-minded desire to arrive at one's destination. The surfeit of movement's potential becomes not choices for exploration, but impediments and distractions from a singular way home. The city as maze—transformed from a field of possibility, memory, and recognition into an "outside," with little to offer one's experience. When Ash Amin and Nigel Thrift argue that "how we experience urban space begins to be mediated by infrastructure in ways that strike at the heart of our experience," this suggests that subjectivity itself is channeled in and through the conduits that move us. [28]

This refiguring of space into one of docile movement, whether "aimless and purposeful" or "disciplined," for Koolhaas does away with the ground's relevance. He states that "the ground is no more. There are too many raw needs to be realized on only one plane." [29] This obliteration through multiplication echoes the representational strategies of *Cities Without Ground*, and the way it's diagrams reconceptualize this plane as an overlapping circulatory "surface across which daily activities and vast circulatory networks occur," rendering the ground itself "elusive and irrelevant." [30] One critic identifies the "obvious paradox" that as "more reference to the ground (outside, in the 'real world') is 'eliminated,' the more valuable that ground becomes." [31] But to describe this as a "paradox" would be to imagine that the forces of private development, politics, and control do not purposefully cohere to propel this dynamic of penury and speculation. Or to imagine that the coincident emptying of the street of characteristics of contingency, potential, and chance was an unforeseen byproduct of that effort and not a motivating objective.

The elimination of the ground is not a paradox so much as a formula for cutting the city off from its more

27. Zhu Tao, "Power of the Ground," 165.
28. Amin and Thrift, *Seeing Like a City*, 51.
29. Koolhaas, "Junkspace," 181.
30. Wilmott, "Book review: *Cities Without Ground*," 254.
31. Rose, "Hong Kong's Shifting Grounds," 65.

uncontrolled and open production. Transparent and legible policies privilege the interiorization of the city, and relegate the ground to an administrative terrain prioritized for vehicular traffic and parceled into overlapping and incoherent domains of administrative functioning. While the interiorized domains of quasi-public life are regulated and policed by the private developers who control and condition how we move through them, streets themselves are administratively overdetermined, with a morcellation and overlapping of responsibility for design, care, and maintenance that allows no one to be responsible for the failures that propel it toward an "irrelevance" that at the same time closes off its role as a site of coming together.

An imagination of "spaces of flow" influences policies, designs, and regulations that govern the circulatory networks of urban life; becoming, for example, a "pedestrianism" of the sidewalk. [32] These may include rules for stopping, staying, and moving that prohibit configurations of bodies for activities such as talking, gathering, protesting, or picketing. "Move along," becomes an ethos that imagines nonstop circulation. When we are told to continue on, that "there is nothing to see here!" it is an assertion that "the space of circulating is nothing other than the space of circulation." [33] This ordering of space, assigning a specific act to a specific place, is Jacques Rancière's "partition of the sensible." It is a distribution, ordering, or rule-setting that divides up the sensible world into parts that are a whole. Rancière calls such a distribution, "the police." For Rancière, the police, in its efforts to partition the common world, leaves certain people unaccounted for. This opens a space for claims that a different "whole" exists, with parts that have not been taken into account. In arguing for a new partition that addresses those not counted, an alternative is imagined and put forward. The possibility of these claims to be made constitutes the political. Rancière's example of an order to "move along" demonstrates how this partition of the sensible includes both space and movement: where, how, in which place, and at what time certain people are able to occupy, traverse, and make their way into and

32. "Pedestrianism understands the sidewalk as a finite public resource that is always threatened by multiple, competing interests and uses. The role of the authorities, using law as needed, is to arrange these bodies and objects to ensure that the primary function of the sidewalk is sustained: that being the orderly movement of pedestrians from point a to point b. Obstacles that impede flow are inherently suspect, according to this logic." Nicholas K. Blomley, *Rights of Passage: Sidewalks and the regulation of public flow* (New York: Routledge, 2011), 3–4.

33. Jacques Rancière, "Ten Theses on Politics," *Theory and Event* 5, no. 3 (2001): para. 22. Also quoted in André Lepecki, "Choreopolice and Choreopolitics: Or, the Task of the Dancer," *TDR: The Drama Review* 57, no. 4 (Winter 2013): 19.

through space. André Lepecki notes the implications of this partitioning when he writes:

> As a political-theoretical concept the police is that which is pregiven in the circulatory organization of the polis as what predetermines pathways, establishes routes for circulation, and fits both into one single mode of being. In that sense it does not hail. Instead, it choreographs. And by doing so the police guarantees that as long as everyone moves and circulates in accord with a general conformity of being-in-circulation, this movement will produce nothing other than a mere spectacle of its own consensual mobility. [34]

While this ordering of movement is already implicit within the distributing functions of the police, Lepecki names this specific partition "choreopolice." The "being-in-circulation" of movement is equivalent to "being-in." Both ontologies are determined by the police. Movement and our capacity to move freely become possible or not based on how rules, orders, and forms of control regulate and order the public realm. When Lepecki speaks of a choreographic imagination of laminar flow subduing the dancer's body, he is also describing a process whereby movement itself is emptied of the collisions, bumps, and frictions that characterize a domain of the political. In this sense, a police that allows certain zones to be inaccessible to certain people, treats those zones as a "whole" or as a "world" that is delimited from some but not others. A claim to access that space contests the not-yet-being-counted within that whole. It is a political revindication for a new world where one is free to move.

INFRASTRUCTURAL PROTEST

Writing in 2011 about protests that had swept across North Africa into the Middle East, Judith Butler questions how the material attributes of a real space of contestation can be reconciled with an idealized sphere of action and political decision-making. She asks how in "seizing and reconfiguring the matter of material environment" we touch upon the political space of appearance that Hannah Arendt theorizes

34. Lepecki, "Choreopolice," 13.

35. Judith Butler, "Bodies in Alliance and the Politics of the Street," Lecture in Venice, Italy as part of the series *The State of Things*, organized by the Office for Contemporary Art (OCA) Norway (7 September 2011): 1, https://scalar.usc.edu/works/bodies/Judith Butler: Bodies in Alliance and the Politics of the Street | eipcp.net.pdf.

36. Ibid.
37. Ibid., 5.
38. Ibid., 4.
39. Ibid., 5.

in *The Human Condition* as a realm of action. [35] Butler argues that protest is always localized within sites that are materially and spatially constituted, and that these sites become actors, at the same time as they are acted upon. She notes that the protests "have depended on the prior existence of pavement, street, and square" sometimes occupying spaces charged with representational political force, such as Tahrir Square in Egypt. [36] In such an instance, protesters "seize upon an already established space permeated by existing power, seeking to sever the relation between public space, the public square and the existing regime. So the limits of the political are exposed, and the link between the theatre of legitimacy and public space is severed." [37] Assembly —as the mobilization of space and the "persistence of the body against those forces that seek to monopolize legitimacy"— is a claim to the "right to have rights" within that space. [38] This struggle makes visceral the agonistic qualities of material emplacement that are missing from the space of appearance as an enacted political realm. In other words, spaces of contestation are never neutral forums for exchange but are striated—in their very material and spatial organization—with relations of control, order, and power that become part of the exchange that takes place. Butler concludes that

> in acting, we bring the space of politics into being, understood as the space of appearance. It is a divine performative allocated to the human form. But as a result, [Arendt] cannot account for the ways in which the established architecture and topographies of power act upon us, and enter into our very action, sometimes foreclosing our entry into the political sphere, or making us differentially apparent within that sphere. [39]

While Butler was writing in response to events more than a decade ago, her essay frames questions that are relevant to the 2019 protests in Hong Kong. How can we think of the role of the street and of the spaces of Hong Kong in the protests? Can we understand the protests as a claim to a space of appearance? I would argue that the infrastructural nature of the protests marks a shift not only from contestations of the city's past, but also of how protest is often conceived in relation to space. The protests were infrastructural in the way bodies, acts, and practices were distributed in space and time. These movements contested an imagination of flows that had come to legitimize the interiorization of the street and the atrophy of the public realm as a site for the civic.

Butler's note on the representational political force of occupied spaces foregrounds an assumption about urban mobilizations: that a claim to a place or space is important to the creation of a space of appearance, for contestation to take place. This occupation can be temporary, over a fixed duration—for example during a march or gathering—or it can endure over days or months in a site that itself becomes linked to the claims themselves. In both cases, the taking over of space becomes the material enactment of a space of appearance. Writing on urban political movements, the geographers Erik Swyngedouw and Lazaros Karaliotas have argued that "a political Idea/Imaginary cannot find grounding without localization. A political moment is always placed, localized and invariably operative in public space." [40] They note that squares, plazas, and other public spaces have historically been sites where contestation can be performed and enacted. "[T]hey are sites of existence, of exhibition, of becoming popular. Without a site, a place or a location, a political idea is impotent." In this formulation, "the political idea" is inextricably linked to the space in which its claim or articulation is staked. Protest is understood to be localized, and in a paradoxical way, immobile in its bound relationship to the spaces or trajectories that define it. Even a march that moves through space is considered to be under control so long as protesters do not exceed the limits of a pre-approved route or surpass an authorized time. It is often those "outbreaks" on the "margins" of contestation that are disavowed.

We can find this close relation between a delimited space and protest in Hong Kong's Occupy Movement. [41] These protests laid claim to one of Hong Kong's most important

40. Lazaros Karaliotas and Erik Swyngedouw, "Exploring insurgent urban mobilizations: from urban social movements to urban political movements?" in *Handbook of Urban Geography*, eds. Tim Schwanen and Ronald van Kempen (London: Edward Elgar Publishing, 2019), 379.

41. The Occupy Movement (also known as the Umbrella Movement or the 2014 Protests) took place in the fall of 2014. It is distinct from

Occupy Central, which was led by a small group camped on the plaza under the HSBC Building for nearly a year beginning in October of 2011. Occupy Central would become one of the longest "Occupy" movements anywhere in the world. See, Elaine Yu, "The Anarchists of Occupy Central," *The New Yorker*, December 10, 2014, https://www.newyorker.com/news/news-desk/original-anarchists-occupy-central.

42. Miguel A. Martínez, "Street Occupations, Neglected Democracy, and Contested Neoliberalism in Hong Kong," *Social Justice* 46, no. 2/3 (2019): 103.

districts—Admiralty— surrounded by government and commercial towers. While activities spread intermittently to other districts in Hong Kong, the movement's global image and logistical base was organized from the arterial routes that cut through the center of the city. The months-long occupation took place in the fall of 2014 and offered images of groups enacting forms of community and sociality amidst the skyscrapers. Protesters squatting on overpasses and under offramps would suggest that "business as usual" had been brought to a halt. But government and office workers found ways to navigate the disruption, and protesters were quick to distance themselves from the anti-capitalist revindications of other Occupy movements in the earlier part of the decade. Instead, they wanted to ensure that the protests were "above all, about having a standard Western-like democratic system in the HKSAR." [42] These assurances were maintained by an organizational structure with visible leaders and centralized messaging that effectively dampened a diversity of views. The political imaginary of the movement found its very grounding amongst the towers of the district, and performed its claims through this seemingly disjunctive superposition. Read through Rancière, the Occupy Movement was a *part-taking* of an urban space in which protesters otherwise felt they did not count: did not count because they were unsatisfed with the participatory mechanisms that constituted and comprised the city's governance. This contestation of a whole in which they did not count, found its representation in a spatial claim as an attempt to open a space for the political.

The 2019 protests were markedly different from the Occupy Movement. Where the latter's imaginary was linked to a delimited space—the Admiralty district of Hong Kong Island—the events of 2019 were dispersed throughout the city. Where Occupy functioned through a literal taking place, the 2019 protests were characterized by movement: they redistributed bodies, temporalities, space, and the very material of the street rather than operating within or against the enforced or chosen stabilization of a specific site or locale. The 2019 protests contested the partition of the city itself: its economy, politics, and the infrastructural systems that made it possible. They challenged a "whole" in which they did not count, and used contestation as a means to open toward a political. That such an opening could not and did not materialize, either within Occupy or in 2019, reveals the thinness of a post-handover political system founded on the propagation of elite consensus, where conflict, agonism, and contention—the necessary debate of democracy—were institutionally bracketed off as anathema to efficient functioning. [43] Where Occupy Movement leaders were identifiable and controlled their message, in 2019, slogans such as "no central stage," "we fight on, each in his own way," and "no snitching, no severing ties" describe flattened relations that explicitly made room for a heterogeneity of views. [44] Real-time messaging technologies allowed for decentralized decision-making, with activities proliferating in time and space.

Displacement and its contestation—at the airport, on highways, and on streets—was central. While Hong Kong's Mass Transit Railway Corporation (MTRC) at first offered extra trains and extended hours to accommodate events, criticism from the government and mainland authorities led to more adversarial relations. This antagonism fed on the close ties between the MTRC—a beneficiary of planning decisions that privilege large-scale, mass-transit-led development—and the government, which is the corporation's single largest shareholder. This relation is indicative of a nexus between government, developers, and construction companies that creates an inevitability around large scale urban projects that interiorize the ground and foreclose alternative civic forms. These interiorized realms became the sites for gatherings and targets for disruption. Protesters shattered glass railings, dismantled escalators, and smashed windows of mainland banks, taking apart these symbols of the smooth flow of people, goods, and capital. In this taking apart of malls, stations, and circulations, the protesters moved beyond the claims to universal suffrage of the Occupy Movement. Flow's disruption threatened the city's image—if not directly blocking digitized and virtualized transactions, then taking apart the physical emplacements that buttressed the city's status as the legal, regulatory, and logistical host of those transactions.

43. See also: Sony Devabhaktuni and Joanna Mansbridge. "Democracy's dislocations: Spaces of protest and the people of Hong Kong." *Public Culture* 34, no. 1 (2022).

44. Agnes Ku, "New forms of youth activism—Hong Kong's Anti-Extradition Bill movement in the local-national-global nexus," *Space & Polity* 24, no. 1 (2020): 113.

The street was emptied of vehicular traffic, with protesters and security forces occupying intersections, carriageways and sidewalks. On elevated walkways, people crowded along the balustrades to watch events taking place on the street below. On Sundays, these crowds included domestic workers who habitually claim these circulatory routes on their government-mandated day off to gather with friends and relax. Later, the walkways became watch stations for security forces. In all of these instances, the arrest of movement reveals how its incessant continuity—with seemingly no place to stop or step to the side—acts itself as a form of control. To be in these spaces otherwise—without moving—is to assert the right to bodily inertia within the public realm. Elsewhere, protesters organized a night-time human chain that replicated the path of three transit lines at the street level. The chains stretched tens of kilometers and overlaid an infrastructure of haptic connection onto the technical circulations that enforced the city's operation. The logistics of organizing, gathering and synchronizing this human connection is a claim to the right of assembly itself and demonstrates a "persistence of bodies" that is life-organizing and sustaining: the support of infrastructure itself.

The protests disrupted imposed orders through infrastructural tactics, and reasserted the ground. The ground here is not the cordoned-off space of the Occupy Movement; its relevance does not register through the contrast it enacts between a city center and its occupation by diverse groups of people. Rather, the ground is an infrastructure of infrastructures, whose elements were rearticulated in a contestation of the sets of relations that control and coordinate life on the street. When Butler speaks of "seizing and reconfiguring the matter of material environment," it is important not to hold our imagination at the abstraction of space. "Matter" and "material" is not that abstraction, but a literal taking apart of the elements that comprise the street: torn up, ripped out, and rearranged, as a recognition of the way they regulate life within the city and enact policies determined through a template that maintains a prevailing and dominant order. The dislodging of hundreds of kilometers of railings made possible certain ways of moving through the city that countered myriad decisions that coagulate through the bureaucratic organigram of an executive government. The unloosening of concrete pavers and their stacking into ordered or unruly piles that blocked circulation also demonstrated a perverse precision founded on an empathy for the material and things of the city. Pavers, railings, security barriers, construction cones, bins, traffic signals, utility boxes, and markings became central characters of contestation. The government was quick to label the protests "riots" and to call for an accounting of the economic damage done to the city's streets; yet, this taking apart was a way of contesting the ways the street acts as a ground for urban life, the way its materials and elements form the basis of the attachment for the city and for each other. In taking the city apart, there was simultaneously a demand to put it back together in other, different ways, to propose a new world. This was a demand for a street that is not simply a surface for managing circulations, but comprises the matter that binds lives together and supports their persistence as bodies that appear in a space that is political. As André Lepecki has argued, a freedom to move (and we could add, to not move) corresponds with movements of freedom, such that if we do not continue to move freely, or act politically, the political itself vanishes from the world. [45]

LOVE AND THE CITY

In his epigraph to *One-Way Street*, Walter Benjamin writes: "The street is named/Asja Lacis Street/after her who/as an engineer/cut it through the author." [46] Love is a street. Its extension is an infrastructural function that requires an engineer's calculation. What is cut into—as a ground—is the city, is Benjamin. There is in *One-Way Street* a relation to cities and to streets that connects affective life to a collective sensing through the ruins of an age. In a description of the child's attraction to the detritus of worksites, Benjamin writes that "the world of things turn directly and solely to them" making it possible through play to assemble new relations that "produce their own small world of things within the greater one." [47] Children have access to methods that allow for a re-actualization of things into other configurations. It is a capacity to see anew that brings past and future into a mediated relation through material.

Benjamin describes a sailor's chest in which "a leather belt from Hong Kong is juxtaposed to a panorama of Palermo and a girl's photo from Stettin." [48] Each keepsake stands in for a city. These objects carry forward into the present.

45. "... in the dancer's activation of freedom within the choreographic plan of composition, the political comes into the world as an enduring movement of obstinate joy." Lepecki, "Choreopolice," 26.
46. Walter Benjamin, *One-Way Street and Other Writings*, trans. Edmund Jephcott and Kingsley Shorter (London: Harcourt Brace Jovanovich, 1978), 45.
47. Ibid., 52.
48. Ibid., 102.

Encountering them in the hands makes that past not a docile, resolved surface but a progenitor of new inscriptions. That active capacity is characterized by anxiety, compulsion, and dread as much as it is by a positive bringing forward of those souvenirs. "For what one has lived is at best comparable to a beautiful statue which has had all its limbs knocked off in transit, and now yields nothing but the precious block out of which the image of one's future must be hewn." [49] The statue, like the souvenirs, is also the cities themselves. Driving in Marseille at dusk to the train station, Benjamin writes that "the city became a book in my hands, into which I hurriedly glanced a few last times before it passed from my sight for who knows how long into a warehouse crate." [50] The shutting of its covers encloses impressions until that moment when the binding splits open and the text can be copied again.

This copying is distinct from reading in the way that travelling a road on foot is different from flying over it. For Benjamin, the "reader never discovers the new aspects of his inner self," and what is opened by the text—like a road cut into him—immediately closes behind. Reading allows the mind to wander, while the copier "submits it to command." [51] The mind's disciplined attention through the act of copying is like walking a road and becoming aware of the way it commands a landscape. "The very scenery that for a flier is an unfurled plain," for the walker of the road "calls forth distances, belvederes, clearings, prospects at each of its turns like a commander." [52] In flight, the body is propelled over the landscape in a distanced and abstracted submission that orchestrates an overall reading. To walk along the road means to engage in a different sort of movement, at once delimited by the road's own commands but also left open to certain choices that walking necessarily affords.

Benjamin described Riga, where he would visit Asja Lacis, as a "huddling city of low wooden booths" with a "dirty stone embankment." [53] The city also appears in the entry "Stereoscope," perhaps alluding to how images of street life are juxtaposed to create a kind of sensorial relief. There are descriptions of shops and signboards and wares being sold. Certain colors of the city—"clay-grey foundation[s]"—are luminescent, "glowing in the cold air," becoming the ground on which "sparse colors melt." [54] There is a kind of note-taking in which language encloses the world in an inventory. The people of the town are alluded to amongst the wares they sell or the objects they carry with them.

49. Ibid., 76.
50. Ibid., 91.
51. Ibid., 50.
52. Ibid.
53. Ibid., 86.
54. Ibid.

The "cheeks of apples," in "housewives' baskets" are compared to a "dark-red church," creating chains of analogy that construct equivalences of sense linked through the material of the city. It is "with such pictures the town is permeated," suggesting that the street cut through Benjamin, is engineered as this overlapping of images. Nevertheless, amongst this stereoscopy of pictures "rise tall, fortress-like desolate buildings evoking all the terrors of Tsarism": the past perduring unmoved, amongst the readily recomposed present of the city and its material. [55]

Yet, to effect this double reading of past and present, this overlapping of image into sense, depends on a kind of impulse that for Benjamin is increasingly estranged from urban life. He argues that the animal's "obscure impulse" to detect "as danger approaches, a way of escape that still seems invisible" is a kind of "insensate intuition" that is no longer accessible to the "mass instincts" that have overcome city dwellers, leaving them instead only with an "animal insensibility." [56] For Benjamin, society is increasingly alienated from these instincts of sense. The city, once an unambiguous urbanity enclosing, like a fortress, the possibility for work, has become an all too comfortable vestibule. [57]

Against this numbing "insensibility," Benjamin also calls for a new relationship with technology: one not founded on a *mastery* of nature but on a relation between "nature and man." He argues that "in technology a *physis* is being organized through which mankind's contact with the cosmos takes a new and different form from that which it had in nations and families." [58] We can understand *physis* here to describe a becoming, put into motion by technology's exploitation of nature. This becoming effectuates a cosmological reordering that for Benjamin is the ground for a redefinition such that "men as a species completed their development thousands of years ago; but mankind as a species is just beginning his." [59] For Benjamin, rending technical progress from imperial mastery is the charge of a proletariat. Having lived through "the nights of annihilation of the last war...shaken by a feeling that resembled the bliss of the epileptic," he foretells that only an "ecstasy of procreation" could make a recollected *physis* possible. [60]

DOUBT AND BEARING

In Benjamin's words there is the ambivalence of today. The darkness of "bliss" is the street cut through him. The instincts of escape along an invisible path also describe a more

55. Ibid., 87.
56. Ibid., 55.
57. Ibid., 59.
58. Ibid., 104.
59. Ibid.
60. Ibid.

61. Ibid., 55.
62. See, Lauren Berlant, "The commons: Infrastructures for troubling times," *Environment and Planning D: Society and Space* 34, no. 3 (2016): 393, https://doi.org/10.1177/0263775816645989. Also: Lauren Berlant, "Sex in the Event of Happiness," keynote lecture, *13th Annual Feminist Theory Workshop*, Department of Gender, Sexuality & Feminist Studies, Duke University, March 22–23, 2019, 22:50, https://gendersexualityfeminist.duke.edu/13th-annual-feminist-theory-workshop.
63. Sampson Wong, "When in doubt, take a walk: crisis, well-being and urban walks," lecture given during the Hong Kong Sessions of *Deep City Climate Crisis, Democracy and the Digital*, symposium organized by Swiss Federal Institute of Technology, Lausanne and the University of Hong Kong, March 25, 2021.

personal flight driven by an understanding that "all close relationships are lit by an almost intolerable, piercing clarity in which they are scarcely able to survive." [61] Benjamin is describing the commingling of bearing those things that we love, even if they may not be good for us, and muddling through the false starts and experiments of a transition through brokenness. Those ideas are Lauren Berlant's in her attempt to understand the kind of life that infrastructure is, and the movements and relations that it organizes, proposes, and creates. [62] The "bearing" that describes the way love—of others, of cities—can happen despite ourselves; or, in other moments, must be borne as a charge to which we have no choice but to submit.

In a talk about what it means to care for Hong Kong after the National Security Law's (NSL) effective criminalization of protest, the artist Sampson Wong referenced a five-meter-long banner unfurled during an illegal march on July 1, 2020—one day after the passing of the NSL. [63] The unattributed banner was stretched open from along its sides and corners by marchers making their way along a route through Hong Kong Island. The banner's message faced upward so that anyone watching from buildings along the route, or from the air, could see it. In a column of white characters on a gray ground—written in a colloquial Cantonese—it read: "We just really fucking love Hong Kong." This visceral "love" describes an intimacy that one has no choice but to bear. It is a love that explains why some protestors, politicians, and civil society members continued their activities despite uncertainty about how the NSL would be applied or transform Hong Kong's governance.

For Wong, this love for the city can be understood as topophilia: a love of place. "Place" here is not an "authentic" Hong Kong rooted in nostalgia or history, but rather coalesces and is constructed around an affective relationship to sites of protest. A relation to these different sites enacted a kind of political agency for the millions of people who took part in marches and the thousands who were caught up in confrontations. For Wong, these events cut through the people of Hong Kong—and that love was of spaces caught up in memory, sadness, anger, or loss. In the months since the NSL came into effect, its ambiguous wording has allowed for ever more copious distribution of illegalities, catching within its vague language, acts, practices, and people from diverse parts of society in a retro- and pro-active criminalization of any seeming contravention.

Wong's response to the uncertainty of how to proceed took the form of the YouTube channel, "When in doubt, take a walk." [64] The channel hosts films that Wong co-produced with the photographer Eric Tsang. Each four- to seven-minute video follows Wong or another single protagonist through a different city neighborhood—identified in the title: through parks, public housing, walkways, stairs, and streets. Along with the sounds of traffic, pedestrian signals, and noises of birds, each film has a musical soundtrack composed by Joshua Chiu that brings a melancholy of discovery to these walks through seemingly familiar neighborhoods. Each video ends with a request to like and share, and directs viewers to information about the places in the video.

The video contains signs of pandemic life in Hong Kong, with police tape closing off playgrounds and recreation areas. Nearly all residents wear masks. The camera's frame is fixed and captures each film's protagonist from all directions as they walk or stop to look. The camera shows us what they see: street life, things collected in the corner, views into the sky or details. Walking in the videos is not the half-attention of the *flaneur*, but rather an expression of that very bearing that Berlant speaks about: the difficult love for a city that forecloses both hope and turning away. The films are, in this sense, a strategy to make it through the "long middle of change" in which any attempt at structuring a response is a provision that allows for a continuing. Wong and his friends are neither resigned to *a* future nor oblivious to ongoing upheaval. That turbulence continues to reorder words, gestures, acts, and practices into opaque and enclosed zones of insensibility and unmeaning. But perhaps it is in their revelation of Hong Kong as a site of continuous re-discovery, that the videos keep the future open.

64. Eric Tsang and Sampson Wong, "When in doubt, take a walk," https://www.youtube.com/c/doubtwalk/about, accessed November 20, 2021.

TRADE CENTRE

Index

Carriageways 142
Drains 144
Curbs 146
Sidewalks 150
Tactile pavers 155
Traffic signs 157
Traffic signals 163
Markings 165
Poles 168
Barriers 170
Railings 173
Bins 176
Trees 179
Access hatches 182
Hydrants 184
Construction 186

INDEX

The index points to elements that make up the street. I use the word "element" following Gilbert Simondon's writing on the nature of technical progress and technology's place in society. Simondon wanted to counter ambivalent and seemingly irreconcilable attitudes toward technology that are still relevant today. These attitudes that view technical objects as either devoid of signification or animated with hostile intentions: phones, refrigerators, and heart monitors as either inert consumables or as a soon-to-be-awakened-into-consciousness robot horde. [1]

Simondon was unsatisfied with these extremes of apathy and fear. He instead argued for a relation to "technical beings" founded on care, that sought to understand the development of these beings amidst the human world. Technology, for him, should be the study of the processes of becoming that characterized this development. Simondon classified technical objects into "elements," "individuals," and "ensembles." Elements are primary tools or instruments that extend the gesture of the body. They can be put together into machines to become "individuals," entering into relations with other elements to create an entity whose functioning becomes concretized in a moment of provisional stability. "Individuals" can then enter into larger arrangements—say a workshop or a construction site—to become "ensembles."

This framework offers a way to think about infrastructure as itself a technical intervention. Simondon argues that our relation to the world is mediated by tools that enact and extend gestures, such that "what resides in the machines is human reality, human gesture fixed and crystallized into working structures." [2] In this sense, elements are this crystallization. From this proposition, we can recognize that infrastructure comprises elements that enact a movement that once comprised a more elaborate human effort (that also brought animals into the service of people). If we take water, for example: reservoirs, pipes, pumps, and faucets, each in their turn, replace a sequence of gestures —the extension of the hands into the river, the cupping of the palms and the retrieval of what is collected there for drinking— that would have been necessary to ensure a supply for human use. Just as the creation of vessels transformed these gestures into others, so infrastructures fixed them into more collective forms.

Speaking of an infrastructural element as being "ready to hand" alludes to this gestural origin: the faucet always available to function with a turn of the wrist. [3] That single localized and instant displacement replaces a sequence of connected exertions that made possible the collection and distribution of water in times past and still today in some parts of the world. Elements of infrastructure, these end points of systems, work in this sense as the crystallization that Simondon describes. The light pole, the railing, or the traffic light immediately call to mind a bodily stance or activity that fulfills the same function.

Simondon was fascinated by the role that technical objects could play as nodal points in larger systems. In an interview from 1968, he reflected on how a television antenna acts as such a point. He first describes the object's components—"nothing but a large, stainless steel dish"—and its disposition: "It is rigid, but it faces a direction. And we see that it looks very far and that it is able to receive signals that are emitted from very far away." From there, Simondon notes that the dish is not only a symbol of what it does, but rather that it seems to represent a gesture of sorts, of an almost magic capacity, a contemporary magic. In this encounter between a place that is high-up and a key-point—a point that is critical for the transmission of high frequencies—there is a sort of *connaturalité* between a human network and the natural geography of the region. This has a poetic aspect, an aspect of meaning and of encounters of meanings. [4]

The "contemporary magic" of the gesture is the overlapping of the natural world and human desire: of a science still dependent on the earthly sphere despite technical developments that would seem to want to overcome that realm. The receiving dish is an infrastructure of communication but it is also a human gesture of calling forth that signals across the landscape. The passage resonates and clarifies Simondon's appeal to "introduc[e] the technical being into culture," by reading the significations of the dish's functioning—where that operation might otherwise be left unattended: inert. [5] As part of culture, entering into "encounters with meaning," the dish is more than a pure techno-instrumentality. Instead, Simondon argues for an understanding—study—of the sets of relations that the technical-being joins together.

The index isolates elements of curb-scale infrastructure in order to propose such encounters with meaning. Elsewhere, I describe these elements as rulers, terminals, and solicitors, each with different forms of address. As elements, they also enter into relations with others to become individuals brought together in ensembles governed by protocols and administrations. These elements are also sometimes the end points of a sequence of gestures that enact infrastructural movements—interactions of "contemporary magic" that comprise the street.

The index reconfigures these elements on the page. Each entry brings together elements that perform within a domain. They are that domain's material orchestration or may be instruments for its deployment. Each domain and the elements themselves are administered by a single government department or, more commonly, implicate overlapping responsibilities. On the street, we encounter these elements in a state of distraction; on the page, we recognize them immediately as part of that world. The page's spatialization gathers the elements into a new sphere of relations. The drawings are analogues not only for the elements but also for decisions that implicate their fabrication, materiality, form, and care. The accompanying texts narrate these decisions. They follow threads that describe the enlivening forces and temporalities that course through each element. Each text is a cut: synthetic, but also finite, like all cuts.

We used observation and the study of standard drawing sets from the Hong Kong government to make the drawings. The drawing sets are available online, attesting to a "transparency" of information on these aspects of Hong Kong's post-handover governance. [6] The standard drawings specify dimensions, materials, details, and histories of changes and amendments to the elements. They are reproduced on websites of mainland factories to simplify orders from private contractors in Hong Kong. They also provide guidance on the installation and disposition of certain elements. Those rules are meant for engineers overseeing work teams. The task of the standard drawing is to offer insurance after the fact: a regulation to be *checked against* rather than a veritable set of instructions. Each index entry narrates how these regulations "reach into individual and organizational lives." [7] The entries speak to hierarchies of value (ecological, economic, human, material) and to the delegation of labor, competence and authority that the standard drawings are meant to enforce. Each entry also brings us into a relationship with the elements—some more technical than others—demonstrating how a study of these beings calls forth an empathy with the street and its infrastructures.

1. Gilbert Simondon, *On the mode of existence of technical objects,* trans. Cécile Malaspina and John Rogove (Minneapolis: University of Minnesota Press, 2017), 17.
2. Ibid., 18.
3. For examples of this framing of infrastructure through the "ready to hand," see Susan Leigh Star, "The Ethnography of Infrastructure," *American Behavioral Scientist* 43, no. 3 (1999), https://doi.org/10.1177/00027649921955326; and Stephen Graham and Nigel Thrift, "Out of Order: Understanding Repair and Maintenance," *Theory, Culture & Society* 24, no. 3 (2007), https://doi.org/10.1177/0263276407075954.
4. The translation is my own. Gilbert Simondon, "Entretien sur la mécanologie," *Revue de Synthèse* 130, no. 1 (2009/03/01 2009): 111, https://doi.org/10.1007/s11873-009-0072-9.
5. Simondon, *On the mode of existence*, 21.
6. See, however: James Ockenden, "Govt Gaslighting on Missing Soho Pedestrianisation Website, Deletes Records," *Transit Jam*, December 16, 2021, accessed January 14, 2022.
7. Susan Leigh Star and Martha Lampland, "Reckoning with standards," in *Standards and Their Stories: How Quantifying, Classifying, and Formalizing Practices Shape Everyday Life*, ed. Susan Leigh Star and Martha Lampland (Ithaca: Cornell University Press, 2008), 7.

CARRIAGEWAYS

thin surfacing

For every kilometer of road surface in Hong Kong, there are approximately 50 kilometers of utilities underneath. [1] This estimate is an average calculated with country park roads that wind through sparsely inhabited areas. The streets in the most built-up parts of Hong Kong are choked with lengths of cables, wires, ducts, tunnels, and pipes all stuffed into ochre-colored dirt below a packed subgrade that supports an asphalt or concrete surface.

This top layer of the carriageway has been the subject of years of debate. In the early 2000s, the Highways Department (HyD) and the Environmental Protection Department (EPD) enlisted a Swedish researcher to study road sound: the bed of urban noise that is the resonation of tires vibrating against the ground's surfacing. In visits between 2005 and 2006, the researcher noted that the most common concrete finish of Hong Kong's roads was "a transversely brushed macrotexture to increase skid resistance... shaped by a broom of steel tines... that was swept across the surface before curing." [2] The researcher added that the texture looked more like a "U.S. tined concrete than... European brushed concrete," and that although the finish seemed to have been phased out on Hong Kong's highways, it was still common on surface streets. [3] He called these concrete roads—still the most prevalent type of carriageway in Hong Kong—"noisy surfaces."

The EPD classifies roads into five major types that are each evaluated for their environmental impact, including noise emissions. Of the five types, three are distributor roads that form the urban neighborhood network. The concrete surfaces of this network are a patchwork of mixes and finishes. Each patch is separated by shallow contraction joints or deeper, 20mm expansion joints capped with petroleum-based sealant. Private contractors working for government departments or private utilities cut into the road and reinstate newly surfaced sections after each job to create the seemingly haphazard pattern. When departments or utilities need to access space underneath the road, they apply for an excavation permit (XP) through an online interface, first uploading a geolocalized vector drawing of the proposed intervention. Utilities and departments use this expedited process if the excavated area is "completely bounded by a circle with diameter of 450m"; otherwise, the work is split into pieces, each with its own permit. [4] Some work requires consultations with the police force or with the Greening Department if "Very Old Trees" are threatened. If the work falls close in space or time to other excavations, the two unrelated jobs are meant to be coordinated into one.

Hong Kong's quietest roads use a polymer modified friction course (PMFC): also referred to as bituminous road base, flexible pavement or asphalt. PMFC comprises a mixture of crushed rock, sand, or gravel with filler and binder. The heated mixture is tipped from a dump truck into piles that are spread evenly with the back of a shovel along a subbase. Voids between the aggregate dampen noise. Over time, with the weight of traffic, these spaces close up, reducing their quieting effect.

Trials of PMFC roads in Hong Kong began as early as the 1990s. In 2015, new HyD "Guidance Notes" set out characteristics that made a stretch of street suitable for this "low noise road surfacing." Traffic volume, gradient, and frequent stopping and starting are all taken into consideration for PMFC retrofitting, leading many road sections in densely trafficked parts of Hong Kong to be deemed unsuitable for the low noise material.

Since 2013, the HyD has also been evaluating the application of "thin surfacing" to road sections where a PMFC retrofit is not possible. These evaluations are ongoing, with "promising findings of the trials...yet to be established." [5] Thin-surfaced roads sometimes develop ragged holes in the topmost layer. The PMFC wears away to reveal the concrete slab below. This wear pattern is one of approximately 28 potential defects in concrete and PMFC road construction identified in the HyD's "Catalogue of Road Defects (CORD)." [6] Among these defects are "spalling," "ravelling," "flushing," and "rutting." "Crocodile cracks" on PMFC road surfaces comprise "interconnected or interlaced cracks forming a series of small polygons." They can also be called "alligator cracks" or "crazing." [7]

1. Audit Commission, "Government's efforts in managing excavation works on public roads," in *Director of Audit's reports*, no. 70, chap. 4 [full report] (April 3, 2018): 1, https://www.aud.gov.hk/pdf_e/e70ch04.pdf.
2. Environmental Protection Department, "Review and evaluation of the low-noise road surface programme for low-speed roads in Hong Kong, Final Report," Ulf Sandberg, HKSARG (March 13, 2008), https://www.epd.gov.hk/epd/sites/default/files/epd/english/environmentinhk/noise/studyrpts/files/LNRS-Mar08.pdf.
3. Ibid., 6.
4. Highways Department, *Excavation Permit Administration Procedure*, chap. 4, sect. 1, rev. 4.1.22, HKSARG, 4.1.1, https://www.hyd.gov.hk/en/publications_and_publicity/publications/technical_document/xppm/manual/.
5. Highways Department, Research and Development Division, "Guidance Notes on Low Noise Road Surfacing," RD/GN/011C, HKSARG (November 2016): 5.
6. Highways Department, Research and Development Division, "Guidance Notes: Catalogue of Road Defects (CORD)," RD/GN/015B, HKSARG (January 2013).
7. Ibid., 26.

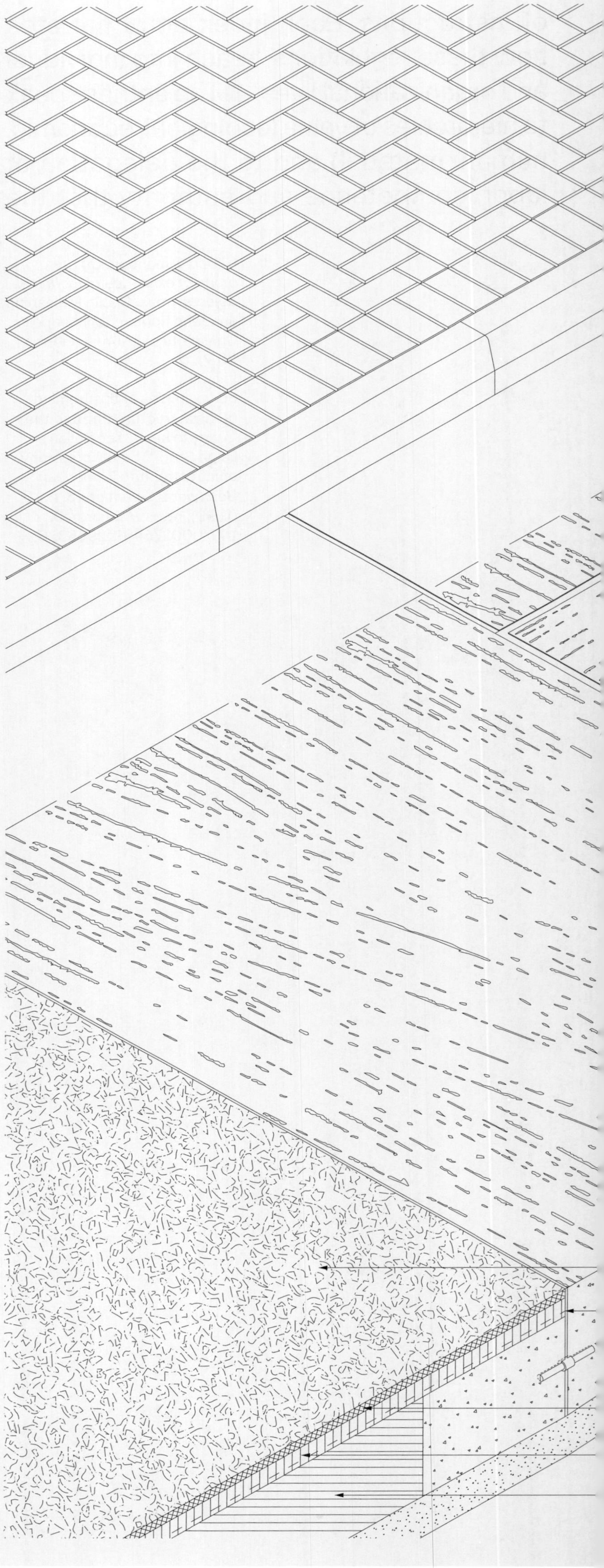

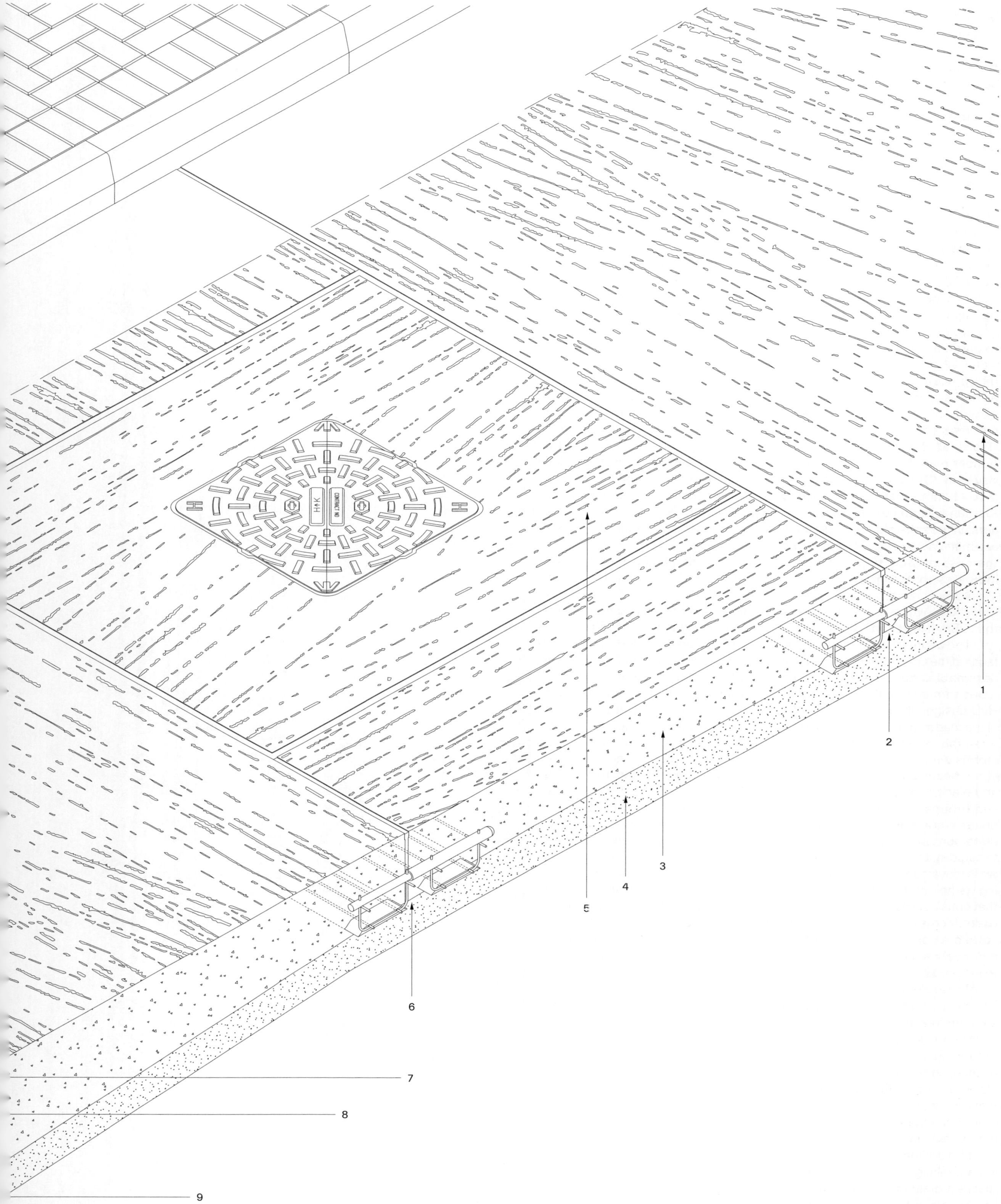

1	concrete pavement	7	bituminous flexible pavement (asphalt)
2	contraction joint	8	GlasGrid
3	concrete slab	9	40 mm wearing course
4	subbase	10	65 mm base course
5	typical layout of box-out slab, isolation joint on four sides	11	road base
6	expansion joint		

DRAINS

residence time

The evacuation of rain from Hong Kong's streets brings together the visible domain of the Highways Department (HyD) with the largely subterranean realm of Drainage Services (DSD). Gully gratings and overflow weirs are the interface between two administrative and technical realms that regulate stormwater. Gully gratings are placed alongside the curb, flush to the carriageway, their diagonal openings meant to be oriented in the direction of the water's flow. Overflow weirs, as their name suggests, act as backups. They replace a unit of the granite or concrete curb adjacent to gratings and catch fast-moving water. Weirs have vertical openings that prevent debris from entering when they are located on a flat piece of road. The openings are parallel to the street—and to rushing water—on slopes. [1] Both units are cast-iron. A more recent "mild steel" grating issued in 2016 is an unoriented grid of 10×10mm square bars welded to a rectangular frame with filleted corners. Where the older iron gratings had manufacturer IDs integrated into the cast surface, the new design indicates that contract numbers should be "painted white, in Arial Black font with characters not less than 25mm in height." [2]

The asphalt and concrete surfaces of the city's streets themselves become drains during storms. Sloped roads turn into shallow rivers. The HyD designs the drainage capacity of the road system to "accommodate a rainfall intensity for heavy rainstorms with a probability of 1 in 50 years occurrence." [3] The design and placement of gullies and weirs—in groups of up to four, at "sag points"—are regulated by "ultimate state considerations" that attempt to avoid instances where the flow of water "overtops" the curb, exceeding its height. A series of formulas that consider "flow height," "flooded width," "crossfall," and the ultimate state are used to calculate where and how many gratings and weirs to install. [4]

These elements evacuate water into tunnels that form a 2,400-kilometer network of conduits of increasingly large diameter that lead to the harbor. This network is buttressed by three underground tanks that can store hundreds of thousands of cubic meters of water during extreme precipitation events, so the system is not overwhelmed by excess runoff. The fifth edition of the DSD's Stormwater Drainage Manual (2018) states that new drainage provisions should be designed to consider climate change effects up to the mid-twenty-first century. Only "if the marginal benefit of the design outweighs the marginal cost" should a projection to the end of the twenty-first century be used. [5]

The DSD maintains a "sewerage" network for domestic waste products as well as the stormwater drainage system. The two systems are governed by different effluvial logics, with the latter conditioned by extreme events—the 50-year storm—and the former designed to maintain constant and predictable movement. The DSD notes that a sewer is not only a pipe for conveying waste products but also "a reactor, inside which microorganisms are breaking down organics and consuming very limited dissolved oxygen." [6] When "the residence time [of sewage in pipes] is long, the temperature...is high and there is a lack of air exchange," the resulting septicity can lead to fatal smells, flammable and explosive gases, and corrosion within the system itself. When pipes are laid at too steep a gradient, the flow can become "supercritical" so that a hydraulic jump ensues when conduits eventually flatten out, leading to "potential damage associated with the uncontrolled energy dissipation." [7]

While the jump between super- and subcritical flow is also relevant to stormwater drainage, the emphasis on extreme precipitation events foregrounds a language of rapid flow: "surcharge," "free-surface," "laminar," and "turbulent." The laminar movement of water comprises "one layer gliding smoothly between the adjacent layers," while turbulent flow is an "erratic motion of fluid particles" that leads to "nearly all practical surface water problems." [8] These considerations regulate the design of the underground network, determining dimensions, slopes, and the junctions of branch and trunk lines. Street access hatches make it possible to inspect underground conduits to ensure that water is not obstructed by silt or objects; these hatches also mark the entrance of stormwater from private residences, parks, and housing estates into the main system. The DSD maintains drawings of this underground double of the street network, with GPS coordinates for each hatch, and the diameters and directions of connecting pipes. [9]

1. Highways Department, Research and Development Division, "Guidance Notes on Road Pavement Drainage Design," RD/GN/035A, HKSARG (February 2020): 17.
2. Highways Department, "H3158A: Mild Steel Gully Grating Type GA1-450," in *Standard Drawings, Section 3: Drainage*, rev. Aug. 2016, HKSARG.
3. Ibid., 2.
4. Ibid., 10-12.
5. Drainage Services Department, *Stormwater Drainage Manual*, 5th ed., HKSARG (January 2018): 33.
6. Drainage Services Department, *Sewerage Manual*, pt. 1, 3rd ed., HKSARG (May 2013): 10.
7. Ibid., 25.
8. Drainage, *Stormwater Manual*, 40.
9. Ibid., 102.

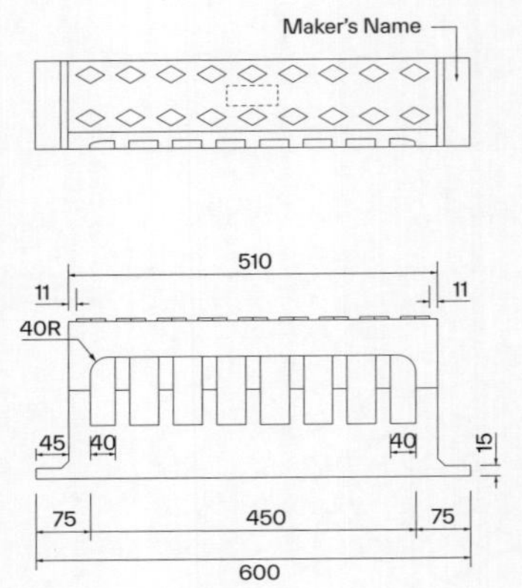

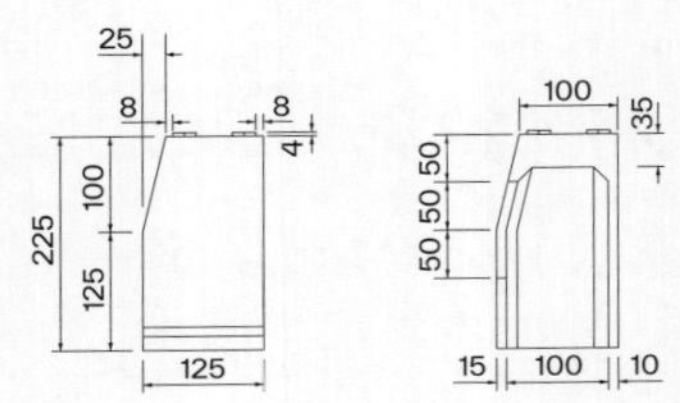

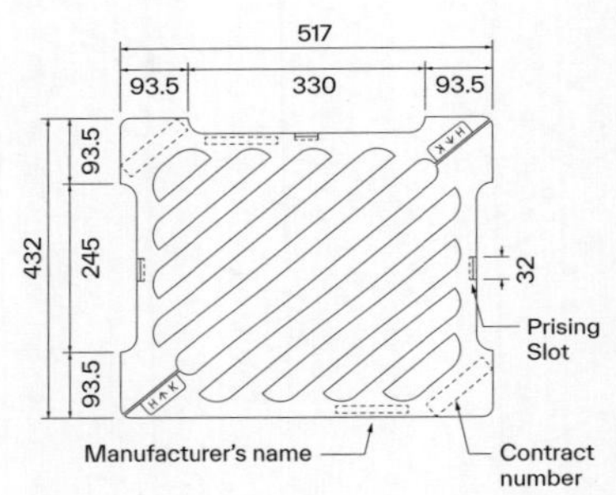

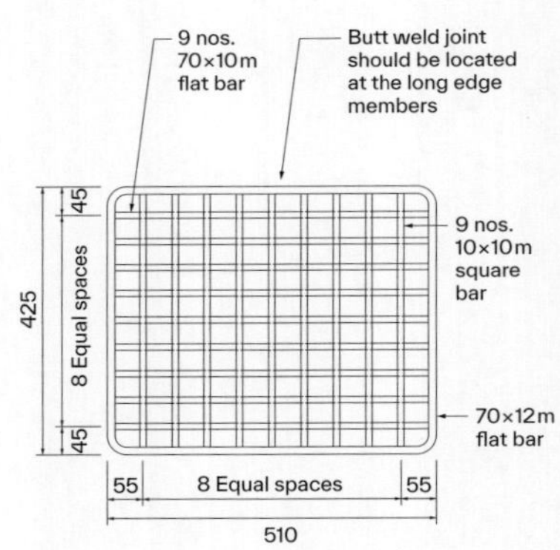

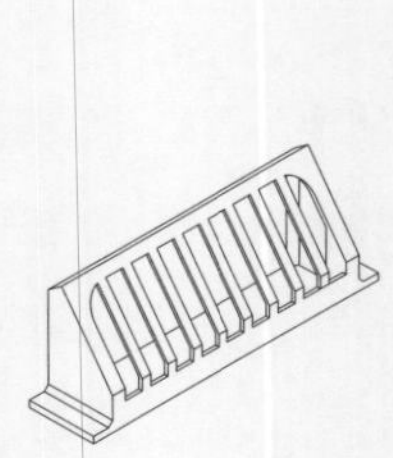
1

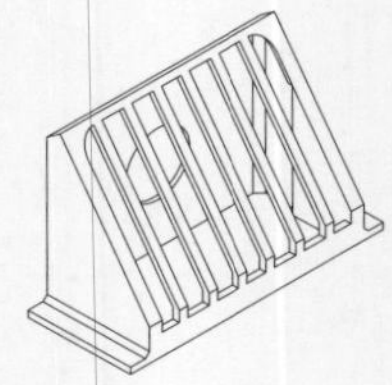
2

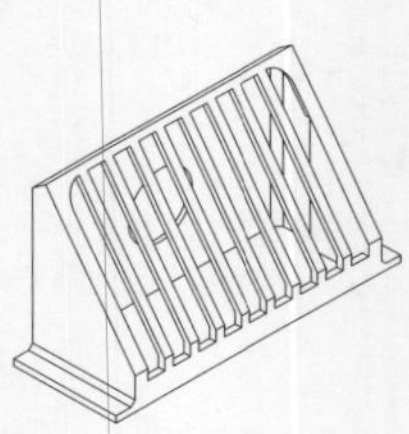
3

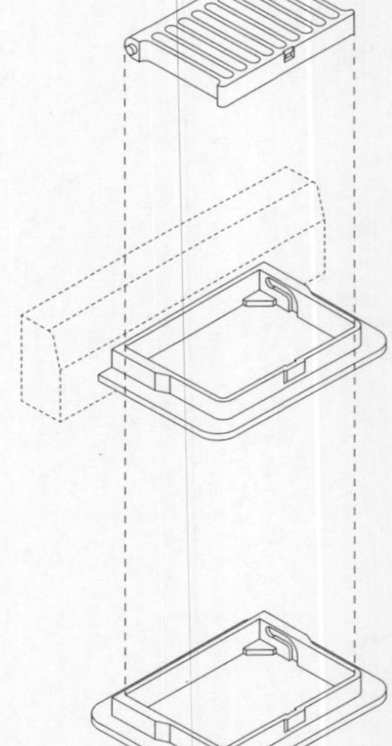
11

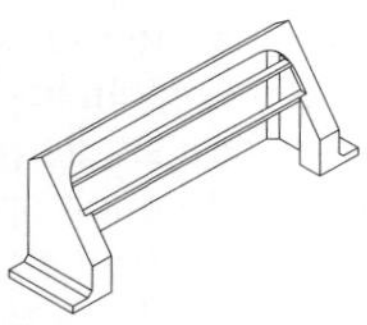

4

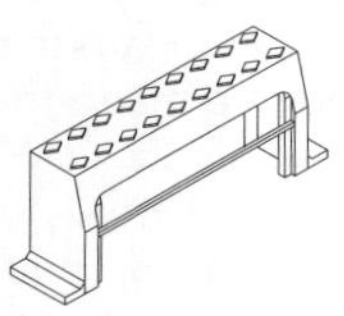

5

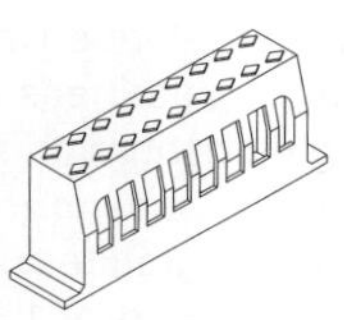

6

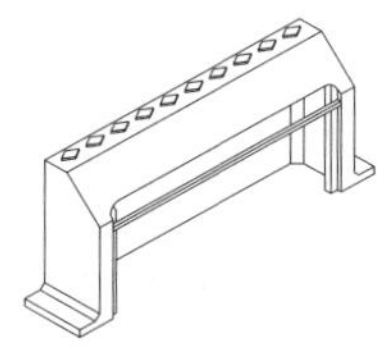

7

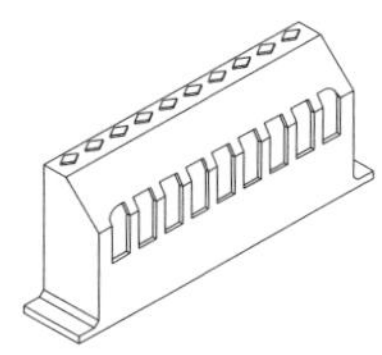

8

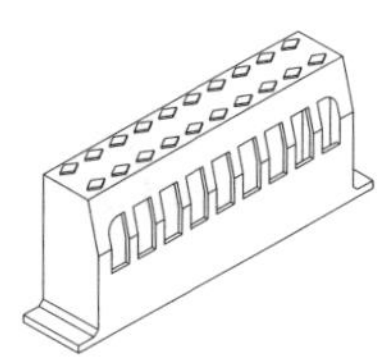

9

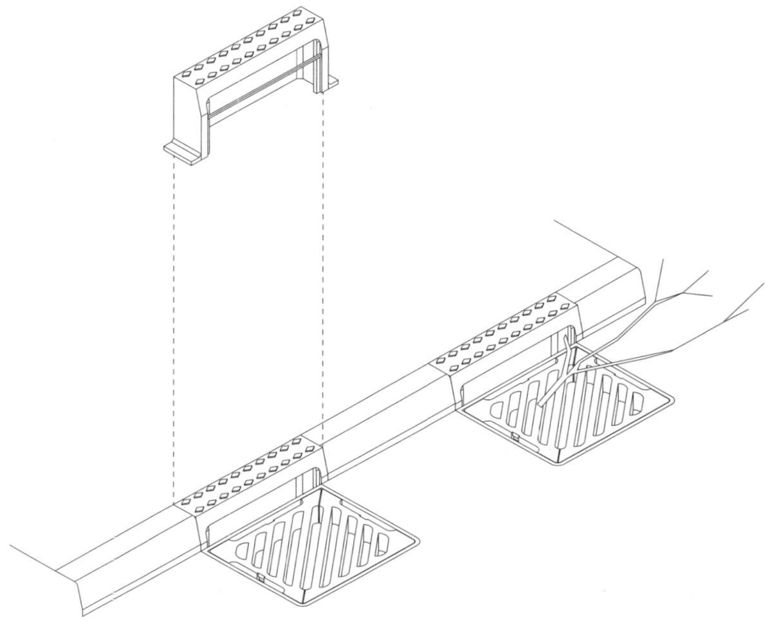

10

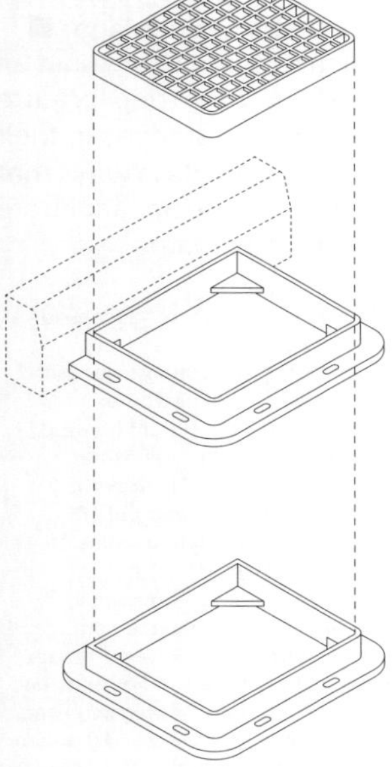

12

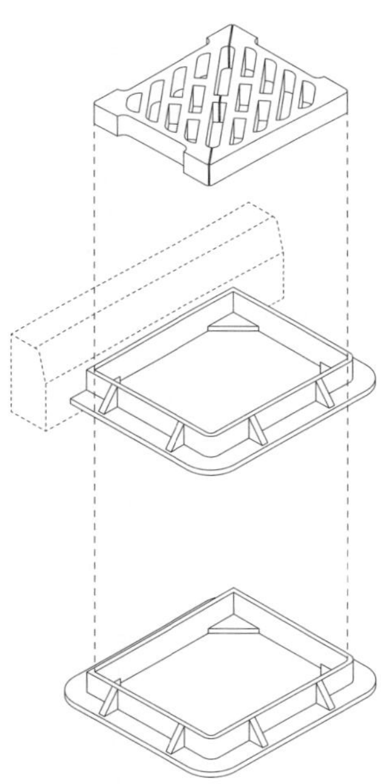

13

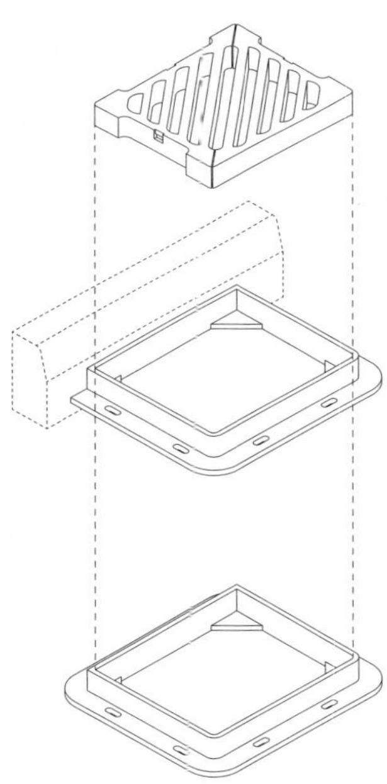

14

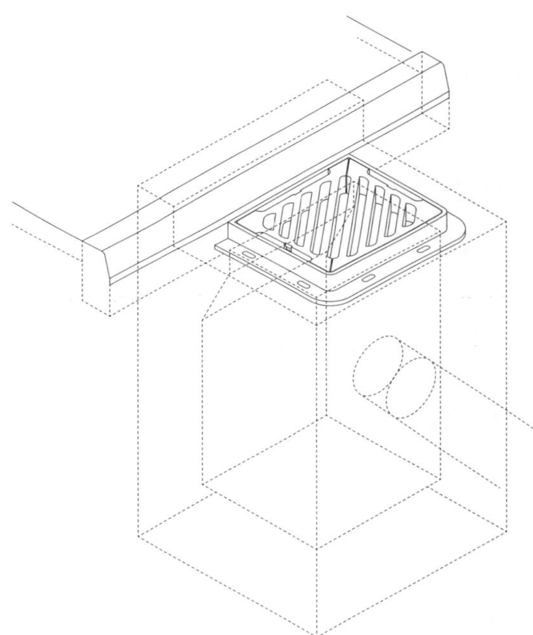

1 curb overflow weir type PR-450V
2 PRS-325V
3 PRS-450V
4 PR-325H
5 K3-325H
6 K3-325V
7 K2-450H
8 K2-450V
9 K1-450V
10 K1-450H
11 gully grating type GA2-325
12 GA1-450 (with two frame types)
13-14 GA1-450, double triangular (with two frame types)

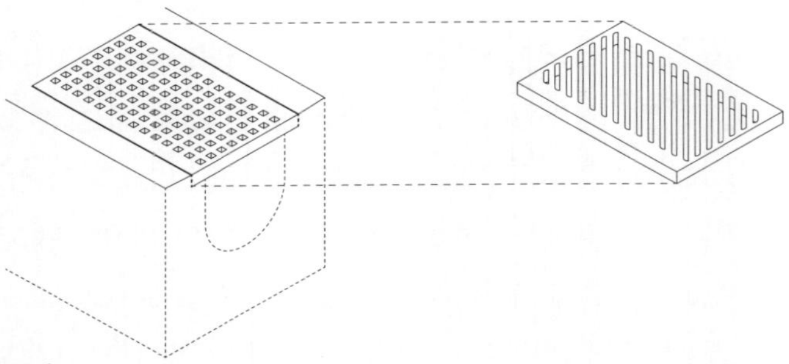

1

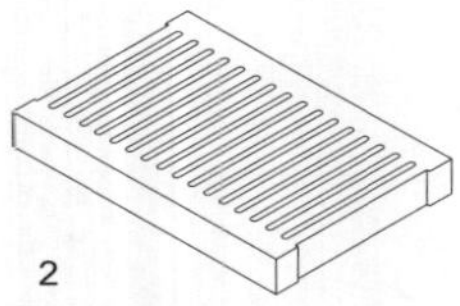

2

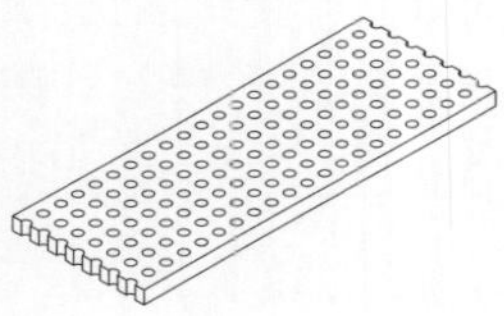

3

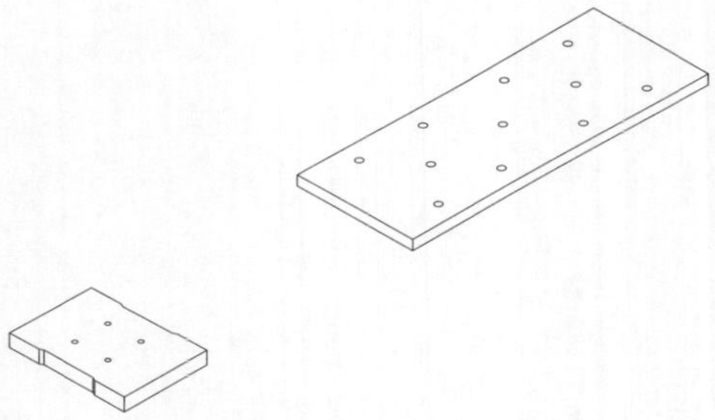

4

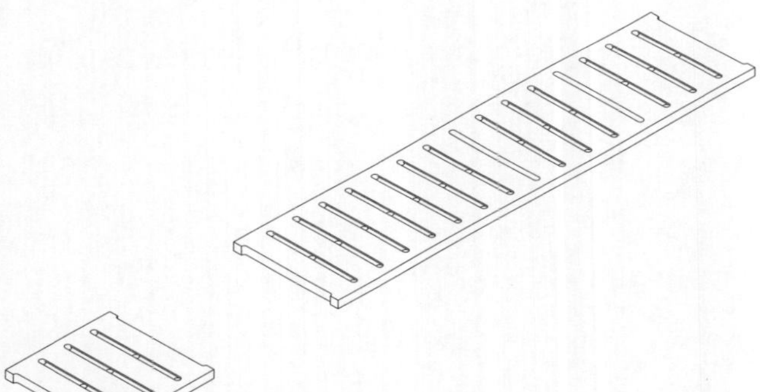

5

1-2 channel grating subject to vehicular load
3 grating at Bank of China Building, Queens Road Central
4 Three Pacific Place, Queens Road East
5 Cheung Kong Center, Queens Road Central

CURBS
kerb

In British English, "curb" and "kerb" have distinct meanings. Curb is the older of the two spellings. It has its origins in the French *courbe* or curve, which describes the geometry of a "chain or strap passing under the lower jaw of a horse" that could be pulled at "for checking an unruly" animal. [1] This usage of "curb" remained common until the 19th century. Washington Irving in *A Tour on the Prairies* (1835)—his account of travels in the United States after 17 years abroad—describes a "fine young animal...reduced to...pass his life under the harness and the curb." In the following decades, this close union between restraint and geometry splits apart, so that "to curb" describes a more general holding back. A now-obsolete usage from mid-19th-century telegraphy describes "a method of signalling through a long cable, by sending a powerful signal followed by one or more weak signals of the opposite sign, the effect of which is to 'curb' or prevent the main signal from lingering in the cable." The "lingering" charge, suggests a certain liveliness to the mechanisms of this early communications infrastructure.

As curb made its way through these meanings, an alternate spelling—"kirb"—also proliferated. In 1797, the architect John Nash filed a patent in London (#2,165) for a system of bridge construction that comprised an assemblage of hollow, plate-iron boxes. These boxes were bolted together and could be over-filled with "Earth, Sand, Stone, Gravel, or other Materials" that formed a road bed. Nash writes that "the skirting[,] or kirb, which keeps in the ground, may be cast or framed with the boxes." [2] An accompanying transversal section shows these lateral "kirb" elements—taller than the hollow box assemblage—holding the earthen road surface in place. Nash's detail articulates a limit that keeps in the ground. By the early 19th century, this new signification would become settled to describe a stone edging that separated the sidewalk from the carriageway. "Kerbs" were also where business was done, or where troublemakers would be kicked. British English also maintained the homonym "curb," with its singular sense of restraint and control. [3]

Hong Kong's administrative departments continue to operate with the inherited structures of colonial language. For example, the technical drawings that comprise the Highways Department's (HyD) primary graphic protocols are detailed in British English; Cantonese or Mandarin versions are unavailable. Drawing standards for granite curbs are classed under: "Maintenance of Existing Installations Only." The last revision to these drawings was made in June 1994, two years before handover. [4] The standards indicate that a granite curb can be anywhere from 150 to 300mm tall and no longer than 60cm. This height and the desired chamfer are to be machine-cut on site, meaning that a single granite profile is tailored to each specific instance. The front, top, and side faces of granite curbs are to be "chisel-dressed," creating a mottled, nonuniform surface. [5] At its squattest height—150mm—the granite curb is flush to the roadway (the element almost entirely embedded in the ground). This means that even drop curbs can be made from the single, specified profile.

When construction calls for granite curbs to be replaced, contractors—working for the HyD or developers—today install precast concrete curbs. These come in one-meter-long sections and are chopped into smaller segments to navigate around curves. Precast curbs are fabricated in the mainland and shipped to Hong Kong or made by detainees in one of Hong Kong's prison workshops. They are untextured and narrower in plan than their their granite counterparts—125mm instead of 150mm. They come in three fixed types: K1 and K2 are 250mm tall and are indicated for "urban areas and where a footway is adjacent to the carriageway" and "rural areas and on high speed roads, where there is no adjoining footway," respectively. K3 is squatter, 200mm, and "should be used only on bridge decks." [6] Precast drop curbs are made with five additional types: K5 and K6 are mirrored by K8 and K9; K7, nearly flush to the carriageway, serves as the middle of the assemblage. [7]

When a K1 butts up against an older, wide, and mottled granite curb, the small differences in their dimensions are legible in ways that the drawings and specifications are unable to communicate.

1. *OED Online*, s.v. "curb, n.," accessed March 2021.
2. The complete patent submission with drawings was published here: "Specification of the Patent granted to Mr. John Nash, of Dover Street, St. James's, Architect," in *Repertory of Arts and Manufactures*, vol. VI (London: Philosophical Societies of All Nations, 1797): 361-67. The bracketed comma appears in a different patent announcement: "Mr. Nash's Iron Bridge: New Patents Enrolled in the Months of February and March," in *The Monthly Magazine and British Register for 1797*, vol. 3 (London: R. Philipps, 1797): 221.
3. I use the North American English spelling of curb except when quoting directly.
4. Highways Department, "H4101: Granite Kerbs," in *Standard Drawings. Section 4: Maintenance of Existing Installations Only*, rev. June 1994, HKSARG.
5. Civil Engineering and Development Department, *General Specifications for Civil Engineering Works*, vol. 2, 2020 edition, HKSARG (July 15, 2021): 11.16.
6. Highways Department, "H1118: Precast Concrete Kerbs (Sheet 1 of 2)," in *Standard Drawings, Section 1: Roads*. Hong Kong: Government of HKSARG.
7. Highways Department, "H1119: Precast Concrete Kerbs (Sheet 2 of 2)," in *Standard Drawings, Section 1: Roads*. Hong Kong: Government of HKSARG.

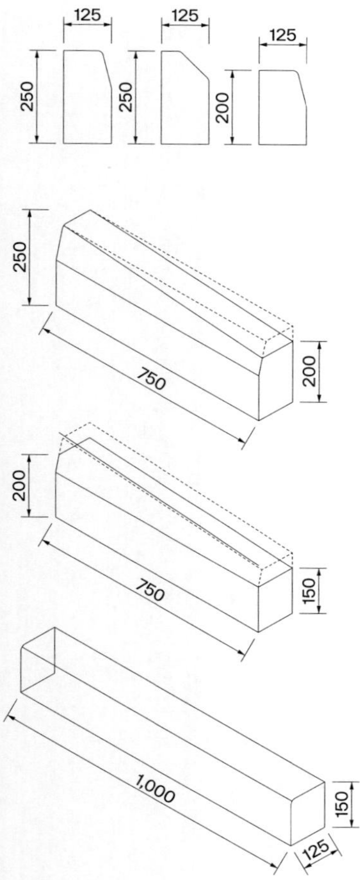

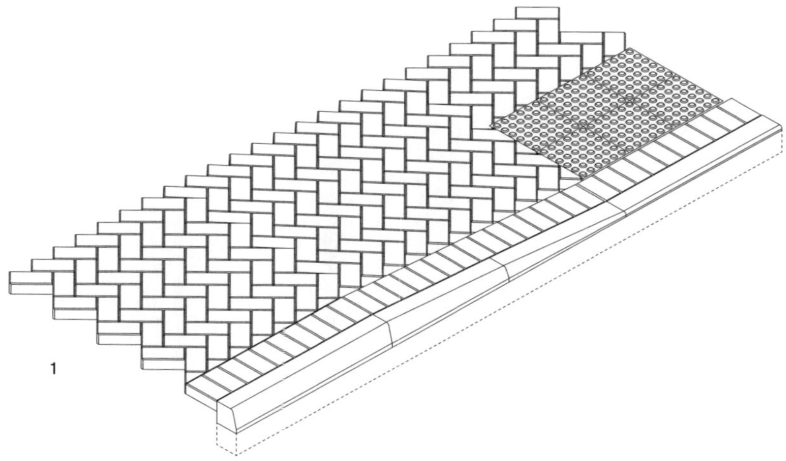

1

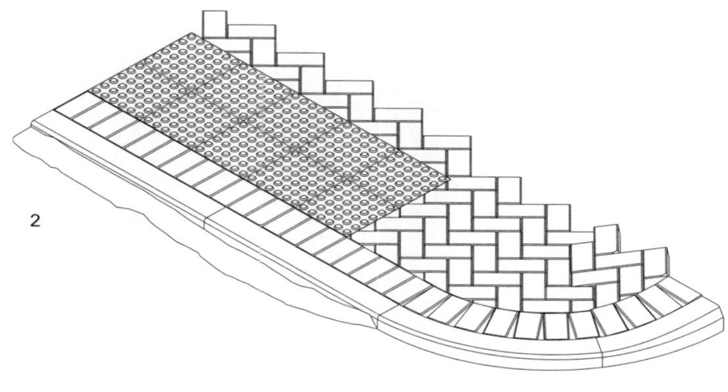

2

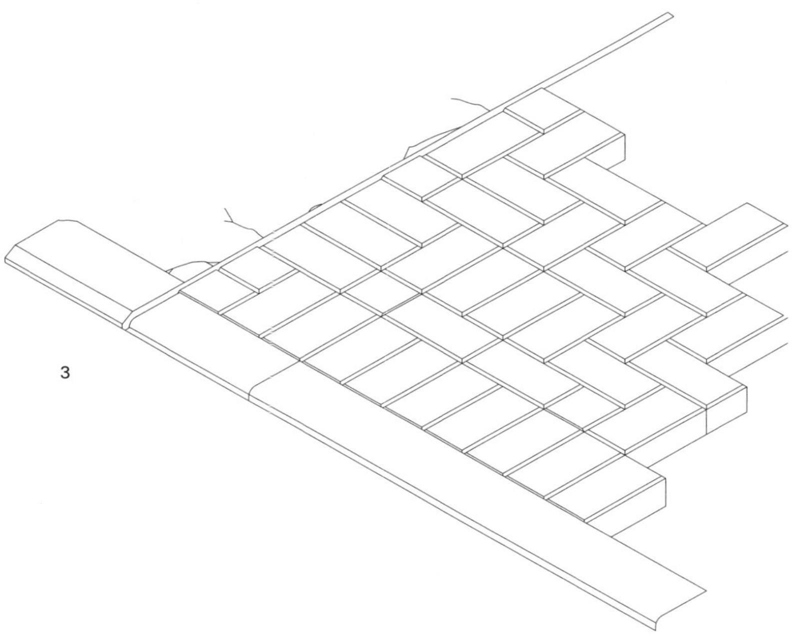

3

1 dropped curb at pedestrian crossing
2 type K3, precast concrete radius curb
3 transition from granite to precast curb

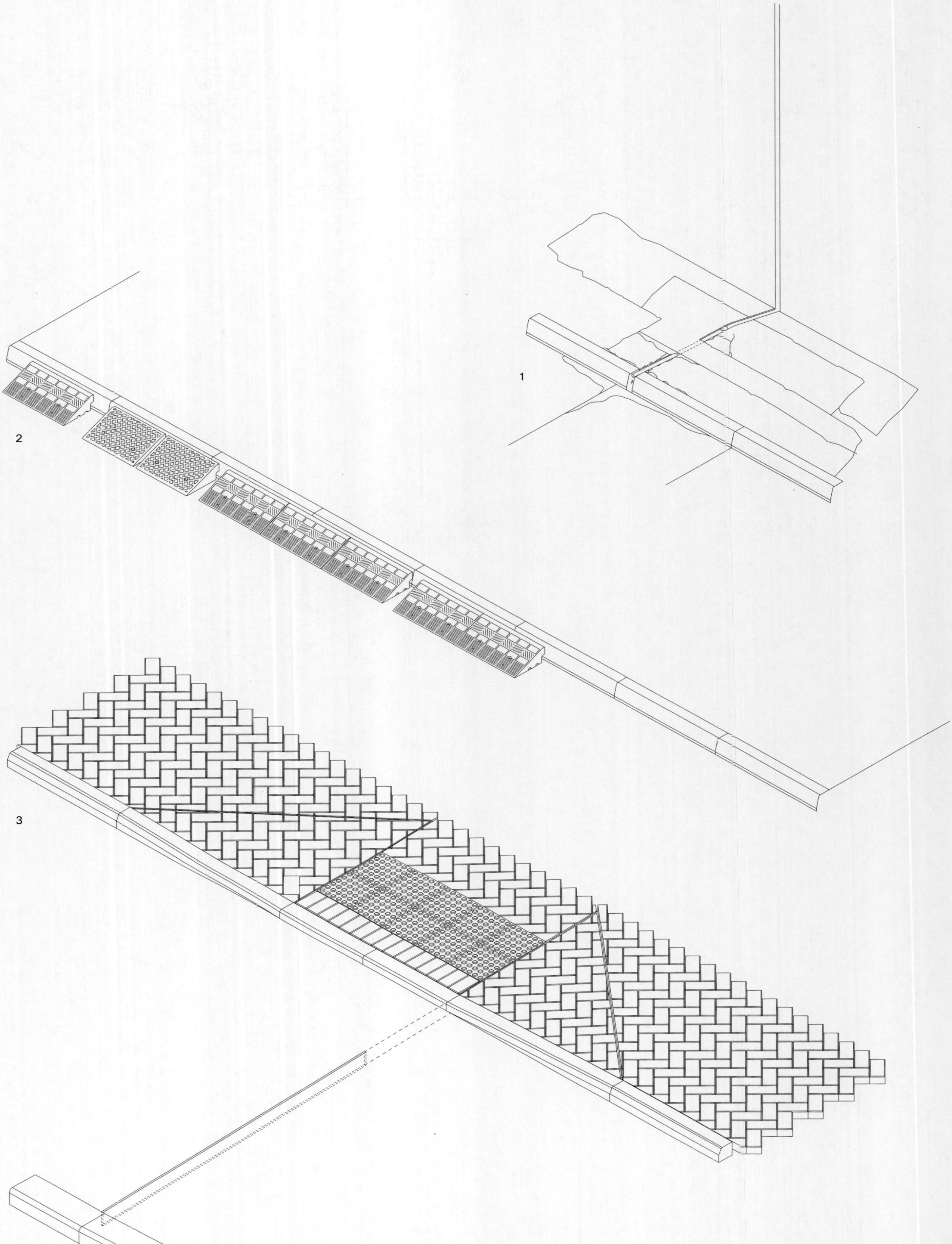
1
2
3

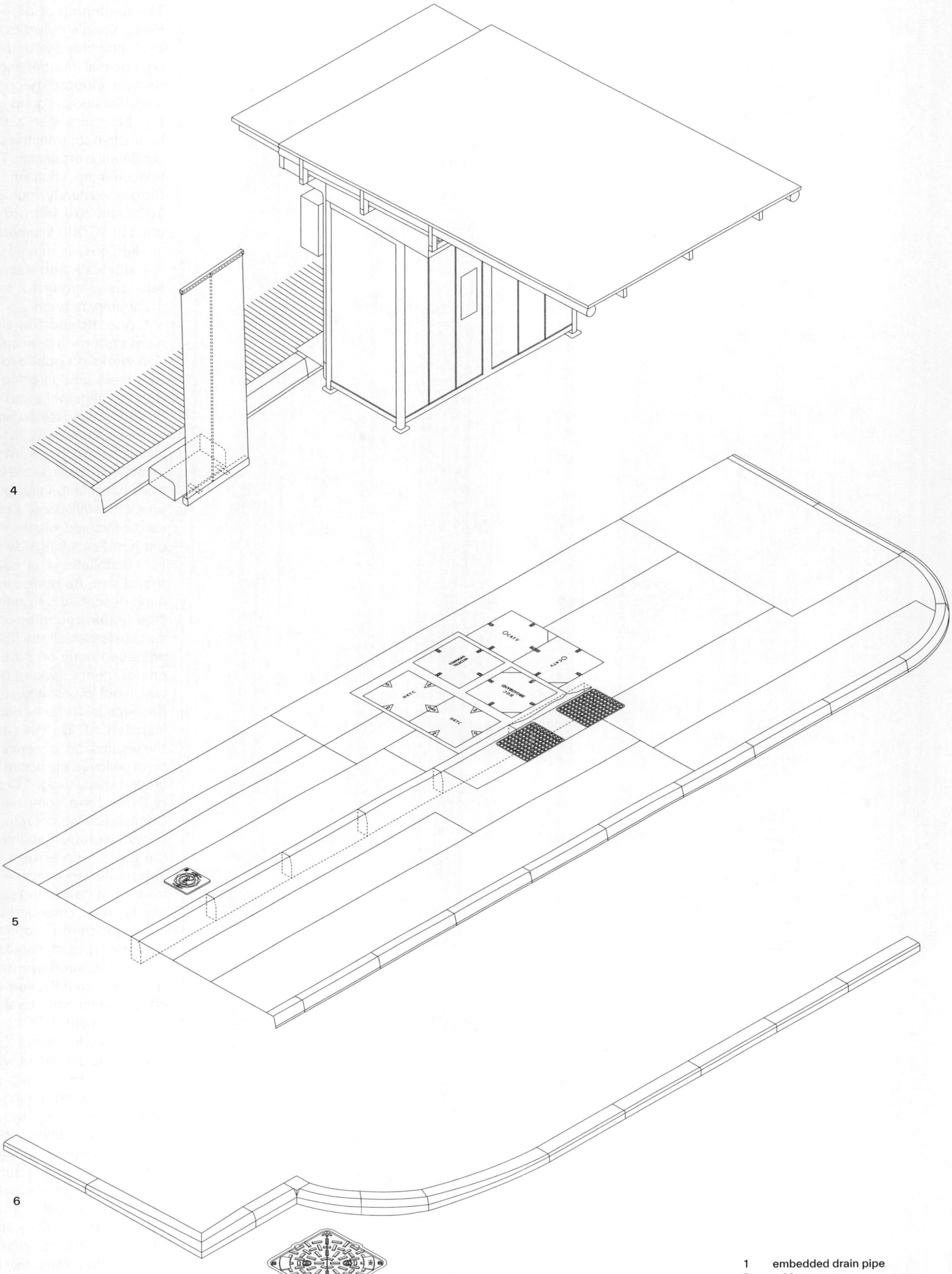

1 embedded drain pipe
2 rubber ramp
3 metal joint in pedestrian dropped curb
4 hawker stall and roll up banner in front of curb
5 extended sidewalk, old curb still embedded
6 corner configuration to avoid access hatch

1

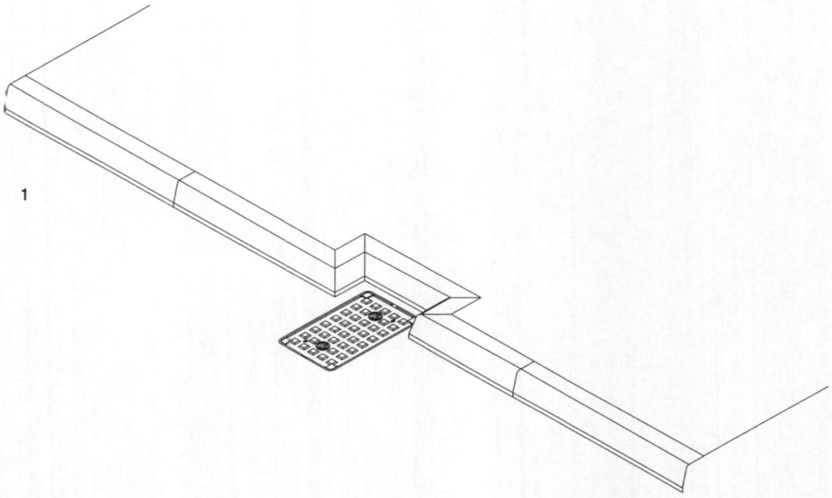

2

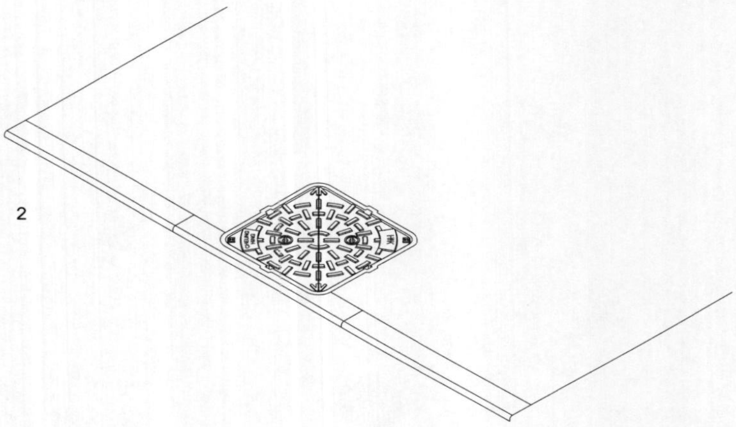

3

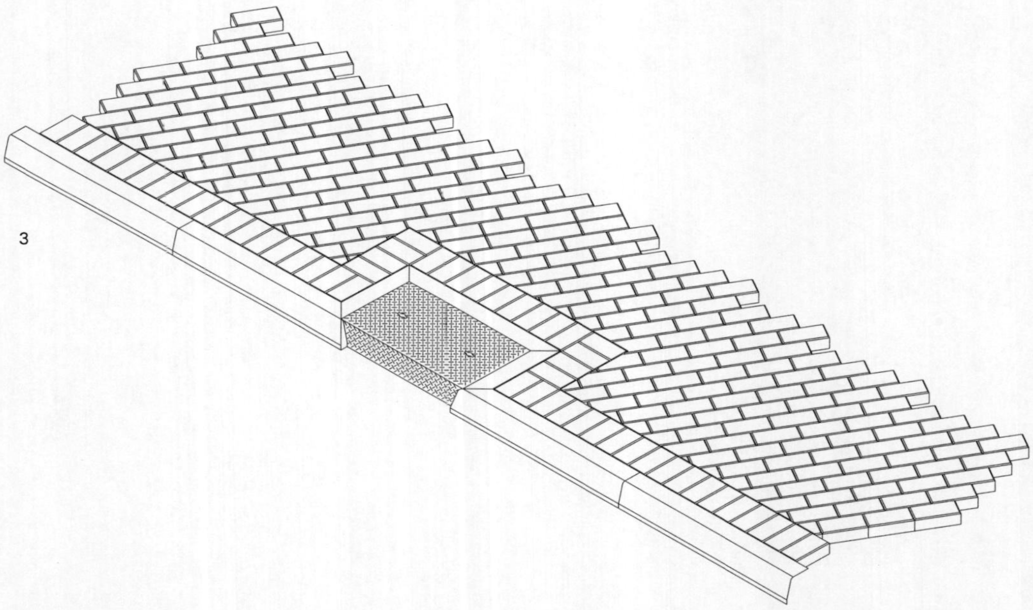

1 notched curb to avoid access hatch
2 access hatch on top of the curb
3 checkered lid covering access hatch, flush to sidewalk

SIDEWALKS
reinstatement

The beginning of deregulation in Hong Kong's telecom industry in 1995 coincided with the launch of commercial internet service. These two developments created a demand for underground utility space that has quickened with advancements in data transmission and the proliferation of telecom. The length of telecommunication infrastructure in the ground nearly doubled between 2006 and 2011, from 26,000 kilometers to 49,000 kilometers. [1] This cabling passes mostly underneath the sidewalk and each individual telecom maintains a map of their proprietary network.

A 2018 audit of the government's efforts in "managing excavation works on public roads" found that there could be "no assurance that the alignment and disposition of underground telecommunications systems have been installed to the satisfaction of the Highways Department [HyD] because the Government does not maintain as-built records on such installations." [2] New cables can be jammed into the earth next to old bundles, alongside a competitor's installations, or near conduits that distribute other services. The audit described a situation in which "the underground space near the surface (especially for [the] footpath) will eventually be saturated with cables/ducts making it very difficult, if not impossible, to go into the deeper sub-surface space for utility installation." [3] This situation was the result of an "absence of government policy on the planning of underground space usage." [4] Instead, the HyD relied on a "compliance" system. Compliance was contingent on the effective promulgation of rules and the good-faith efforts of telecom companies to oversee their contracted installation teams. These teams, in turn, needed to abide by minimum-depth requirements for different types of installations. Ultimately the audit warned that the situation "could result in adverse effects on the structural integrity of road pavements." [5]

The proliferation of cables underground has coincided with a policy to resurface Hong Kong's sidewalks with paving units, which now cover nearly 30 percent of the city's footpaths. The remaining sidewalks are covered in concrete slabs similar to the carriageway itself. The new pavers can be of precast concrete, recycled aggregate, or natural and artificial granite. They are easier to take up for access to the ground underneath without the noisy demolition required of concrete slab pavement. Workers responsible for reinstating the pavement come from the many private contractors that bid for HyD jobs. To work as a certified bricklayer, contractors need to ensure that their employees "have satisfactorily completed at least 14 hours of training in the past 3 years on laying of pavers." [6] Workers without such training are regarded as "helpers."

Along with detailed drawings for many standard paving units, the HyD has "Guidance Notes" on their installation. After going through the "Types of Paving Units," a section on "Aesthetics" breaks the subject into "themes" and "attributes." Paving themes "could affect coherence and harmony of footways" and are themselves governed by "detailed attributes, such as laying patterns and textures." [7] Attributes are further broken down and include rhythm —"repetitive features at regular intervals"—and rhyme.

In its introduction to rhyme, the notes make a definitional aside: "Rhyme, or 'likeness tempered with difference', gives variation on an object without breaking its rhythm." This is followed by two photographs that serve as illustrations of this phenomenon. In the Guidance Notes "likeness tempered with difference" is set off by quotes but unattributed. The quoted fragment likely comes from an often referenced dialogue from 1865 by the Victorian poet Gerard Manley Hopkins: "On the Origin of Beauty." Hopkins was still a student when he wrote the text. In the fictional discussion between an Oxford professor who is chair of Aesthetics and a colleague, it is *rhythm* that the interlocutors agree is "likeness tempered with difference," and rhyme that is defined as a "proportion of disagreement joined with agreement": like *cat* and *hat*. Hopkins's dialogue is reproduced by Cambridge University animal behaviorist N. K. Humphrey in his 1973 essay "The Illusion of Beauty." Humphrey is looking for a "biology of aesthetics," and turns to Hopkins and other earlier theories of beauty in his search. [8]

Detailed measured drawings show common standard arrangements for the concrete pavers on the city's sidewalks. These include "herringbone," "stretcher," and "basket weave" configurations—or "bonds"—that reference centuries-old brickwork patterns. Drawings illustrate every potential circumstance: from the treatment of edges and curves, to the cutting of pavers to meet drains or poles. Additional photos provide side-by-side examples of problems and their rectification: solutions identified with a red check mark.

The use of high-pressure water jet cleaning on *pavered* surfaces has led to the erosion of the cement that holds them together. Water makes its way into joints, seeping into the sand underneath. Traces of organic matter sprout into plants that push up between cracks, causing deformations. This problem has led to the use of a joint stabilizer sealer in highly trafficked areas. Worries about the adherence of pavers also led government officials to authorize the application of an even stronger glue in sidewalk paver joints near government headquarters before Xi Jinping's 2017 visit. [9] During the 2019 protests, pavers were taken up from 22,000 square meters of sidewalks. Some of the bricklike blocks were repositioned in the street in seemingly precise groupings: menhirs, cairns, trilithons, and more unruly piles that formed a traffic-blocking, scaleless protoground.

1. Audit Commission, "Government's efforts in managing excavation works on public roads," in *Director of Audit's Reports*, no. 70, chap. 4 [full report] (April 3, 2018): 46.
2. Ibid., ix.
3. Ibid., 65.
4. Ibid., 12.
5. Ibid., 54.
6. Research and Development Division, "Guidance Notes on Design and Construction of Pavements with Paving Units," RD/GN/044B, HKSARG (November 2020): 43.
7. Ibid., 4.
8. N. K. Humphrey, "The Illusion of Beauty," *Perception* 2, no. 4 (1973): 429–39.
9. Clifford Lo, "Hong Kong applies simple solution amid elaborate security plans for Xi Jinping's visit," *South China Morning Post*, June 28, 2017, https://www.scmp.com/news/hong-kong/politics/article/2100347/hong-kong-applies-simple-solution-amid-elaborate-security.

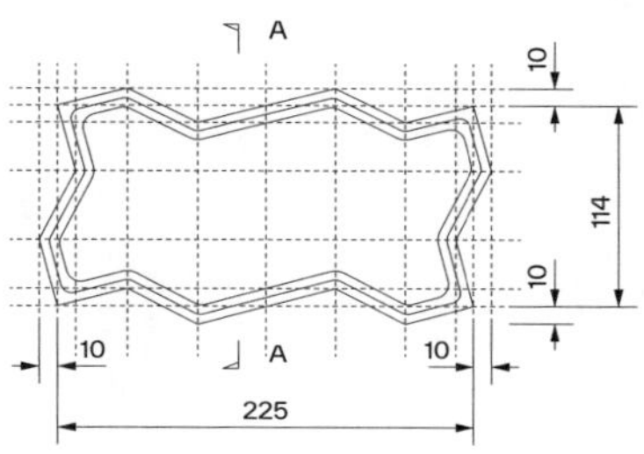

PLAN

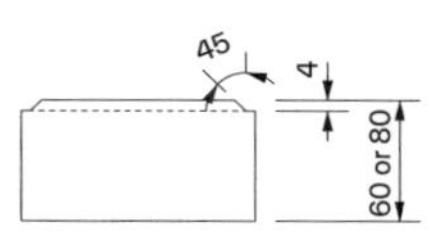

SECTION A-A

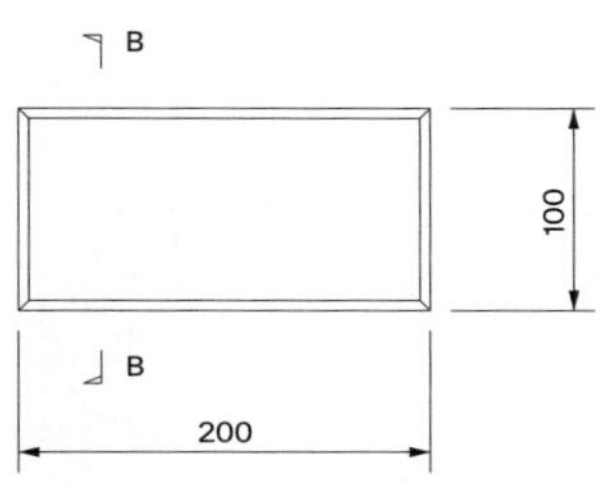

PLAN

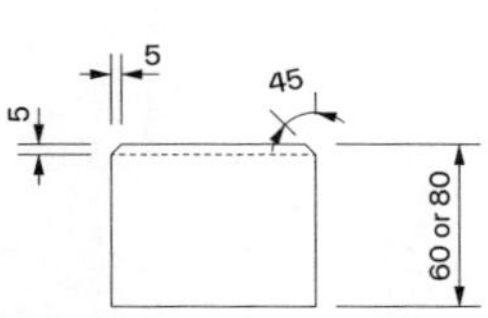

SECTION B-B

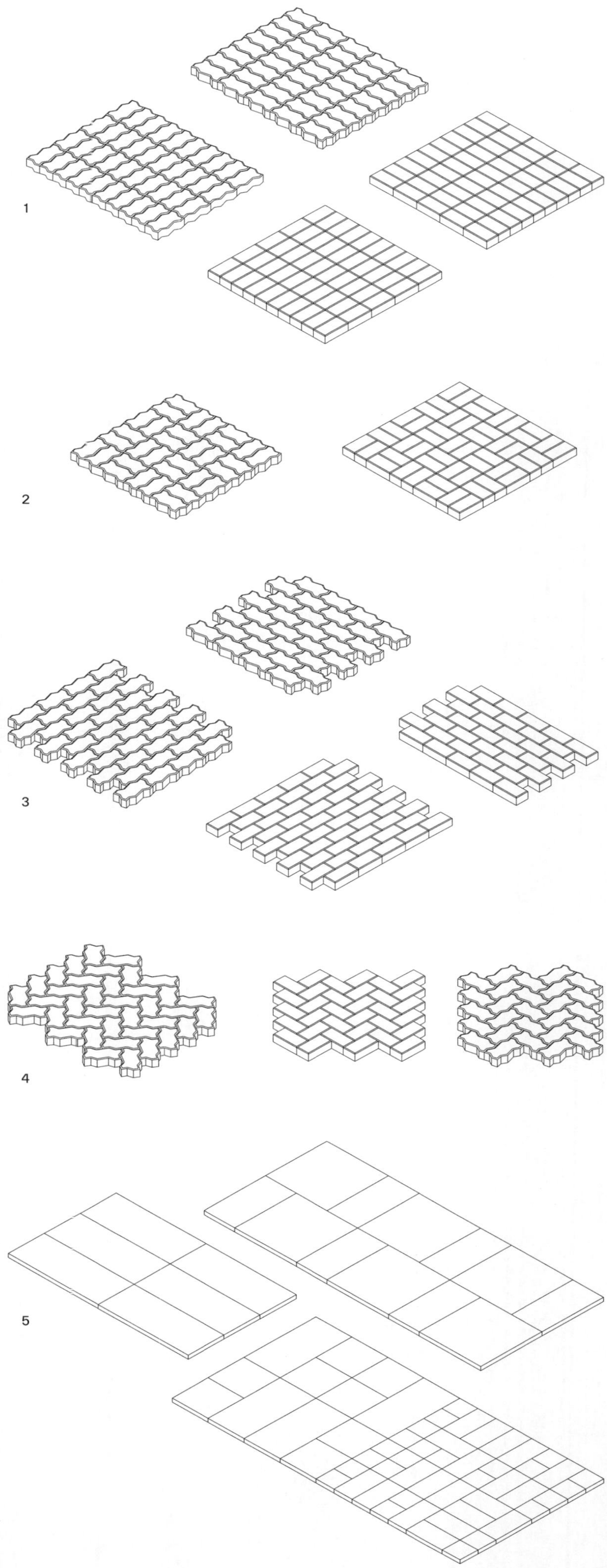

1 stack bonding
2 basketweave
3 stretcher
4 herringbone
5 stone paving slabs

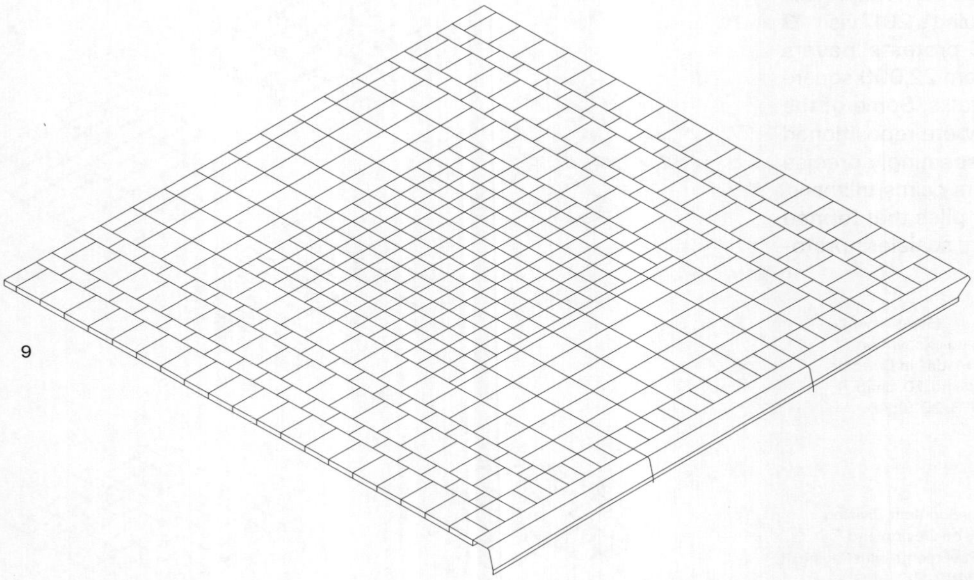

9

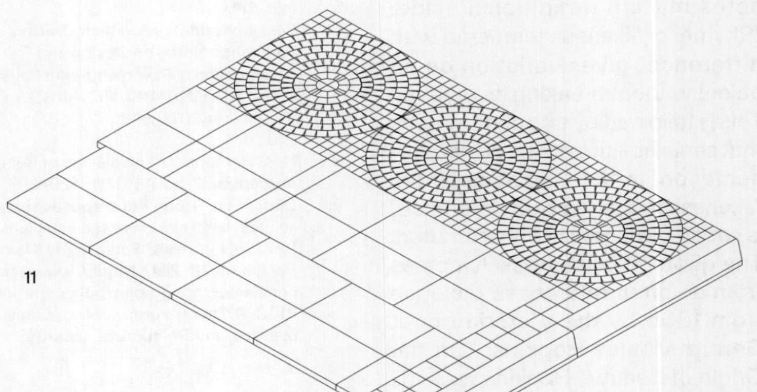

11

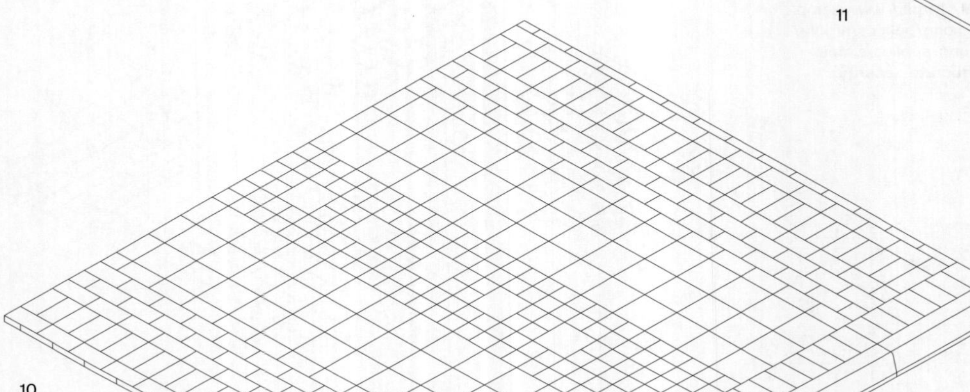

10

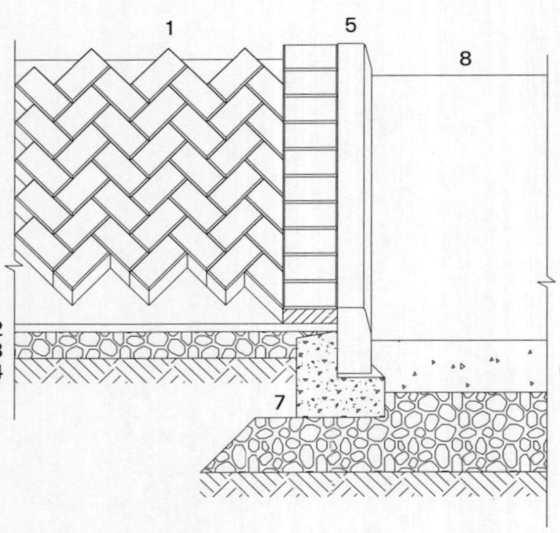

12

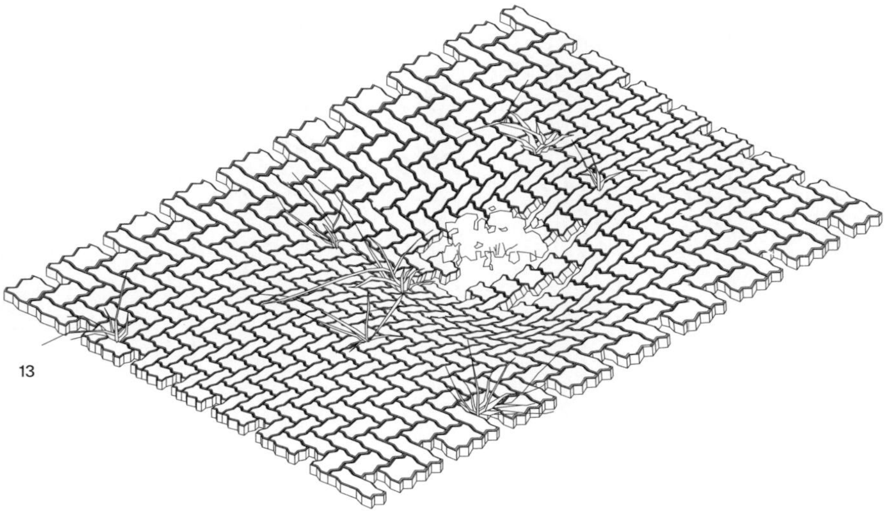

13

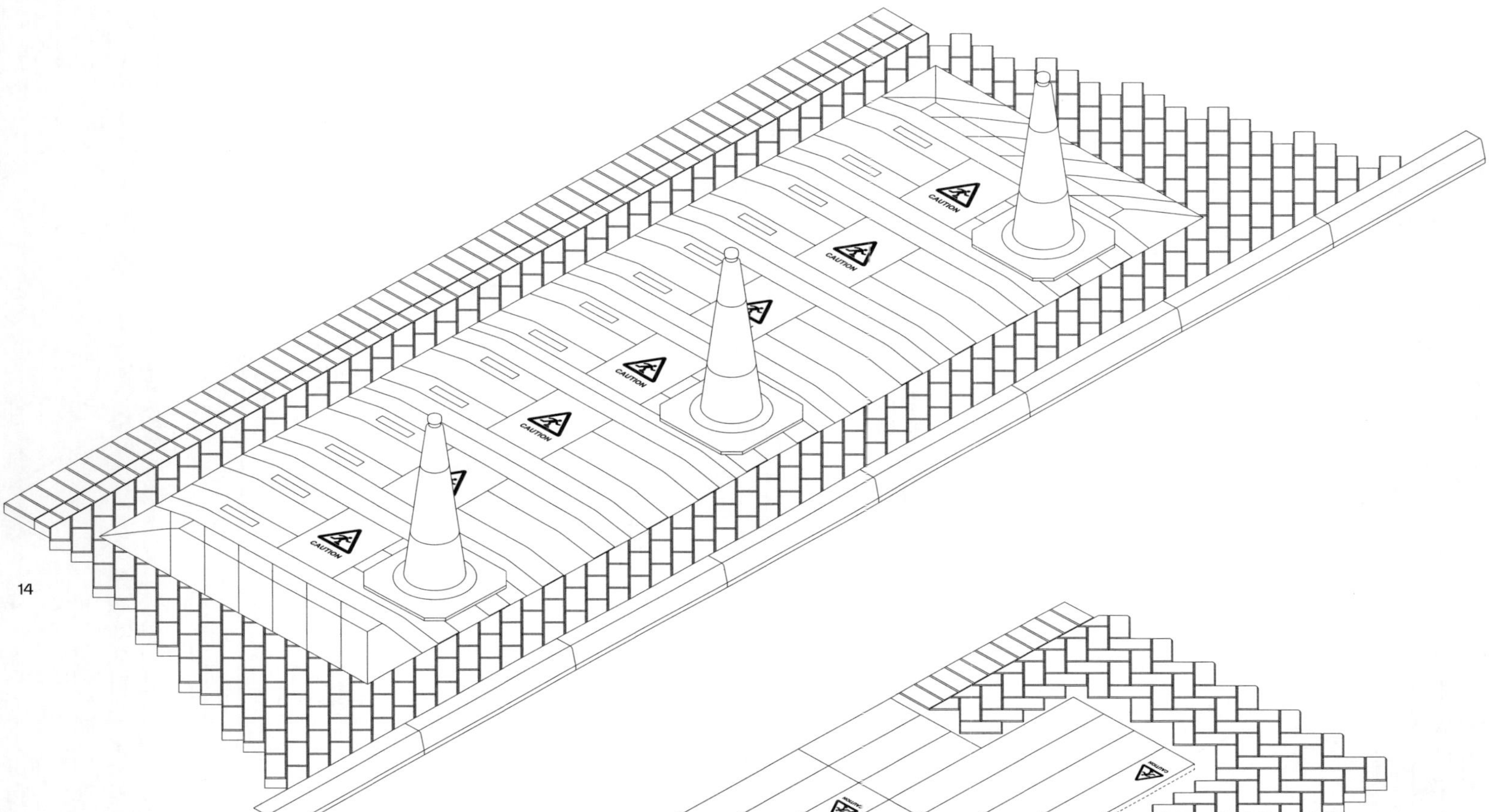

14

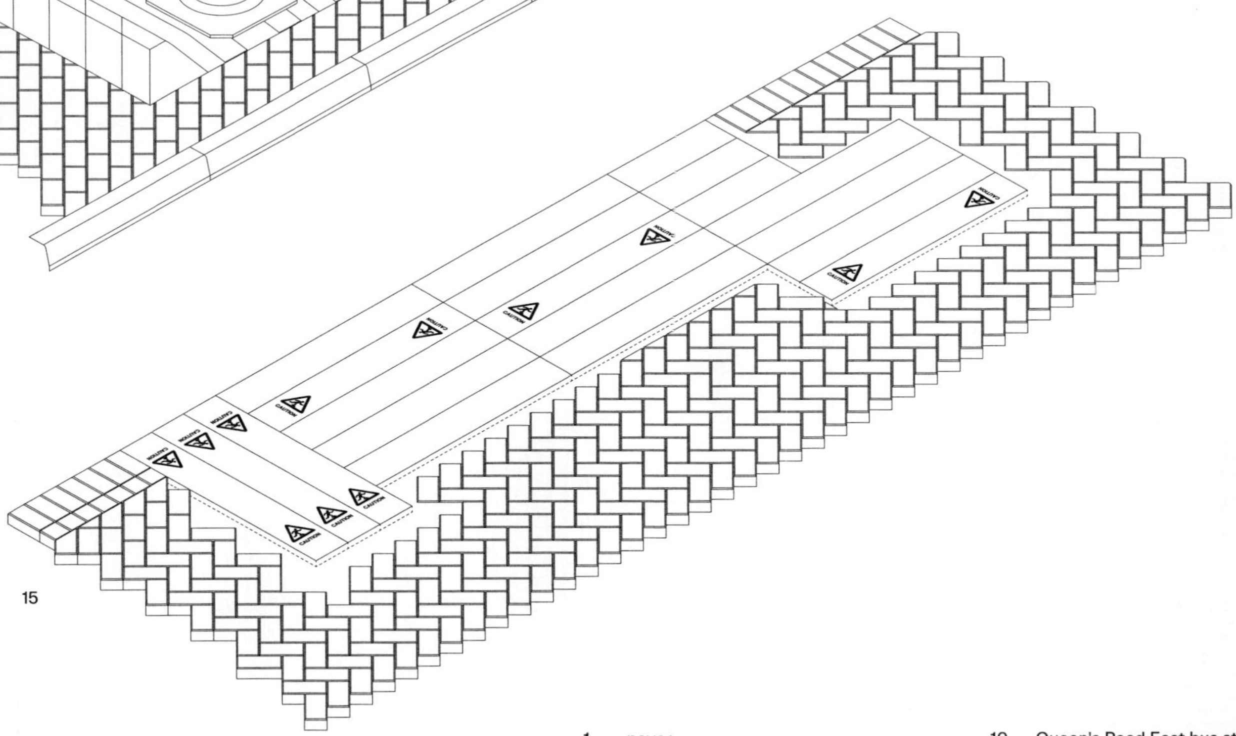

15

1 paver
2 sand course, sand, and cement bedding
3 subbase
4 earth
5 curb or other edge restraint
6 cement mortar (10 mm - 40 mm)
7 concrete backing and foundation
8 concrete slab (carriageway)
9 Three Pacific Place
10 Queen's Road East bus stop
11 Dominion Garden
12 Wan Chai historical coastline marker, Queen's Road East
13 blockwork defects – depression/ uneven surface/wild vegetation
14 temporary pedestrian trench cover
15 embedded wooden panels for excavation work

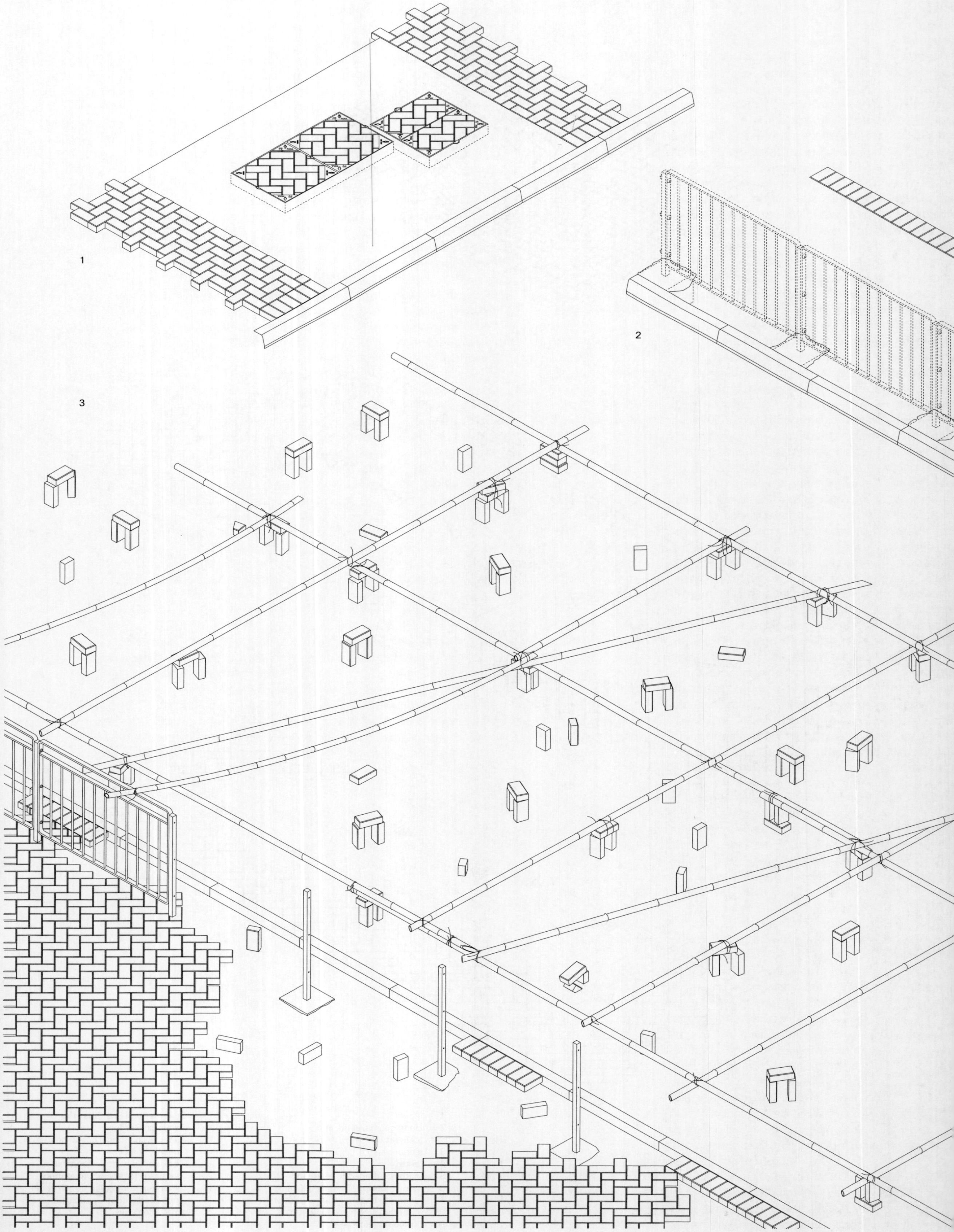
1
2
3

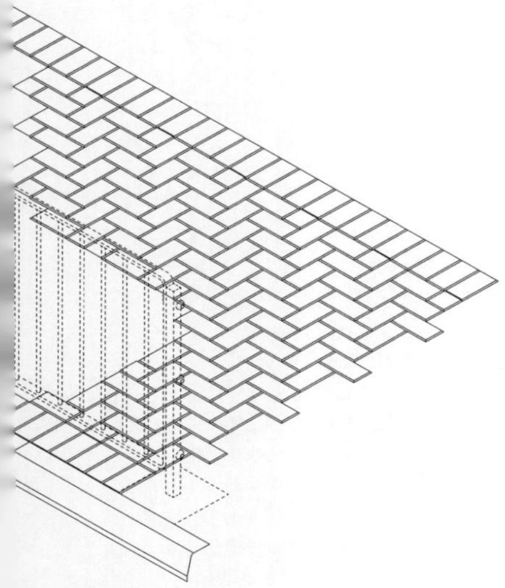

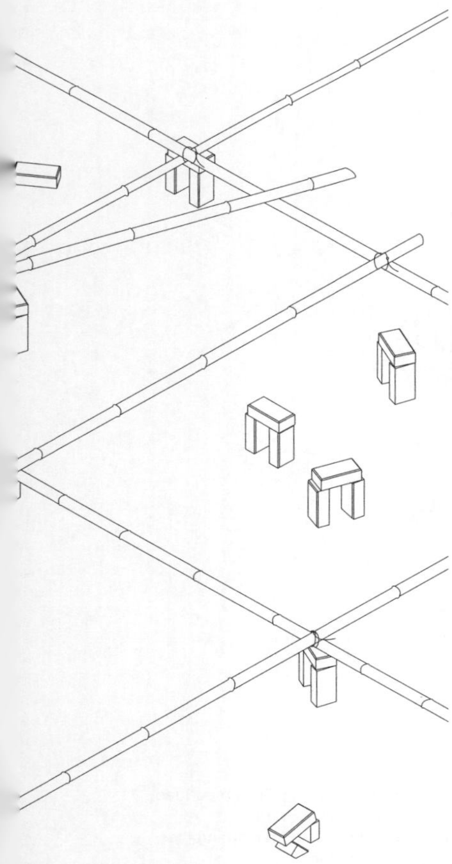

1 temporary sidewalk repair, concrete fill
2 asphalt fill
3 brick and bamboo roadblock

TACTILE PAVERS
strips

The codes governing the design and installation of tactile pavers in Hong Kong replicate standards that date from their invention and use in Japan in the mid-1960s. Legislation on tactile pavers appeared in Hong Kong almost immediately after handover in a revision to the "Building (Planning) Regulations (Cap. 123F)" that appeared on September 20, 1997. Amendments included a change to the title of the "Third Schedule" from "Disabled Persons" to "Persons with a Disability"; new text required "tactile warning strips...at the head and foot of a ramp" or "at landings and at the bottom and top ends of a staircase." A "tactile guide path" leading to "lift zones and functional areas" of buildings "intended to be used by the public" was also newly indicated. [1]

This language remained unchanged until 2008, when an "Interpretation" section was introduced to the beginning of the Third Schedule. [2] This new section defined a number of terms, including "tactile guide path" and "tactile warning strip." Both definitions reference drawing figures included in the legislation. The illustrations replicate ones that first appeared in the Transport Department's *Transport Planning Design Manual* which were also the basis for a set of five Highways Department (HyD) technical drawings that appeared in 2001. The HyD set addresses the fabrication, disposition, and installation of tactile pavers on the city's streets. In 2002, the set was appended with the addition of a new drawing on "Typical Fixing Details of Tactile Warning Strip"; and again in 2003 with "Tactile Warning Strip at Curved Pedestrian Crossing."

The seven drawings that currently comprise the set specify a system that is faithful to the original Japanese invention. The design comprises three different types of pavers: directional (for guidance), positional (for a change in direction) and warning. These three designs are distinguished by variations in their raised patterns, which are drawn to the millimeter in the HyD drawings. Drawing number H5118E, the first in the set, further classifies tactile pavers as "tiles," "slabs," or "blocks," with thicknesses of 15mm, 60mm, and 60mm, respectively. The edges of "tiles" and "slabs" have a 3mm chamfer, while block edges are square. Note 4 requires that pavers be made of precast concrete; note 7, that all pavers "contrast visually with adjoining surfaces." Note 8, updated in May of 2021, requires a "Wet Pendulum Test" to verify slip resistance; an accompanying chart indicates acceptable results for specified gradients. [3]

Additional drawings describe the disposition of "warning" pavers at crosswalks (perpendicular to the crosswalk and not necessarily parallel to the curb) and details for five types of sidewalk paver installations, including situations when pavers are nested into recessed access hatch covers. The notes and drawing sheets speak to the different phases of fabrication, design, installation, and maintenance implicated by the introduction of tactile pavers into the street. This information makes its way from those who draw and redraft these standards to the engineers overseeing their implementation, to the contractors, subcontractors, work teams, and maintenance workers who are directly responsible for their proper execution.

The adoption of tactile pavers in Asia saw many cities copying early Japanese mistakes or adopting habits suitable to Tokyo sidewalks with few encumbrances. [4] In other parts of the world, the spread of tactile pavers led to new designs and standards. This proliferation has been explained by the relative ease with which tactile pavers can be integrated into existing sidewalks or into new projects, where they are often applied when work is nearly complete. In this sense, the pavers are expedients that make universal access a requirement to fulfil, rather than an organizing principle. They make it possible to avoid a radical rethinking of street life around "natural leading elements" and a "simple and logical organization of the built environment" conceived for people with different forms of mobility. [5] In a chapter that addresses "Facilities for People with Disabilities," a 2001 edition of the Hong Kong Transport Department's planning and design manual notes that "the width of all footways should not be less than 2m and preferably wider." [6] Despite the decades that have passed, many sidewalks in both old and new parts of the city fail to achieve this measure.

1. Legislative Council, "Cap. 123F. Building (Planning) Regulations," September 20, 1997, HKSARG.
2. Legislative Council, "Cap. 123, section 38. Building (Planning) Regulations," December 1, 2008, HKSARG.
3. Highways Department, "H5118E: Tactile Pavers: Tactile Tiles / Slabs / Blocks," *Standard Drawings. Section 2: Street Furniture*, rev. May 2021, HKSARG.
4. Tomomi Mizuno, Arisa Nishidate, Katsumi Tokuda, and Kunijiro Arai, "Installation Errors and Corrections in Tactile Ground Surface Indicators in Europe, America, Oceania and Asia," *IATSS Research* 32, no. 2. (January 2008): 68–80, https://doi.org/https://doi.org/10.1016/S0386-1112(14)60210-7.
5. Aud Tennøy, Kjersti Visnes Øksenholt, Nils Fearnley, and Bryan Matthews, "Standards for Usable and Safe Environments for Sight Impaired," *Proceedings of the Institution of Civil Engineers—Municipal Engineer* 168, no. 1 (2015): 25, https://doi.org/10.1680/muen.13.00043.
6. Transport Department, "Facilities for People with Disabilities," in *Transport Planning & Design Manual*, vol. 6, chap. 8 (2001), HKSARG, 8.3.2.1.

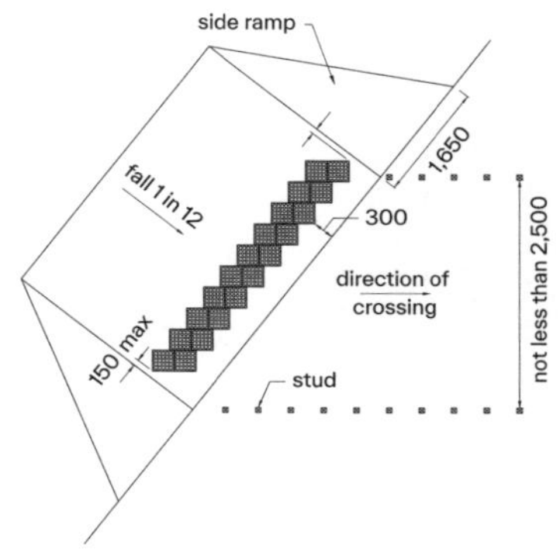

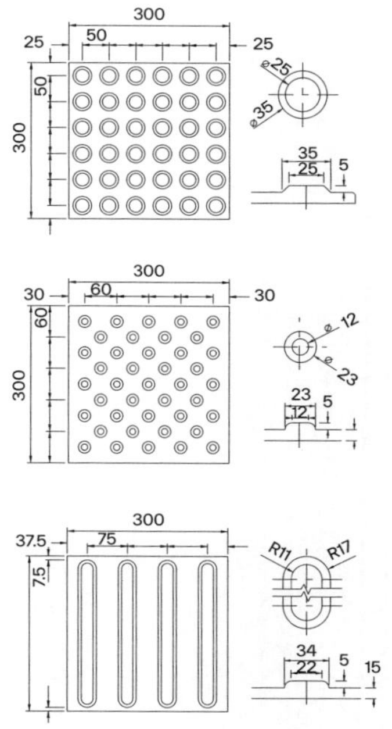

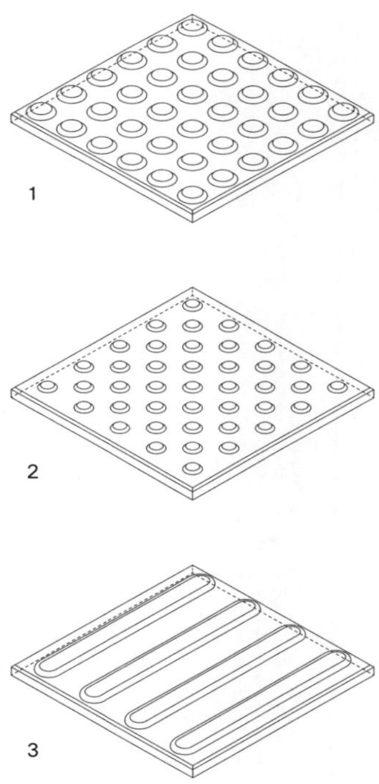

1 hazard warning tile
2 positional tile
3 directional tile

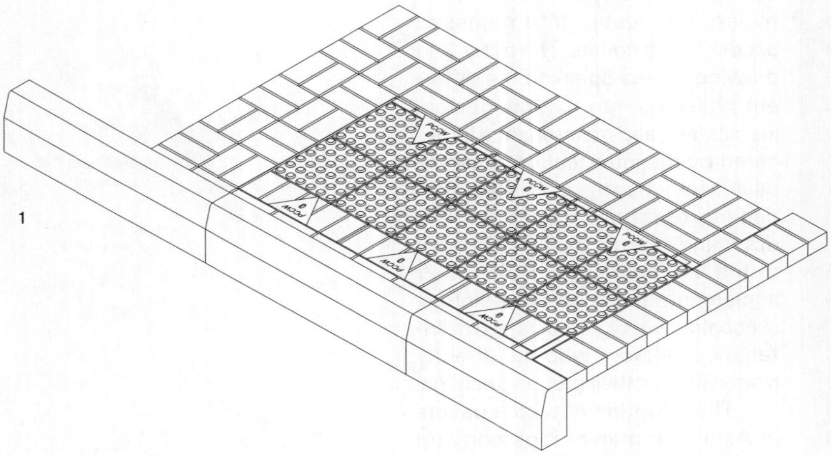

1

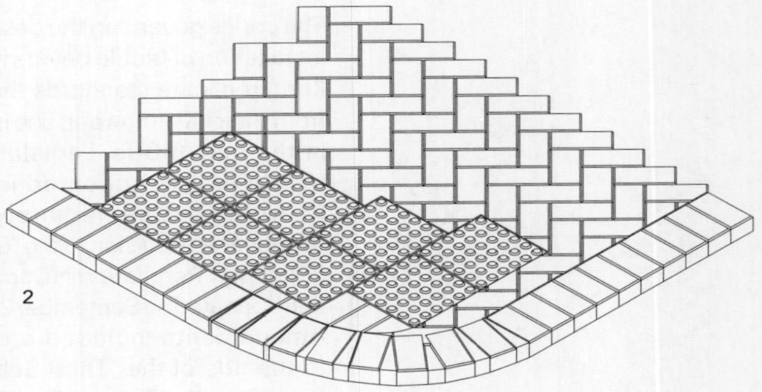

2

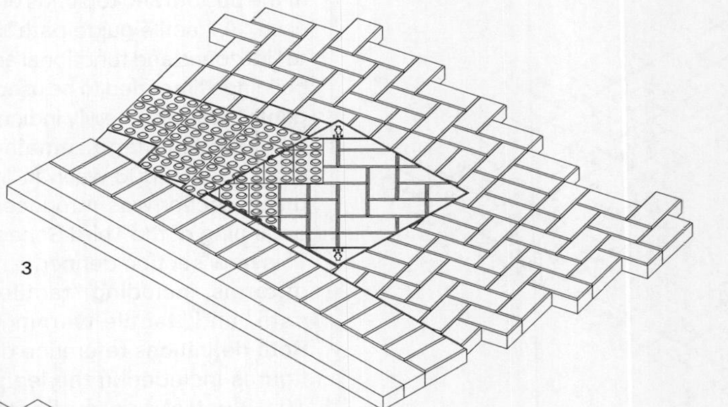

3

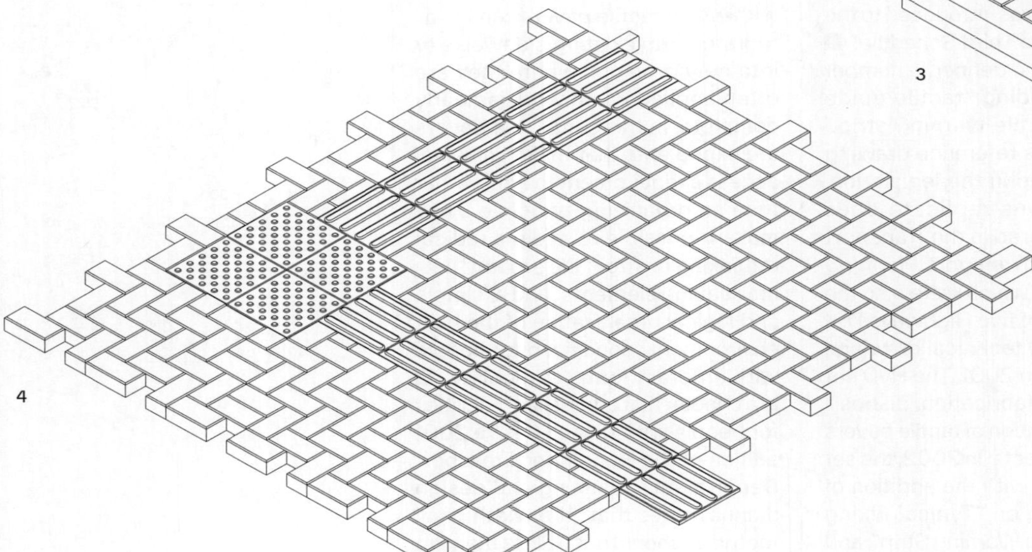

4

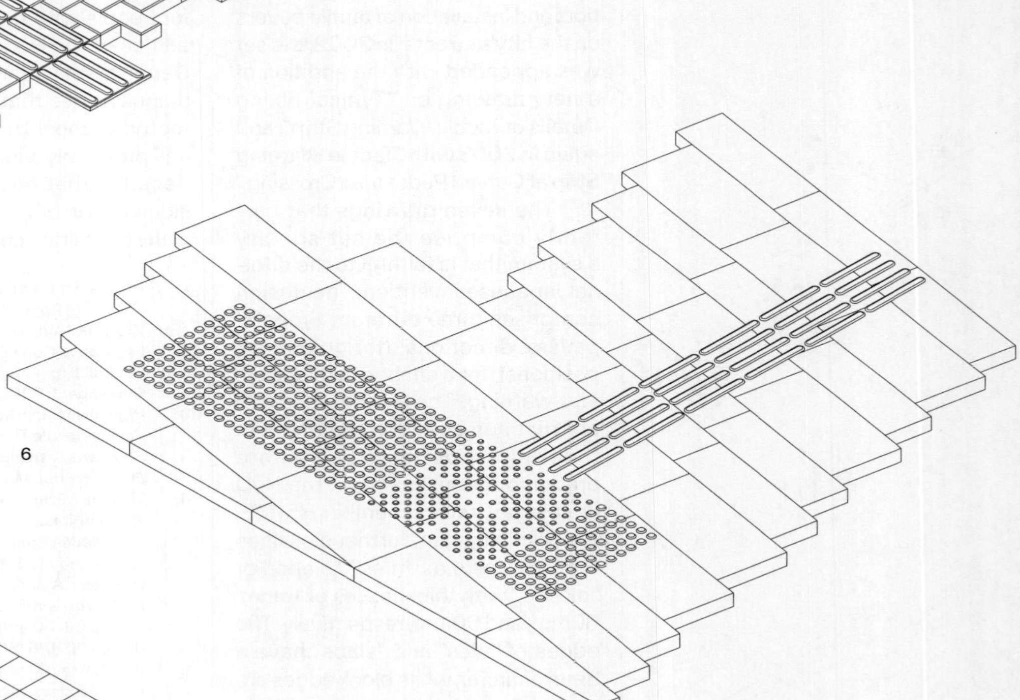

6

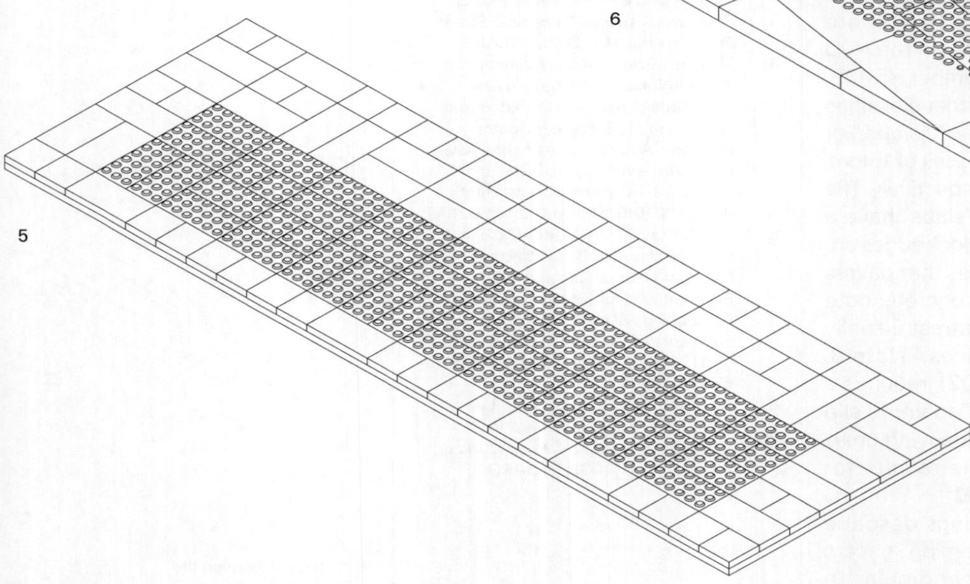

5

1 hazard warning tiles embedded in access hatch tray
2 staggered hazard warning tiles at the corner
3 misaligned warning tiles
4 positional tiles indicating change in directional guide path
5 hazard warning tiles on concrete pavers
6 junction of three tactile markings on stone paving slabs

TRAFFIC SIGNS
post congestion

The Lands Department is responsible for naming streets in Hong Kong and maintaining a registry of their geographic definition. The Director of Lands promulgates a "Declaration of a Street Name" each time a new street is created. The announcement includes at least one plan and a text description of the intersections where the new street starts and ends, and its length. [1]

Street nameplates are one of two kinds of signs that appear on Hong Kong's roads. The second type are rule-giving, traffic signs that are part of the "language of the road" set out in the Transport Department's "Road Users' Code." The Highways Department (Hyd) maintains standards for the nameplates and for the rule-giving signs. These standards also describe how the two types of signs are to be disposed on the street and fixed onto poles.

The signs themselves are made in one of 14 workshops maintained by the Correctional Services Department (CSD). A 2015 government audit of these "rehabilitation services," found that the most profitable workshop was the laundry service; in 2013 and 2014, it made a net contribution of HK$118.9 million to government finances. Sign making employs roughly 135 people at any one time and loses the government HK$8.3 million each year. A precast concrete workshop that produces pavers, curbs, and tactile strips numbers 29 people and runs a yearly deficit averaging HK$8.8 million. [2] Prisoners make between HK$45 and $192 a week, depending on their assigned trade. Until 1997, when the sign-making workshops switched to digital processes, prison workers cut letters by hand in a font that has now disappeared from Hong Kong's roads. [3]

The current design for street nameplates dates from January 2004, when the HyD began including building numbers. At the time, they also announced that nameplates should be fixed on both the front and back of curbside posts so that the street name could be seen from the sidewalk as well as the carriageway. [4] Depending on the number of letters and characters in a street's name, the 3mm-thick, 324mm-tall aluminum nameplates measure between 750 and 2,000mm, growing in 50mm increments. A black border around the nameplate thickens to form an arrow pointing in one direction if the nameplate is situated at the start or end of the street: it thickens to point in both directions if it is situated along a street's course. [5] Roman letters appear in a font derived from the "Transport" typeface first developed by the United Kingdom's Department for Transport. Traditional characters are 98mm-high in "Quanzhen BoldHei." This font was developed by Vector Technology Co., Ltd., a Taiwanese company founded in 1990 that got its start in pre-press typesetting. The traditional characters are straddled on either side by building numbers that correspond to their direction on the street. The English street name appears above.

Signs are mounted to hollow steel poles. Single-sign poles are 76.1mm in diameter, while poles with multiple signs are 88.9mm. These poles are anchored into foundations whose size and depth also varies based on the number of signs. In May of 2018, a revision to the HyD's drawings indicated that a length of 40mm square steel should be housed inside the pole, projecting at least 800mm above the ground, presumably adding stability under lateral impact. [6] In February of 2019, another revision called for a "detachable dome shape cap" to be added to the top of the pole. A separate drawing specifically for this "cap" calls for it to be fixed to the pole with a stainless steel bolt and washer. Text indications call for drill holes that pierce the pole to be "protected by two coats of zinc rich paint and with transparent sealant at the edge to prevent ingress of rainwater into the CHS [circular hollow section] steel tube." [7]

The HyD does not limit the *number* of street signs attached to any given pole. Instead, standards indicate a "maximum total projected area of sign plates in any direction" of 1.28m². This "total projected area" also determines the dimensions and depth of concrete footings: from 700mm to 1,100mm deep. [8] Rules for the disposition of nameplates on city streets are detailed in a diagram showing a fictional "Road A." Block lengths and road widths determine their spacing and required number. [9] The proliferation of signs on city streets led to a HyD note in 2006 indicating that "post congestion" was to be avoided and that "pedestrian movement and sightlines... should not be adversely obstructed as far as possible." [10] The note also mentions that installations should take care to avoid underground utility services, many of which run under the sidewalk.

1. See Lands Department, "Survey and Mapping: Government Notices and Plans for Street Naming," HKSARG, last update: July 30, 2021, https://www.landsd.gov.hk/en/survey-mapping/mapping/street-geographical-place-naming/street-naming.html.
2. Audit Commission, "Rehabilitation services provided by the Correctional Services Department," in *Director of Audit's Reports*, no. 64, ch. 8 [full report], HKSARG (April 1, 2015): 78–80.
3. Yau Yick Cheung Gary and the Road Research Society documented and publicized the font that came out of CSD's sign-making workshops. Yau dubbed it "Prison Gothic," and has popularized it as an element of Hong Kong's disappearing visual identity. See Yau Yick Cheung Gary, 香港道路探索—路牌標誌 × 交通設計 = *Hong Kong Road Study: Signage & Highway Design*, 1st ed., (Hong Kong: Extraordinary Publishing Company/Fei Fan Publish, 2019).
4. Highways Department, Research and Development Division, "Guidance notes on Installation of New Street Name Plates Inscribed with Building Numbers," RD/GN/031B, HKSARG (January 2006): 2.
5. Highways Department, "H2206C: Street Name Plate With Building Numbers," *Standard Drawings. Section 2: Street Furniture.* rev. March 2018, HKSARG.
6. See, for example, Highways Department, "H2199D: Single Post Traffic Sign Support (Using Off-Centered Method) (Sheet 2 of 4)," *Standard Drawings. Section 2: Street Furniture,* rev. Feb. 2019, HKSARG.
7. Highways Department, "H2300: Detachable Dome Shape Cap for Traffic Sign Post," *Standard Drawings. Section 2: Street Furniture,* rev. Feb. 2019, HKSARG.
8. Highways Department, "H2228E: Single Post Multi-Sign Support for Street Name Plates and Centre-Mounted Traffic Signs," *Standard Drawings. Section 2: Street Furniture,* rev. Feb. 2019, HKSARG.
9. Highways Department, "H2207: General Method of Assigning Building Number to Street Name Plates," *Standard Drawings. Section 2: Street Furniture,* rev. March 2004, HKSARG.
10. Highways Department, Research and Development Division, *Guidance Notes on Installation of New Street Name Plates Inscribed with Building Numbers.* RD/GN/031B, HKSARG (Jan. 2006): 3.

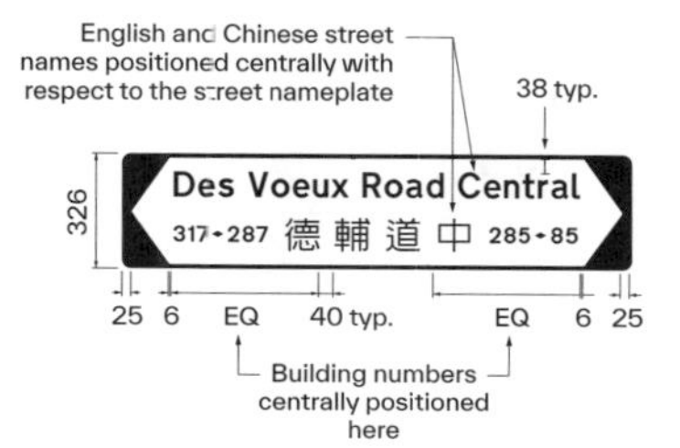

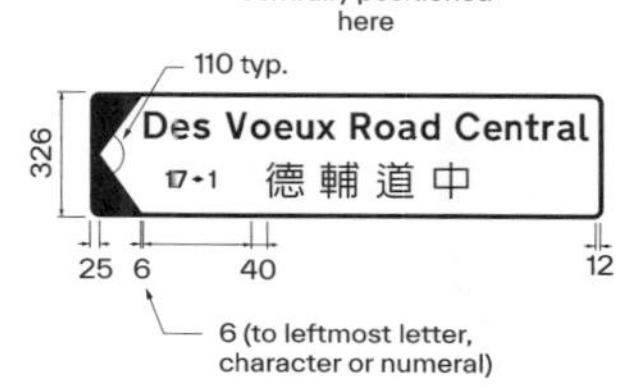

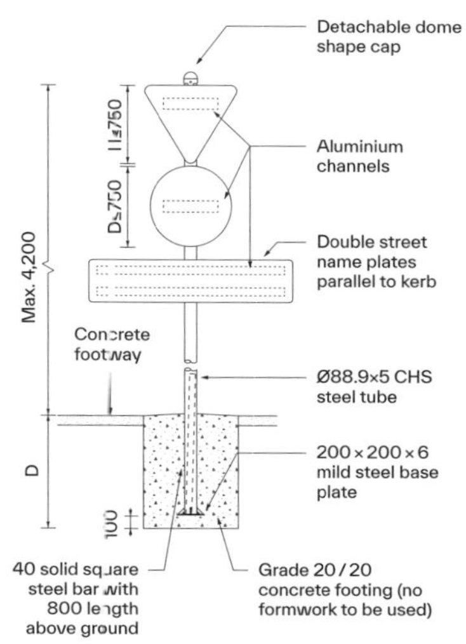

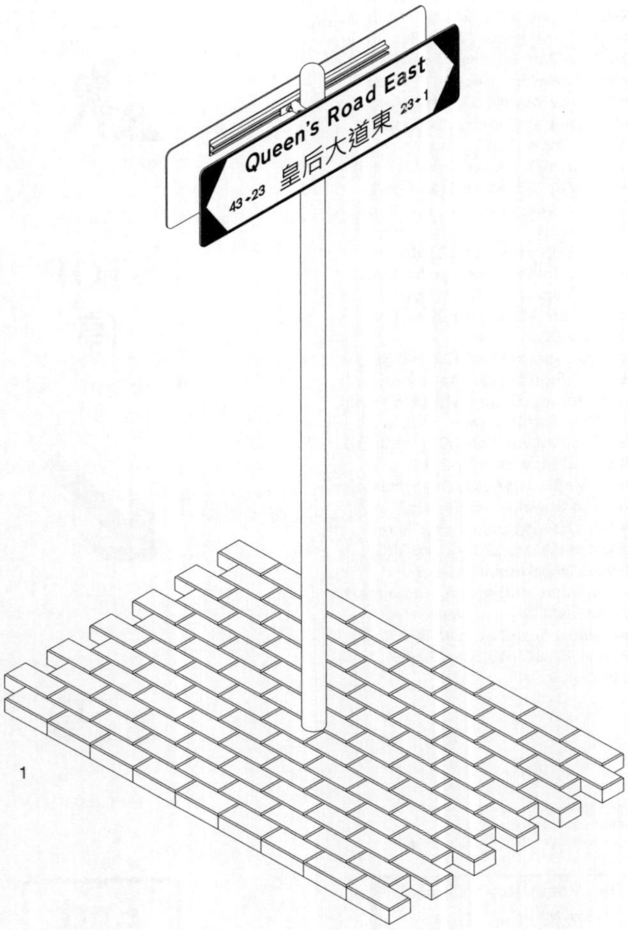
Queen's Road East
43-23 皇后大道東 23-1

1

St. Francis Street
聖佛蘭士街

2

Lun Fat Street
聯發街

3

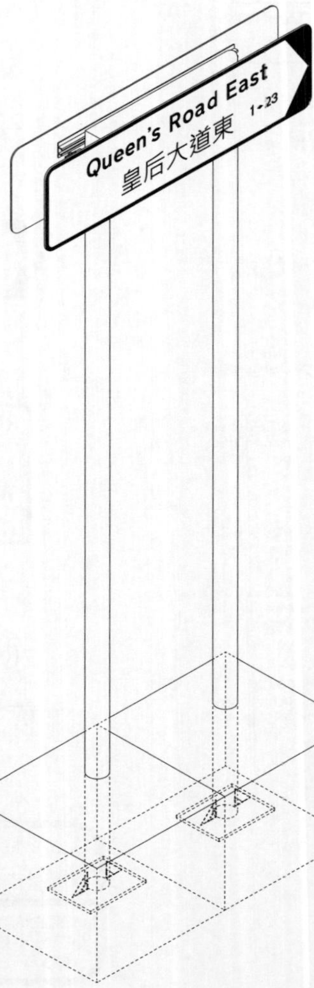
Queen's Road East
皇后大道東 1-23

4

Queen's Road East
92-112 皇后大道東 118-136

5

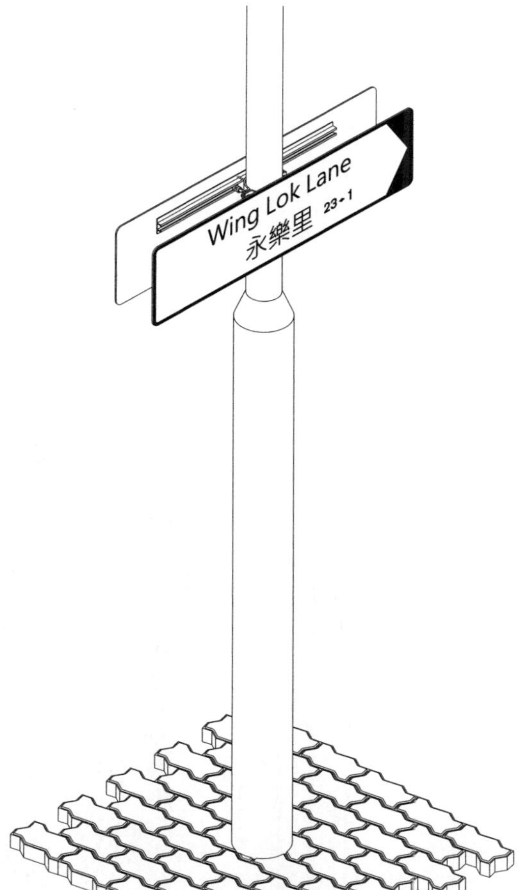

6

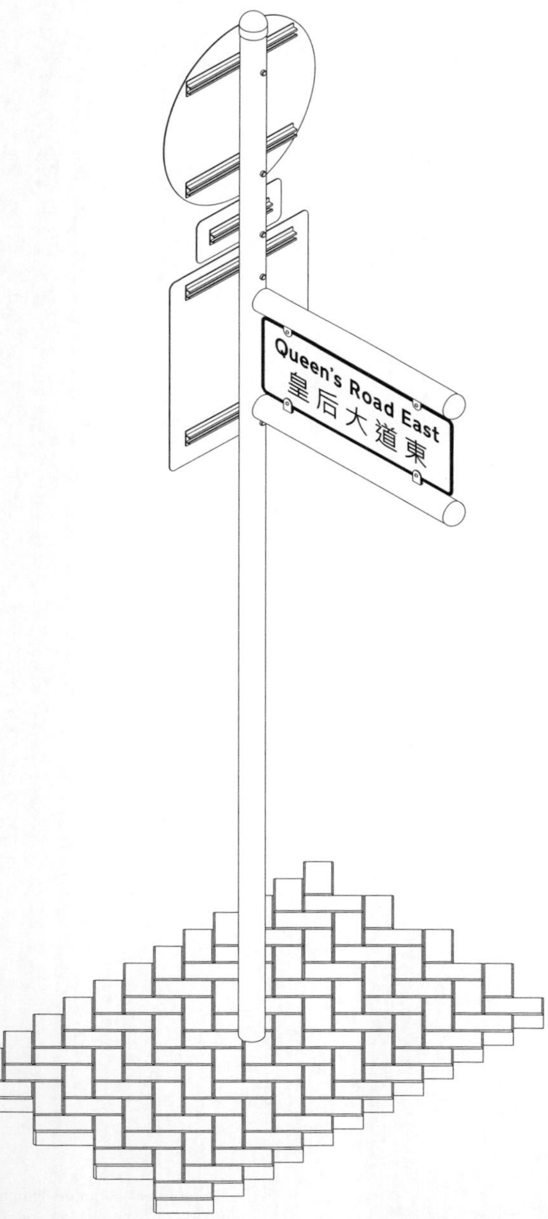

7

8

1 single post, center-mounted double street nameplate
2 wall-mounted nameplate, eight-screw attachment
3 two-screw attachment
4 double street nameplate on double post, base plate reinforcement in concrete footings
5 center-mounted double street name-plate on single post, traffic sign
6 on lamppost
7 double sided street nameplate on single post, traffic signs
8 roadside directional sign, Water Street

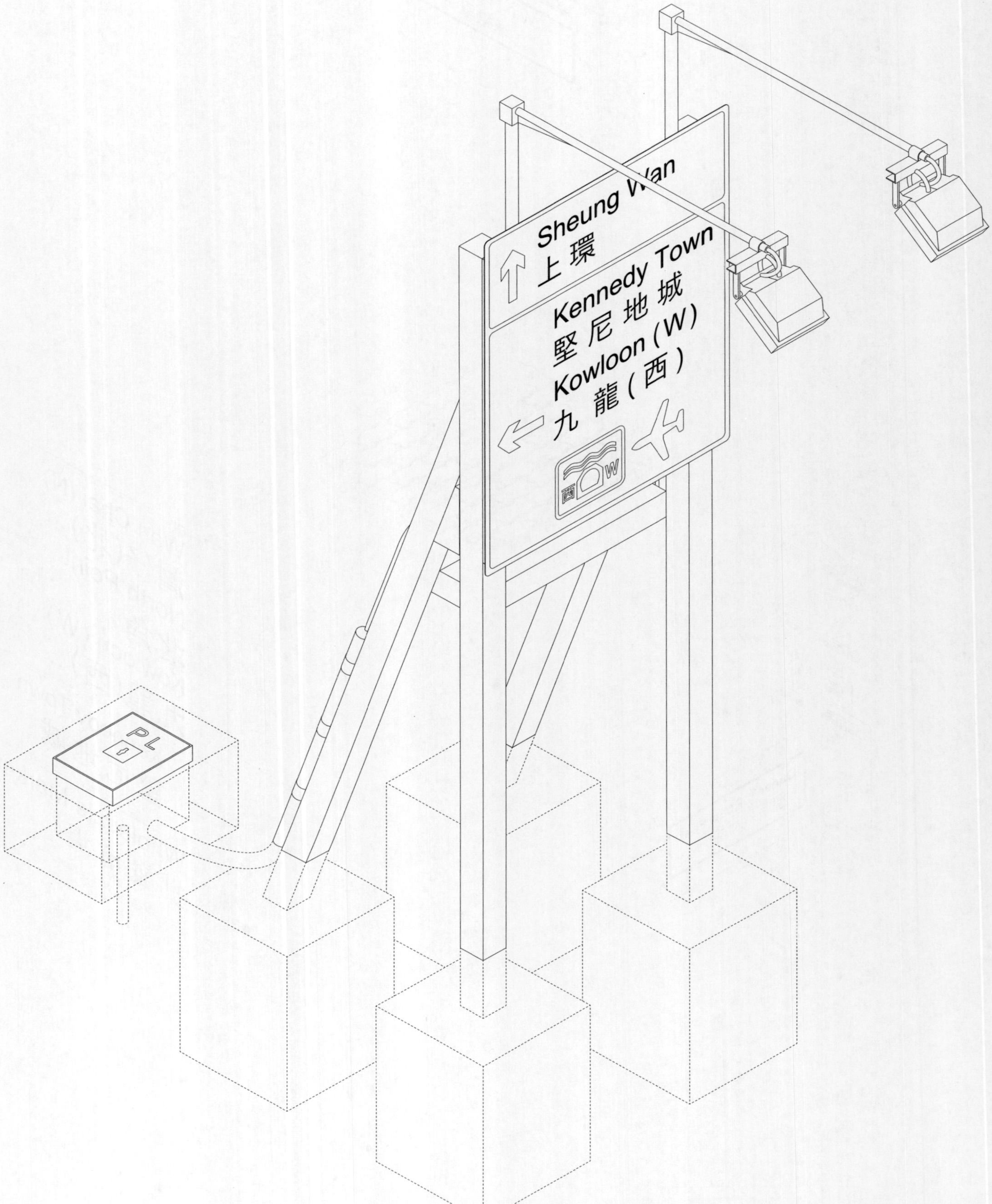

Junction Ahead Signage illuminated roadside directional sign, foundations, ducts, and power source

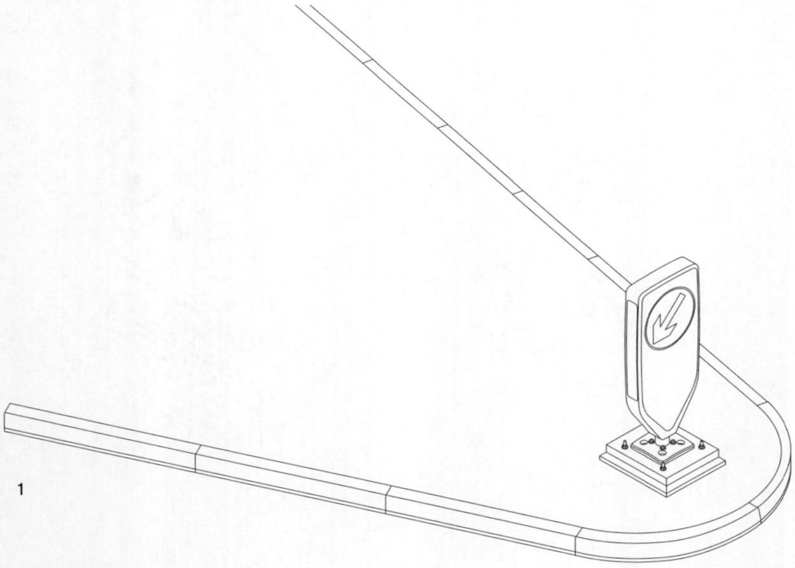

1

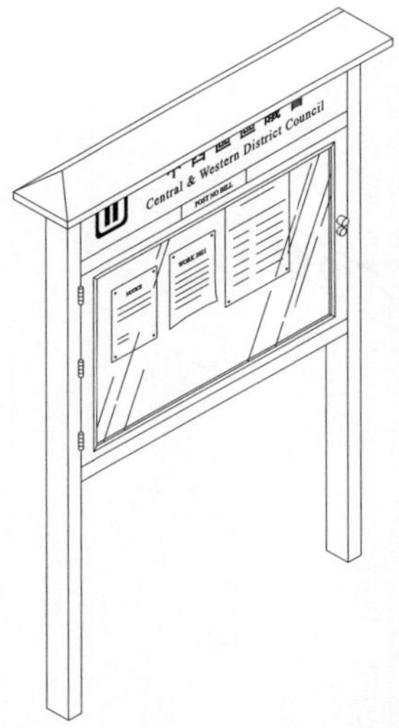

2

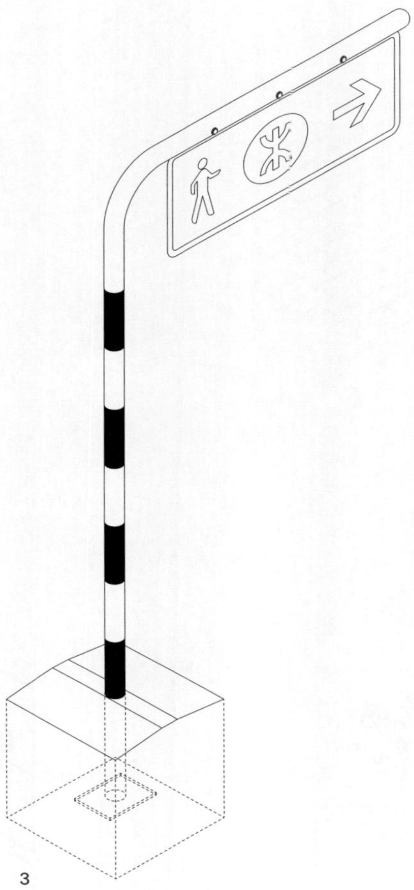

3

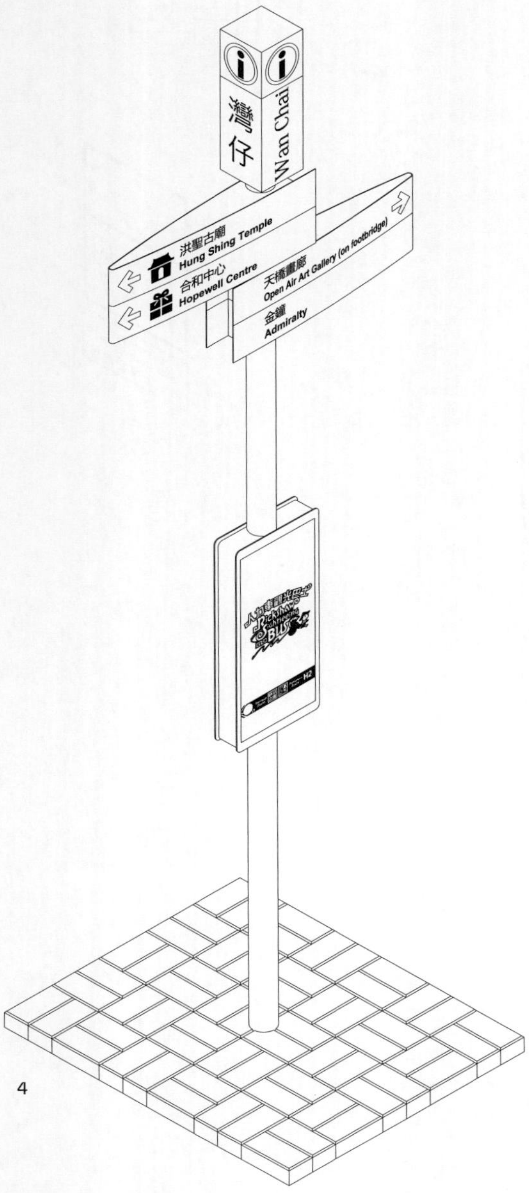

4

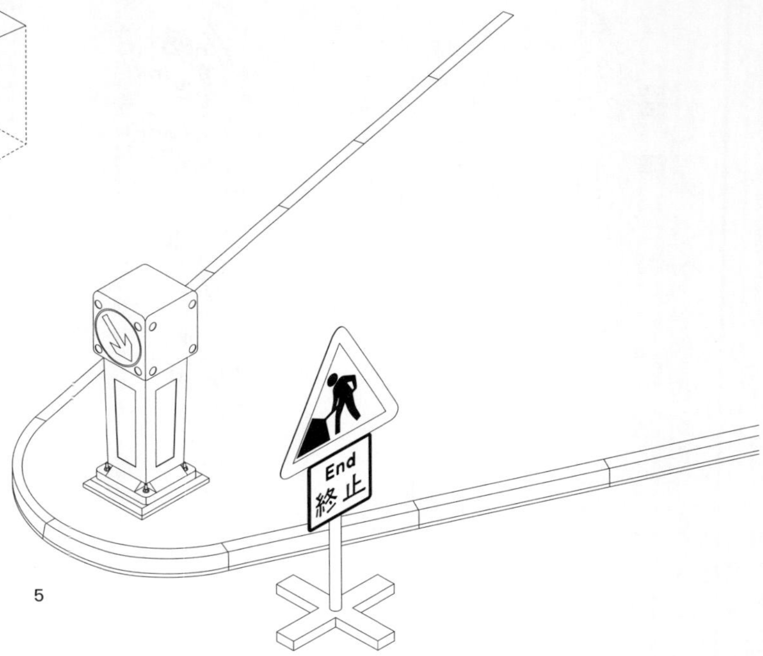

5

1 retro-reflective self-righting traffic island bollard
2 civic bulletin board
3 MTR directional signage
4 directional signage for visitors, Queen's Road East
5 illuminated traffic island bollard

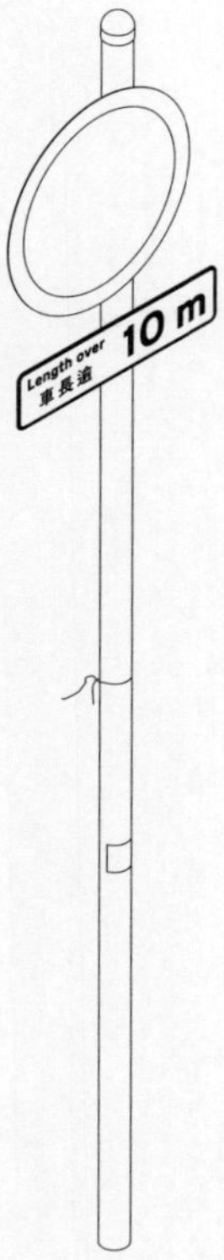
Length over
車長逾
10 m

1

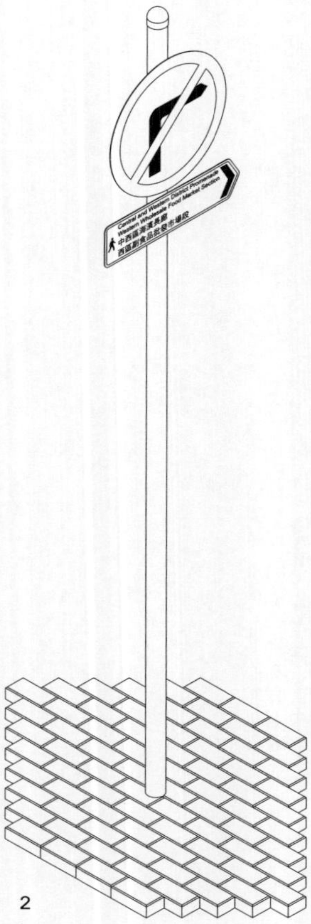

2

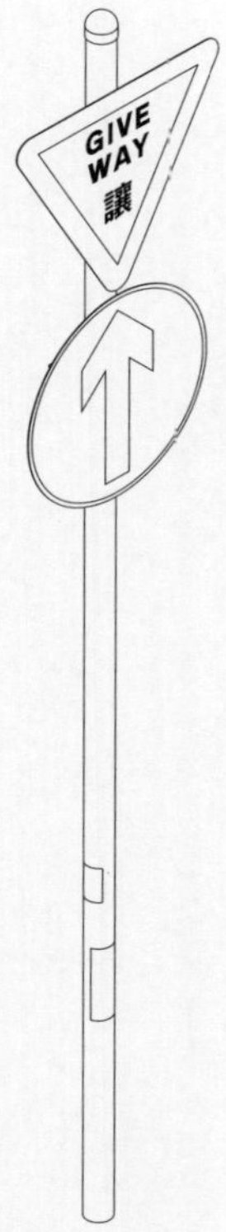
GIVE
WAY
讓

3

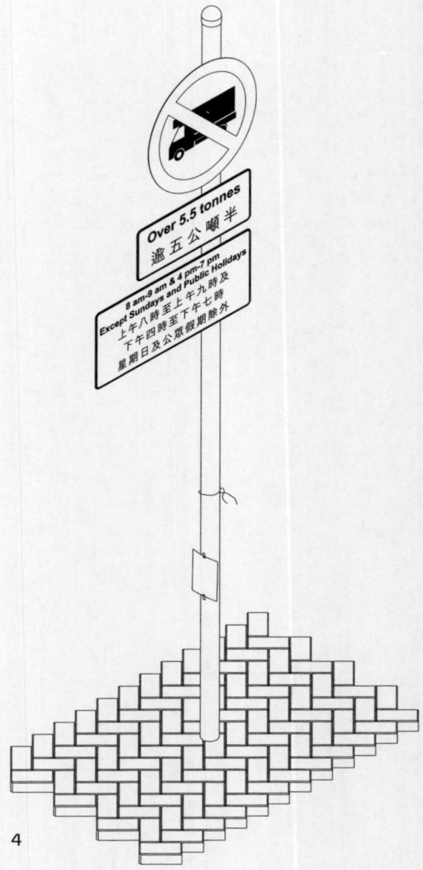
Over 5.5 tonnes
逾五公噸半
8 am–9 am & 4 pm–7 pm
Except Sundays and Public Holidays
上午八時至上午九時及
下午四時至下午七時
星期日及公眾假期除外

4

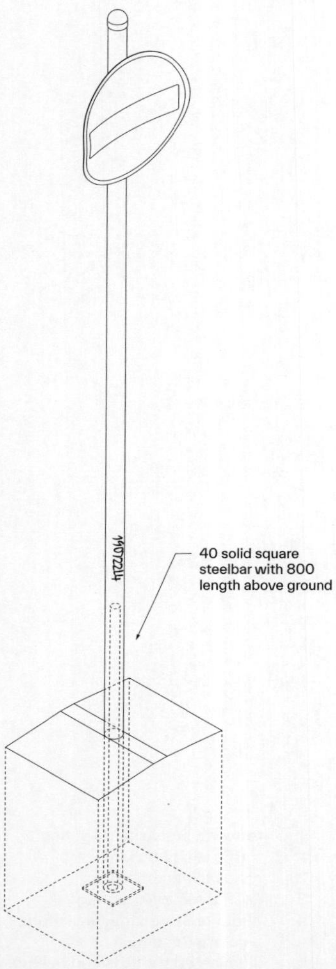
40 solid square
steelbar with 800
length above ground

6

10
m
Private Road
私家路
3.3m

7

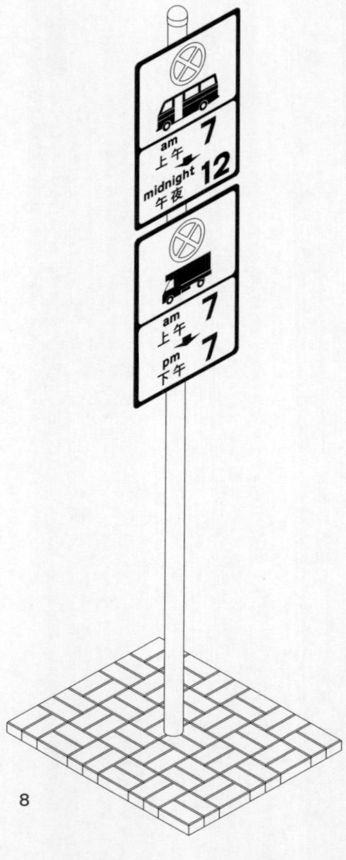
am
上午
7
midnight
午夜
12
am
上午
7
pm
下午
7

8

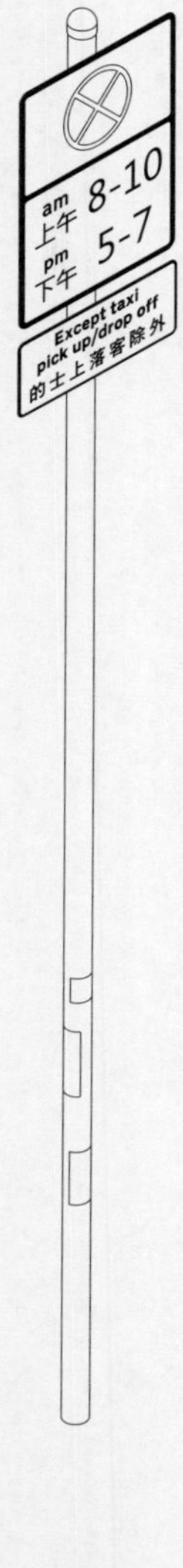
am
上午
8-10
pm
下午
5-7
Except taxi
pick up/drop off
的士上落客除外

9

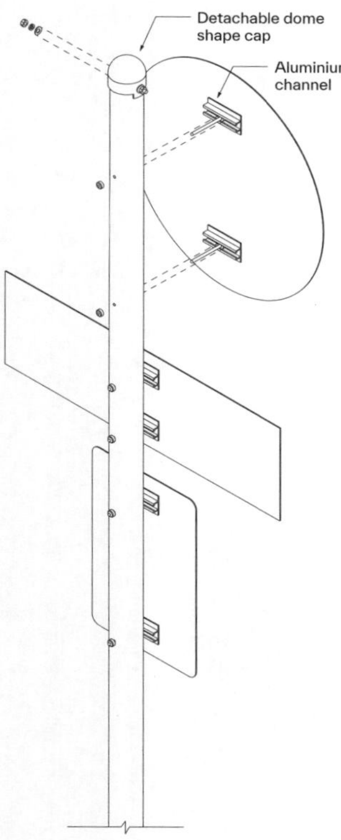

5

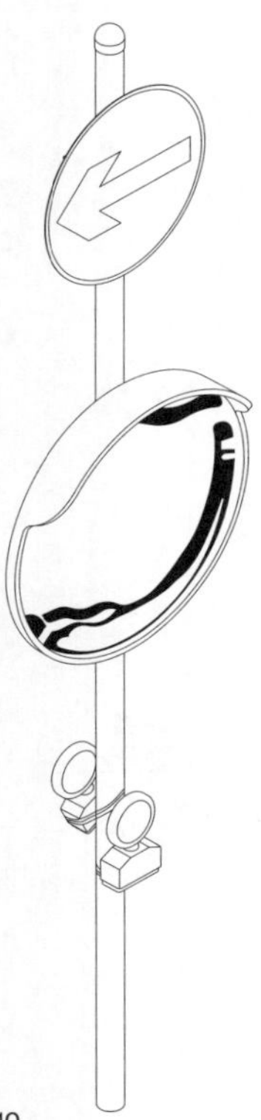

10

1 no vehicles over 10 m
2 no right-turn for traffic, directional signage for visitors
3 "give way," ahead only
4 off-center mounted plates, no goods vehicles, weight limit, time limit
5 assembly showing detachable cap on single post
6 post with solid steel bar reinforcement, no entry for all vehicles
7 length limit, "private road," children going to and from school, height limit
8 cluster of no stopping signs
9 no stopping "except taxi pick up / drop off"
10 turn left, convex mirror, hazard warning lanterns

TRAFFIC SIGNALS
controllers

Hong Kong's traffic control system is part of an "Intelligent Transport System" (ITS) managed by the Transport Department (TD). ITS encompasses an array of mechanisms to regulate the circulation of vehicles on the city's streets and highways. These include, for example, toll booths, electronic parking meters, an "Unmanned Aircraft System" of traffic-monitoring drones, and a contactless payment system—Octopus—first developed for mass transit fares.

Among the most visible elements of this system are the more than 1,900 signalized junctions that control how vehicles and pedestrians share the street. These are part of an Area Traffic Control System (ATCS) that also comprises detector loops embedded in the street at selected junctions, and more than 800 CCTV cameras. Tall, slim, gunmetal-gray "controller" cabinets positioned adjacent to the curb near junctions regulate these different elements and gather data. Controllers are set on a concrete plinth with chamfered edges whose dimensions are specified in a Highways Department standard drawing. [1] The plinth elevates the controller 150mm or 200mm from the sidewalk and is buried up to 550mm into the ground, enclosing a void. This void allows conduits to pass up and into the cabinet. A small square access hatch marked "ATC" is never far away. The hatch opens to a "draw pit" housing data transmission lines that link to an Area Traffic Control Centre (ATCC). At the ATCC, in a high-ceilinged room oriented toward rows of large screens, technicians monitor traffic. The duration of the "green" signal shortens and lengthens over the course of the day based on the history of observed traffic patterns, but can also be manually programmed to respond to contingencies.

Pedestrian "walk" indications, however, always remain constant. These indications comprise both visual and audible cues. In the past decade, adaptations to this system have responded to criticism that the policy favors car traffic over pedestrian safety. Trials include countdown timers for crosswalks, animated pedestrian symbols, and "Smart Devices" that allow pedestrians to add time onto the walk signal by tapping an Octopus card registered to a person who is elderly or disabled. In its description of the Smart Devices, the TD notes that they will be placed "near locations where the elderly or the disabled usually visit, and at non-busy junctions to avoid serious traffic congestion," creating some ambiguity about whether these two criteria need overlap. [2]

More common at crosswalks are "Electronic Audible Traffic Signals" (eATS). An eATS comprises both a speaker attached discreetly just below the traffic lights, and a smaller unit mounted at pedestrian "elbow level," that vibrates to indicate the signal state at the same time that the speaker emits a distinctive noise. [3] The sequence of chirping—slow then rapid when it is possible to walk—is one of several types of audible systems available globally for crosswalks. The volume of the "tic-tac" adjusts automatically depending on ambient noise conditions. In the early days of its implementation, the TD tested five different pitches with groups advocating for persons who are visually impaired, and adjusted the eATS's upper and lower sound threshold in response to these consultations. [4]

In 2008, incandescent traffic light lamps were replaced with LED technology. The new "Futurit" lamps were supplied by Supremetech Engineering and fabricated by Swarco, an Austrian traffic engineering group. The LED lamps reduced power consumption by a third and increased service life from one to ten years. While the TD oversees the ATCS, the traffic lights themselves are maintained by the Engineering Services branch of the Electrical and Mechanical Services Department (EMSD). The EMSD touches on nearly all aspects of Hong Kong's electrical and mechanical infrastructure in its mission to "ensure that E&M [electrical and mechanical] and energy technologies are harnessed in a safe, reliable, economical and environment-friendly manner." [5] This includes looking after elevator safety, amusement park rides, energy and gas delivery, and fleet maintenance for Hong Kong's specialist security forces.

Of the nearly HK$66 million in protest-related repairs announced by the government, almost two-thirds was allotted to traffic lights, security cameras, and the controllers. [6] After periods of intense protests, intersections were left without functioning traffic lights; drivers negotiated through intersections by making eye contact or following instructions from volunteers or security forces directing traffic. Reinstated controllers are now sometimes housed in a cagelike armature of horizontal, stainless steel rods. The housing prevents the steel cabinets from being pried open but doesn't spare their surfaces from graffiti or stickers. The most well-known of such tags in Hong Kong's recent history was the calligraphy of Tsang Tsou Choi. He covered gray steel controllers with political commentary and fictions of his family's claims to Kowloon. His characters transform the box and plinth from a discreet sentry into a recollecting. [7] One of his interventions, the *19th Ancestor Tsang Pen Kam...*(1999), was removed from the street, and is now part of the collection of the Rockbund Art Museum in Shanghai. When it is displayed, the box sits directly on the gallery floor, unmoored from its plinth.

1. Highways Department, "H2163B: Details of Controller Plinth (Type C 2000 & C 3000 for Use on Hong Kong Island Only)," in *Standard Drawings. Section 2: Street Furniture*, rev. March 2018, HKSARG.
2. Transport Department, "Smart Device for the Elderly and the Disabled," last updated April 15, 2021, https://www.td.gov.hk/en/transport_in_hong_kong/pedestrians/pedestrian_crossing_facilities/smart_device/index.html.
3. Transport Department, "Electronic Audible Traffic Signal," last updated April 13, 2021, https://www.td.gov.hk/en/transport_in_hong_kong/pedestrians/pedestrian_crossing_facilities/electronic_audible_traffic_signal/index.html.
4. Environment, Transports and Works Bureau, "Legislative Council Panel on Transport: Electronic Audible Traffic Signals (eATS)," LC Paper No. CB(1)1413/03-04(01), HKSARG (March 2004): 3.
5. Electrical and Mechanical Services Department, "About Us: Regulatory Services," last updated April 1, 2021, https://www.emsd.gov.hk/en/about_us/vision_mission_values/regulatory_services/.
6. Sum Lok-kei, "Hong Kong protests: government spent more than HK$66 million to repair damaged public facilities," *South China Morning Post*, June 10, 2020, https://www.scmp.com/news/hong-kong/politics/article/3088459/hong-kong-protests-government-spent-more-hk66-million.
7. See Hans Ulrich Olbrist, "A Protest Against Forgetting," in *King of Kowloon: The Art of Tsang Tsou Choi*, edited by David Spalding (Hong Kong: Vermillion Art Collections, 2013): 1–9.

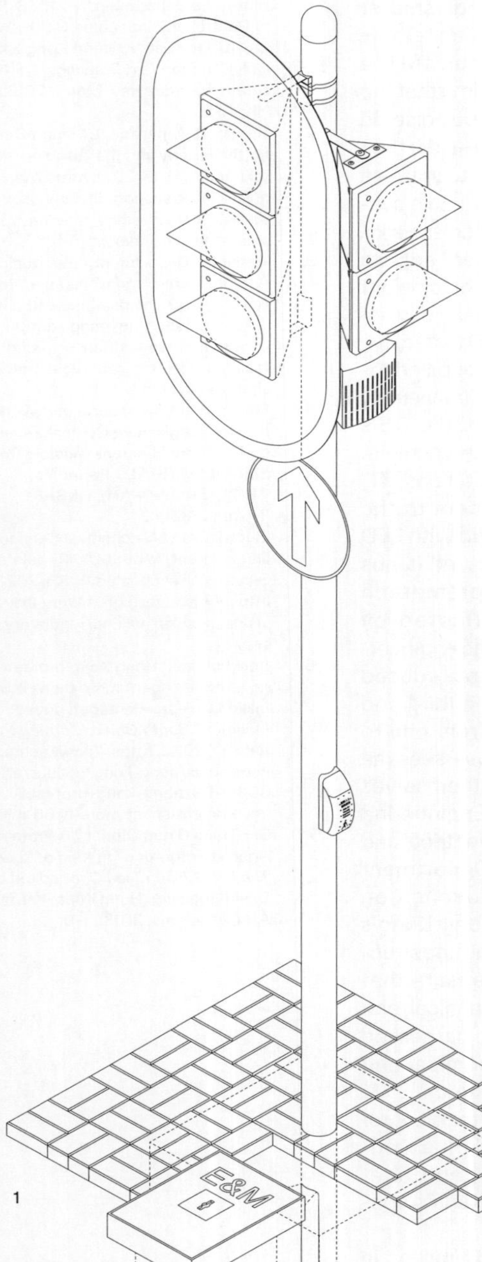
E&M

1

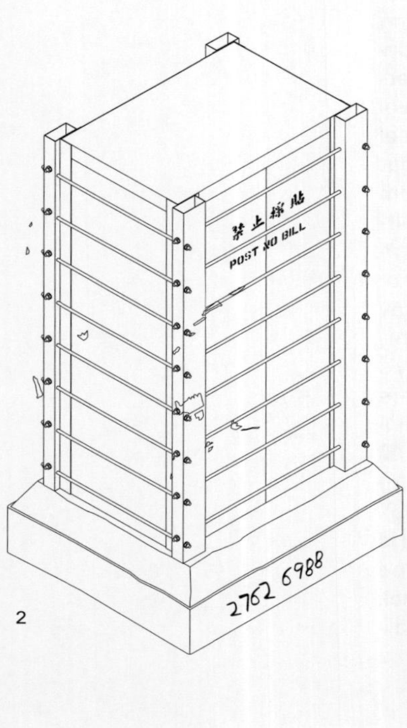
禁止標貼
POST NO BILL
2762 6988

2

3

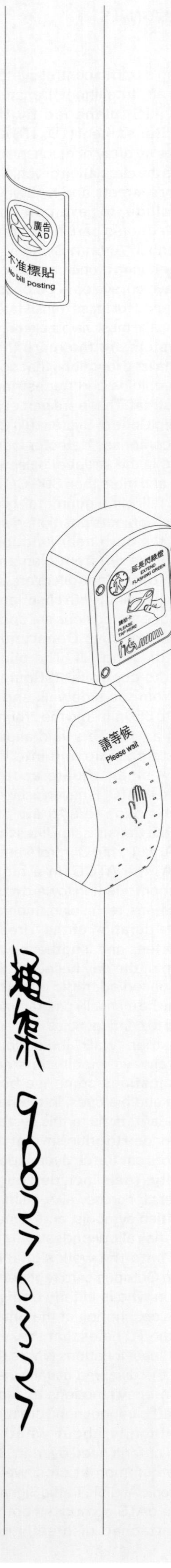
廣告
AD
不准標貼
No bill posting
延長閃綠燈
EXTEND FLASHING GREEN
請等候
Please wait

4

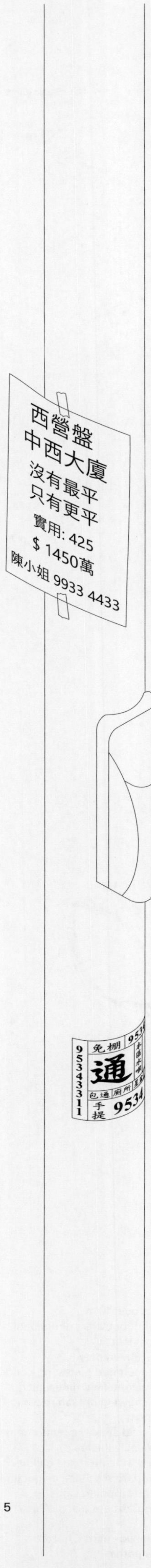
西營盤
中西大廈
沒有最平
只有更平
實用: 425
$ 1450萬
陳小姐 9933 4433
視障人士輔助設施
Aids for Visually Impaired Persons
通

5

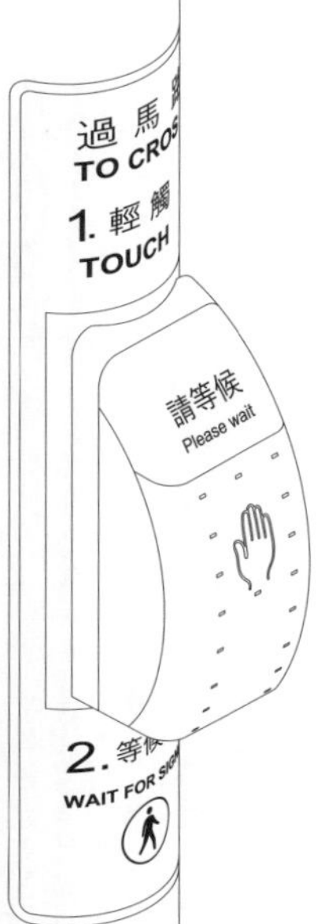

6

1 traffic signals for cars and people, E&M drawpit
2 roadside traffic controller cabinet
3 smart parking meter
4 "No bill posting," Octopus "please tap here" Smart Device, touch-enabled eATS, phone number for a plumbing emergency
5 apartment for sale, eATS, plumbing emergency
6 eATS

MARKINGS
microspheres

The Highways Department (HyD) announced a switch from painted road-marking to thermoplastic in 1984 with Road Note No. 7. [1] Thermoplastic markings were first used in the United States in the late 1950s. The durability, anti-skid properties and potential for reflectivity of thermoplastic markings have made them a preferred marking method in much of the world despite higher initial costs.

The thermoplastic road markings used in Hong Kong are defined by the Civil Engineering and Development Department (CEDD) as a "substance supplied in block, granular or powder forms, which can be heated to a molten state and then applied with an appropriate hand or mechanical applicator, and form a cohesive film by cooling." [2] Workers also sometimes use thermoplastic *tape* that is either preformed or cut into requisite shapes. Thermoplastic precursors are heated to 200° Celsius on-site in a mixing drum whose temperature needs to be closely monitored. "Guidance Notes" from the HyD cite a "common mishap" that occurs when overheating to above 300°: the excess heat reacts with the precursors to release a gas whose pressure causes the drum cover to rocket off with molten plastic following behind. If a mishap leads to contact with the skin, bystanders should "flood affected part of the injured person's body with cold water until the thermoplastic is cold" and then immediately proceed to a hospital. [3]

While the material is being heated, glass beads—also called microspheres—are added to the mixture. In Hong Kong, either a hand-pulled screed box or a larger screed machine is used to apply the mixture onto a prepared road surface. Hand screeding for smaller markings requires highly skilled operators who must "maintain the speed of the screeding operation as constant as possible in order to achieve an even thickness." [4] Screed operators can use metal or cardboard molds with straight or flexible guiding edges, but otherwise the work is a delicate operation where the demands of an even thickness—requiring a constant speed—run up against the desire for well-shaped markings. In Hong Kong, road markings are to be no more than 4mm thick. When they are renewed, worn-out markings should be heated and scraped off with the tip of a shovel or ground away before applying a new layer.

In addition to mixing glass beads into the heated thermoplastic mixture, a critical final step is the dispersal of beads on top of the newly laid, still molten markings. A precise and timely application is critical to activate the reflective qualities of the microspheres and their anti-skid properties. Too few microspheres or a poor distribution, and the beads no longer bounce light back at drivers to give markings their illuminated glow. Too many "would render the reflected light being shadowed by the excessive beads." If beads are applied when the newly laid markings are too hot, they will sink into the surface. Workers need to be able to master quantities, velocities, and vectors of distribution. [5] After the initial application, time and traffic wear away particles of thermoplastic, revealing beads embedded in the material and activating their reflectivity.

Glass beads were first added to painted road markings in 1934. They are up to one micron in diameter and are made from crushed, often recycled, glass that is heated to 1,200°C to precipitate the formation of liquid microspheres. These perfectly orbital bodies are sieved into sizes and remixed according to various specifications. One of the world's leading producers of "premium" microspheres with higher rates of reflectivity is M. Swarovski GmbH, today part of Swarco, an Austrian "traffic technology group" that "offers one of the most complete solution portfolios for road marking, signage, urban traffic management, parking, highway and tunnel management, and public transport." [6] Microspheres are made throughout Europe, and in the United States, Japan, and China. Between 2015 and 2019, Hong Kong imported an average of 205 metric tons of glass microspheres a year; Belgium was consistently the lead supplier. [7]

While glass beads have other applications, their use in road markings is the most quantity intensive. Debate on the sustainability and life cycle assessment of various road marking systems suggests that durability is the most important indicator of a marking technology's environmental impact. While thermoplastics mark an improvement over solvent- and water-based paint in this regard, new "cold plastic" technologies offer additional durability and a reduced environmental impact over their life cycle. [8] Glass beads and thermoplastic are carried away by rains when they wear; in Hong Kong they eventually make their way into the drainage system and the harbor. Some beads may also be picked up by the wind. The use of microspheres corresponds with the growth of road systems and the rise of the automobile. This concordance in time, the physical and chemical stability of glass beads, and their ubiquity in marine and terrestrial sediment makes microspheres a potentially reliable stratigraphic marker for the Anthropocene. [9]

1. Highways Department, Research and Development Division, "Guidance Notes on Road Markings," RD/GN/036A, HKSARG (January 2016): 3.
2. Civil Engineering and Development Department, *General Specification for Civil Engineering Works*, vol. 1, 2020, HKSARG, 12.10.
3. Highways, "Road Markings," 15.
4. Ibid., 9.
5. Ibid., 10.
6. SWARCO, "About Us," 2021, https://www.swarco.com/about-us.
7. Glass spheres of less than 1mm. See World Integrated Trade Solution, "Hong Kong, China Glass microspheres; not exceeding 1mm in diameter imports by country in 2015 [-2019]," last updated August 14, 2021, https://wits.worldbank.org/trade/comtrade/en/country/HKG/year/2015/tradeflow/Imports/partner/ALL/product/701820.
8. Marisa Cruz, Alexander Klein, and Viviana Steiner, "Sustainability Assessment of Road Marking Systems," *Transportation Research Procedia* 14 (2016): 869–75, https://doi.org/10.1016/j.trpro.2016.05.035.
9. Agnieszka Gałuszka and Zdzisław M Migaszewski, "Glass Microspheres as a Potential Indicator of the Anthropocene: A First Study in an Urban Environment," *The Holocene* 28, no. 2 (2018): 323–29, https://doi.org/10.1177/0959683617721332.

1
2
3
4
5
6
7
8
9
10
11
12
13
14
15
16
17
19
20
21
23
LOOK RIGHT
望右
LOOK LEFT
望左

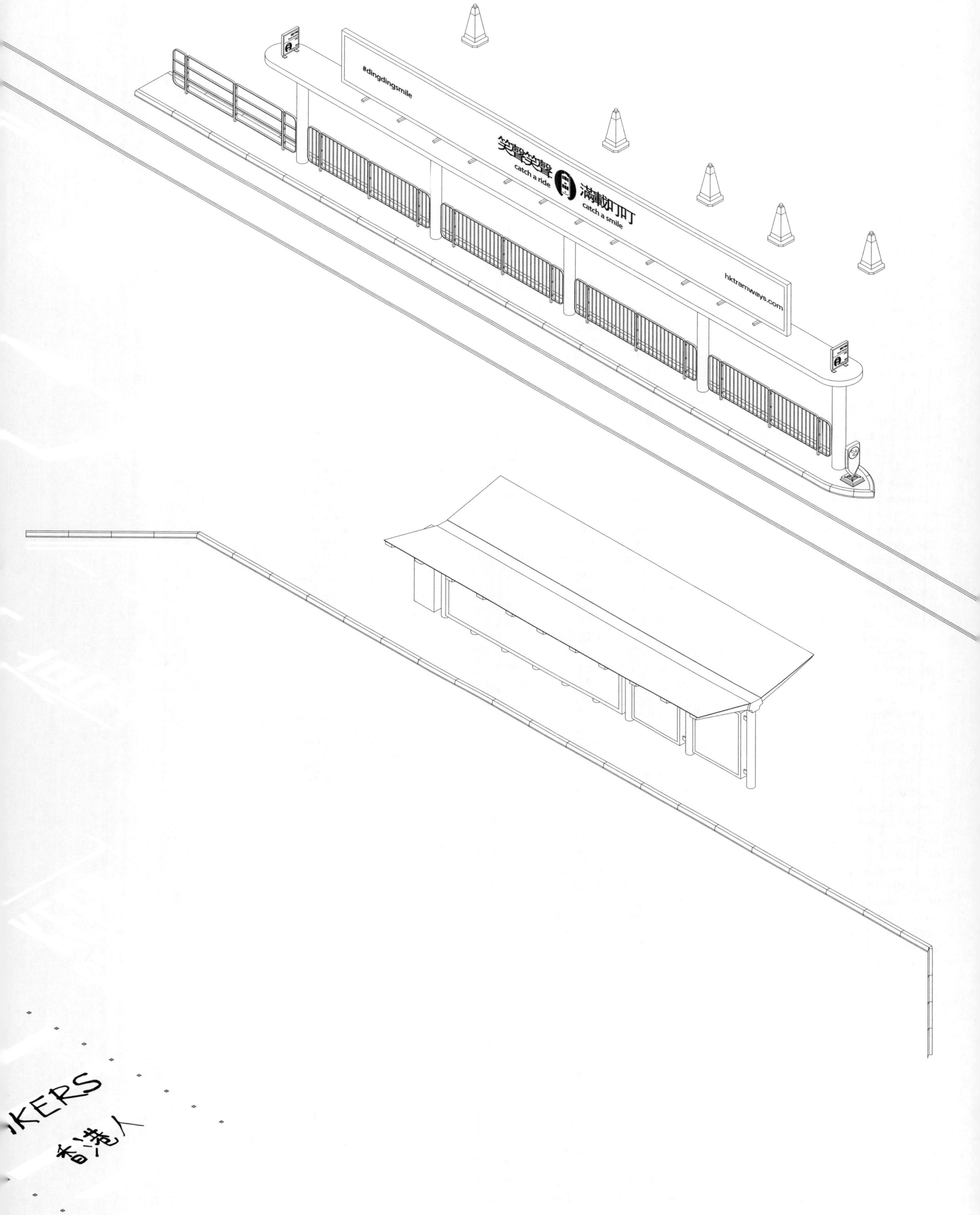
#dingdingsmile
catch a ride
catch a smile
hktramways.com
KERS
香港人

POLES
iAM smart

In a question posed to the government in April 2017, a legislative council (LEGCO) member inquired about progress on energy efficient LED street lighting. While the Highways Department (HyD) had concluded that retrofitting the city's street lighting system would not be cost effective after trials in 2009, the LEGCO member noted that LED prices had dropped significantly since that time and that "quite a number of overseas countries and the Mainland in some of their road lighting systems" had made the switch to LED.

The Secretary for Transport and Housing provided a response. He noted that since the 2009 trials, the HyD had "continued to monitor the technical and market development of LED road lights, and carry out various trial schemes for LED road lights to provide [a] technical basis for the extensive use of LED road lights in the future." These additional trials included the installation and monitoring of 171 road lights, three gantry road signs, and, in 2015 and 2016, "LED tubes in 20 subways." The trials showed various levels of energy saving and improvements in color rendering and visibility. Along with these evaluations, HyD representatives "visited London and Mainland cities like Zhuhai, Shanghai and Ningbo" in 2016 and 2017 to "exchange ideas with the institutions of lighting professionals and road lights manufacturers there." The Secretary announced that with the information gleaned from these trials and consultations—along with the downward trend in LED prices—the HyD would begin a wholesale replacement of the high-pressure sodium lamps, which numbered around 146,000 at the time, that had been in place since the 1990s. [1]

The city's standard lighting columns vary in dimension along seven parameters, including the height of the column, the diameter of the concrete foundation, and the length of the bracket arm. The column comprises two parts: a narrow shaft that supports the bracket arm and a wider base that projects up to 2.5 meters into the ground. The base rises anywhere from 1,655mm to 2,485mm, flaring inward at its top to meet the circumference of the shaft, where the joint between them is welded. Inside the base, a 6mm steel plate holds the shaft in place with additional welds. [2] Four drawing sheets detail different "embellishment kits" and "decorative brackets" that can be added to the standard column and shaft assemblage.

The HyD is also responsible for other types of poles. These include poles for tramline infrastructure, CCTVs, and wireless data equipment. In 2010, Hong Kong Broadband (HKBN), a private company, installed 487 poles in densely populated neighborhoods in Kowloon and Hong Kong Island. These poles brought broadband service to buildings where ground laid cables were impractical. [3] HKBN used the Highways Department's online application system to obtain a small-scale works excavation permit (SSWXP). The SSWXP was put in place to expedite small excavation works, and involved minimal direct oversight. It was, however, not meant for excavation works destined for the installation of sidewalk encumbrances—like poles. The HyD and the Lands Department saw HKBN's gambit as an abuse of the system. They ordered the poles removed and the sidewalks reinstated.

In August of 2019, protesters dismantled "smart lampposts" that they feared were being used for various forms of surveillance and data collection. [4] This followed an assurance from the government that the lampposts did not include facial recognition and that technologies for license-plate identification and video monitoring of illegal industrial waste dumping would not be activated. The lampposts would solely be used to provide traffic and weather data to various public departments. [5] The lamppost project was directed by the Office of the Government Chief Information Officer (OGCIO) and was part of a larger "Smart City Blueprint" released in December 2017. The "Blueprint" also included the "iAM Smart" electronic identity ("eID") to manage government interactions with residents and a government cloud infrastructure ("GovCloud"). [6]

In March of 2020, the "Technical Advisory Ad Hoc Committee on Multi-functional Smart Lampposts" released a report unanimously affirming the lampposts "as a key digital infrastructure in smart city development" noting that "many other cities are pursuing similar projects." [7] The report noted the public's privacy concerns and identified a series of measures to "regain the trust of the public on the whole initiative." [8] This would include making decisions and approval processes for the installation of new lampposts—as well as test results for electromagnetic radiation and human radiation exposure—"transparent to the public." [9]

Standard Drawing sheets for the smart lamppost were issued in February 2021. The hot-dipped galvanized steel poles comprise a single column planted up to 1,600mm into the earth and fixed in place by a concrete foundation of up to 800mm in diameter. Three donut-shaped polycarbonate attachments housing smart devices are fixed at specified heights where power and data cables connect from within the pole. [10] A separate drawing sheet details the "SL-A Bracket" that is familiar from protest images: two tubular arms projecting in arcs on either side of the pole. [11] The street-facing arm is 60mm in diameter and supports an LED lantern, while the shorter arm over the sidewalk has no lamp. Both arms support a decorative, leaf-shaped armature. No mention is made in the drawing specifications of this figurative design, or of the nonfunctional role of the design's second, shorter "leaf." In a "Smart Lamppost 3D Model" on the OGCIO website, additional monitoring devices—a thermal detector and a meteorological sensor—are attached to the leaf, suggesting a potential future use. [12]

1. GovHK, "LCQ4: Public Lighting System," April 26, 2017, HKSARG, https://www.info.gov.hk/gia/general/201704/26/P2017042600277.htm.
2. Highways Department, "HLDSDGE01-CL002J: Standard Dimensions for Public Lighting Columns," Lighting Division Standard Drawings, rev. June 2018, HKSARG.
3. Olga Wong, "Transmission poles break rules, officials tell broadband firm," *South China Morning Post*, April 3, 2010, https://www.scmp.com/article/710435/transmission-poles-break-rules-officials-tell-broadband-firm.
4. "Hong Kong: anti-surveillance protesters tear down 'smart' lamp-post-VIDEO," *The Guardian*, August 26, 2019, https://www.theguardian.com/world/video/2019/aug/26/hong-kong-anti-surveillance-protesters-tear-down-smart-lamp-post-video.
5. Kris Cheng, "Hong Kong gov't deactivates functions on new lampposts amid privacy concerns," *Hong Kong Free Press*, July 17, 2019, https://hongkongfp.com/2019/07/17/hong-kong-govt-deactivates-functions-new-smart-lampposts-amid-privacy-concerns/.
6. Office of the Government Chief Information Officer, "Update on Smart City Development," LC Paper No. CB (1)876/18-19(03), HKSARG (April 16, 2019): 1.
7. Office of the Government Chief Information Officer, "Report of the Technical Advisory Ad Hoc Committee on Multi-functional Smart Lampposts," HKSARG (March 2020): 11.
8. Ibid., 13.
9. Ibid., 17–19.
10. Highways Department, "HLDSDGE07-CL0053: Standard Dimensions for Smart Lamppost Column (Sheet 1 of 4)," Lighting Division Standard Drawings, rev. Feb. 2021, HKSARG.
11. Highways Department, "HLDSDGE07-CL0057: Details of Type SL-A Bracket for Public Lighting Column," Lighting Division Standard Drawings, rev. Feb. 2021, HKSARG.
12. Office of the Government Chief Information Officer, "Smart Lamppost 3D Model," last updated March 31, 2021, https://smartlamppost.ogcio.gov.hk/3DModel/index_en.html.

1

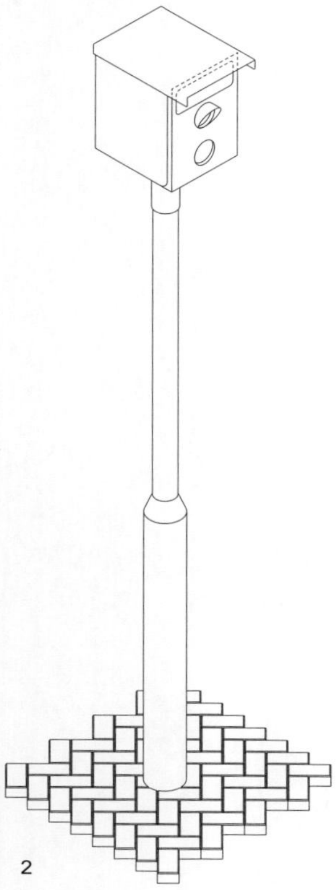

2

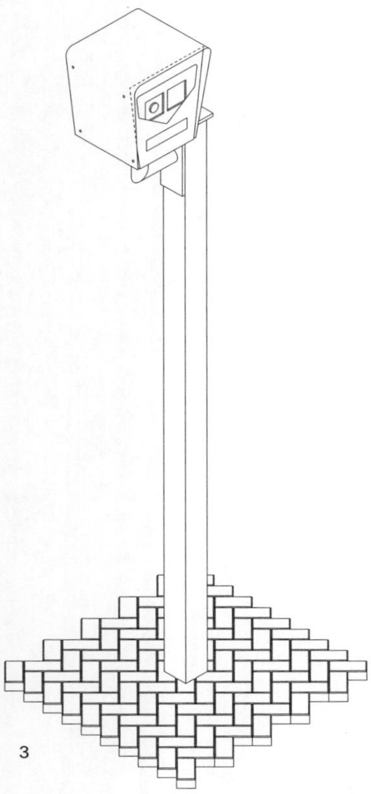

3

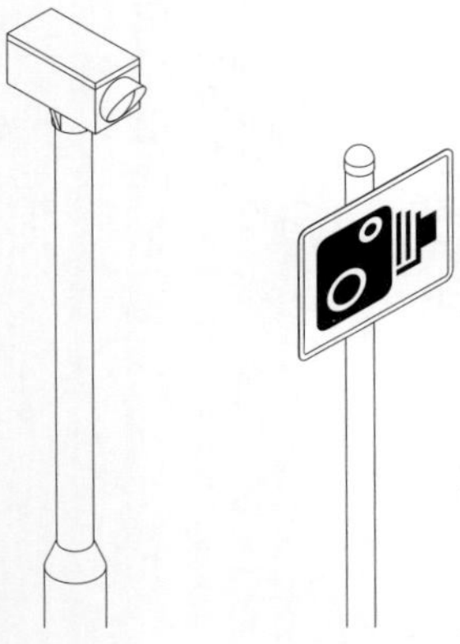

4

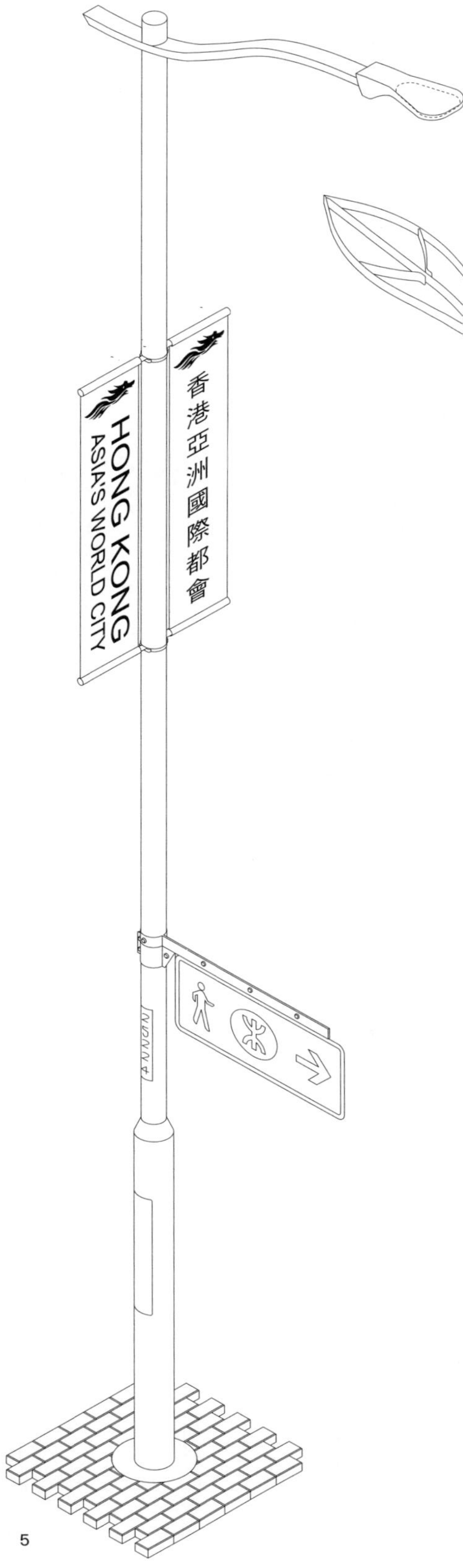

5

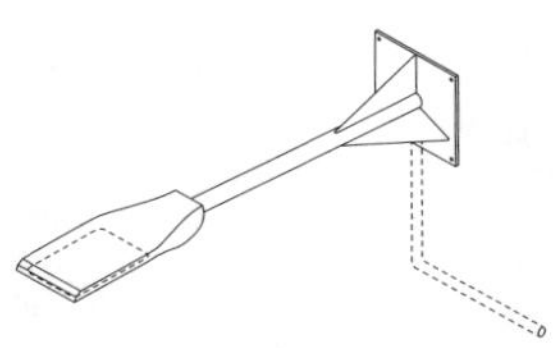

6

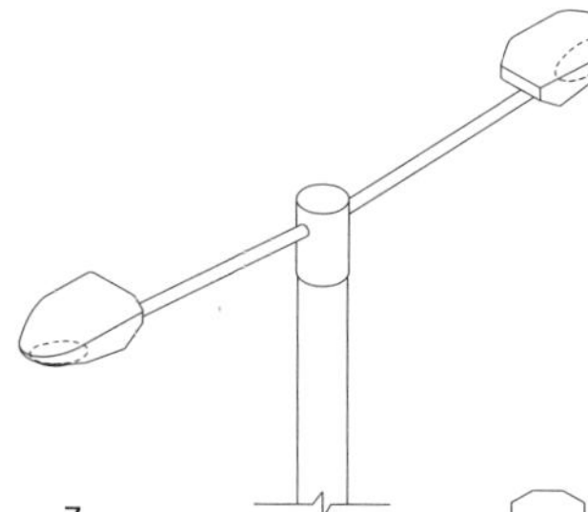

7

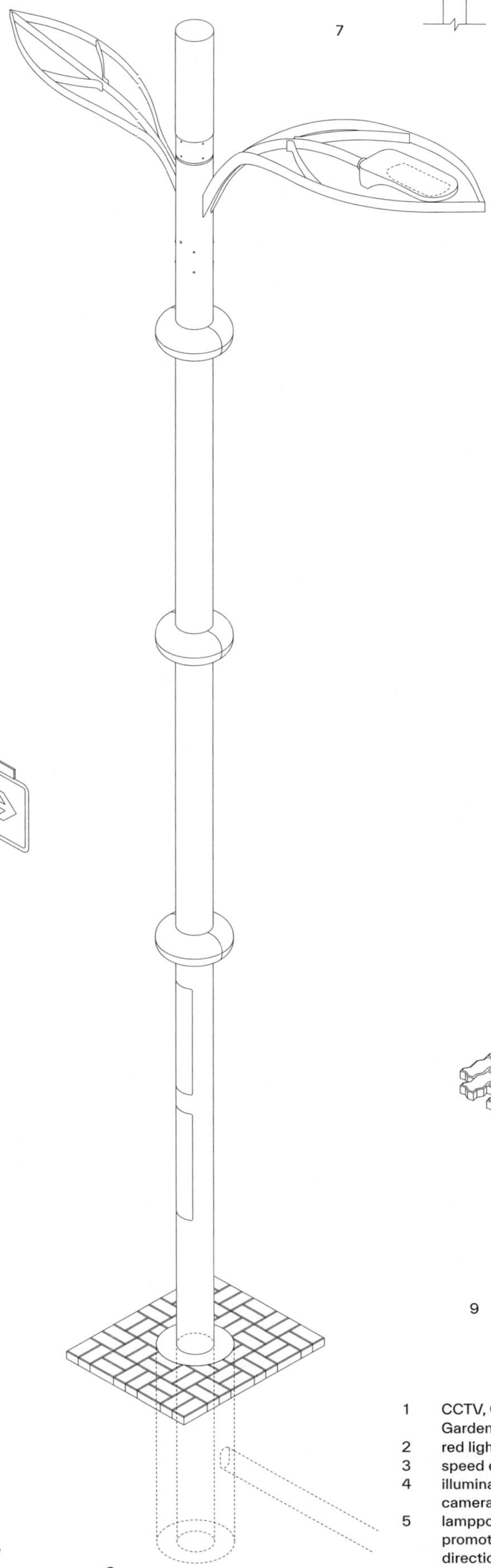

8

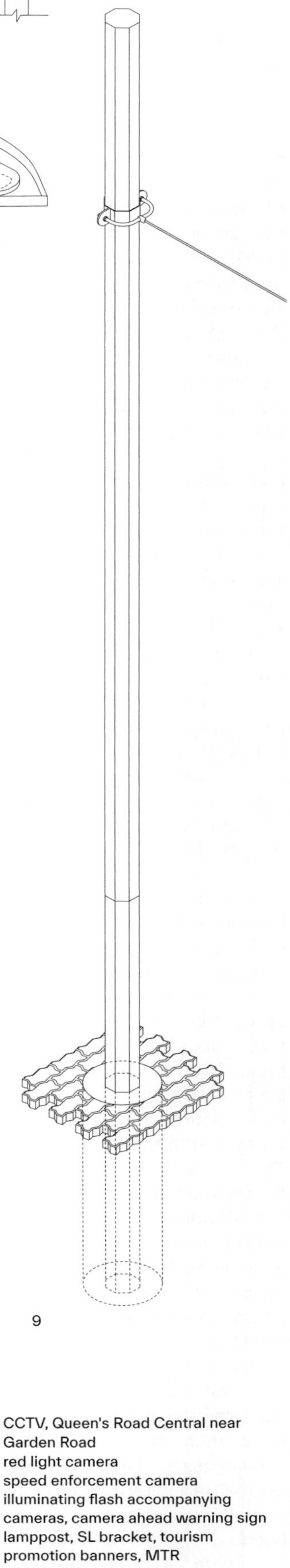

9

1 CCTV, Queen's Road Central near Garden Road
2 red light camera
3 speed enforcement camera
4 illuminating flash accompanying cameras, camera ahead warning sign
5 lamppost, SL bracket, tourism promotion banners, MTR directional sign
6 LED public lighting installed on building facade
7 double arm sodium-vapor lamp
8 Multi-functional Smart Lamppost, SL-A bracket and smart device housings
9 pole for overhead tram cables

BARRIERS
beam barrier

For months after the 2019 protests the entrances to local police stations were cordoned off by plastic barriers, often displacing pedestrians from the sidewalk. The barriers are relatively easy to transport and install when they are empty, but immovable when filled with water or sand. Their bulging design suggests overfull bellies. In May of 2020, a lawmaker triggered a debate within the Legislative Council by pointing out that the water barriers blocked access routes for people who are disabled or visually impaired. The city's then Secretary of Security retorted that "rioters and their violent acts" were to blame. [1] In 2012, environmental groups protested that two-meter-high barriers—erected for the visit of then Chinese President Hu Jintao—were a waste of water. Each required one ton of fresh water. If filled, the water in the 200 assembled barriers could provide 900 adults with a daily supply. [2]

The water-filled barriers are used when barriers made of concrete—portable or permanent—are too cumbersome. Precast concrete units are more often found blocking worksites or as permanent barriers between the carriageway and the sidewalk. The units are cast with two V-shaped lifting bars embedded upside down into the concrete, leaving a hook of 50mm at the top of the barrier. Highways Department (HyD) drawings indicate that the barriers can be made permanent by planting each unit 250mm into the ground. The hook is then cut and its housing capped with joint sealant. [3]

The impact of a fast-moving car against these permanent concrete barriers separating sidewalks from carriageways propels it into the air or causes it to crumple. Sometimes these dividers are assembled with a corrugated beam of hot-dip galvanized steel to create a low "beam barrier." Rectangular or hollow section posts with concrete or compacted earth footings support the beam as it runs along the edge of the curb. The standard drawings indicate that footings can be up to 300mm square and 900mm deep and should begin deep enough under the surface to accommodate a layer of paving units on footpaths. [4] Toward its end, the beam hinges downward and away from the adjacent carriageway, until it enters into the ground or joins a concrete anchor. Beam barriers are used along the carriageway to protect the columns of overhead walkways or overpasses. They also replace pedestrian railings on curved roads that make their way through neighborhoods with high foot traffic.

Beam barriers can also be found doubled up with pedestrian railings, presumably preventing residents from jumping into traffic and fast-moving cars from veering onto the sidewalk. The notion that railings are for pedestrian safety is undermined by the very existence of the beam barriers. Rather than putting in place measures to slow traffic, the barriers act as a mechanism that, at the same time, assumes and authorizes a certain speed for cars, buses, and trucks and imagines the inevitable mishap. The beam barriers evoke the speed of the highway and a violence of impact that makes their place on city streets an aggressive warning. They condition a certain hostility and enforce a hierarchy of movement where the pedestrian puts his or her own life in peril in the name of the passenger moving from one point of the city to another. In this sense, the here of a neighborhood street corner loses out to the abstraction of an elsewhere.

Other barriers include the temporary tubular fencing that appears with excavation or repair work. These tubular assemblages are red, yellow, and white, with interlocking attachments and removable footings that allow them to be positioned on uneven ground. Spacing between the horizontal tubes is used to attach signage. Round, blinking yellow lanterns are clipped to the top bar. The HyD's specifications note that while the tubular fencing should be sturdy enough to "not be easily toppled or moved by pedestrians or slipstreams of moving traffic," they nevertheless "shall not cause excessive damage" to a vehicle that hits them. In January of 2021, a revision to the drawing indicated that tubular fencing should be made of plastic rather than steel. [5]

1. Natalie Wong, "Hong Kong protests: security chief John Lee lays blame for water-barrier obstruction across city on 'rioters'," *South China Morning Post*, May 21, 2020, https://www.scmp.com/news/hong-kong/politics/article/3085348/hong-kong-protests-security-chief-john-lee-lays-blame-water.
2. Simpson Cheung, "Protest barriers a waste of water, say greens," *South China Morning Post*, July 7, 2012, https://www.scmp.com/article/1006099/protest-barriers-waste-water-say-greens.
3. Highways Department, "H2104/1B: Standard Precast Profile Barrier," in *Standard Drawings, Section 2: Street Furniture*, rev. Oct. 2019, HKSARG.
4. Highways Department, "H2119E: Untensioned Beam Barriers with Concrete Footings for Post Spacing 4,000mm (Sheet 2 of 3)," in *Standard Drawings, Section 2: Street Furniture*, rev. Nov. 2016, HKSARG.
5. Highways Department, "H6112E: Temporary Tubular Barrier," in *Standard Drawings, Section 6: Miscellaneous*, rev. Jan. 2021, HKSARG.

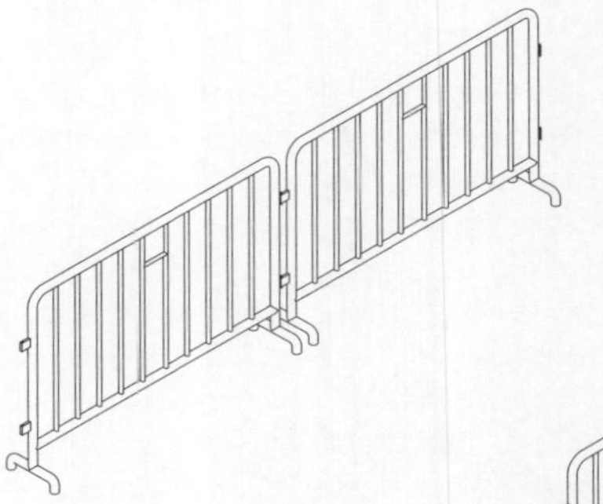
1

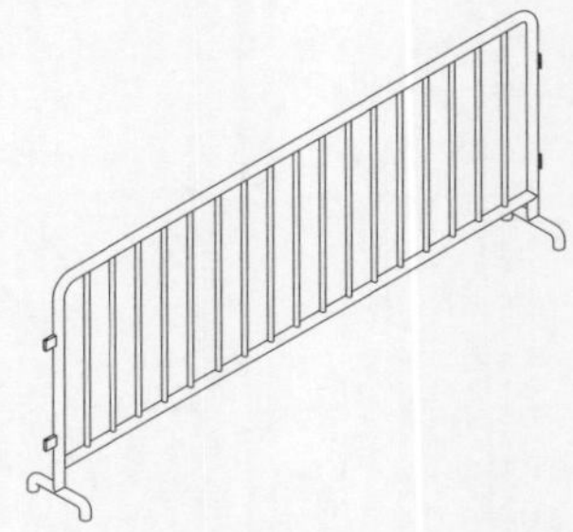
2

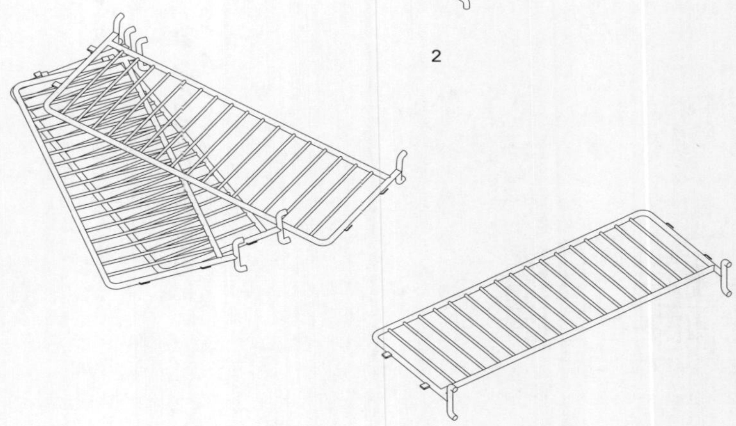

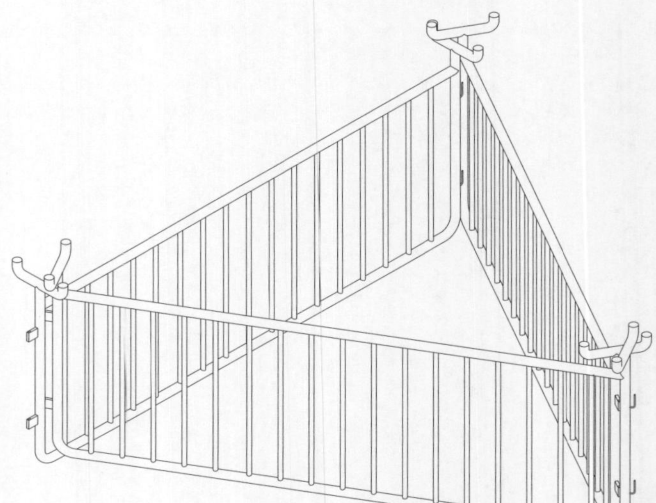
3

4

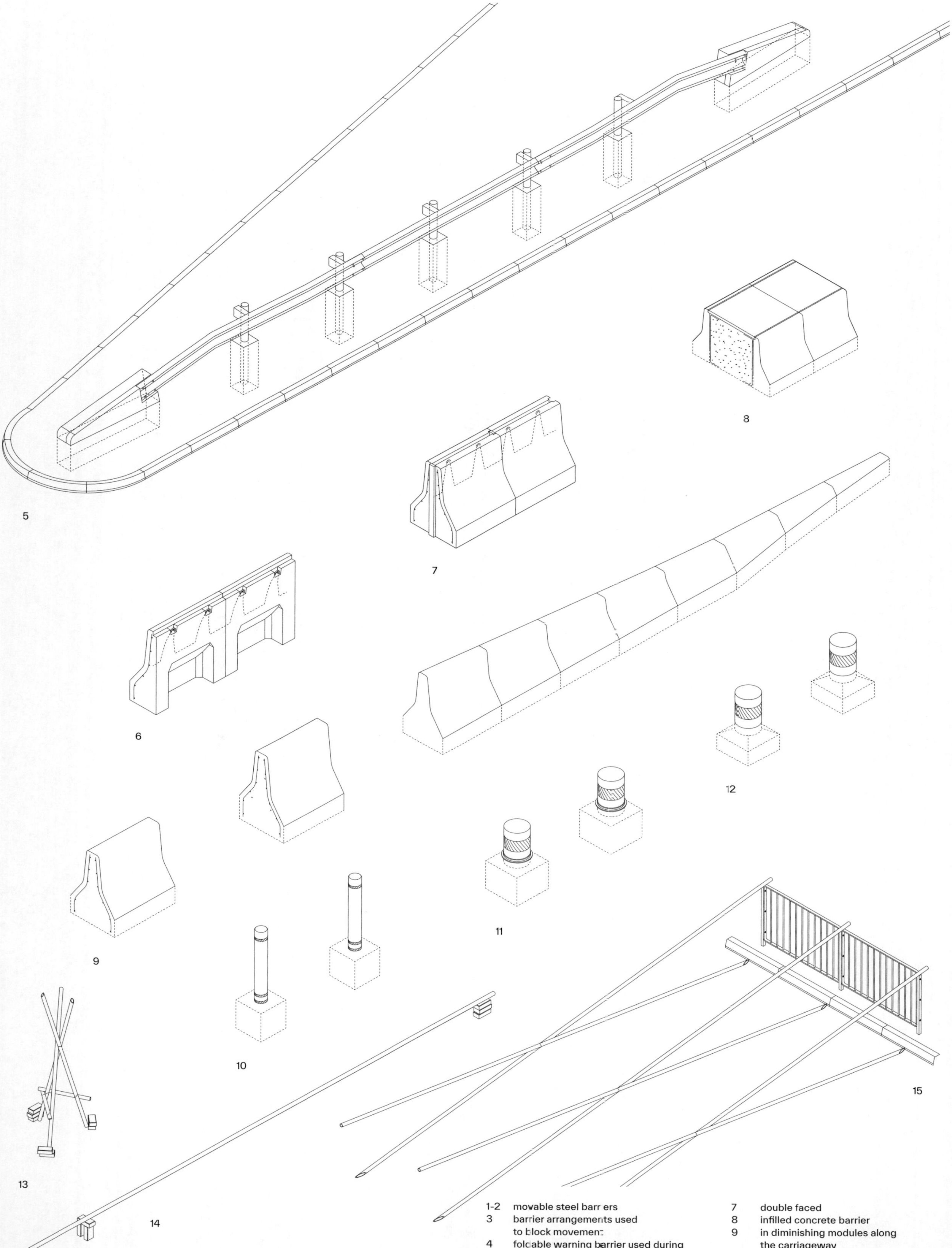

1-2	movable steel barriers	7	double faced
3	barrier arrangements used to block movement	8	infilled concrete barrier
4	foldable warning barrier used during high-pressure water jetting	9	in diminishing modules along the carriageway
5	anchored, flared beam barrier	10	metal bollards
6	standard precast concrete barrier, single faced	11-12	concrete bollards with metal trim
		13-15	improvised roadblocks

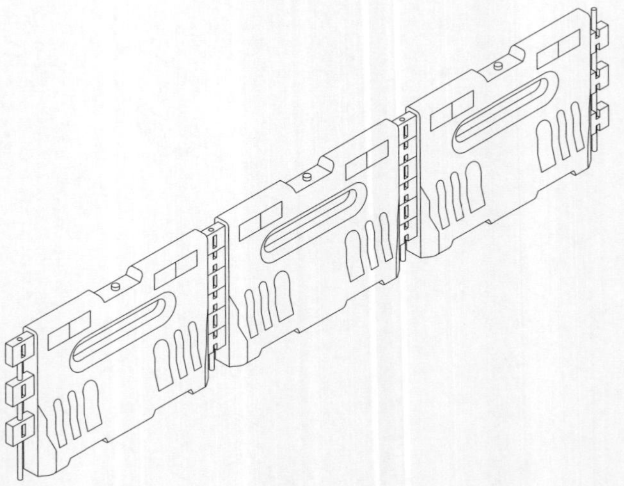

1

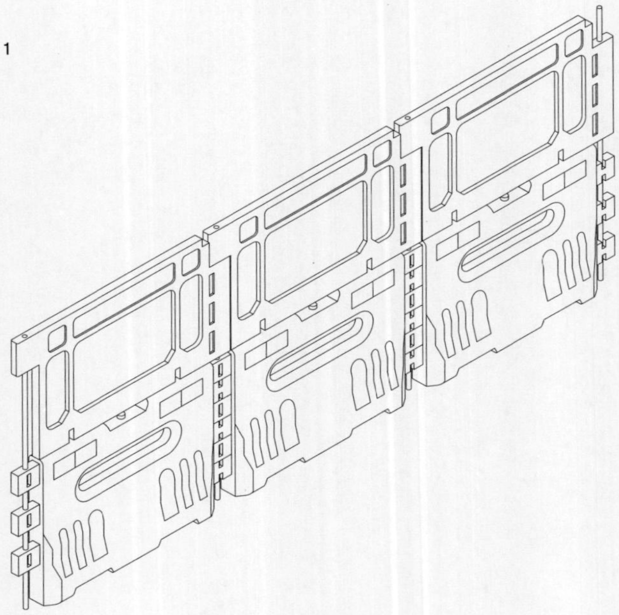

2

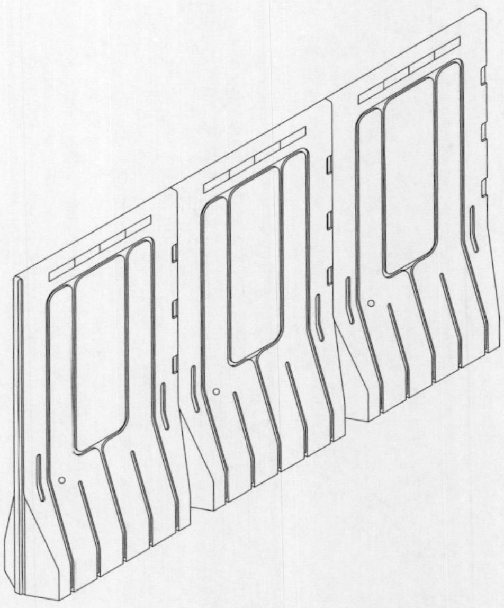

3

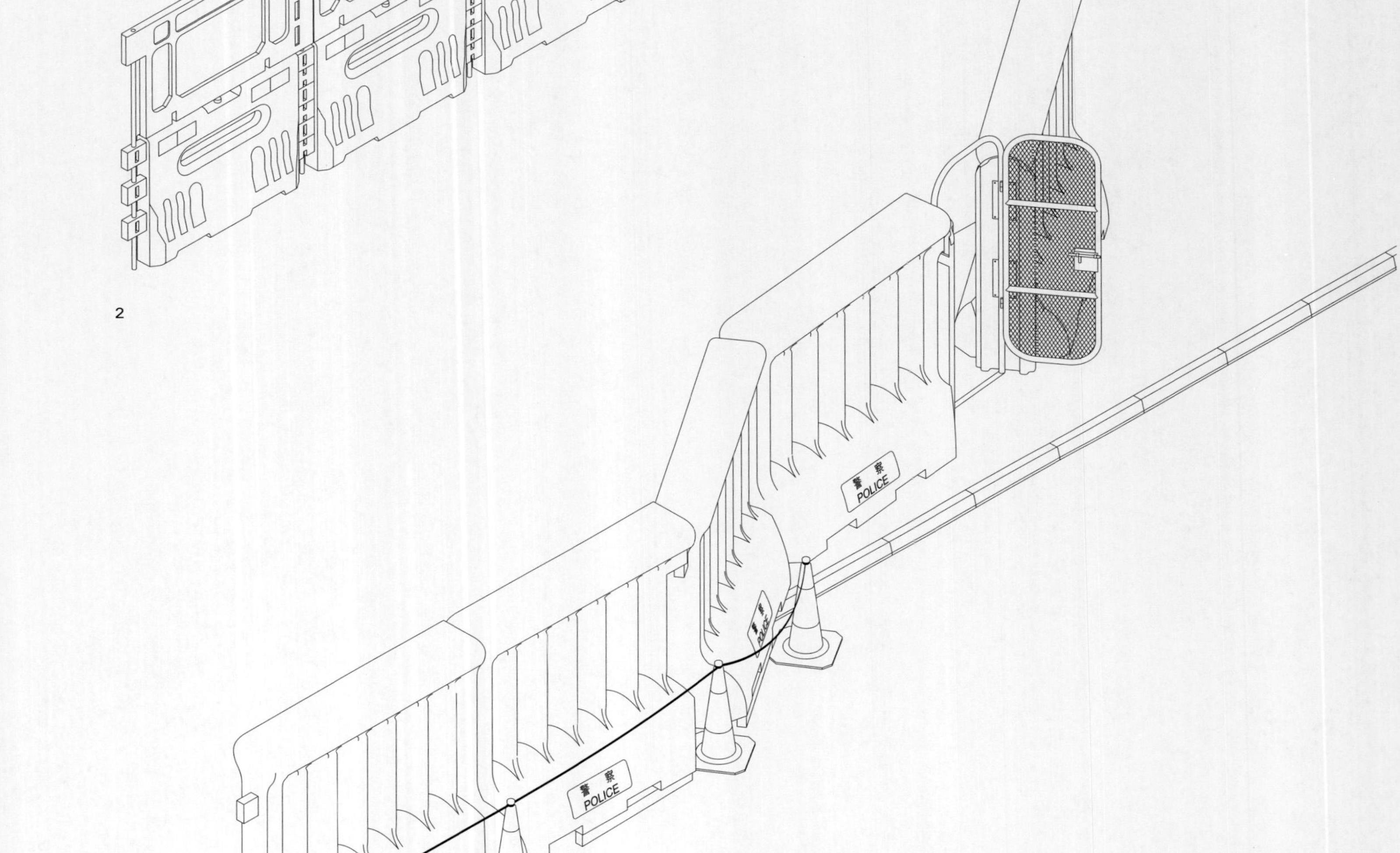

4

1-3 various water horse barriers
4 with integrated security gate

RAILINGS
control purposes

The Transport Department (TD) is responsible for verifying the "need, purpose, and type of railings on public roads" while the Highways Department (HyD) oversees their "design and erection." [1] In a joint circular released in July 2017, the TD and HyD noted that "railings are not designed to protect pedestrians from vehicular impact but to control and guide pedestrians for road safety and traffic management purposes." This observation is evident when a yet-to-be-replaced railing panel has crumpled into metal ribbon, marking a gentle collision.

Earlier in that same month, Transport for London released findings of a study that monitored the safety of 70 junctions and crossings where pedestrian railings had been taken down. The report found no increase in pedestrian accidents with the removal of barriers and noted that without the railings, people crossed in more locations on an "ad hoc" basis and drivers slowed down in response. [2]

The joint TD, HyD statement notes that the circular was being released to offer additional guidelines after a review of "current practices." Importantly, it states that "railings should not be considered as the only measure to achieve" road safety and traffic management and warned against their "overuse." The circular called for railings to be "simple," "unobtrusive," and "coherent with the surrounding environment using minimum materials," yet also noted that "to enhance streetscape, customised railing designs are required near historical buildings." A little less than a year after the release of the circular, the HyD published new standard drawings for pedestrian railings that respond to this call for customization.

In the period between 2010 and 2020, the length of railings on city streets increased from 730 kilometers to 1,500 kilometers. [3] From June to October of 2019, protesters removed 45.6 kilometers from city streets. Railing panels were piled up in barricades or removed to prevent crowds from getting crushed in a sudden swell. Reporters and civic groups observed an enhancement to circulation in the city, and urged a rethinking of the government's policy toward pedestrian railings or specific decisions about their placement. [4] Where protesters left the vertical railing posts, the HyD almost immediately used red plastic chain or police tape to link them. Cable ties in the bolt holes held the chains in place. In parts of the city where posts were also removed, streets were railing-free for weeks.

The HyD moved quickly to address this transformation; a reinstatement of all removed railings was accompanied by a revision of standard drawing H2130 that addressed "Type 2 Railings - For Control Purposes." The revision—dated June of 2020—comprised two important modifications: the addition of base plates to the railing posts and changes to the details of bolts and nuts. The base plates are welded to the end of the poles, and the assemblage is embedded in a concrete footing that lodges it into the ground. [5] The new bolt and nut details are specified in a separate drawing sheet and comprise a "dome shaped stiffener," six-pointed, star-shaped "steel torx" bolts, and "anti-theft shear nuts" that are to be deformed after installation. [6] These components replaced the standard flat bolt and nut assemblage that could be removed with a wrench. [7] Apart from these revisions, the railings were reinstated exactly as before, their top edge 1,000mm above the ground—too high to be accessible as a handrail—and at least 20cm in from the curb edge, reducing the width of sometimes already narrow sidewalks. [8]

In the summer of 2020, months after the protests, one neighborhood group in Causeway Bay held discussions with the TD and district council members about leaving open a crossing that had been created by the removal of railings. In the midst of these discussions, they discovered one morning that HyD contractors had closed it off. [9] In November of that same year, a Legislative Council Panel on Transport received a paper arguing for increased staffing for the "Walkability Project Management Office" and for regional offices of the HyD to help coordinate the government's "Walk in HK" policy, aimed at developing Hong Kong into a "Walkable City." As part of this policy, the paper identified "rearranging traffic signs and removing non-essential railings" in the neighborhoods of Sham Shui Po and Central as trial measures for enhancing walkability. [10]

1. The title page of the circular, available on the HyD website, lists both TD and HyD reference numbers. I cite both here. Highways Department, "Technical Circular No. 2/2017: Guidelines for the Provision and Design of Pedestrian Railings," HYD GR/1-50-1, HKSARG (July 10, 2017).
   Transport Department, "Departmental Circular No. 3/2017: Guidelines for the Provision and Design of Pedestrian Railings," TD DS/6-5/1, HKSARG (July 10, 2017).
2. Transport for London, "Collisions Before and After the Removal of Pedestrian Railings at 70 Junctions and Crossings on the Transport for London Road Network," Street Behavior, Report No. SB257, Greater London Authority (July 2017): 12.
3. The total length of Hong Kong's public road network is 2,184 kilometers: Highways Department, "Hong Kong Road Network," HKSARG (August 9, 2021), https://www.hyd.gov.hk/en/road_and_railway/existing/road_network/road.html.
4. See for example: Walk DVRC, "Railing over Railings," June 2020, https://walkdvrc.hk/upload/files/research/20200624120139_108.pdf.
5. Highways Department, "H2130: Type 2 Railings - For Control Purposes," in *Standard Drawing, Section 2: Street Furniture*, rev. June 2020, HKSARG.
6. Highways Department, "H2131D: Type 2 and Type 4 Railings - Details," *Standard Drawing, Section 2: Street Furniture*, rev. June 2020, HKSARG.
7. A tweet sent out by *Transit Jam*, a registered Hong Kong newspaper dedicated to sustainable transport, noted that a Transport Department repair crew of three people needed an angle grinder powered by a petrol generator to cut through the new bolts. Transit Jam (@Transit_Jam), "Remember those fancy new bolts Transport Department put on all the railings last year to stop people removing them with simple spanners?" *Twitter*, December 8, 2021, 7:48 a.m., https://twitter.com/Transit_Jam/status/1468472498975277056.
8. For the Transport Department's regulations on railing installation, see Transport Department, "Railings" in *Transport Planning and Design Manual: Highway Design Characteristics*, vol. 2, chap. 3 (2001): 3.9.2.
9. James Ockenden, "Surprise Railing Deployment Ends Crossing Battle," *Transit Jam*, August 1, 2020, https://transitjam.com/2020/08/01/surprise-railing-deployment-ends-crossing-battle/.
10. Legislative Council Panel on Transport, "Staffing Proposal for the Walkability Project Management Office and the Regional Offices of the Highways Department," LC Paper No. CB(4) 139/20-21(06), HKSARG (November 20, 2020): 5.
    More recently, the government's commitment to "walkability" has been called into question after the disappearance of consultancy studies from the Transport Department website following pedestrian deaths in dense neighborhoods. See: James Ockenden, "Govt Tongue-Tied on Soho, San Po Kong Walkability Deaths," *Transit Jam*, January 6, 2022, https://transitjam.com/2022/01/06/govt-tongue-tied-on-soho-san-po-kong-walkability-deaths/.

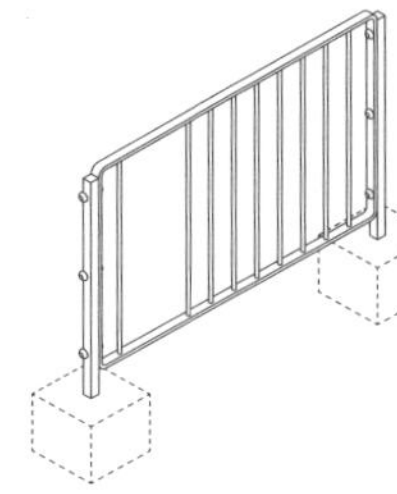
1

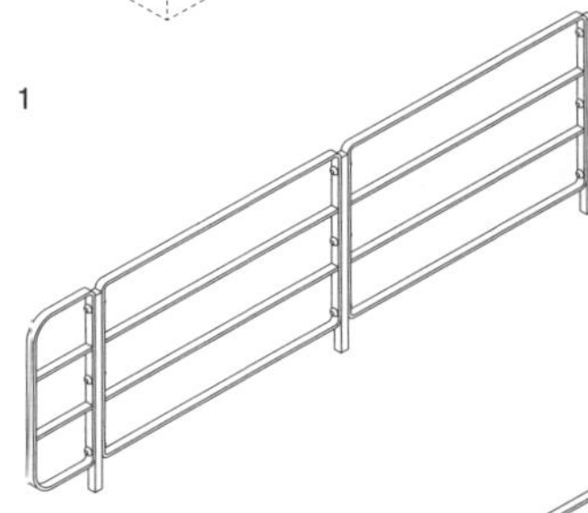
2

3

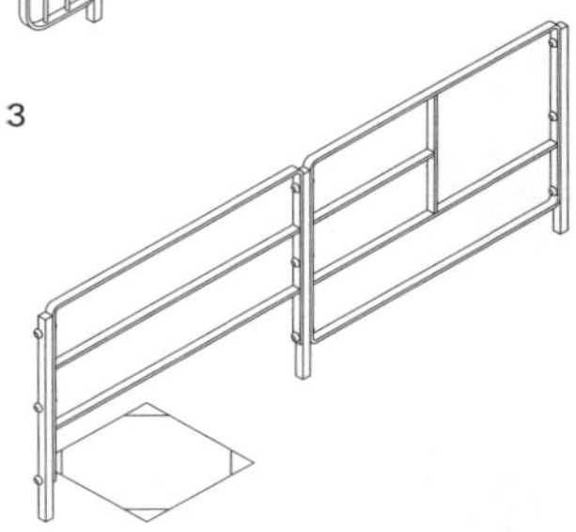
4

5

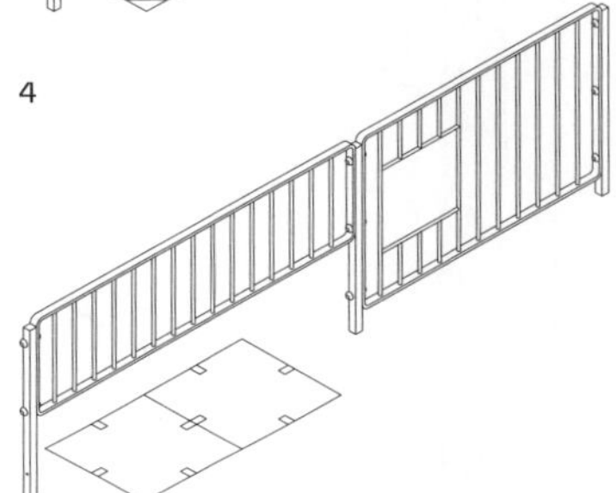
6

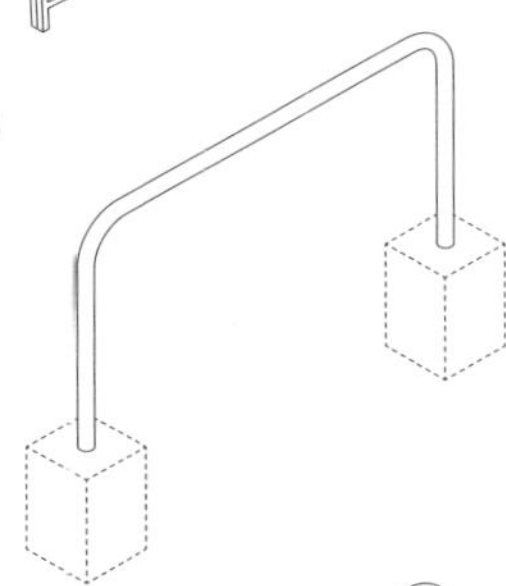
7

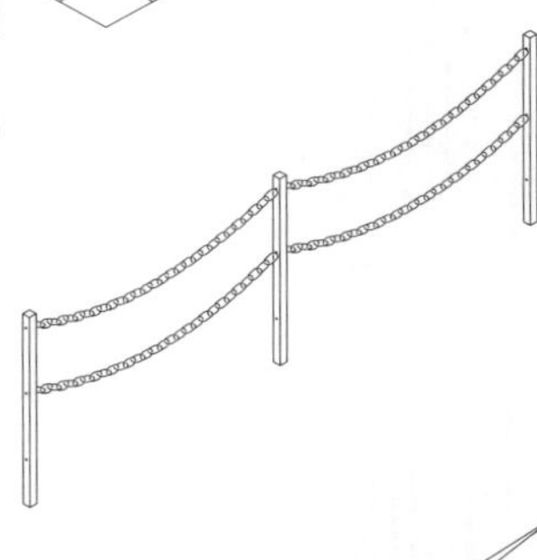
8

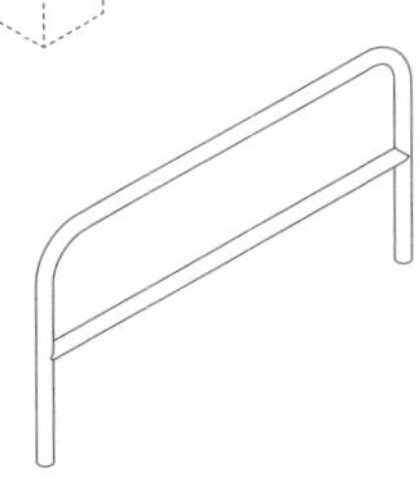
9

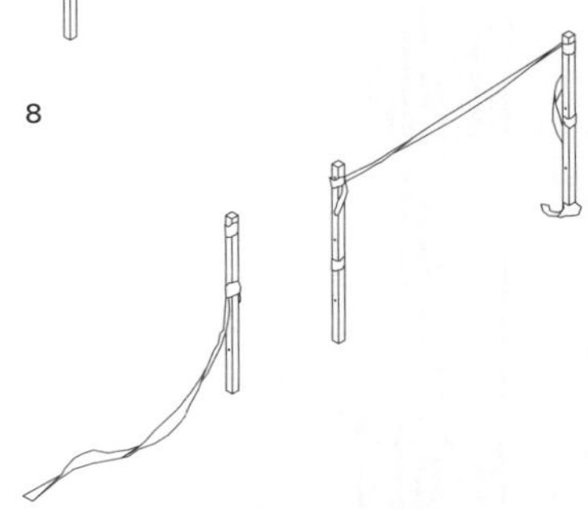
10

1 type 2 vertical railing, rods removed for hydrant access
2 type 2, flat horizontal members to allow through-visibility
3 type 4
4 type 2 horizontal railing, half panel for access hatch
5 wooden ladder chained to posts stripped of railing panels
6 type 2 vertical railing, half panel
7 tubular amenity railing, concrete footings
8 chain-linked railing for guidance purpose
9 amenity railing, additional horizontal member
10 police tape connecting posts stripped of railing panels

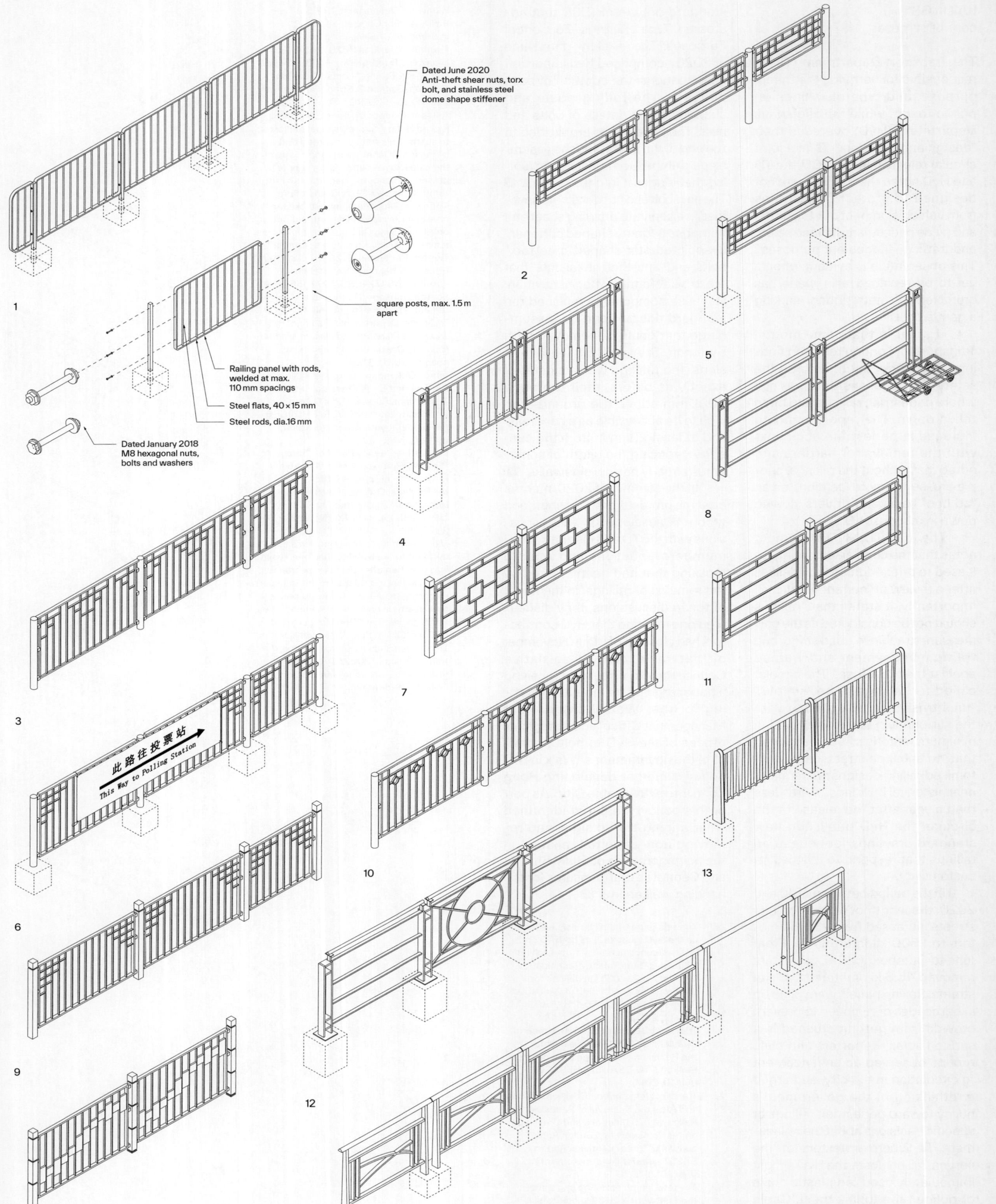

1 standard type 2 railing nstallation, concrete footings, old and new bolt assemblage
2 type 10 (half panel)
3 type 10
4 type 12, footings
5 type 5 (half panel), footings
6 type 7, district council elections voting banner, footings
7 decorative railing
8 type 13 (high visibility panel), trolley left overnight
9 type 9
10 type 11
11 decorative railing
12 type 13, decorative panel, footings
13 decorative railing, Cheung Kong Center, footings
14 Three Pacific Place, footings

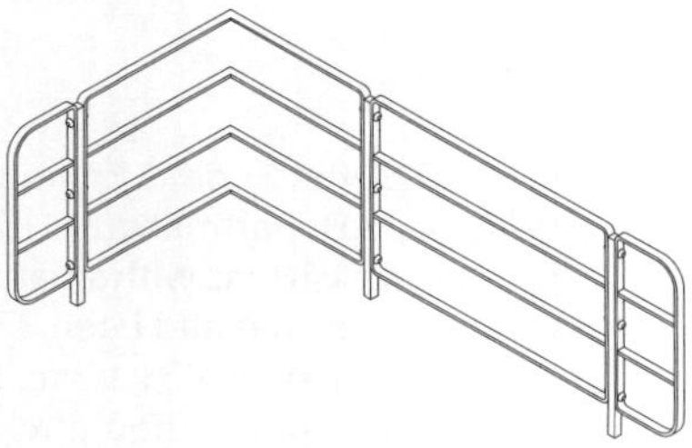

1

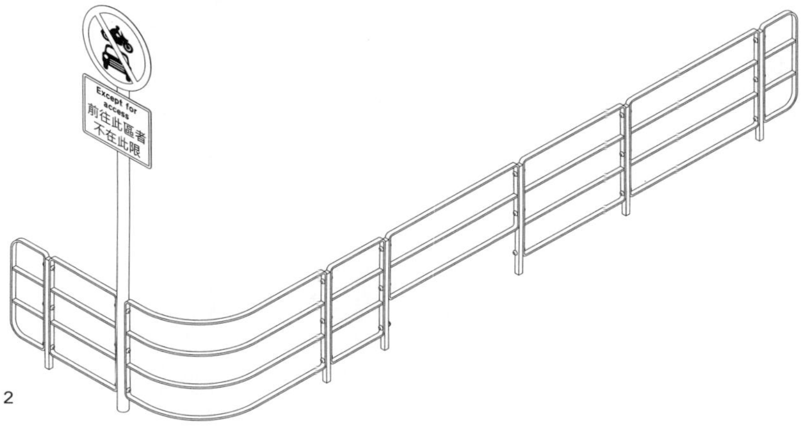

2

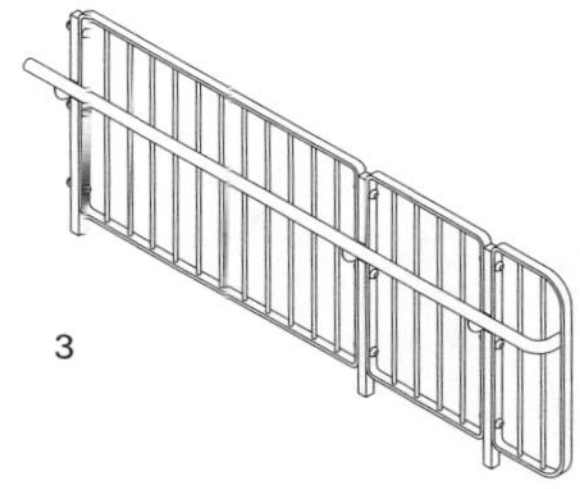

3

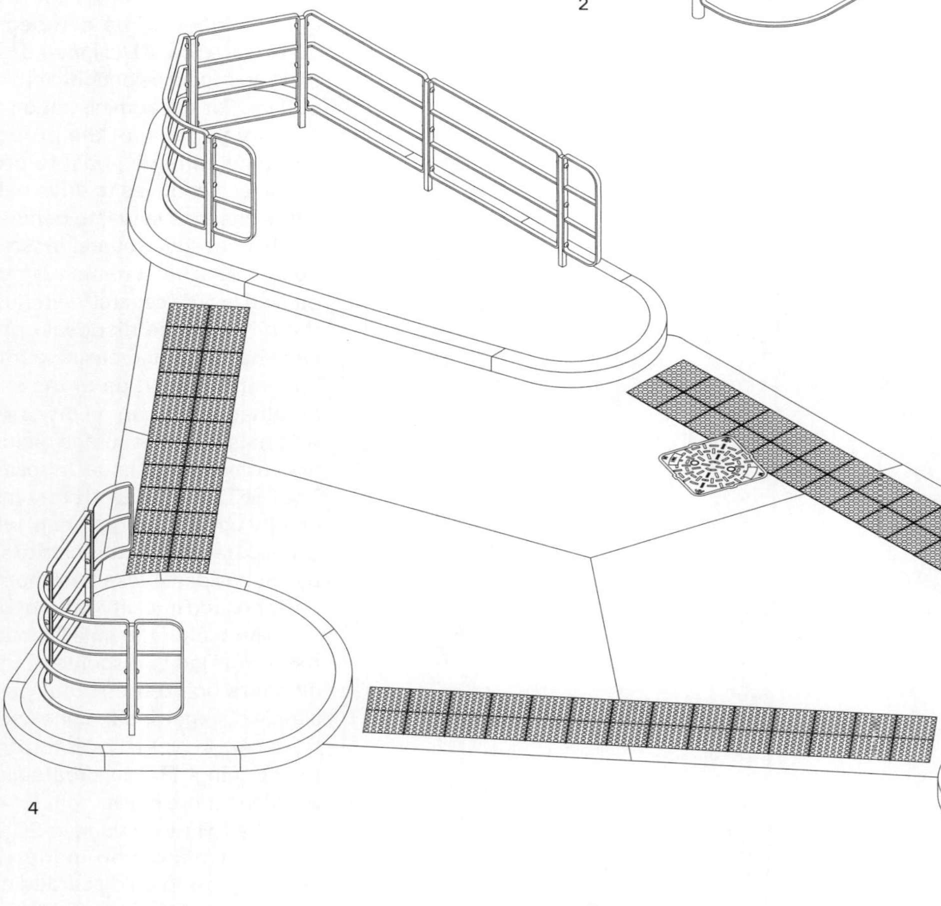
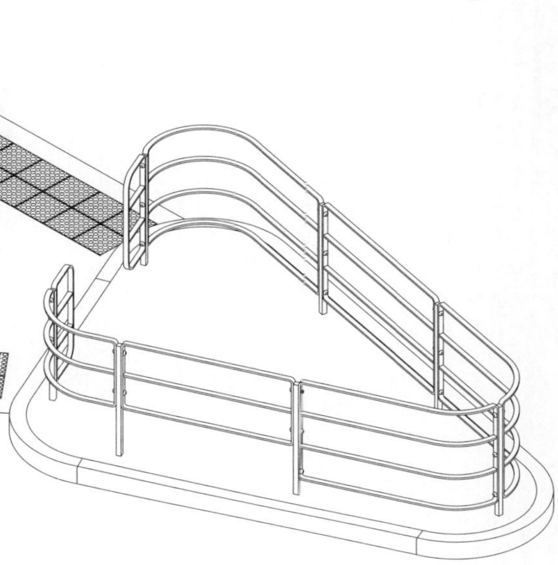

4

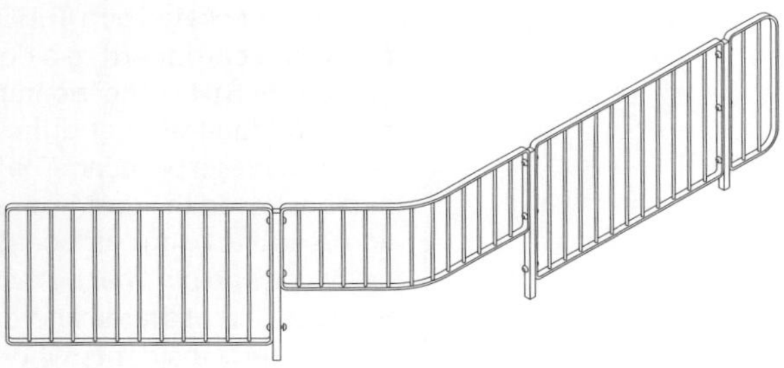

5

7

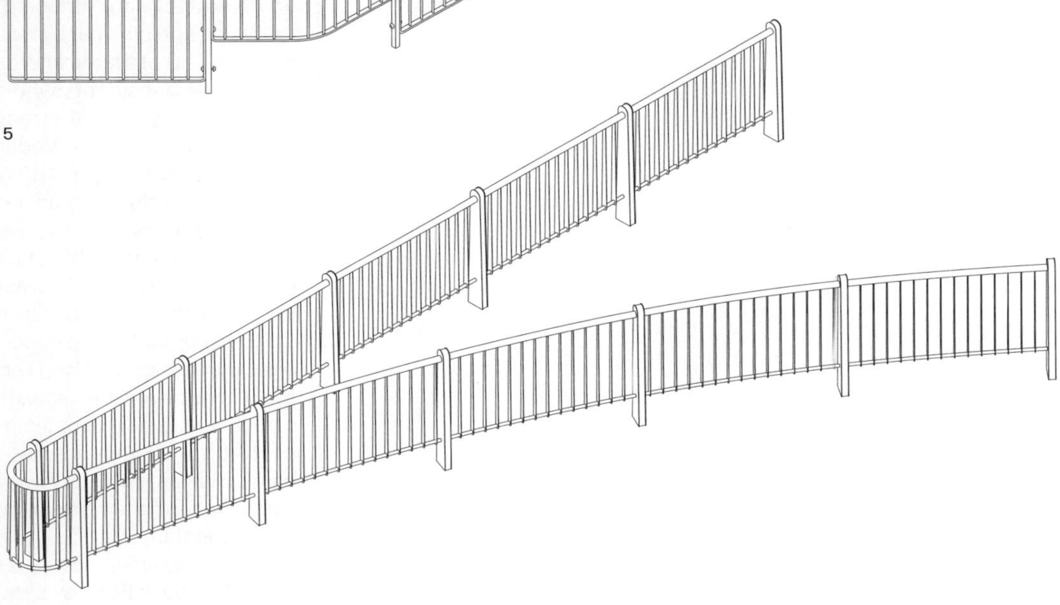

6

1 angled corner railing
2 curved corner railing, integrated post
3 railing, accessible handrail for persons with reduced mobility
4 railings enclosing pedestrian islands
5 curved railing, half panel to accommodate access hatch
6 curved traffic island railing, Cheung Kong Centre
7 pleats resulting from vehicle impact

1 bollards with chains, guidance purpose
2 staircase railing, Kwong Fung Lane
3 amenity bus stop railing, Castle Peak Road
4 staircase amenity railing, Pound Lane

BINS
frontline

In 2016, the Food & Environmental Hygiene Department (FEHD) tested new rubbish bins with smaller openings: holes that had been 37 × 19cm were reduced to 23 × 15cm. The new design also included stickers announcing fines for leaving trash on the sidewalk. The bins were introduced in preparation for a solid waste charging scheme first discussed in public consultations in 2012. The idea was that all trash would need a "designated label" or be dumped in a "designated bag." Designated labels and bags could be bought from retail outlets. For the administration, "the primary purpose of the proposed charging scheme [was] to create financial incentives to drive behavioural changes in waste generation and hence reduce overall waste disposal." [1] The scheme was to be phased in over several years, just as the city's waste disposal options were becoming increasingly critical. The implementation of the small-mouthed trash can on city streets was meant to discourage residents from using bins for large disposables. The FEHD also reduced bin numbers on city streets, citing Japan, where curbside receptacles are hard to come by and residents take trash home to be deposited into city-bought bags.

The trial of the small-mouthed trash cans led to discontent. Street cleaners pointed out that people simply disregarded the fine and left trash next to bins if it was too big for the opening. [2] This created more work and more mess.

The following year, in 2017, an elderly woman who made extra income picking up discarded cardboard was ticketed by a FEHD officer for selling cardboard to a domestic worker for $1HK. The woman faced a fine and jail time and the officer confiscated her pushcart. The woman had borrowed the cart from a friend and used it to bring cardboard to a local buyer who paid her by the kilo. [3] She was part of a large informal sector of elderly residents who sustain themselves by collecting recyclable waste—most often cardboard. The news was widely reported, with stories about "cardboard grannies" making their way through the media. [4] In that same year, China tightened curbs on imports of solid waste. This led to a continuous decline in prices for scrap paper, with more paper-based products ending up in Hong Kong landfills, where they are the second-largest component. Other countries in Southeast Asia soon implemented import bans on waste products as well, leading to the further deterioration of the wastepaper market.

The new small-mouth redesign was followed in 2019 by bins developed by the Agriculture, Fisheries and Conservation Department, working with the FEHD and the Environmental Protection Department

(EPD). These bins and containers can be strapped to barricades, making them tip-proof, and their lids operate with a foot pedal, making them difficult to open. These features "prevent raids from wild pigs or monkeys" on the territory's urban fringe. [5]

Meanwhile, economic uncertainty brought on by the protests and the pandemic forestalled the passage of the waste charging scheme; only in June 2020 did debate on the scheme's implementation resume in the Bills Committee of the Legislative Council. After three meetings in which 3 out of 37 clauses to the amendment bill were discussed, certain committee members expressed concern about the slowness of the proceedings. Ultimately, the government, citing a lack of time, terminated the proceedings and dissolved the committee. [6]

On October 22, 2020, a *new* Bills Committee was formed to study the waste charging scheme's implementation as well as the government's performance on environmental issues. [7] An "Information Note" addressed to the committee from the EPD outlined several measures being taken to address ongoing concerns about waste reduction and recycling. [8] Among the various measures, the EPD noted that it had taken over the management of curbside recycling bins from the FEHD. [9] This change came after reports from citizen groups that FEHD contractors were depositing recyclable materials into waste streams designated for landfills. The EPD promised to "increase...efficiency and strengthen the public's confidence in the proper handling of recyclables." [10]

The EPD also detailed a scheme designed to rejuvenate the collapsed wastepaper market. The program involved 17 contractors with HK$440 million in funding to collect, screen, sort, and bail wastepaper. These contractors were required to maintain a 70 cent per kilo price "to collect waste paper (including cardboards, newspapers, and office papers) from street corner recycling shops, mobile recyclers and frontline collectors, etc. across the territory." [11] The "frontline collectors" include the elderly men and women who collect cardboard. [12] Along with this and other programs to promote the financial viability of the recycling industry, the city is moving forward with the extension of three landfills that, when completed, should serve the city's waste disposal needs into the 2030s. [13] A "Waste Blueprint for Hong Kong 2035" published by the Environment Bureau, to which the EPD belongs, argues that the city cannot hope for further extensions and should aim for a "0 Landfill" policy in the coming years. [14]

1. Legislative Council Secretariat, "Report of the Bills Committee on Waste Disposal (Charging for Municipal Solid Waste)(Amendment) Bill 2018," LC Paper No. CB(1)849/19-20, Ref. CB1/BC/2/18, HKSARG (July 2020): 12.
2. Chantal Yuen, "New rubbish bin design 'creating more work' for street cleaners," *Hong Kong Free Press*, June 14, 2016, https://hongkongfp.com/2016/06/14/street-cleaners-say-new-small-hole-rubbish-bins-are-creating-more-work/.
3. Elson Tong, "Elderly woman faces up to HK$5k fine and jail after selling cardboard to domestic worker for HK$1," *Hong Kong Free Press*, June 15, 2017, https://hongkongfp.com/2017/06/15/elderly-woman-faces-hk5k-fine-jail-selling-cardboard-domestic-worker-hk1/.
4. Matthew Keegan, "Hong Kong's 'cardboard grannies': the elderly box collectors living in poverty," *The Guardian*, April 24, 2018, https://www.theguardian.com/cities/2018/apr/24/hong-kong-cardboard-grannies-elderly-box-collectors-recycling-poverty.
5. Gov HK, "Press Releases: AFCD rolls out wildlife-resistant refuse collection facilities (with photos)," October 24, 2019, HKSARG, https://www.info.gov.hk/gia/general/201910/24/P2019102300643.htm.
6. See: Legislative Council Secretariat, "Report of the Bills Committee on Waste Disposal," 4.
An opposition lawmaker cited "total government failure in terms of environmental policy" and mentioned that meetings had "prioritised debate over the national security law, the national anthem law and infrastructure projects over social issues such as environmental protection." See Kathleen Magramo, "Hong Kong waste charging scheme dumped as time runs out on long-delayed bill," *South China Morning Post*, June 22, 2020, https://www.scmp.com/news/hong-kong/health-environment/article/3090115/hong-kong-waste-charging-scheme-dumped-time-runs. The National Security Law was eventually passed on June 30, 2020.
7. The waste charging scheme was passed by the Legislative Council in August of 2021 and will come into effect in early 2023.
8. Environmental Protection Department, "Information Note: Waste Reduction and Recycling Complementary Measures Launched by Environmental Protection Department and their Progress," LC Paper No. CB(1)187/20-21(01), HKSARG (November 2020): 1.
9. Ibid., 6.
10. Gov HK, "Press Releases: EPD to take over recycling bins," September 30, 2020, HKSARG, https://www.news.gov.hk/eng/2020/09/20200930/20200930_171427_696.html.
11. Environmental Protection Department, "Information Note: Waste Reduction," 1.
12. Gu Mengyan, "Recycling to nowhere," *China Daily Hong Kong*, February 5, 2021, https://www.chinadailyhk.com/article/157039#Recycling-to-nowhere.
13. Environmental Protection Department, "Problems and Solutions," updated May 12, 2020, https://www.epd.gov.hk/epd/english/environmentinhk/waste/prob_solutions/landfill.html.
14. Environment Bureau, "Waste Blueprint for Hong Kong 2035," HKSARG (February 2021).

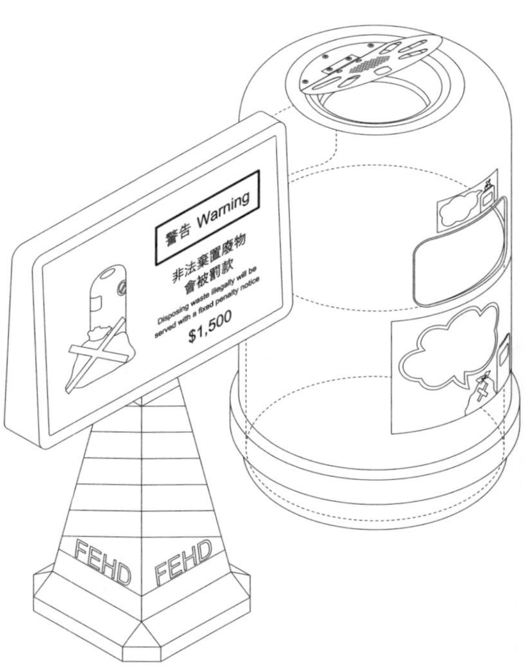

1

2

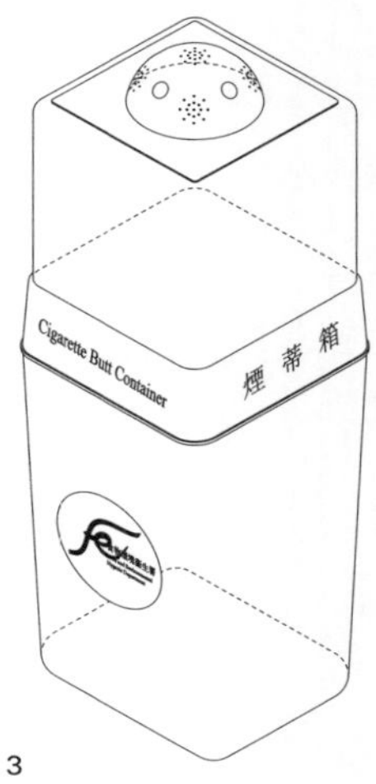

3

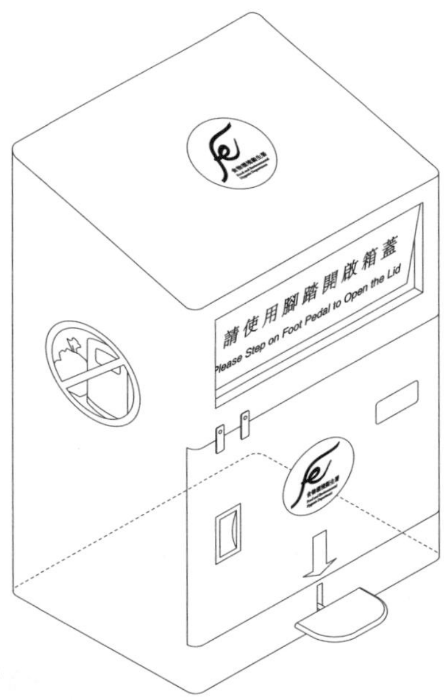

4

1 small-mouth litter container
2 dog excreta container
3 cigarette butt container
4 step-on-foot-pedal-to-open litter container

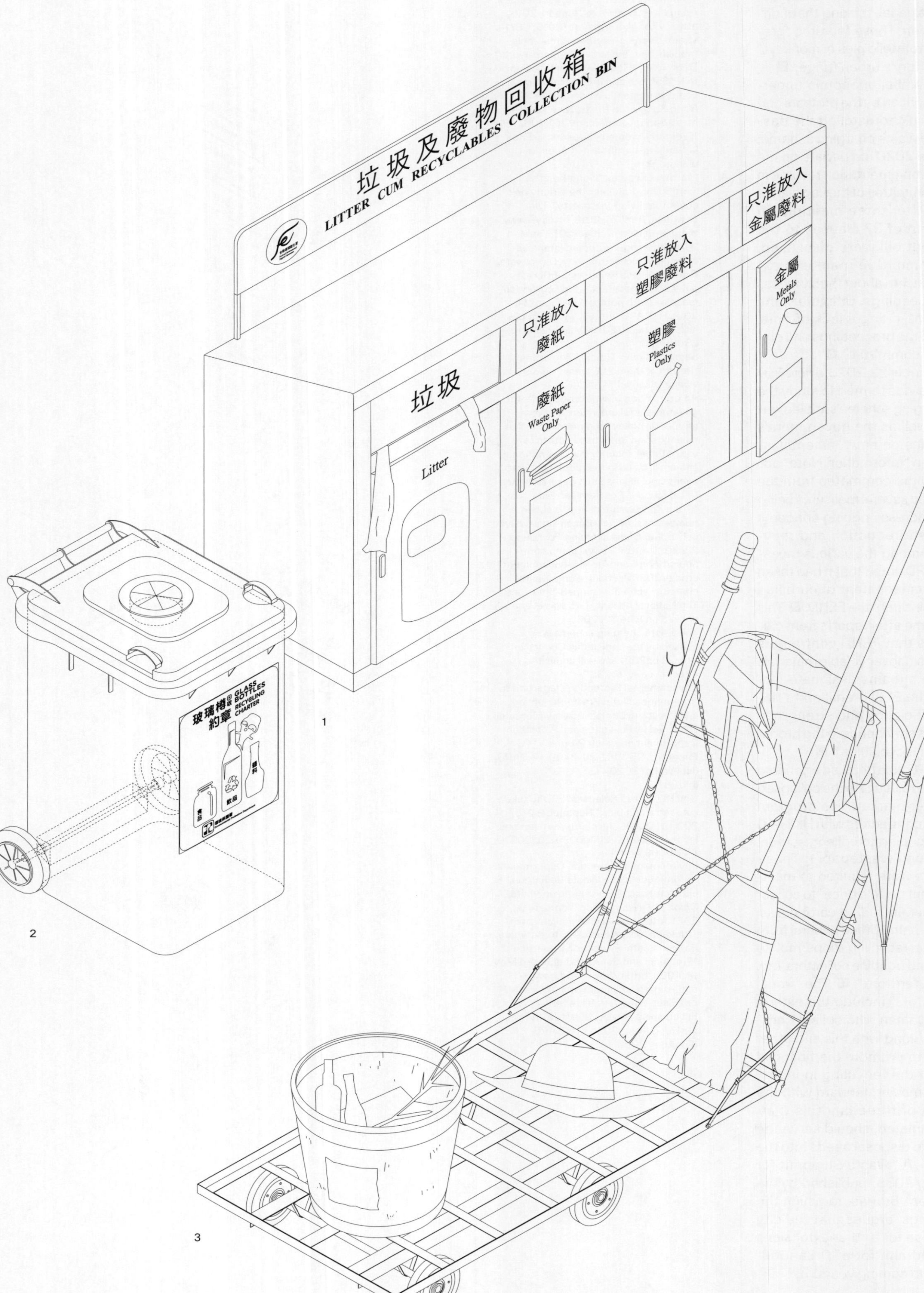

1 litter and recyclables bin
2 glass bottle recycling
3 street cleaner trolley

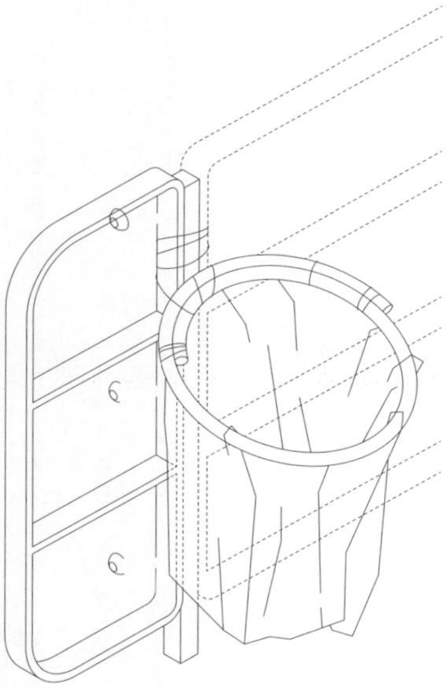

1

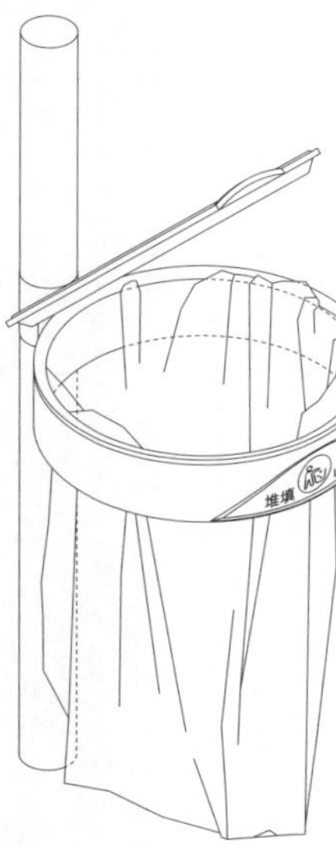

2

3

1 temporary plastic bag ring support, attached to railing
2 temporary cylindrical ring support with lid, fixed to post
3 temporary scissor frame, chained

TREES
tell-tales

Hong Kong does not have legislation on trees. In place of laws, the Secretary of Development noted to the Legislative Council Panel on Development that the care of trees falls on departments to "follow the requirements for tree management and maintenance promulgated through policies, relevant ordinances, technical circulars, guidelines, codes of practice, etc." **1** As for trees on private land, the Secretary noted that they are looked after by legally binding tree protection clauses written into lease conditions; the government is concerned that private landholders might face additional financial burdens from legislation on trees, particularly due to the insufficient capacity for tree inspection and maintenance work in the city. The secretary argued that this, in turn, could lead private landowners to forego planting new trees.

Since 2010, the management and coordination of tree maintenance and care in Hong Kong has fallen under the Development Bureau's Greening, Landscape and Tree Management Section (GLTMS). As part of its "Greening Efforts" the GLTMS maintains a list of 459 "Old and Valuable Trees" (OVT) growing on government land. A tree's size, age, and species determine inclusion on the list, as does "cultural, historical or memorable" significance. This last category could comprise a "well-known Fung Shui or landmark tree" or a tree "associated with special memories such as those planted by a senior government official." **2** OVTs also appear on the "Tree Register," a searchable database of 847 trees. **3** The database localizes OVTs, "Tree[s] with Brown Root Rot" or "Stone Wall Tree[s]." Trees with Brown Root Rot suffer from a highly transmissible white fungus. Stone Wall Trees grow from the retaining walls of hillside terraces. Arborists and engineers from the GLTMS continuously monitor for brown root rot disease and use tell-tales to check for the structural displacement of retaining walls. Tell-tales are no larger than a glass slide and are placed astride cracks to measure the movement of walls in and on which roots nestle. Trees may sometimes be cut down if they are "assessed to be of imminent danger to the public"; these "Removed Trees" are not registered in the database, but instead vanish. **4**

While the GLTMS *oversees* care, the routine maintenance of trees is distributed among 17 administrative services who are responsible for "managing the trees in the facilities and lands under their purview." **5** These include the Police Force and the Postal Department. Each of the 17 departments has their own tree management teams who employ private contractors to conduct tree risk assessments and maintenance. With the Tree Register, it is possible to identify 11 OVTs under the Highways Department's authority. Nine of these trees are *Ficus microcarpa*, or Chinese banyan. The banyans' aerial roots begin as a hanging veil of branches; upon touching the ground, they organize their growth into the earth and thicken into muscly columns.

In 2020, building on the success of the Tree Register, the GLTMS launched additional web-based tools. The Tree Management Common Platform (TMCP) allows scattered work teams to access geolocalized information and submit tree inspection reports. For the public, a system of QR-coded tree labels will make it possible by 2022 to "report problematic trees" and access "educational information" on nearly 200,000 trees along footpaths. GLTMS is also working with private funders and a university research team to develop a "smart tree tilt measuring and monitoring system for sensing tree movement" that could potentially identify trees at risk of collapse. **6**

The government has also sought to address public concerns about the care and pruning of trees with efforts to boost the training and certification of arborists and horticulture experts. In an incident in 2017, 21 of 29 nesting young egrets and herons were killed by a tree pruning team contracted by the Leisure and Cultural Services Department (LCSD). An investigation found, among other faults, "insufficient supervision and manpower of the tree team's subteam" and concluded that the subteam "failed to exercise common sense and awareness on wild animal protection nor stop the work when they noticed that the nests of the birds would be affected." **7**

1. Secretary of Development, "Landscape and Tree Management Work in Hong Kong," Legislative Council Panel on Development, LC Paper No. CB(1)776/17-18(01), HKSARG (April 4, 2018): 2.
2. Additional criteria can be found here: Development Bureau, "Old and Valuable Trees," Greening, Landscape & Tree Management Section, updated April 8, 2020, https://www.greening.gov.hk/en/departments_greening_efforts/old_and_valuable_trees.html.
3. Development Bureau, "Tree Register," Greening, Landscape & Tree Management Section, updated August 16, 2021, https://www.greening.gov.hk/treeregister/map/treeIndex.aspx.
4. Secretary of Development, "Landscape and Tree Management," 2.
5. Ibid., 6.
6. Development Bureau, "Annex A: Applications of Technologies in Tree Management," in "Urban Forestry Management Work in Hong Kong," LC Paper No. CB(1)909/20-21(03), Legislative Council Panel on Development, HKSARG (May 25, 2021).
7. Gov HK, "LCSD completes investigation of Tai Po tree pruning incident," December 1, 2017, HKSARG, https://www.info.gov.hk/gia/general/201712/01/P2017120100315.htm.

1

2

1 tree tag
2 smart tree health sensor

stone wall tree, intersection of
Fuk On lane and Tai On Terrace

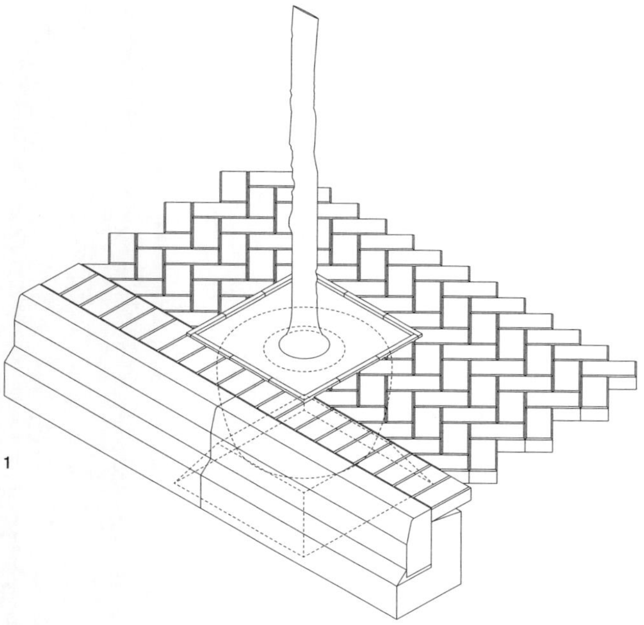

1

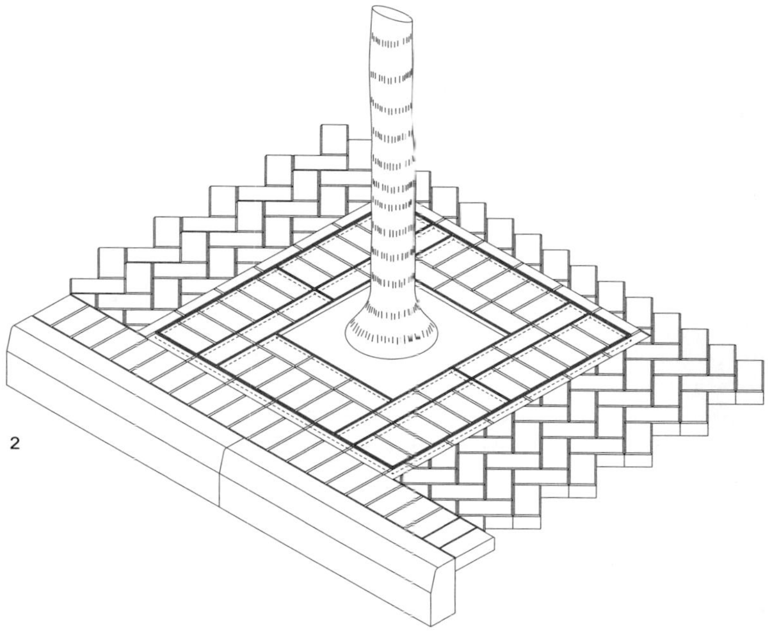

2

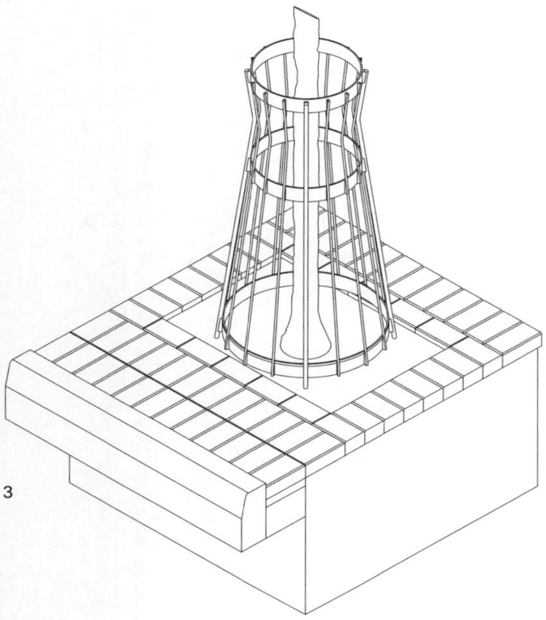

3

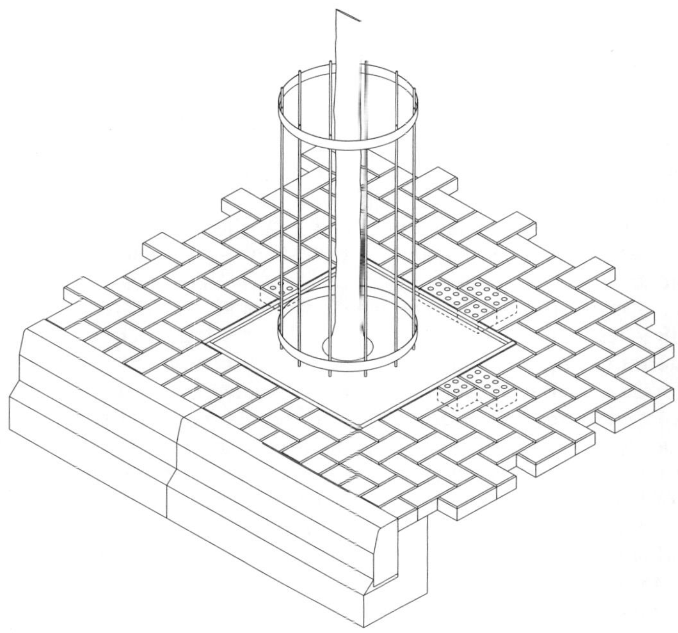

4

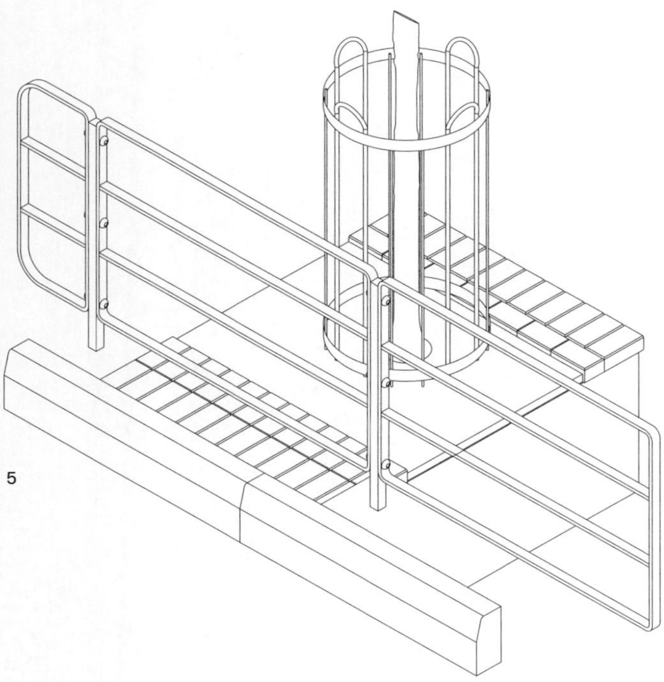

5

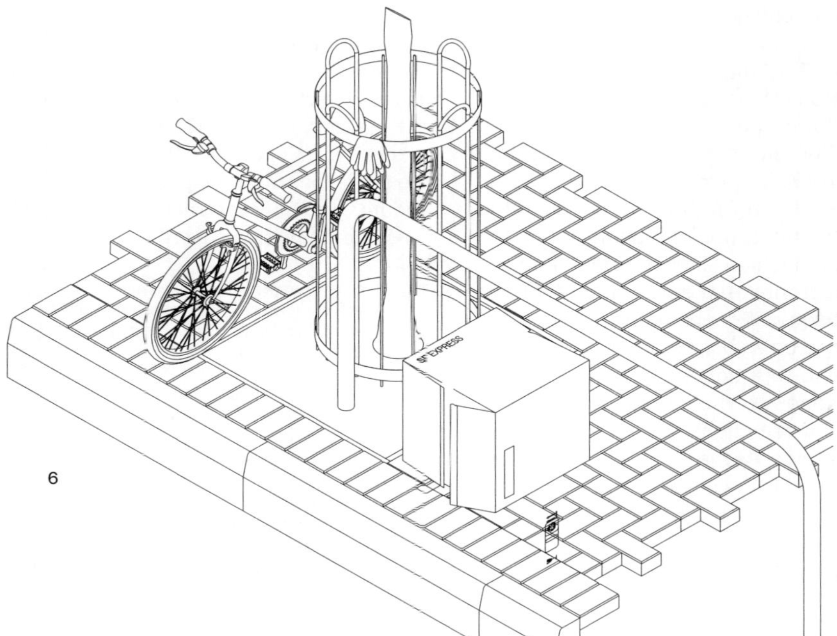

6

1 typical tree pit
2 tree pit with reinforced paving
3 with guard
4 porous bricks
5 pedestrian railing
6 tubular railing

ACCESS HATCHES
keyhole

Many of the access hatches scattered across Hong Kong's streets are overseen by the Drainage Services Department (DSD). They are specified in drawing sets that were reviewed in February, 2001, and "Redrawn by CAD" in August of the same year. While revisions to Highways Department (HyD) drawings are identified by month and year, DSD drawings are annotated with a specific date. The drawings provide specifications for access hatches and the cavities they conceal. Cast-iron hatch covers, nestled in a frame, open into reinforced, precast concrete chambers set into the earth. At the base of the chambers, conduits for water or waste intersect and can be inspected. When access hatches are situated on concrete carriageways or sidewalks, they are set in slabs delimited by sealed, 10mm isolation joints cut the full depth of the concrete. These slabs require both a different grade of concrete and a different sub-base from the remainder of the street. In a bituminous road surface, asphalt comes to the edge of an access hatch, with no discontinuity and the immediate depth of earth around the chamber is reinforced with brickwork.

The outbreak of plague in Hong Kong in 1894 led to the development of a subterranean system for waste and water. Stormwater and sewage were separated into two streams and troughs were moved underground to mitigate the breeding and spread of bacteria. Access hatch covers with radial or circular patterns today indicate stormwater, while raised studs in a square grid are for foul water. Older covers include information about the name and contract number of the hatch's manufacturer; a manufacturer could be in England or India, as well as in Hong Kong. In the 1950s, local production moved to districts in the city's northern New Territories, and in 1991, the enforcement of the Air Pollution Control Ordinance led to the relocation of foundries to mainland China. These details and the histories that surround them have been well documented in exhibitions and on websites devoted to historic and rare access hatches in Hong Kong. **1** The more iconic of these can be bought as laser printed miniatures. As the city itself is razed and re-built, the covers endure as traces of an otherwise disappearing history. That they are inscribed with distinguishing marks also suggests a time when fabrication at a large scale did not foreclose customization.

Apart from sewage and stormwater covers, streets are checkered with access hatches of varying sizes and orientations. Some of the installations guarded underneath include: switches for the delivery of gas and drinking water; cables for the Transport Department's Area Traffic Control System; guard control valves for fire hydrants; and wiring for the public lighting system. The covers to these hatches are sometimes no larger than a book and are marked with acronyms that identify their function or the utility that oversees them.

Access hatches also proliferate on sidewalks. These accommodate the telecom installations that have burgeoned over the past decades with new residential and office towers and updates in technology. Recessed covers are increasingly replacing cast-iron hatches on sidewalks. These covers comprise a hollow, steel removable tray, that slots into a frame fixed into the ground. The tray has a depth of 100mm and is filled with material to blend into the surrounding sidewalk. **2** Concrete pavers, cement, asphalt, granite, and tactile strips that continue indications from adjacent sidewalks, are all used as infill. When recessed covers are incorrectly replaced after maintenance, these indications are disrupted.

The recessed covers are marked at their corners or along their narrow sides by a triangular area of steel that is cut through with a hole. A keyhole such as this exists on nearly all access hatches to allow for their displacement with a lifting hook, or "key." Following a series of explosions in which trapped underground gases launched access hatch covers into the air, design changes were made to increase the keyholes' venting capacity. New guidelines were put in place by the Communications Authority (CA) to regulate telecommunications services provided by fixed network operators (FNOs). In their update to guidelines for the recessed covers, the CA noted that FNOs "shall comply with safety requirements which may be prescribed from time to time by the CA and any directions of the CA in relation to the safety matter." **3** In addition to this design change in the covers, the guidelines detail inspection procedures and indicate which type of gas detector is to be used.

1. See, for example: The Conservancy Association Centre for Heritage, "Manhole Covers Exhibition," http://cache.org.hk/blog/manhole_covers_ex/.
2. Highways Department, "H2186C: Fabricated Steel Recessed Cover And Frame For ATC/E&M Drawpit Opening From 400×400 To 600×600 (Sheet 2 Of 3)," in *Standard Drawings, Section 2: Street Furniture*, rev. July 2010, HKSARG.
3. Office of the Communications Authority, "Implementation Guidelines on Mitigating the Risk of Gas Explosion in Telecommunications Manholes," GN-14/2016, July 29, 2016, HKSARG.

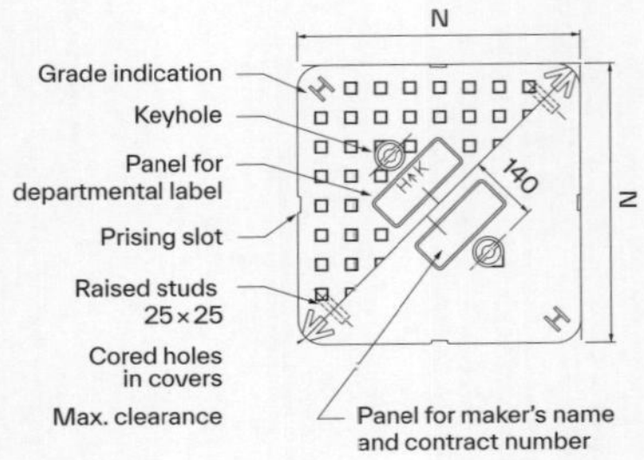

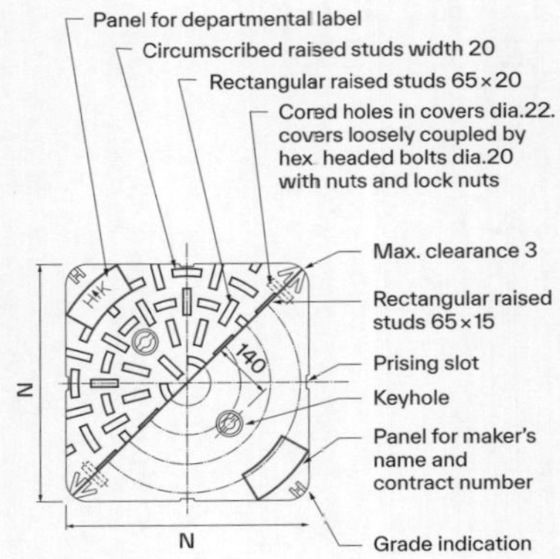

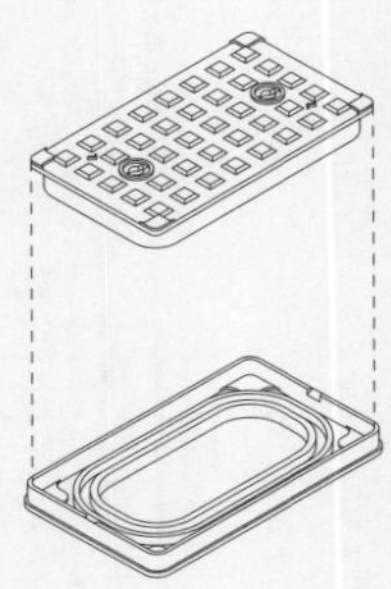

1

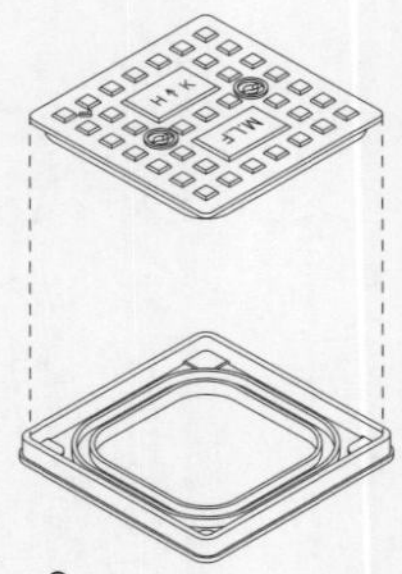

2

9

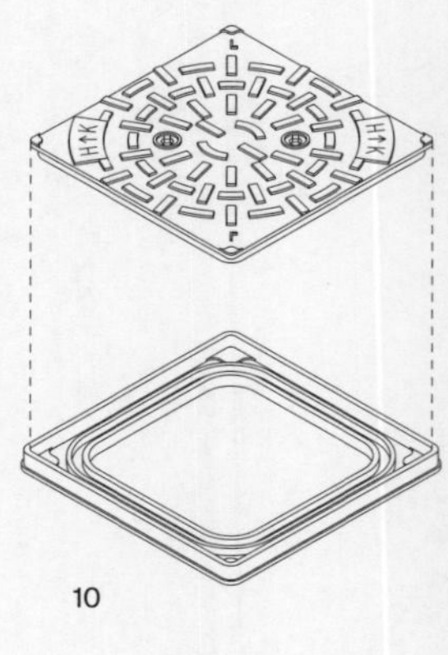

10

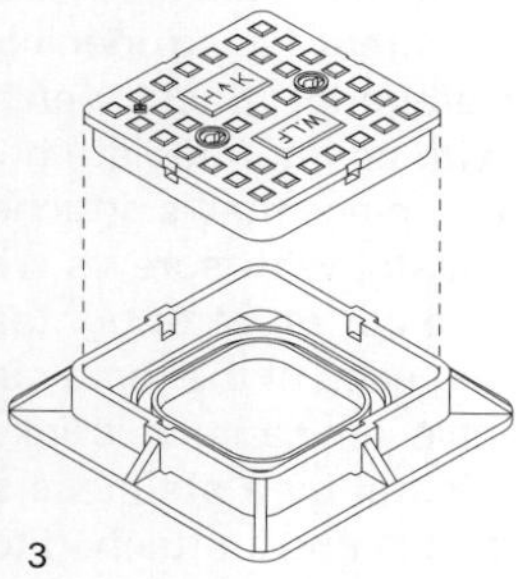

3

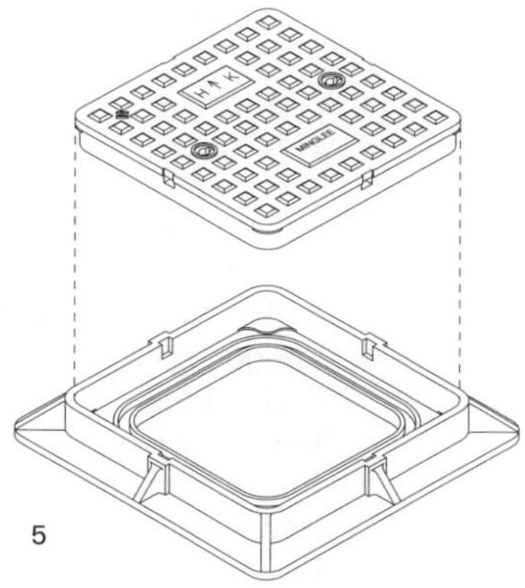

5

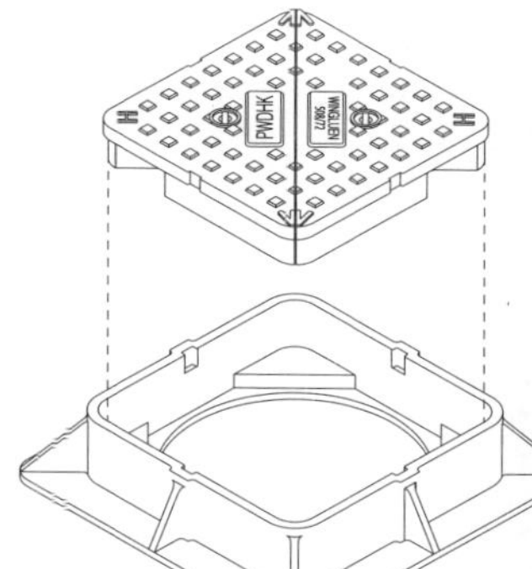

7

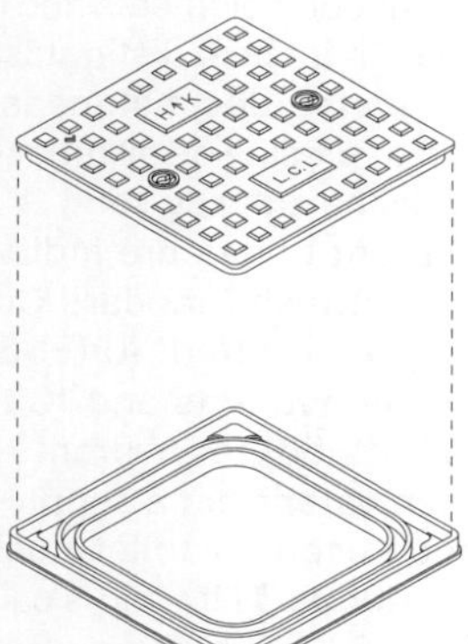

4

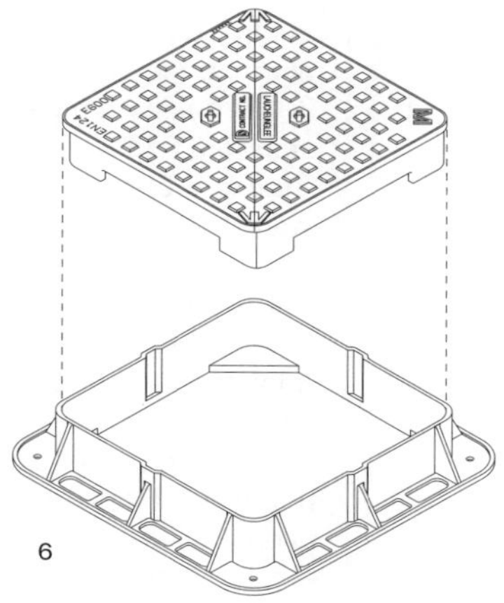

6

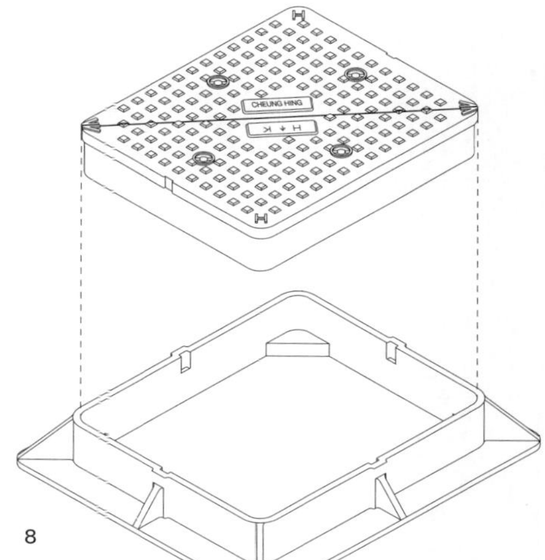

8

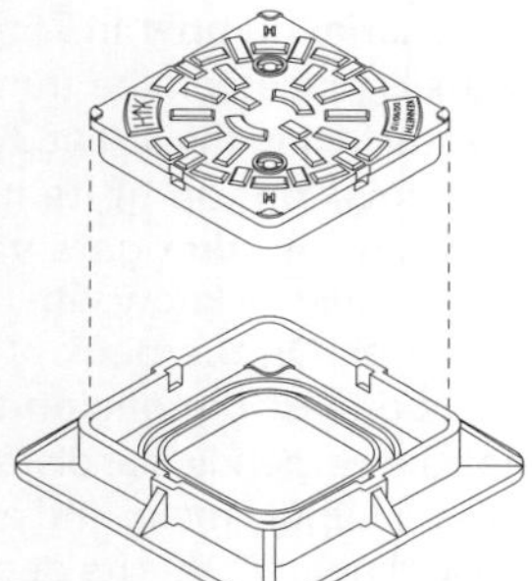

11

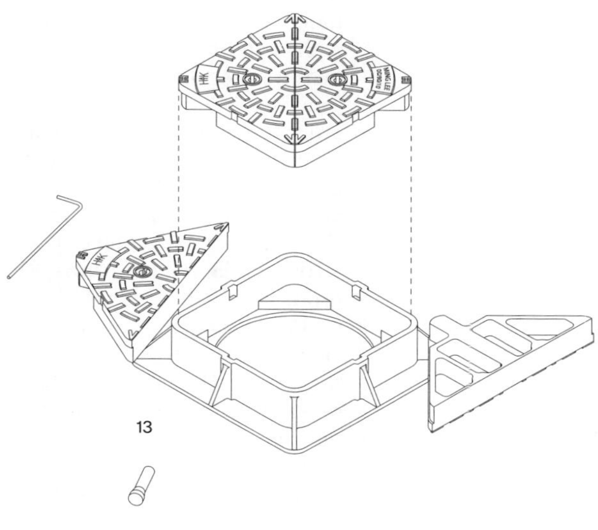

13

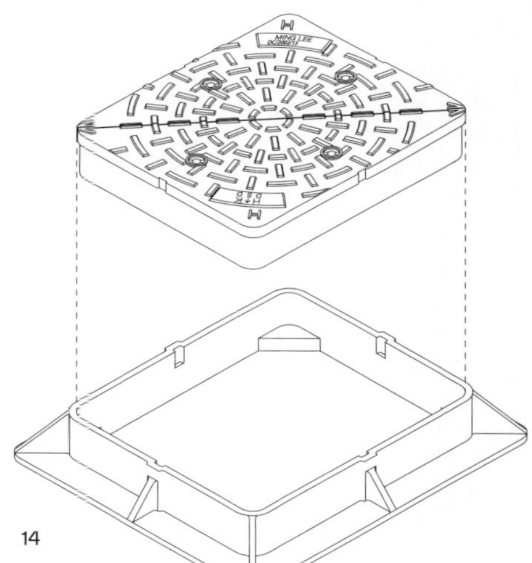

14

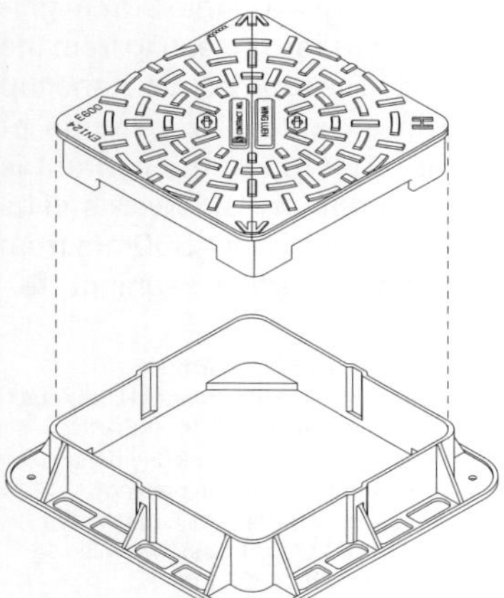

12

1 double seal terminal sewer access hatch type MC2-40/18A (square grid pattern)
2 MC2-29/29A
3 MA2-29/29A
4 MC2-45/45A
5 MA2-45/45A
6 standard 675, double triangular ductile iron access hatch
7 double triangular access hatch
8 desilting access hatch
9 double seal terminal stormwater access hatch type MC2-29/29B (radial pattern)
10 MC2-45/45B
11 MA2-29/29B
12 standard 675 square double triangular ductile iron access hatch
13 double triangular access hatch, key
14 desilting access hatch

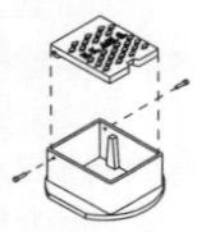

1

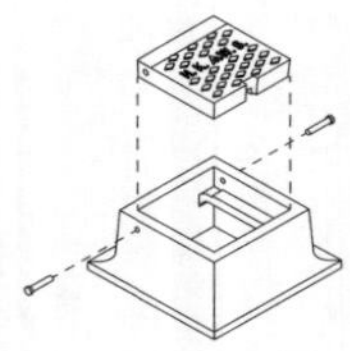

2

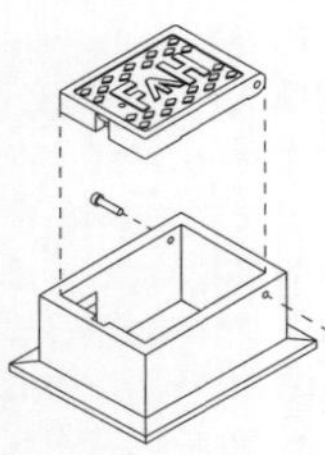

3

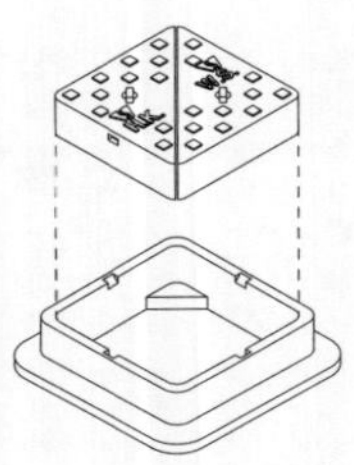

4

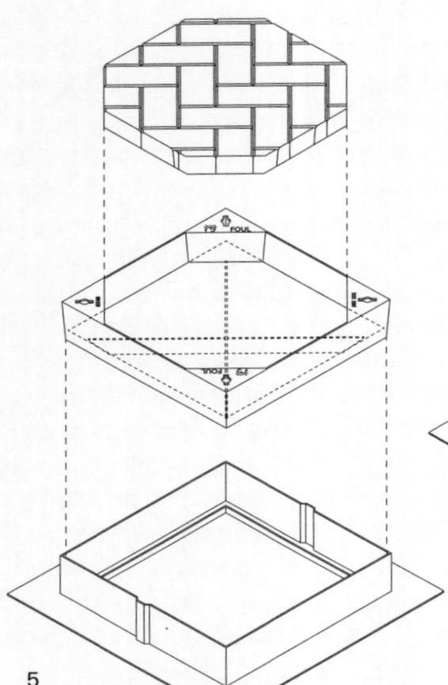

5

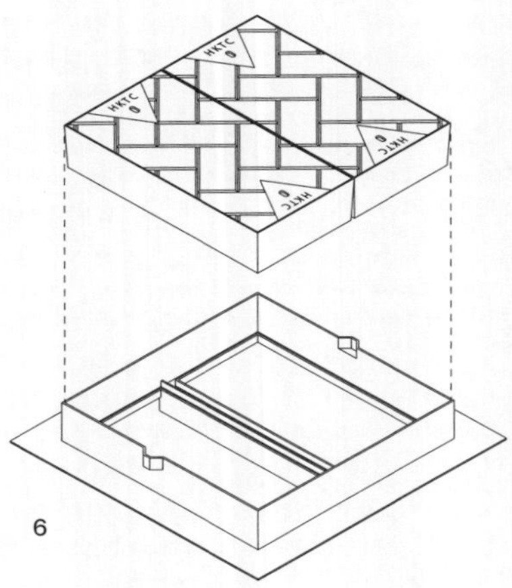

6

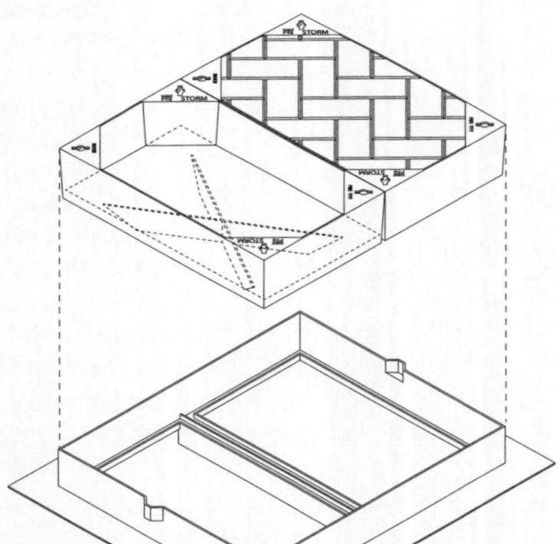

7

1 light grade ductile iron surface box
2 180 square surface box
3 fire hydrant surface box
4 300 square surface box
5 550 square recessed access hatch, paver infill, tray, frame
6 infilled tray, frame
7 desilting access hatch, in-filled tray, frame

HYDRANTS
round-head

Hydrants are part of a system of waterworks overseen by the Water Services Department (WSD). This network includes pumping stations, service reservoirs, water treatment works, and mainlaying. Each of these categories has its own section in the WSD's publicly available standard drawings. Access roads and security measures also have relevant drawings. In notes amended to the documentation, the department website states that the drawings "give guidance on suitable design details and for direct reference in waterworks contracts," noting that they "form part of the Design Division's quality documentation complying with the requirements of ISO 9001: 2000 quality management system standard." [1] An abstract from the iso.org website explains that the standard can be relevant for organizations that deliver a product that "meets customer and applicable regulatory requirements," and which "aim[s] to enhance customer satisfaction...including processes for continual improvement." [2] The WSD notes also indicate that "[a] number of controlled copies [of the drawings] are kept in the Design Division's Document Control Centre" and welcome feedback or suggestions from users that incorporate information in the drawings into tender bids. [3]

Two sets of drawings in the "mainlaying" section describe the design and finish of fire hydrants. The "round-head" hydrant's cylindrical pedestal is 150mm in diameter. This cast-iron housing flares at the bottom and then narrows into a notch before flattening into a flange with eight screw holes. [4] The underside of the flared material sits on the ground while the notch and flange are in the earth. The screw holes of the hydrant flange align with that of a vertical piping element. This vertical pipe is stabilized by a "concrete thrust block" measuring 600 × 900 × 750mm. [5] The pipe turns 90 degrees within its concrete housing and then passes through a "gate valve" chamber about 200mm under the ground. Opening the gate valve releases water into the hydrant. The gate valve assemblage is housed in a void enclosed by precast concrete units stacked onto a poured in-situ surround that sits on a precast concrete slab. Once past the gate valve, the pipe turns perpendicular to the curb and runs into the street where it passes through another concrete thrust block and crosses a second gate valve assemblage before joining the main water supply.

The hydrant's position in relation to the curb depends on the design speed and cross fall of the carriageway. It can be anywhere from 500 to 1,000mm from the curb-line. Nevertheless, a note stipulates that the absolute minimum distance should be 200mm on the "district and local distributor roads" that comprise the majority of neighborhood streets. [6]

The hydrant pedestal has three outlets: a street-facing opening and two lateral ones. Each opening is fitted with an intermediate bronze connector piece that is attached to the pedestal with screws whose heads are cut off after tightening. Enclosing each of the three outlets is a ductile iron cap that is linked to the pedestal by a stainless steel chain that keeps it attached to the hydrant when it is unscrewed. The bronze connector piece and its cap come in two different types—one for the lateral openings and another for the front whose interior diameter is considerably larger. The dimensions of the connector elements and caps are given in inches, distinguishing them from the decimal measurements that preside on all other indications in the drawing set.

Hydrant colors are indicated using the British Standard Colour Chart: "Carnival Red" (04E56) for freshwater hydrants and "Canary Yellow" (10E55) for hydrants that draw seawater from a supply that has been used for toilet flushing since the 1950s. [7] If a cap is painted in "Mermaid" blue, the hydrant is recently installed and not yet in service; a "White" band around the base means the hydrant is connected to a trunk main—one of the large tunnels that brings treated water to reservoirs before it is distributed by gravity. A serial number in 75mm-high digits is placed on the trunk of the pedestal facing the street. A "V-shaped arrow" on top of its head points toward the first gate valve so fire crew quickly know where to release water. On the back of the hydrant is an "H" dimension that indicates the perpendicular distance to the water supply main; and a "D" dimension that indicates its depth.

"Swan neck" hydrants are installed on water distribution mains that are too small to provide pressure for round-heads. They can also supplement a main hydrant. Swan necks comprise a single 80mm galvanized iron pipe projecting from the sidewalk. The tube bends at the top to form an arc with a radius of 230mm. The top of the hydrant is 1,000mm from the sidewalk and its head stretches about 300mm from the axis of its vertical segment. [8]

1. Water Services Department, "Notes for the WSD Standard Drawings," 1, updated July 18, 2008, HKSARG, https://www.wsd.gov.hk/filemanager/en/content_1452/StdNotes.pdf.
2. International Standards Organization, "ISO 9001:2000," https://www.iso.org/standard/21823.html.
3. Water Services, "Notes," 1.
4. Water Services Department, "WSD 1.54: Details of Cast Iron Round Head Fire Hydrant," in *Standard Drawings, vol. 1: Mainlaying*, rev. May 22, 2015, HKSARG.
5. Water Services Department, "WSD 1.17D: Typical Arrangement of DN150 Fire Hydrant (Sheet 2 of 2)" in *Standard Drawings, Vol. 1: Mainlaying*, rev. Jun. 9, 1992, HKSARG.

6. Water Services Department, "WSD 1.17D: Typical Arrangement of DN150 Fire Hydrant (Sheet 1 of 2)" in *Standard Drawings, Vol. 1: Mainlaying*, rev. Sept. 5, 2003, HKSARG.
7. Water Services Department, "WSD 1.34B: Painting on Fire Hydrant (Sheet 3 of 3)," in *Standard Drawings, Vol. 1: Mainlaying*, rev. Nov. 20, 1995, HKSARG.
8. Water Services Department, "WSD 1.55A: Swan Neck Fire Hydrant and Cap (Type II)," in *Standard Drawings, Vol. 1: Mainlaying*, rev. Feb. 3, 2021, HKSARG.

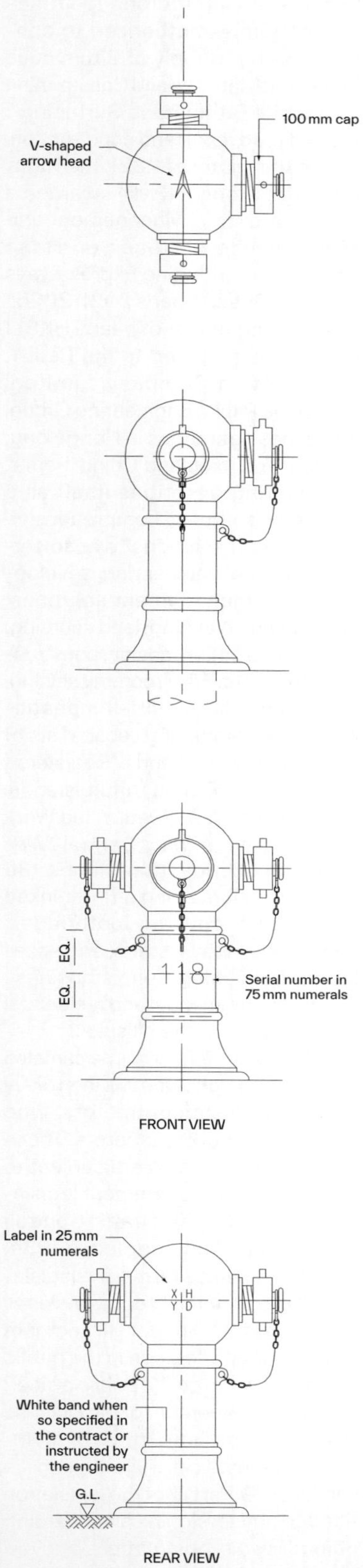

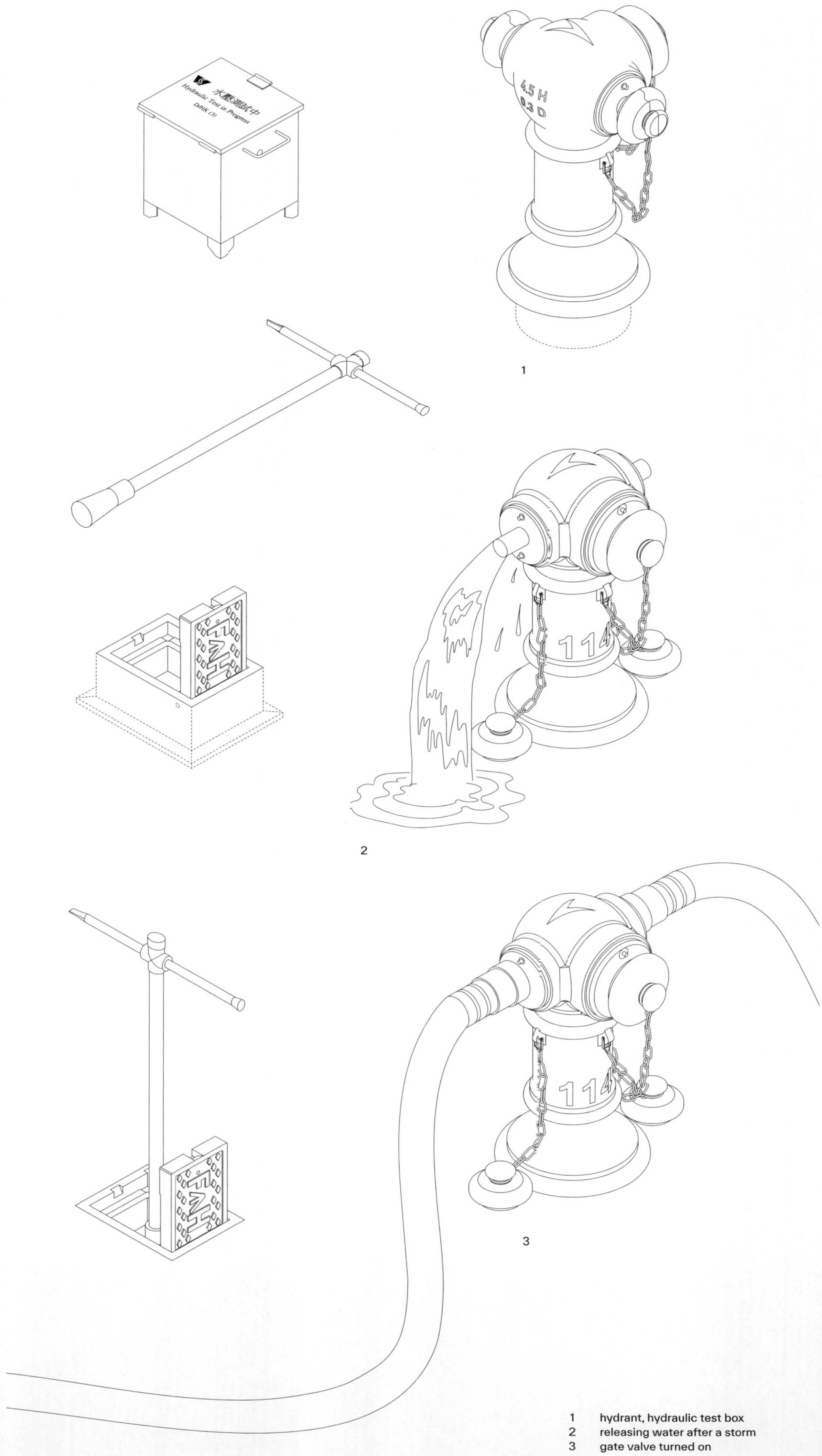

1 hydrant, hydraulic test box
2 releasing water after a storm
3 gate valve turned on

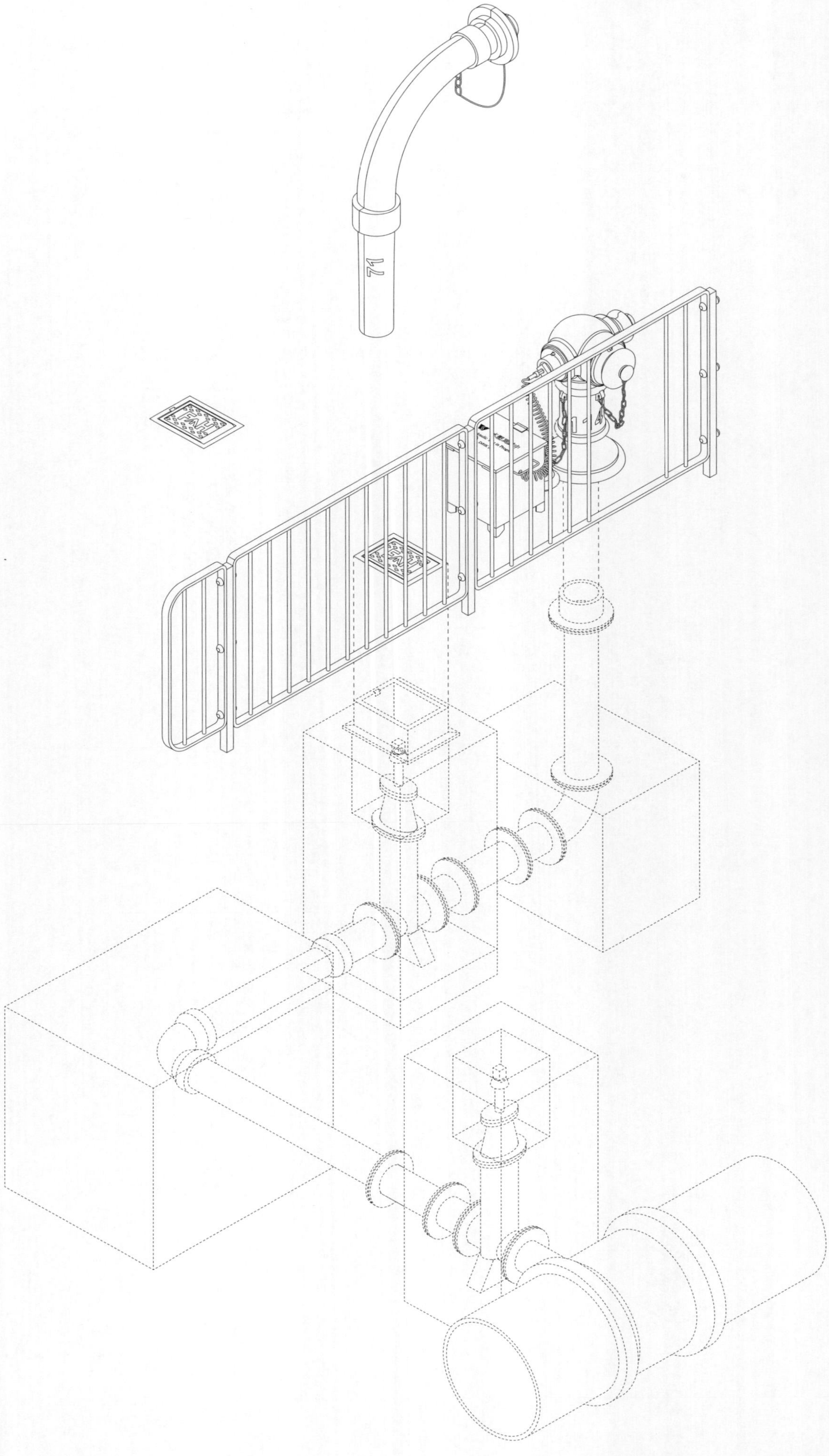

curb-side and underground hydrant configuration

CONSTRUCTION
RGWs

The Development Bureau (DB) oversees the construction sector and maintains a list of over 300 private contractors permitted to bid for public works contracts. These include "buildings," "port works," "site formation," and "roads and drainage." One hundred and seventy contractors are authorized to bid on this last category of work. [1] A separate list of "Specialist Contractors" identifies six companies authorized to contract for the "Supply of Bituminous Pavement Materials and Construction of Special Bituminous Surfacing": asphalt road repair and construction.

In the winter of 2021, the Highways Department (HyD) awarded a contract for the "Management and Maintenance of Roads on Hong Kong Island excluding Expressways and High Speed Roads 2021–2025." The winning tender of nearly HK$1.1 billion was awarded to the Paul Y. Construction Company, Limited, part of the Paul Y. Engineering Group, which has operations in Hong Kong, Macau, and mainland China. Paul Y. Engineering describes itself as a "one-stop source of comprehensive construction solutions" whose services include "engineering, development and management solutions; concept and planning; land sourcing; asset appreciation; design; construction; fitting out; E&M; commissioning; marketing and facilities management." The company's website lists 19 "Principal Bankers" and a "Registered Office" in the British Virgin Islands. From 1991 to 1995, Paul Y. led work on the kilometer-long "Central-Mid-Levels Escalator" that climbs 135 meters in height along an interlinked sequence of covered footbridges, moving walkways, stairs, and escalators, from Hong Kong's business district to commercial and residential areas further up the hillside.

The Paul Y. tender will be parceled out to contractors, who will then divvy it up among subcontractors, who then assign work to laborers. These different work teams are subject to rules set out by government legislation on "Road Traffic (Traffic Control) Regulations" first adopted in 1984. Among numerous terms, the legislation's "Interpretation" section includes definitions for "Director" (Director of Highways) and "person in the public service of the State" (a public officer; as of 2012, "a member of the Chinese People's Liberation Army"; or members of fire, medical, civil aid, or police services). [2] Part IV of the legislation titled "Lighting, signing and guarding of road works, obstructions and excavations" includes its own "Interpretation" section with a single term: the "'person responsible' in relation to any road works, obstruction or excavation means the person under whose supervision or direction the road works are carried out or the obstruction or excavation is caused or made." [3]

The text of the legislation forms the basis of the HyD's *Code of Practice for the Lighting, Signing and Guarding of Road Works*. This document notes that the "person responsible" becomes "liable to prosecution" upon failure to ensure the safety and functioning of the worksite. [4] The *Code* also indicates that the "the name of the person responsible must appear in English and Chinese on the back of each sign" on a worksite, along with the work contract number, the name of the private utility or public department undertaking the works, the name of the contractor, and a telephone number for complaints. [5] Section five addresses the "Arrangement of Traffic Management Devices for Road Works" and includes tables that advise on distance, spacing, and numbers of barriers, traffic cones, signboards, lights, etc. Fifteen drawings —some in plan, others in axonometric—illustrate typical arrangements. The person responsible is charged with making decisions about any actual on-site configuration.

Work crews comprise a construction industry labor force that the government has warned is aging and insufficient in number. Statistics maintained by the Construction Industry Council (CIC) are broken down into "skilled" and "semi-skilled workers." Between August 2020 and July 2021 there were 292 "Paving Block Layers" registered in the system, all of whom were skilled, and more than 48 percent of whom were over 60 years old. [6] The largest category of trades in the CIC database, however, is the unskilled "Registered General Worker"(RGW). RGWs comprise more than half of all registered workers. To register, an RGW pays HK$100 and must hold a "green card" attesting to completed safety training courses. Much of the work done by RGWs is daily wage labor, and not all RGWs are active within the industry on a regular basis. Road repair and excavation work carried out on city streets can comprise work teams with multiple RGWs assisting with the moving around of earth. [7]

A background brief summarizing Legislative Council discussions on these issues listed measures to attract people to the industry. These measures sought to counteract "a host of issues including wage and welfare problems, a lack of job security, sub-contracting, long working hours, poor working environment and inadequate compensation for industrial accidents." [8] The brief noted that the government's Supplementary Labour Scheme (SLS) had been enhanced to allow "imported skilled workers" across various public sector works projects, and that discussions with the CIC were targeted at attracting more women and ethnic minorities. Other government measures sought to address concerns that imported workers would depress wages and exacerbate working conditions. [9] For example, workers imported on the SLS program are required to receive a monthly wage payment. This requirement has led the Hong Kong Construction Association to describe the SLS program as "rigid" and "not suitable for compact multiple intermittent crossover trade demands of construction projects." [10]

1. Development Bureau, "Contractors," last updated, August 16, 2021, https://www.devb.gov.hk/en/construction_sector_matters/contractors/index.html.
2. Hong Kong e-Legislation, "Road Traffic (Traffic Control) Regulations (Cap. 374 section 11)," HKSARG, https://www.elegislation.gov.hk/hk/cap374G.
3. Highways Department, *Code of Practice for the Lighting, Signing and Guarding of Road Works*, Fifth Issue (2017), HKSARG, 2, https://www.hyd.gov.hk/en/publications_and_publicity/publications/technical_document/code_of_practice/index.html.
4. Ibid., 8.
5. Ibid., 12.
6. Construction Industry Council, "Demographics of Registered Workers," in *Statistics of Registered Construction Workers*, accessed August 17, 2021, http://www.cic.hk/common/StatisticofReg-Workers/dashboard.aspx?lang=en-US.
7. Hong Kong Construction Association, "Advocacy and Views," accessed August 17, 2021, https://www.hkca.com.hk/advocacy-and-views.
8. Legislative Council Secretariat, "Updated background brief on construction manpower in Hong Kong," LC Paper No. CB(1)1086/18-19(04), Ref. CB1/PL/DEV, May 21, 2019, Panel on Development, HKSARG, 6.
9. Ibid., 4–6.
10. Hong Kong Construction Association, "Advocacy and Views."

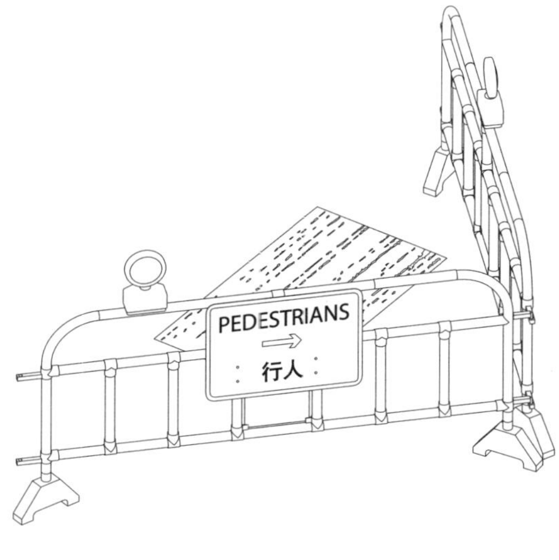

1

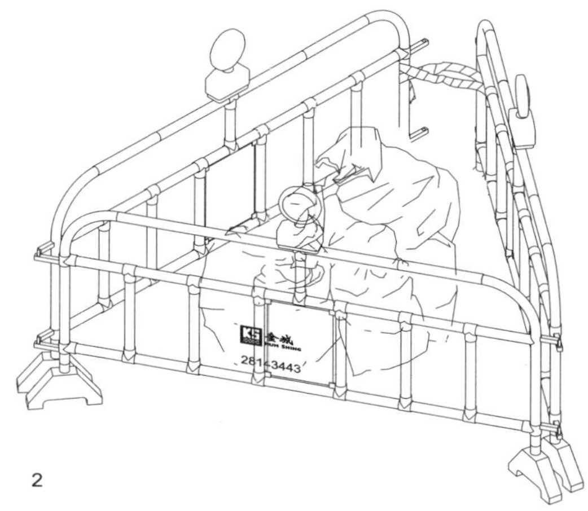

2

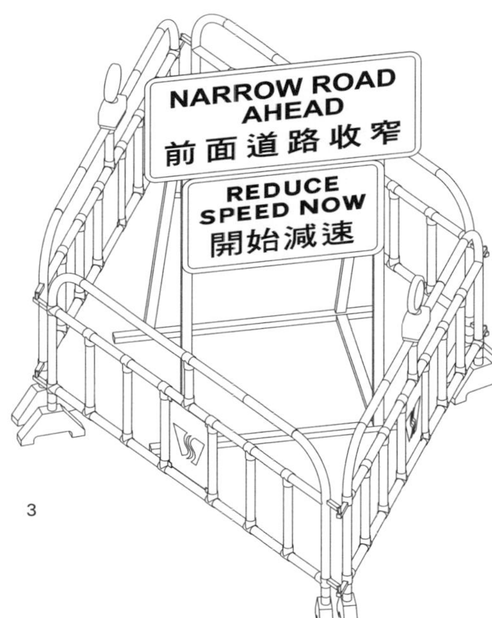

3

1 temporary enclosure for wet concrete
2 for construction material
3 for warning sign

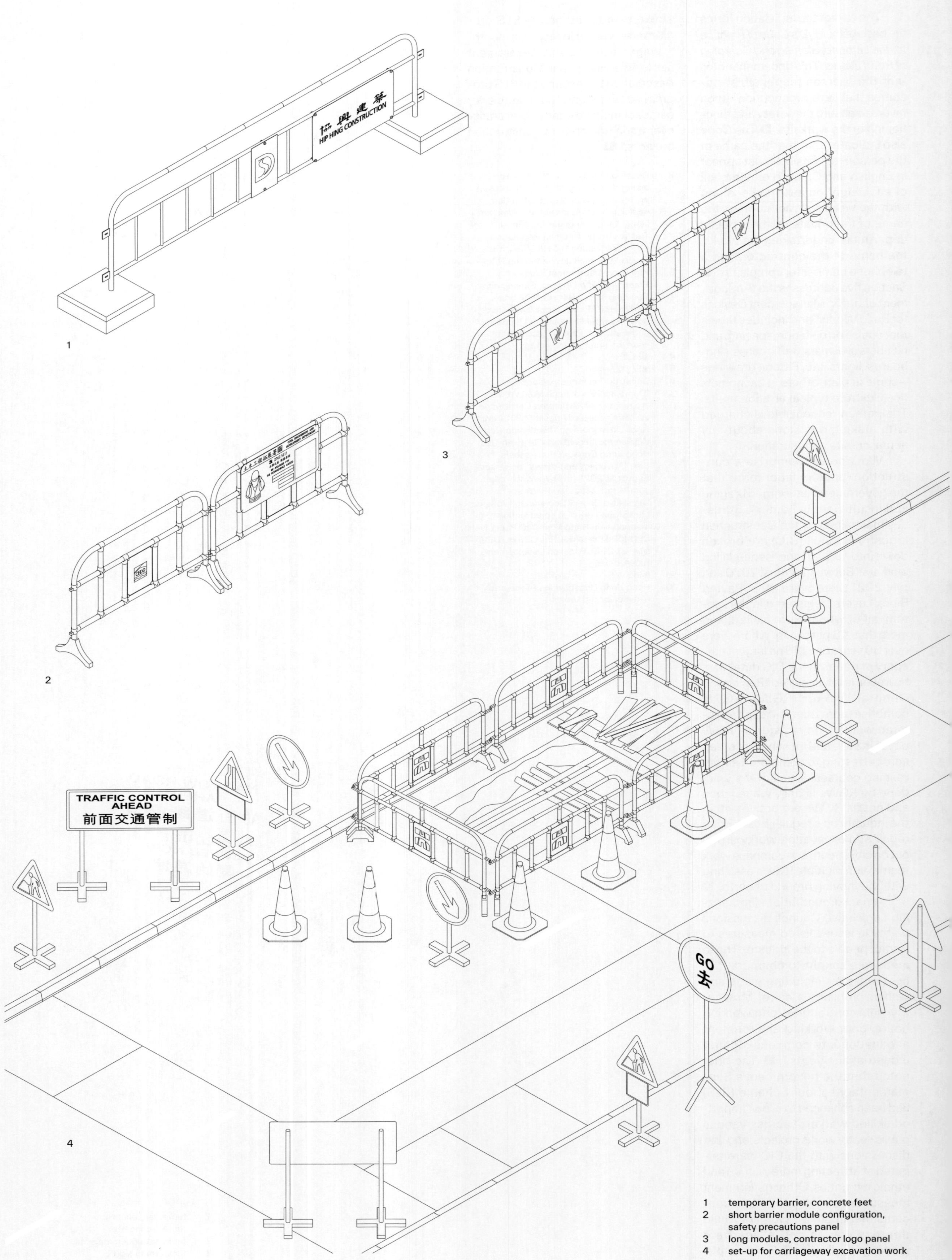

1 temporary barrier, concrete feet
2 short barrier module configuration, safety precautions panel
3 long modules, contractor logo panel
4 set-up for carriageway excavation work

Street

Drawing

誠信中心
ANYTIME FITNESS
Open 24hrs
Select
V-Power

STREET DRAWING

TYPICAL SECTIONS

In his introduction to *Streets for People* (1969), Bernard Rudofsky laments the poor condition of streets in American cities. He is flabbergasted that "not even architects and planners are interested in them beyond the call of duty." [1] His book—"*a primer for Americans*"—was more specifically addressed to New York City, where Rudofsky lived from 1935 until his death in 1988, all the while despairing the metropolis's inability to apply European urban examples. *Streets for People* brought together photos from Rudofsky's travels and writing, which were prepared for a series of exhibitions at the Museum of Modern Art, where he was a curator. The 1961 exhibition *Roads* surveyed the highway's impact on cities and culled lessons to limit damage, noting that "the true utopia may be a road for pedestrians." [2] Work gathered for the cancelled exhibition *Streets, Arcades and Galleries* (1967) formed much of the basis for *Streets for People*, extending Rudofsky's celebrated contributions to dwelling by considering "the street as a propelling force toward collective living." [3] The street was for Rudofsky a kind of public home: a possibility for being together in the city recalled from his youth and witnessed during his travels. Rudofsky's writing, while never "anti-American" in tone, did "question American habits more than those of other countries" and also explored "why people did things in a particular way." [4] Rudofsky never missed a chance to escape New York. *Streets for People* suggests he felt nothing but disappointment for the culture he continually returned to, dumbfounded by technocratic policies and laissez-faire economics that left little possibility for spaces of city life. He wrote of this failure in specific, material terms:

> street pavements represent the low-water mark of the urban environment —square miles of patched asphalt of no discernible texture and color, erratically perforated by metal grilles through which

1. Bernard Rudofsky, *Streets for People: A Primer for Americans*, 1st ed. (Garden City, NY: Doubleday, 1969), 16.
2. The Museum of Modern Art, "*Roads*, New Exhibition at Museum of Modern Art," Press Release no. 91, August 15, 1961, https://www.moma.org/momaorg/shared/pdfs/docs/press_archives/2878/releases/MOMA_1961_0093_91.pdf.
3. Ugo Rossi, "The Road and the House: The possible salvation of urban living," in *Congresso Internacional de Habitação Coletiva*, eds. Josep Maria Montaner Sustentável, Zaida Muxí, and Paulo Bruna (São Paulo: Fundação Armando Alvares Penteado, 2016), 157.
4. Wim de Wit, "Rudofsky's Discomfort: A Passion for Travel," in *Lessons from Bernard Rudofsky: Life as a Voyage*, edited by Architekturzentrum Wien (Basel: Birkhäuser Verlag AG, 2007), 117.

5. Rudofsky, *Streets for People*, 265. *Streets for People* includes an epigraph from *Architecture Without Architects* that begins, "It simply never occurs to us to make streets into oases rather than deserts." The original paragraph has an additional opening sentence that is missing from the epigraph: "Above all, it is the *humaneness* of this architecture that ought to bring forth some response in us." Rudofsky's insistence on the relationship between the material and spatial fabrication of cities and dwellings returns to this question of the "humane," in the sense of showing compassion and benevolence, a caring for each other that is another way of describing the common.

6. Ibid., 16.

> escape the stenches of the sewers, carried aloft on clouds of tepid steam. ...[S]treets are torn up in an eternal ritual, baring a netherworld of pipes and strands of cables, as ugly and mysterious as the great Cretan labyrinth. [5]

In allotting blame to architects and planners, Rudofsky noted that "on their drafting boards streets appear as nothing more striking than parallel lines." [6] In his mind, if architects didn't care to draw the street, then it was unlikely that other "technical diagnosticians" would take up the problem. Alternately, his resignation could derive from a sense that *even if* architects *did* draw the street, their diminished role in its articulation would render such effort meaningless. In either case, the reduction of the street to parallel lines suggests a territory that has been abandoned and unattended. Left blank on the page as a projected emptiness, the actually existing street was disposed through the force of habit or policy rather than as the result of a reflection enacted through drawing. The page's blankness both resulted from and produced a lazy imagination that fell back on thinking about a street given over to circulation—a surface divided into functional zones. Rudofsky's lament is a call for an active speculation to challenge this reduction. It is a call to recognize the complexity of the infrastructural elements that make place for themselves in the realm of the street. And critically, through this recognition, to acknowledge that these elements influence our relation to the city and to each other. Architecture's failure, through the incapacity of drawing, was a failure to see the street as a valuable ground for the projection of possibility.

The relation between the street and architectural concerns has not always been distant. In classical architectural treatises, prescriptions for street layouts and widths exist alongside architectural details as a continuous, linked domain of the building arts. In the 11th century, the *Yingzao Fashi* firmly encodes road building in the hands of a professionalized guild system of craftsmen that links these activities to the state's control of development. Where roads were earlier built by "unpaid labor," the move to standardize and regulate their construction in the hands of artisan families suggests their importance as resource-intensive infrastructures. [7] Also from the 10th to the 11th century, the south Indian Hindu treatise the *Mayamatam* describes the disposition and naming of streets for cities and villages. Streets become part of a larger cosmology that regulates social and infrastructural relations through measure and adjacency. [8] Leonardo da Vinci's sketches for an ideal city, and Andrea Palladio's plan view showing a tripartite division of the street, are other examples of the street as a realm of concern: in the first as an infrastructure, and in the second in relation to its elements. [9] Drawing enters into these latter examples as an analytical and projective tool, and will become central to architecture's engagement with the street through the development of the typical section in the 18th century.

The typical section brought together the infrastructural thinking of Leonardo's sketches with Palladio's engagement with materiality. The most celebrated example appears in Pierre Patte's treatise of 1769, *Mémoires sur les objets les plus importans de l'architecture*. Patte's typical section describes subterranean voids that regulate effluvia and liberate street traffic. [10] His drawing and description contributed to machinic, anthropomorphic, and hygienic discourses that continue to influence how we speak about the city. [11] Patte's drawings pre-date sectional illustrations in popular nineteenth-century journals that linked streets to interiors, revealing correspondences between social and spatial strata: empty, wet pavements contrasting with bawdy crowds gathered in small rooms. [12] The cut through

7. Qinghua Guo, *Chinese Architecture and Planning Ideas, Methods and Techniques* (Stuttgart: Axel Menges, 2005), 90–96.
8. Bruno Dagens, *Mayamatam: Treatise of Housing, Architecture and Iconography* (New Delhi: Indira Gandhi National Center for the Arts, 1994).
9. See Éric Alonzo's comprehensive history of the road in European and North American architecture, *L'architecture de la voie: histoire et théories* (Marseille: Parentheses, 2018). For Leonardo's ideal city sketches, see Manuscript B, *Leonardo da Vinci Manuscripts*, 1485–1488, MS 2173, pp 16, 36, Library of the Institute of France, Paris. https://minerva.bibliotheque-institutdefrance.fr/. For Palladio's "Large Road Paved with Stone," see Book III, plate 1: Andrea Palladio, *The Four Books of Architecture*, trans. Richard Schofield and Robert Tavernor (Cambridge, MA: MIT Press, 2002).
10. Patte's section and its revelation of an underneath arrives at the same time as what Rodolphe el-Khoury describes as the peak of the "miasmic threat" that led to an eighteenth-century keenness for a "sanitary 'coating' of the surface." These coatings comprised "stone, plaster and even paint" that were thought to deodorize and seal in "noxious effluvia." We could understand the impulse to manage the depths through technical infrastructures as an alternative to sealing in the offending depths. See Rodolphe el-Khoury, "Polish and Deodorize: Paving the City in Late Eighteenth-Century France," *Assemblage* 31 (December 1996): 6–15.
11. See the chapter on Patte: Antoine Picon, *French Architects and Engineers in the Age of Enlightenment* (Cambridge, UK; New York: Cambridge University Press, 1992), 186–210.
12. The two referenced drawings come at the end of the first chapter. See Pierre Patte, *Mémoires sur les objets les plus importans de l'architecture: Ouvrage enrichi de nombre de Planches Gravées en taille-douce* (Paris: Pozet, 1769), 70, https://gallica.bnf.fr/ark:/12148/bpt6k5701519t.texteImage. In her study of these illustrations, Diana Periton contrasts

the street rendered the hidden city visible, revealing that social relations had a spatial organization and linking them to the infrastructural conduits undergirding the city. [13] Patte's section appeared at a moment when this analytical imagination was part of a larger effort to reconceive the city as a problem of technical management, with engineered solutions developing as a form of expertise. [14] Patte's use of the section attests to this circulation of knowledge and suggests "the presence of a real international network of savants interested in solving the problems of the urban street together." [15] This development of the city as a technical problem would soon involve increasingly specialized domains, beginning the architect's marginalization from this realm.

Patte's contribution to the technical planning of the street is sometimes summarized by a discussion of his typical section. The double-page plan that accompanies it has received less attention. [16] This plan drawing comprises an oblong portion of road that a graphic scale measures out to approximately 31×13 *pied* (9.8×4.2 meters). The street begins at a quay, intersects with a road of greater width and continues off the page. The drawing's linear proportion makes it difficult to grasp the entire scene at once. Letters stamped onto the plan's surface correspond to labels on the section and notes in Patte's text. Where the section describes how conduits underneath the street are linked to rooms within the adjacent architecture, the plan denotes buildings as

the interior crowds to the unoccupied voids of Patte's section. She compares the emptiness to early photographs of Paris from a century later: "[Charles] Marville's photograph is taken from close to ground level, with a long exposure time, capturing only that which visibly endures. As in Patte's ideal, that which circulates disappears." See Diana Periton, "The 'Coupe Anatomique': sections through the nineteenth-century Parisian apartment block," *Journal of Architecture* 22, no. 5 (2017): 948n52, https://doi.org/10.1080/13602365.2017.1351805. The unpeopled state of Patte's section "emerges as a site of orderly urban potential, promising that crowds can be both contained and rationally understood." See Emily Eastgate Brink and William M. Taylor, "Architecture and Crowd-Less Streets: Urban and Environmental Order, Absence, and Risk in Pierre Patte's Profil d'une rue (1769)," *Architectural Theory Review* 23, no. 2 (2019): 179, https://doi.org/10.1080/13264826.2019.1656267.

13. Patte's work on theater design would also have made him familiar with sectional interior representations. For example, Charles-Nicolas Cohin's 1765 *Projet d'une salle de spectacle pour un théâtre de comédie* includes sections that reveal the social classes stratified within the auditorium—each in their own small rooms—and a lateral cut through the stage that shows the void underneath. For a description of Patte's work on theater design, see Pannill Camp, "Le coup d'œil du spectateur: Spectatorial Function and Stage Space in French Theatre Design, 1760–1784," *Journal for Eighteenth-Century Studies* 32, no. 4 (2009), https://doi.org/10.1111/j.1754-0208.2009.00223.x.

14. After the great Portuguese earthquake of 1755, engineers used the typical section to demonstrate earthquake-resistant construction techniques. See: Andrew J. Tallon, "The Portuguese Precedent for Pierre Patte's Street Section," *Journal of the Society of Architectural Historians* 63, no. 3 (2004), https://doi.org/10.2307/4127976.

15. Tallon, "The Portuguese Precedent for Pierre Patte's Street Section," 374.

16. Picon includes the plan alongside the section in his chapter on Patte without commenting on the plan: Picon, *French Architects and Engineers in the Age of Enlightenment*, 199. El-Khoury includes Patte's plan as an example of the 18th century obsession with paving (See note 9): El-Khoury, "Polish and Deodorize," 31. Eric Alonzo includes both plan and section in his history of roads, and describes the logic of flows that motivates the details of the plan, Alonzo, *L'architecture de la voie*, 242–47.

a *poché*d inert mass. In one *poché*d building plan, we pass through a *porte cochère* to a courtyard fitted out with a latrine and a fountain. Another mass is cut into with two identical spaces accessed from the street: public toilets. Apart from these links to the world outside, the spaces within the architecture of the plan remain abstracted and inaccessible.

The plan describes infrastructural movements with small ruptures in the street's surface: holes designed to collect water or covered pits for the deposit of household waste. Where the oblique voids of the section perform liquid transfers, the plan describes these exchanges in a coded language: a hatch parallel to a crease at the meeting of the sidewalk and street, or dotted lines for an underground sewer and for the household pipes that feed into it. The section relies on the coincidence of the vertical axis of the page with gravity to signify its functioning. The virtualization of that performative axis, and the horizontal spread of x and y, mean that gravity's pull in the plan is latent in the code of the drawing, and activated only through its relation with the section. Where the section is syncopated by voids connected across space—each linear conduit filled with the echoing sound of its functioning—the silence of the plan is contained within the singular void of the street. Where the section manages connections between the domestic and the urban, flattening space as an instant of time, the plan speaks of a temporality outside of the well-functioning network of parts. The plan resists a flattened, technical reading and introduces the possibility of a multiplicity of unrelated events taking place over and across time, less dependent on the instant of fluvial projection that the section awaits. The typical section produces space through its potential translation into the page's depth. The plan resists that possibility. Its ideality comes from being a model or an inventory of configurations rather than its potential for repetition. The section reveals a topology: of fluids, air, and light through linked chambers. Yet the plane of the sectional drawing reveals this continuity without being coincident to it: it cuts against that smoothness. The plane of the street plan is parallel to the ground of movement. As a drawing, it extends through space in time parallel to lived experience.

The design of Patte's ideal intersection is drawn from accounts of cities in Europe and elsewhere. He attends to several aspects of streets in foreign cities, including their width, partitioning for pedestrians and traffic, and the composition of paving. Patte notes that streets in China are up to 120 *pied* (39 meters) wide and divided into three parts with pedestrians occupying a central raised lane. [17] Despite this generous width, he deems the arrangement insufficient, both because the central lane is unshaded and because pedestrians need to navigate traffic on either side of their path to reach their destination. Such assessments contribute to his plan's ultimate configuration: large paving stones defining a space for pedestrian traffic alongside buildings, and smaller pavers—offering better traction for horses—on the carriageway. The drawing's surface orchestrates the movement of people, machines, water, and refuse, suggesting how the separation of traffic was already a concern. This desire to regulate flows became ever more important to the economic functioning of the city. [18]

The circulation of goods and people that undergirds trade bracketed decisions about urban development. As traffic moved faster, the potential violence done to the body became greater, and the economic stakes more significant. With the arrival of the automobile, this trend accelerated. "Machine space" occupied an increasingly larger share of the ground and traffic engineers developed models to manage the movement of cars. [19] The street plan became a regulatory tool for enforcing a division between the prioritized movement of mechanized goods traffic, over pedestrians. Displacement between distant points (in a car) trumped the life taking place in districts and neighborhoods along that trajectory. One of the results of the technical management of the street was that drawings themselves needed to adapt. Rather than a description in which the excess of life registered as a surface teeming with description, drawings of the street became an "over-coded territory" in which signs and symbols notated the city as "knowable, neatly layered, and hierarchical, even though its actual expression may be chaotic and complex." [20] Traffic diagrams, flow volumes, and the isolation of infrastructural networks from their relational condition predominated. In this new, abstracted, and over-coded language, representation destroys liveliness and contingency, excluding those things that enter into conflict with its preferred narratives.

17. Patte, *Mémoires sur les objets*, 20.
18. See Alonzo's chapter on "flow": Alonzo, *L'architecture de la voie: histoire et théories*, 233-351.
19. Ronald J. Horvath, "Machine Space," *Geographical Review* 64, no. 2 (1974): 167–88, https://doi.org/10.2307/213809.
20. Cattoor and Perkins, "Re-cartographies of Landscape: New Narratives in Architectural Atlases," *The Cartographic Journal* 51, no. 2 (2014): 167.

This development provided a context for Bernard Rudofsky's pessimism and for the way architectural drawings would turn away from the street. Almost a decade after *Streets for People*, Stanford Anderson, working under the aegis of the Institute for Architecture and Urban Studies, edited a collection of essays titled *On Streets* (1978). The book included a bibliography of references classed into sixteen sections: for example, "Streets: Dark Sides," "Environmental Conditions: Noise, Wind, Light, Microclimate," and "Semiotics of Urban Space." An entry on Rudofsky's *Streets for People* notes that "it contributed to the notably extended concern with streets that appeared in the seventies," but also that it was "marred by its bitterness that America is not Europe." [21] A last section in the bibliography called "Streets: Notation Systems, Representation" lists works from Lawrence Halprin and E. T. Hall, two essays from Kevin Lynch, a special issue of *Kenchiku-Bunka* on "Street Semiology," edited by Minoru Takeyama, and the entry: "Nolli, Giambattista. Roma. (Famous map, engraved Rome, 1748)." [22] These references offer a snapshot of a disciplinary moment, each proposing descriptive methods that have since been normalized or discarded.

This last section of the bibliography also includes a chapter from the "Manual of Photographic Interpretation" published by the American Society for Photogrammetry. The chapter is titled "Photo Interpretation in Urban Area Analysis," and includes aerial photos of Peoria, Illinois drawn over with streets, rail lines, buildings, and borders. [23] It describes how to identify building types in these images and how to visualize data. The chapter prefigures contemporary "mapping" and the influence that new ways of thinking about the map, as well as the availability of visualization technologies and data sets, would have on how we draw cities. James Corner's "The Agency of Mapping" (1999) articulated this potential to "engender the re-shaping of worlds" by the "uncovering of realities previously unseen or unimagined even across seemingly exhausted grounds." [24] In this making visible, mapping opened toward a recognition that any map suppressed certain realities as it uncovered others.

21. Stanford Anderson (ed.), *On Streets*, 2nd ed. (Cambridge, MA: MIT Press, 1986), 385.
22. Ibid., 399–340.
23. James R. Wray, "Photo Interpretation in Urban Area Analysis," in *Manual of Photographic Interpretation* (Washington: American Society of Photogrammetry, 1960), 667-716.
24. James Corner, "The Agency of Mapping: Speculation, Critique and Invention," in *The Map Reader: Theories of Mapping Practice and Cartographic Representation*, eds. Martin Dodge, Rob Kitchen, and Chris Perkins (Chichester, UK: John Wiley & Sons, 2011), 213.

Corner's allusion to "seemingly exhausted grounds" suggests that what is "exhausted" is not the real itself as an object of study through drawing, but the methods used to describe it. Mapping interceded as a reproof to that exhaustion, interlacing data, scales, localizations, and images to open imaginations to relational adjacencies between distance and epochs. It visualized virtual diagrams that acted on and reproduced the world and simultaneously held out the promise that design could thread into these reified relations to remake potentials.

While mapping continues to transform drawing, the methods and technologies that inform it can also sometimes operate at a remove from that "seemingly exhausted ground." The capacity to "look close from a distance" makes it possible to analyze violence or unrest from afar or to spatialize indicators of justice and equity. [25] This actualizes an imagination of zooming introduced in the *Powers of Ten* by Charles and Ray Eames: an Earth ready for its close-up performs itself as a remote object of inquiry. [26] Reinhold Martin argues that in introducing the seemingly objective distance of scientific observation, the *Powers of Ten* "elegantly and disarmingly...domesticates unruliness" and "converts the cosmos and the microcosmos into a continuum of number." [27] Martin's ambivalence suggests the way mapping techniques smooth out shifts in point of view that make it more difficult to recognize the value of things not fitting together. This is not to say that "looking from afar" does not also incorporate other scales and techniques of investigation; instead, I want to suggest that zooming and other technologies of distance limit the way we see cities and the street in important and sometimes unquestioned ways. Digital technologies and mapping techniques allow for a mastery of scales, temporalities, and materialities that resolve multiplicity, agonism, and a "throwntogetherness" in sometimes illusory coherences where solutions are themselves not the answers. [28] They do, inevitably, also displace descriptive prerogatives that attend to different scales of relations or material attributes: a city not reduced to geo-localized data sets, satellite images, or "street-views."

25. On looking from afar, see Laura Kurgan, *Close Up at a Distance: Mapping, Technology, and Politics* (Brooklyn, NY: Zone Books, 2013); and her work on mapping justice, equity, and exclusion: the Center for Spatial Research, Columbia University, http://c4sr.columbia.edu.
26. A "rough sketch" of the film was completed in 1968. The final, better-known version was finished in 1977.
27. Reinhold Martin, *The Urban Apparatus: Mediapolitics and the City* (Minneapolis: University of Minnesota Press, 2016), 21.
28. Doreen B. Massey, *For Space* (London: Sage, 2005), 141.

Nevertheless, in the decades since mapping churned up exhausted grounds with its descriptive and projective imaginations, other architects have continued to use drawing to describe the street using orthographic projections that rely on normative architectural conventions. Allan B. Jacobs's *Great Streets* (1995) and more recently Robert Mantho's *The Urban Section* (2014) use plans and section to examine exemplary streets that, for them, hold lessons. [29] Jacobs's case studies include fifteen European and North American cities along with Beijing; the chapter "Street and City Patterns" also includes pages of figure ground plans of a wider array of cities, drawn to the same scale. Each city plan is reduced to an image of its organization. Mantho's "data sets" for *The Urban Section* include cities from around the world; the book juxtaposes city transects in plan and section with larger-scale drawings of each case study street. The plans use thick outlines for buildings and detail the ground to indicate divisions between sidewalk and carriageway. The sections show a continuity between street and ground floor. While Jacobs's book concludes with a chapter on "Making Great Streets," split into three parts that include "Requirements" and "Qualities," Mantho is less interested in identifying models than in proposing a method of analysis that brings together different types of architectural drawing. For both authors, the street is an object that can be understood through a comparative approach that sets disparate examples next to one another. Lessons of the street are primarily spatial and programmatic. Drawing operates through the reduction of the ground to zones of different dimensions, material characteristics, and programmatic appropriations. [30]

Vittorio Lampugnani's two-volume *Atlas for Urban Planning* (2018) is similar to these earlier works in its comparative approach and in the lessons it hopes to proffer by studying the street. [31] Lampugnani attends, however, to the detail, arguing that the public realm is an object of fabrication and design. The volume on European streets passes through different types—from representational, city-center

29. Allan B. Jacobs, *Great Streets* (Cambridge, MA: MIT Press, 1993); Robert Mantho, *The Urban Section: An Analytical Tool for Cities and Streets* (London: Routledge, 2015).
30. *Great Streets* and *The Urban Section* function in certain ways as "street manuals," which along with "standard drawings" are important graphic tools for the management of the street. Although recent work on graphic standards and on building manuals has contributed to a better understanding of their role in the circulation of cultures of architecture and building, the histories of how "street manuals" and "standard drawings" developed specifically in relation to ideas about the public realm remain open to further research.
31. Vittorio Lampugnani, Harald R. Stühlinger, and Markus Tubbesing, *Atlas Zum Städtebau: Stressen*, vol. 2 (Munich: Hirmer Verlag GmbH, 2019).

boulevards to suburban lanes—demonstrating how urban ideas cohere between them. Each street is drawn at three levels of closeness. The most detailed scale records paving patterns and indicates the grade of sidewalks. Drains and access hatches appear intermittently to demonstrate how these intrusions from below are resolved into the surface. The method casts urban planning as a craft that brings together the intuitions of a tacit, artistic knowledge and the procedural rigor of investigation. Drawing becomes a mode of reasoning that can resolve the problems of the city through the planning of its material, tectonic, and spatial assemblages. Reasoning first operates through observation and then by attending to the street with measure as a tool that unearths *designer-ly* logics of precision. These are exemplary spaces. The street here is controlled to the smallest detail. Exceptions to that mastery are noted to demonstrate their resolution. The din of the street's infrastructural overlaps is silenced by the well-tailored surface.

In earlier writing from the book *Hong Kong: The Aesthetics of Density* (1993), Lampugnani identifies qualities that ostensibly could distinguish Hong Kong's streets from the European exemplars in the *Atlas for Urban Planning*.

> The beauty of Hong Kong, that is to say, however undisputable and stirring, is of a totally different sort from that, for example, of a city laid out during the Renaissance. The latter corresponds to a precise political and artistic purpose, and follows a plan implemented over a long period of time; the former, on the other hand, has emerged, and continues to emerge, largely without reference to human purpose, and at best from the superimposition and conflict of various purposes. Even if not without a plan, it is still a capitulation to that which is highly complex, and thus resistant to planning. [32]

In this framing, Hong Kong stands apart from historical European cities. Its plan functions as a kind of happenstance, rather than as a willed representational figure that coalesces into a "precise political and artistic purpose."

32. Vittorio Lampugnani, *Hong Kong Architecture: The Aesthetics of Density* (Munich: Prestel, 1993), 11.

It is an accidental plan that emerges through conflict without a teleology that drives its development. Where a European city plan is the key to reading civic intention, Hong Kong is better understood by other manifestations of urban complexity that appear as by-products of less directly operable forces: "the aesthetics of density." Lampugnani describes these forces by noting that "a metropolitan organism such as Hong Kong…is an artificial product, formed by the uncheckable power of money, technology and the human imagination." [33] This reading marks out two categories of cities: one that is historical, purpose-driven and coherent, and another that is ahistorical, scattershot, and ridden with strife. Planning, and the meaningful plan, are operative only for the former. I would argue that this opposition makes us less attentive to the exclusions, accidents, and contradictions of cities in one part of the world, and, on the other hand, to the ways in which a city "resistant to planning" reflects, in its plan, very precise political and economic decisions linked to histories of exploitation, trauma, and colonial administration. The ad hoc condition of Hong Kong's streets, in that sense, does not describe a lack of human purpose, but instead is the perfect representation of a specific vision of the city that privileges certain values over others to the detriment of the civic, the shared, or the common, in every possible instance.

Lampugnani's reading of Hong Kong foregrounded the density of its architectural assemblages viewed from above or afar. More recent works examine closer to the ground, with some arguing for its very irrelevance; the diagrams of *Cities Without Ground* describe continuous pedestrian networks that comprise quasi-public, private, and commercial zones that at once serve transit, commerce, entertainment, and residential functions. [34] The smooth topology is the counterpart to Lampugnani's density: an unwilled result of economic forces stripped of any political purpose or planning. That the drawings recall diagrams found in Hong Kong's MTR stations and shopping malls speaks to the way they are reconciled to a civic life subsumed within seemingly endless consumption and connection. Other drawing projects from the recent past situate a possibility for cultural and social life within the street itself, describing how the ground affords informal appropriations that constitute a kind of minimum civic-ness. Melissa Cate Christ, in a series of projects that culminated in the book *Step Up: Hong Kong Stairs as Productive Public Spaces*, documented outdoor

33. Ibid., 12.
34. Adam Frampton, Clara Wong, and Jonathan Solomon, *Cities Without Ground: A Hong Kong Guidebook* (San Francisco: ORO Editions, 2012).

staircases as spatial figures of "extreme topography" that link to the city's history through changing practices of appropriation. [35] Axonometric drawings isolate each staircase and adjoining buildings from their context, rendering them into autonomous figures. An inventory valorizes these artifacts as remnants of the city's heritage: at once spatial, material, and intangible. The graphic designer Brian Kwok used axonometric drawing and illustration to look at the spatial tactics of street hawkers in his book *I Am a Street Ethnologist: Street Culture in Fa Yuen Street* (2016). These tactics functioned through appropriations, arrangements, and practices. Graphic description made these tactics legible. This method required embedded, everyday observation: a fieldwork concerned with human exchange as primary to the urban.

Kwok's method echoes the work of Japanese architect Kon Wajiro, whose sketches and photographs of the aftermath of the 1923 Great Kanto Earthquake began a practice of "modernology" that foregrounded human and nonhuman relations in different scales of community with chance being the "operative principle for documenting everything he encountered": from villages to urban settings. [36] This openness would influence generations of Japanese artists, architects, and urbanists, interested in the happenstance of the city. For example, The Street Observation Society (ROJO)—a group active in the mid 1980s—used drawing, photography, and text to record their observations; they wandered the city looking for "readymade 'artworks' lying latent in the streets of Tokyo." [37] The influence of this modernist history of ethno-*graphic* recording, has more recently been re-asserted in an exhibition organized at the Japan Pavilion of the 2018 Venice Biennial by Kaijima Momoyo, Laurent Stalder, and Yu Iseki. *Architectural Ethnography* brought together work from 42 international practices that share in this attitude toward drawing relations, and to some extent partake in the impulse for "documenting everything." In the exhibition catalog essay, "A Drawing Is Not a Plan," Laurent Stalder and Andreas Kalpacki distinguish these drawings from normative architectural representations. They write:

35. Melissa Cate Christ, Anita Dawood, and Stephanie Liu, *Step Up: Hong Kong Stairs as Productive Public Spaces* (Hong Kong: Mosses Books, 2018).
36. Lisa Hsieh, "Architecture's Disquieting Ghosts," *Log*, no. 41 (2017): 32, http://www.jstor.org/stable/26323713.
37. Thomas Daniell, "Just Looking: The Origins of the Street Observation Society," *AA Files*, no. 64 (2012): 60, http://www.jstor.org/stable/41762306.

> The geometrical basis of orthogonal projections allows for the extrapolation of the information they contain, making them an accurate tool for communicating a design intention. But this has never stopped architects from reaching for alternative representational techniques to suit their particular needs... These alternative kinds of drawings speak of an endless variety of "perceptual worlds" whose boundaries have to be measured and re-measured to get a fix on their individual temporal and spatial qualities. [38]

Many of the works in the *Architectural Ethnography* exhibition—including diagrams from *Cities Without Ground*—upset expectations that architectural drawings should function as facsimiles of a certain, measured reality. Instead, new modes of description register immaterial conditions, relations, and events to assert a different function for architecture that privileges the recording of life itself. The exhibition drawings include mappings from a distance, but also close-up observations. The drawings encompass an "everything" that includes the nonhuman world of animals, insects, and blades of grass, as well as the affective qualities of things strewn apart or piled together. [39]

STREET DRAWINGS

Susan Leigh Star famously described her essay "The Ethnography of Infrastructure" as "a call to study boring things." [40] To draw the street as an infrastructure of infrastructures heeds this call. This book's drawings attend to the street's "seemingly exhausted grounds" by snapping a habit of inattention. They also counter the habit of assigning activity to moving things (cars, people, electrical current), which, Keller Easterling argues, gets in the way of recognizing how "physical objects in spatial arrangements, however static, also possess an agency that resides in relative

38. Momoyo Kaijima, Laurent Stalder, and Yu Iseki, *Architectural Ethnography* (Tokyo: Totoshuppan, 2018), 15–16.
39. See for example "Maiden Survey" by Bureau A, a record of the Euromaiden demonstrations in Ukraine in 2013; "Livre Invisible: A Guidebook on Mon(s) Invisible" by Constructlab; or the floating worlds of Map Office's "Hong Kong Is Land." In Kaijima, *Architectural Ethnography*.
40. Susan Leigh Star, "The Ethnography of Infrastructure," *American Behavioral Scientist* 43, no. 3 (Nov/Dec 1999), 377–91.

41. Keller Easterling, *Extrastatecraft: The Power of Infrastructure Space* (London; Brooklyn, NY: Verso, 2014), 72.
42. Ash Amin and Nigel Thrift, *Seeing Like a City* (Cambridge, UK; Malden, MA: Polity Press, 2017), 27.
43. Ibid.
44. Momoyo Kaijima, et al., *Architectural Ethnography*, 15–16.

position." [41] The drawings could be part of Nigel Thrift and Ash Amin's "alternative science" of the city, which "concerns itself with making visible, rather than taking for granted." [42] While this science can look into "the hidden work of algorithms, machines, [and] codes behind the city's many sociotechnical systems," the drawings contribute a method of scrutinizing what is taken for granted in the street, a seeing that only drawings as a descriptive tool renders legible. [43]

In rendering this visibility, the drawings leave out appropriations of the street: pushcarts secured to a drainpipe or poles; a signboard at the edge of the sidewalk in front of a salon; plastic, water- and soil-filled bottles, cut in half and hung on railings to grow flowers; clothes on cords strung between street signs; heavy, household plants left overnight along the curb; or folding chairs stored in a corner. The chairs may belong to people who take care of the street, or to a group of elderly friends. Like other appropriations, they enable practices of the social, the civic, and the domestic. They make possible everyday events of space that comprise worlds themselves: market streets, the gatherings of domestic workers, and the watch repairmen, engravers, and shoe shiners who operate in stalls outside of metro exits. The choice to draw streets emptied of these encounters was a question about whether a description of the street's physical elements could point toward those lives despite their absence; about the capacity of drawing to make the vitality of those appropriations present, although they were missing. It was a question also about how staking out such a claim could inform an imagination of the city.

The plans are surcharged with dimension. They propose that immeasurable, relational qualities can appear despite the normalization of convention, rule, and code. In this sense, a plan is also a drawing that opens toward the "perceptual worlds" to which "alternative representational techniques" would seem to have purchase. [44] In attending to drains, pavers, hydrants, and other infrastructures of the street the drawings invert hierarchies of agency. Rather than existing as a background, these physical elements—their overlaps and configurations—become the very material of the city's production. The drawings articulate the street as a fabrication that supports or subdues forms of intelligence, affect, and relation. As descriptions, the drawings make the density of that fabrication legible.

Drawing everything or drawing things as they are, alters the negotiation that takes place between description, as a part of architectural drawing, and abstraction. The cliché that all drawing is abstract misses the point that abstraction is never total or complete, but always exists in relation to a descriptive residue—the part of visual depiction and likeness that a drawing either slips loose from or integrates. Abstraction's relation to drawing is, in this sense, one of *kind*: not of being "more abstract" or less, but about how a drawing is used to attend to certain things and not to others. What kind of abstraction do we aim at? What is ignored, simplified or exhausted? What is described in ways that attempt to reproduce likeness, or communicated with a code? What is removed from its context or situated within a field; isolated, clarified through reduction, or let spill over in a seeming mess? The drawings in this book chase after likeness; they turn toward description as an impossible program of reproducing the world—the street—in all of its liveliness.

In her study of description in modernist writing, Dora Zhang discusses its meager status, noting Willa Cather's remark that "every writer who is an artist knows that his 'power of observation' and his 'power of description,' form but a low part of his equipment." [45] She points out that this sentiment was common throughout the history of Western literature, and becomes more pronounced in the 20th century. She identifies a "narrate/describe" paradigm that led to modernist writing's dismissal of description as pure surface matter. Narration was where things happened, whereas description could be skipped over. There was a sense, as well, that the intellectual content of a literary work did not reside in blocks of descriptive prose. Zhang argues that this *setting against* of the two modes of writing misses the ways in which description and narration are imbricated one in the other. Importantly, description has the capacity to propel action and reveal intentions despite its seeming interest in the visible. Zhang counters this oppositional stasis, by arguing that for some modernist writers—Woolf, James, Proust—"the very idea of what it means to describe becomes reconceptualized such that a new standard of likeness emerges, one that breaks from visual depiction and directs us to 'see' the relations between things." [46] This break from visual depiction means that the writers "rethink

45. Dora Zhang, *Strange Likeness: Description and the Modernist Novel* (Chicago: University of Chicago Press, 2021), 18.
46. Ibid., 9.

visuality *in language*," leading to new frameworks. [47] Zhang additionally points out that for some early modernist teachers of literature, observation—description's other couple—meant "a careful and thorough inventory of details," while for others "the mark of a writer's perceptual skill was precisely the ability to 'see' what was not visible." [48] In this sense, all of these modes of perceiving and reproducing the world hinge on that question of visibility and appearance: of making what is real for us, appear, both when it is visible and when it is not.

Where drawn description bears an additional responsibility compared to the task of writing, is in its relation to the surface of the page. Despite the demonstrated futility of the tattered Borgesian map, the page of a drawing arguably remains coincident to the space that it describes. Here, Doreen Massey's call to disavow ourselves from the notion that space is a surface becomes ever more critical: to wrest our imagination of space from the horizontality of the page. In imagining that what we are drawing on the surface of the page is space itself, we exhaust space of its becoming—of its condition of always changing. We pin down space in opposition to the accepted mutability of time, making it a "safe haven from the temporal" stripped of the possibility that is necessary and inherent to the political. [49] Massey argues that maps, charts, and drawings that flatten space—while offering the chance for us to walk across them in our imagination, allowing us to locate ourselves and find our way—nevertheless represent a closed system: a "sphere of completed horizontality." [50] For Massey, space is no more a "passive surface" to be inscribed than time waits to effectuate its movements. [51]

What is space then if not a surface of inscription: the map or plan that mediates between the impression left by the ground and the projection imprinted upon it? Massey's call demands a change in our imaginative reckoning of space whose order of magnitude is not insignificant, particularly within the realm of architecture. She argues that rather than space as surface, we consider space as a multitude of trajectories that comprise practices and processes that are in a constant act of reconfiguration. These practices and processes comprise "stories-so-far": about encounters down the street, about rocks moving across continents over time, or materials forged into becoming the things around us. [52] Space as not-a-surface is a constant retelling of stories-so-far; it upholds the contingent, imagining the future as always waiting to be inscribed: politically, relationally,

47. Ibid., 15.
48. Ibid., 20.
49. Massey, *For Space*, 28.
50. Ibid., 107.
51. Ibid., 83.
52. Ibid., 189.
53. Ibid., 116.

materially. [53] This new imagination of space offers a challenge to drawing which inevitably, almost by its nature, fixes space (and time) within the limited frame of a sheet or a screen. Massey's call for space counters that stilling, flattening, and quieting down. This book is one attempt at what can only be a practice: of drawing the street (space) as a contingent openness whose trajectories usurp the hold of the page.

CA	Communications Authority
CAD	Civil Aviation Department
CCTV	Closed-circuit television
CIC	Construction Industry Council
CORD	Catalogue of Road Defects
COVID	Coronavirus disease 2019
DB	Development Bureau
DSD	Drainage Services Department
eID	Electronic identification
E&M	Electrical and mechanical
EPD	Environmental Protection Department
FEHD	Food and Environmental Hygiene Department
FNOs	Fixed network operators
GLTMS	Greening, Landscape & Tree Management Section Development Bureau
GovCloud	Government Cloud Platform
HK	Hong Kong
HKD	Hong Kong dollar
HKBN	Hong Kong Broadband Network Limited
HKSAR	Hong Kong Special Administrative Region of the People's Republic of China
HKSARG	Government of the Hong Kong Special Administrative Region
HSBC	The Hong Kong and Shanghai Banking Corporation
HyD	Highways Department
ISO	International Organization for Standardization
ISS	International Social Service
LandsD	Lands Department
LCSD	Leisure and Cultural Services Department
LED	Light-emitting diode
LEGCO	The Legislative Council of the Hong Kong Special Administrative Region
MTR	Mass Transit Railway
MTRC	MTR Corporation/Mass Transit Railway Corporation
NSL	National Security Law
OGCIO	Office of the Government Chief Information Officer
OVT	Old and Valuable Trees
PMFC	Polymer modified friction course
PPP	Public Private Partnership
QR	Quick response
RGW	Registered general worker
SLS	Supplementary Labour Scheme
SSWXP	Small-scale works excavation permits
TD	Transport Department
TMCP	Tree Management Common Platform
WSD	Water Supplies Department
XP	Excavation Permits

SECONDARY SOURCES

Abbas, M. Ackbar. *Hong Kong: Culture and the Politics of Disappearance*. Hong Kong: Hong Kong University Press, 1997.

Alonzo, Éric. *L'architecture de la voie: histoire et théories*. Marseille: Editions Parenthèses, 2018.

Amin, Ash, and N. J. Thrift. *Seeing Like a City*. Cambridge, UK: Polity Press, 2017.

Anderson, Stanford. *On Streets*. Cambridge, MA: MIT Press, 1986.

Arendt, Hannah. *The Human Condition*. Chicago: University of Chicago Press, 1958.

Belanger, Pierre. "Landscape As Infrastructure." *Landscape Journal* 28, no. 1 (2009): 79–95.

Benjamin, Walter. *One-Way Street and Other Writings*. Translated by Edmund Jephcott and Kingsley Shorter. London: Verso, 1979.

Benjamin, Walter, and Rolf Tiedemann. *The Arcades Project*. Cambridge, MA: Belknap Press, 1999.

Bennett, Jane. "Powers of the Hoard." In *Animal, Vegetable, Mineral*, edited by Jeffrey Jerome Cohen, 237–70. Washington, DC: Oliphaunt Books, 2012.

- *Vibrant Matter: A Political Ecology of Things*. Durham, NC: Duke University Press, 2010.

Berlant, Lauren. "Sex in the Event of Happiness." *13th Annual Feminist Theory Workshop*, Department of Gender. Sexuality & Feminist Studies, Duke University. March 23, 2019. Video of lecture, 1:34, https://youtu.be/h7X6j0af7Bo.

- "The Commons: Infrastructures for Troubling times." *Environment and Planning D: Society & Space 34,* no. 3 (2016): 393–419.

Blomley, Nicholas K. *Rights of Passage: sidewalks and the regulation of public flow*. New York: Routledge, 2011.

Borges, Jorge Luis, and Andrew Hurley. *Collected Fictions*. Translated by Andrew Hurley. New York, NY: Viking, 1998.

Brink, Emily Eastgate, and William M. Taylor. "Architecture and Crowd-Less Streets: Urban and Environmental Order, Absence, and Risk in Pierre Patte's *Profil D'une Rue* (1769)." *Architectural Theory Review* 23, no. 2 (2019): 178–94.

Brown, Stephen, and Christine Loh. *Hong Kong: The Political Economy of Land*. Hong Kong: Civic Exchange, 2002.

Buck-Morss, Susan. *The Dialectics of Seeing: Walter Benjamin and the Arcades Project*. Cambridge, MA: MIT Press, 1989.

Butler, Judith. "Bodies in Alliance and the Politics of the Street." Paper presented at *The State of Things*. Organized by the Office for Contemporary Art (OCA) Norway. Venice, Italy. September 7, 2011. https://scalar.usc.edu/works/bodies/Judith Butler: Bodies in Alliance and the Politics of the Street | eipcp.net.pdf.

Camp, Pannill. "Le Coup D'œil Du Spectateur: Spectatorial Function and Stage Space in French Theatre Design, 1760–1784." *Journal for Eighteenth-century Studies* 32, no. 4 (2009): 493–513.

Carax, Leos, director. *Les Amants du Pont-Neuf*, 1991. 2hr. 5 min.

Cattoor, Bieke, and Chris Perkins. "Re-cartographies of Landscape: New Narratives in Architectural Atlases." *Cartographic Journal* 51, no. 2 (2014): 166–78.

Christ, Melissa Cate. "Evidence of Action: Towards an Ecology of Objects." In *Specifics: ECLAS 2013 International Conference Proceedings*, edited by Christiane Sörensen and Karoline Liedtke, 276–81. Berlin: Jovis Verlag GmBh, 2014.

Christ, Melissa Cate, and Anita Dawood. *Step up: Hong Kong Stairs as Productive Public Spaces* = 拾級：活用香港 樓梯公共場所. Hong Kong: Mosses, 2018.

Cochin, Charles Nicolas. *Projet D'une Salle De Spectacle Pour Un Théatre De Comédie*. Londres: Charles-Antoine Jombert, 1765. https://gallica.bnf.fr/ark:/12148/bpt6k97716210/f11.item.textelmage.

Corner, James. "The Agency of Mapping: Speculation, Critique and Invention." In *Mappings*, edited by Denis Cosgrove, 213–52. London: Reaktion Books, 1999.

Cruz, Marisa, Alexander Klein, and Viviana Steiner. "Sustainability Assessment of Road Marking Systems." *Transportation Research Procedia* 14 (2016): 869–75. https://doi.org/10.1016/j.trprc.2016.05.035.

Dagens, Bruno. *Mayamatam: Treatise of Housing, Architecture and Iconography*. New Delhi: Indira Gandhi National Center for the Arts, 1994.

Daniell, Thomas. "Just Looking: The Origins of the Street Observation Society." *AA Files* 64 (2012): 59–68. http://www.jstor.org/stable/41762306.

Devabhaktuni, Sony and Joanna Mansbridge. "Democracy's dislocations: Spaces of protest and the people of Hong Kong." *Public Culture* 34, no. 1 (2022).

De Wit, Wim. "Rudofsky's Discomfort: A Passion for Travel." In *Lessons from Bernard Rudofsky: Life as a Voyage*, edited by Architekturzentrum Wien, 98–125. Basel: Birkhäuser Verlag AG, 2007.

Dung, Kai-cheung. *Atlas: The Archaeclogy oof an Imaginary City*. Translated by Dung Kai-cheung, Anders Hansson, and Bonnie S. McDougall. New York: Columbia University Press, 2012.

Eames, Charles, and Ray Eames, directors. *The Powers of Ten: A Film Dealing with the Relative Size of Things in the Universe and the Effect of Adding Another Zero*, 1977. 9 min.

Easterling, Keller. *Extrastatecraft: The Power of Infrastructure Space*. London; Brooklyn, NY: Verso, 2014.

El-Khoury, Rodolphe. "Polish and Deodorize: Paving the City in Late-Eighteenth-Century France." *Assemblage* 31 (1996): 7–15.

Felson, Alexander J., and Linda Pollak. "Situating Urban Ecological Experiments in Public Space." In *Ecological Urbanism*, edited by Mohsen Mostafavi and Gareth Doherty, 352–363. Zurich: Lars Müller Publishers, 2010.

Frampton, Adam, Clara Wong, and Jonathan Solomon. *Cities without Ground: A Hong Kong Guidebook*. Novato, CA: ORO Editions, 2012.

Gałuszka, Agnieszka, and Zdzisław M. Migaszewski. "Glass Microspheres as a Potential Indicator of the Anthropocene: A First Study in an Urban Environment." *Holocene* 28, no. 2 (2018): 323–29. https://doi..org/10.1177/0959683617721332.

Graham, Stephen, and Nigel Thrift. "Out of Order." *Theory, Culture & Society* 24, no. 3 (2007): 1–25.

Guo, Qinghua. *Chinese Architecture and Planning: Ideas, Methods, Techniques*. Stuttgart: Edition Axel Menges, 2005.

Hayes, Brian. *Infrastructure: A Field Guide to the Industrial Landscape*. New York; London: Norton, 2005.

Horvath, Ronald J. "Machine Space." *Geographical Review* 64, no. 2 (1974): 167–88.

Hsieh, Lisa. "Architecture's Disquieting Ghosts." *Log* 41 (2017): 27–36.

Humphrey, N. K. "The Illusion of Beauty." *Perception* 2, no. 4 (December 1973): 429–39. https://doi.org/10.1068/p020429.

Ingold, Tim. "The Temporality of the Landscape." *World Archaeology* 25, no. 2 (1993): 152–74.

Jacobs, Allan B. *Great Streets*. Cambridge, MA: MIT Press, 1993.

Karaliotas, Lazaros and Erik Swyngedouw. "Exploring Insurgent Urban Mobilizations: From Urban Social Movements to Urban Political Movements?" In *Handbook of Urban Geography*, edited by Tim Schwanen and Ronald van Kempen, 369–82.

Edward Elgar Publishing, 2019. https://doi-org.eproxy.lib.hku.hk/10.4337/9781785364600.00037

Kaijima, Momoyo, Laurent Stalder, and Yu Iseki. *Architectural Ethnography*. Tokyo: Totoshuppan, 2018. Exhibition catalog.

Koolhaas, Rem. "Junkspace." *October* 100 (2002): 175–90.

Ku, Agnes S. "New Forms of Youth Activism – Hong Kong's Anti-Extradition Bill Movement in the Local-national-global Nexus." *Space & Polity* 24, no. 1 (2020): 111–17.

Kurgan, Laura. *Close up at a Distance: Mapping, Technology, and Politics*. Brooklyn, NY: Zone Books, 2013.

Kwok, Brian, 《我是街道觀察員 — 花園街的文化地景》 [*I am a Street Ethnologist: Street Culture in Fa Yuen Street*]. Hong Kong: Joint Publishing, 2016.

Lam-Knott, Sonia. "Carving Enclaves of Alternative Urbanisms in Hong Kong." In *Enabling Urban Alternatives*, 223–46. Singapore: Springer Singapore, 2018. https://doi.org/10.1007/978-981-13-1531-2_11.

Lampugnani, Vittorio, et al. *Atlas Zum Städtebau: Strassen*, vol. 2. Munich: Hirmer Verlag GmbH, 2019.

• *Hong Kong Architecture: The Aesthetics of Density*. Munich: Prestel, 1993.

Larkin, Brian. "Promising Forms: The Political Aesthetics of Infrastructure." In *The Promise of Infrastructure*, edited by Nikhil Anand, Akhil Gupta, and Hannah Appel, 175–202. Durham: Duke University Press, 2018.

• "The Politics and Poetics of Infrastructure." *Annual Review of Anthropology* 42, no. 1 (2013): 327–43.

Latour, Bruno. "Paris, Invisible City: The Plasma." *City, Culture and Society* 3, no. 2 (2012): 91–93.

Latour, Bruno and Émilie Hermant, "Paris Ville Invisible." *Les Annales de la recherche urbaine* 85 (1999): 58–62.

Lee, Francis. "Digital Media and Social Movements." *Architecture, Urbanism and Humanities Initiative Speaker Series*, Department of Architecture, University of Hong Kong. April 20, 2021. Video. https://www.arch.hku.hk/event_/francis-lee-李立峯/?subcat=auhi.

Lee, Kim Ming, Benny Ho Pong To, and Kar Ming Yu. "Financialization and Economic Inequality in Hong Kong: The Cost of the Finance-led Growth Regime." In *Hong Kong 20 Years after the Handover*, 127–51. Studies in the Political Economy of Public Policy. Springer International Publishing, 2017. https://doi-org.eproxy.lib.hku.hk/10.1007/978-3-319-51373-7_6.

Lepecki, André. "Choreopolice and Choreopolitics: Or, the Task of the Dancer." *TDR: The Drama Review* 57, no. 4 (2013): 13–27.

• *Singularities: Dance in the Age of Performance*. London: Routledge, 2016.

Lo, Wai Han. "Governmentality and Neoliberalism: A Study of Media Discourse on Poverty in Hong Kong." *The Journal of Poverty and Social Justice: Research, Policy, Practice* 28, no. 1 (2020): 55–78.

Loh, Christine. "The Revolution Needed to Achieve Carbon Neutrality 2050." *Architecture, Urbanism and Humanities Initiative Speaker Series*, Department of Architecture, University of Hong Kong. April 13, 2021. https://www.arch.hku.hk/event_/the-revolution-needed-to-achieve-carbon-neutrality-2050/?subcat=auhi.

Mantho, Robert. *The Urban Section: An Analytical Tool for Cities and Streets*. Abingdon, Oxon; New York: Routledge, 2015.

Martin, Reinhold. *The Urban Apparatus*. Minneapolis: University of Minnesota Press, 2017.

Martínez, Miguel A. "Street Occupations, Neglected Democracy, and Contested Neoliberalism in Hong Kong." *Social Justice* 46, no. 2/3 (2019): 101–24.

Massey, Doreen B. *For Space*. Thousand Oaks, CA: Sage, 2005.

Mattern, Shannon. "Maintenance and Care." *Places Journal* (November 2018). https://placesjournal.org/article/maintenance-and-care/?cn-reloaded=1

Meyboom, Annalisa. "Infrastructure as Practice." *Journal of Architectural Education* 62, no. 4 (2009): 72–81.

Mizuno, Totomi, Arisa Nishidate, Katsumi Tokuda, and Kunijiro Arai. "Installation Errors and Corrections in Tactile Ground Surface Indicators in Europe, America, Oceania and Asia." *IATSS Research* 32, no. 2. (January 2008): 68–80, https://doi.org/10.1016/S0386-1112(14)60210-7.

Ng, Mee Kam. "Transformative Urbanism and Reproblematising Land Scarcity in Hong Kong." *Urban Studies* (Edinburgh, Scotland) 57, no. 7 (2020): 1,452–68.

Olbrist, Hans Ulrich. "A Protest Against Forgetting." In *King of Kowloon: The Art of Tsang Tsou-Choi*, edited by David Spalding, 1–9. Hong Kong: Vermillion Art Collections, 2013.

Palladio, Andrea. *The Four Books of Architecture*. Translated by Richard Schofield and Robert Tavernor. New York: Dover Publications, 1965.

Patte, Pierre. *Memoires sur les objets les plus importans de l'architecture*. Paris: Rozet Librarie, 1769. https://gallica.bnf.fr/ark:/12148/bpt6k5701519t.texteImage.

Peckham, Robert. "Hygienic Nature: Afforestation and the Greening of Colonial Hong Kong." *Modern Asian Studies* 49, no. 4 (2015): 117–209.

Periton, Diana. "The 'Coupe Anatomique': Sections through the Nineteenth Century Parisian Apartment Block." *Journal of Architecture* 22, no. 5 (2017): 933–48.

Picon, Antoine. *French Architects and Engineers in the Age of Enlightenment*. Cambridge, UK: Cambridge University Press, 1992.

Poon, Alice. *Land and the Ruling Class in Hong Kong*. Richmond, BC: A. Poon, 2005.

Pryor, Mathew Robert. "Street Tree Planting in Hong Kong in the Early Colonial Period (1842–98)." *Journal of the Royal Asiatic Society Hong Kong Branch* 55 (2015): 33–56.

Rancière, Jacques. "Ten Theses on Politics." *Theory & Event* 5, no. 3 (2001): 1–33.

Raxworthy, Julian and Jessica Blood. *The MESH Book: Landscape/Infrastructure*. Melbourne: RMIT Publishers, 2004.

Rose, Julie. "Hong Kong's Shifting Grounds." *Log* 27 (Winter/Spring 2013): 59–66.

Rosenbaum, J. "The problem with poetry: Leos Carax," *Film Comment* 30, no. 3 (May 1994): 12–23.

Rossi, Ugo. "The Road and the House: The possible salvation of urban living." In *Congresso Internacional de Habitação Coletiva*, edited by Josep Maria Montaner Sustentável, Zaida Muxí, and Paulo Bruna, 156–61 (São Paulo: Fundação Armando Alvares Penteado, 2016).

Rudofsky, Bernard. *Streets for People: A Primer for Americans*. Garden City, NY: Doubleday, 1969.

Santos, Telma João. "On Turbulence: In between Mathematics and Performance." *Performance Research* 19, no. 5 (2014): 7–12.

Schwartz, Hillel. "Torque: The New Kinaesthetic of the Twentieth Century." In *Incorporations*, edited by Jonathan Crary and Sanford Kwinter, 70–126. New York: Zone Books, 1992.

Shannon, Kelly, and Marcel Smets. *The Landscape of Contemporary Infrastructure*. Rotterdam: NAi Publishers, 2010.

Simmel, Georg. "Bridge and Door." *Theory, Culture & Society* 11, no. 1 (February 1994): 5–10. https://doi.org/10.1177/026327694011001002.

Simondon, Gilbert. "Entretien sur la mécanologie." *Revue*

de Synthèse 130, no.1 (2009): 103–32.

- *On the mode of existence of technical objects.* Translated by Cécile Malaspina and John Rogove. Minneapolis: University of Minnesota Press, 2017.

Stalder, Laurent, and Andreas Kalpakci. “A Drawing is Not a Plan.” In *Architectural Ethnography*, edited by Momoyo Kaijima, Laurent Stalder, and Yu Iseki, 15–17. Tokyo: Totoshuppan, 2018.

Star, Susan Leigh. “The Ethnography of Infrastructure.” *The American Behavioral Scientist* 43, no. 3 (1999): 377–91.

Star, Susan Leigh, and Martha Lampland. “Reckoning with standards.” In *Standards and Their Stories: How Quantifying, Classifying, and Formalizing Practices Shape Everyday Life*, edited by Susan Leigh Star and Martha Lampland, 3–24. Ithaca: Cornell University Press, 2008.

Tallon, Andrew J. “The Portuguese Precedent for Pierre Patte's Street Section.” *Journal of the Society of Architectural Historians* 63, no. 3 (2004): 370–77.

Tennoy, Aud, Kjersti Visnes Oksenholt, Nils Fearnley, and Bryan Matthews. “Standards for Usable and Safe Environments for Sight Impaired.” *Proceedings of the Institution of Civil Engineers. Municipal Engineer* 168, no. 1 (2015): 24–31.

Terranova, Tiziana. *Network Culture: Politics for the information* age. London: Pluto Press, 2004.

The Conservancy Association Centre for Heritage. “Manhole Covers Exhibition.” April 27, 2018.http://cache.org.hk/blog/manhole_covers_ex/.

Tsang, Eric and Sampson Wong. “When in doubt, take a walk.” YouTube channel. https://www.youtube.com/c/doubtwalk/about.

Unger, Roberto Mangabeira. “The Better Futures of Archtecture.” In *Anyone*, edited by Cynthia Davidson, 28-37. New York, NY: Rizzoli, 1991.

Wilmott, Clancy. “Cities Without Ground: A Hong Kong Guidebook by Adam Frampton, Jonathan D. Solomon, and Clara Wong (review).” *Cartographica* 48, no. 3 (2013): 254–55.

Wong, Sampson. “When in doubt, take a walk: crisis, well-being and urban walks.” *Deep City: Climate Crisis, Democracy and the Digital*. Swiss Federal Institute of Technology, Lausanne and the University of Hong Kong. March 25, 2021. Zoom talk.

Wray, James R. “Photo Interpretation in Urban Area Analysis.” In *Manual of Photographic Interpretation*, 667–716. Washington, DC: American Society of Photogrammetry, 1960.

Xi Xi, and Eva Hung. *My City: A Hongkong Story*. Hong Kong: Chinese University of Hong Kong Press, 1993.

Yau, Yick Cheung Gary. 《香港道路探索 — 路牌標誌x交通設計》 [*Hong Kong Road Study: Signage & Highway Design*]. Hong Kong: Extraordinary Publishing Company/Fei Fan Publish, 2019.

Yu, Elaine. “The Anarchists of Occupy Central.” *The New Yorker*, December 10, 2014. https://www.newyorker.com/news/news-desk/original-anarchists-occupy-central.

Zhang, Dora. *Strange Likeness: Description and the Modernist Novel*. Chicago: University of Chicago Press, 2020.

Zhu Tao. “Power of the Ground.” In *The Social Imperative: Architecture and the City in China*, edited by H. Koon Wee, 164–70. Barcelona: Actar, 2017.

PRIMARY SOURCES

Aikin, John, ed. “Mr. Nash's Iron Bridge: New Patents Enrolled in the Months of February and March.” *The Monthly Magazine and British Register for 1797*, vol. 3 (London: R. Philipps, 1797): 221.

Assemblée Nationale. “Séance du jeudi 2 décembre 1875.” *Journal officiel de la République française* (Paris). December 3, 1875. Online Archive. https://gallica.bnf.fr/ark:/12148/bpt6k62103230.

Assemblée Nationale. “Séance du vendredi 3 décembre 1875.” *Journal officiel de la République française* (Paris). December 4, 1875. Online Archive. https://gallica.bnf.fr/ark:/12148/bpt-6k6210324d.

Audit Commission. “Government's efforts in managing excavation works on public roads.” *Director of Audit's reports*, no. 70, chap. 4 (April 3, 2018). https://www.aud.gov.hk/pdf_e/e70ch04.pdf.

- “Rehabilitation services provided by the Correctional Services Department.” *Director of Audit's Reports*, no. 64, chap. 8 (April 1, 2015). https://www.aud.gov.hk/pdf_e/e64ch08.pdf.

Buildings Department. “Public Open Space.” Last updated, November 25, 2021. https://www.bd.gov.hk/en/resources/codes-and-references/public-open-space/index.html.

- “Public open space: Central and Western District.” Last updated, November 25, 2021. https://www.bd.gov.hk/en/resources/codes-and-references/public-open-space/HK/dedicated_areas_HK_CW.html.

Cheng, Kris. “Hong Kong gov't deactivates functions on new lampposts amid privacy concerns.” *Hong Kong Free Press*, July 17, 2019. https://hongkongfp.com/2019/07/17/hong-kong-govt-deactivates-functions-new-smart-lamp-posts-amid-privacy-concerns/.

Cheung, Simpson. “Protest barriers a waste of water, say greens,” *South China Morning Post*, July 7, 2012. https://www.scmp.com/article/1006099/protest-barriers-waste-water-say-greens.

Civil Engineering and Development Department. *General Specifications for Civil Engineering Works*, vol. 1. 2020 edition (July 15, 2021): 12.16.

- *General Specifications for Civil Engineering Works*, vol. 2. 2020 edition (July 15, 2021): 11.16.

Construction Industry Council. “Demographics of Registered Workers.” *Statistics of Registered Construction Workers*. Interactive Database. http://www.cic.hk/common/StatisticofRegWorkers/dashboard.aspx?lang=en-US.

Da Vinci, Leonardo. “Manuscript B.” *Leonardo da Vinci Manuscripts, 1485–1488*. MS 2,173. Library of the Institute of France, Paris. https://minerva.bibliotheque-institutdefrance.fr/.

Development Bureau. “Annex A: Applications of Technologies in Tree Management.” *Urban Forestry Management Work in Hong Kong*. LC Paper No. CB(1)909/20-21(03). Legislative Council Panel on Development (May 25, 2021). https://www.legco.gov.hk/yr20-21/english/panels/dev/papers/dev20210525cb1-909-3-e.pdf.

- “Contractors.” Last updated, August 28, 2021. https://www.devb.gov.hk/en/construction_sector_matters/contractors/index.html.
- “Old and Valuable Trees.” Greening, Landscape & Tree Management Section. Last updated, April 8, 2020. https://www.greening.gov.hk/en/departments_greening_efforts/old_and_valuable_trees.html.
- “Tree Register,” Greening, Landscape & Tree Management Section. Last updated, August 16, 2021. https://www.greening.gov.hk/treeregister/map/treeIndex.aspx.

Drainage Services Department. *Sewerage Manual*, pt. 1, 3rd ed. (May 2013).

- *Stormwater Drainage Manual*, 5th ed. (January 2018).

Electrical and Mechanical Services Department. “About Us: Regulatory Services.” Last updated, April 1, 2021. https://www.emsd.gov.hk/en/about_us/vision_mission_values/regulatory_services/.

Environment Bureau. "Waste Blueprint for Hong Kong 2035." (February 2021).https://www.enb.gov.hk/sites/default/files/pdf/waste_blueprint_2035_eng.pdf.

Environment, Transports and Works Bureau. "Legislative Council Panel on Transport: Electronic Audible Traffic Signals (eATS)." LC Paper No. CB(1)1413/03-04(01) (March 2004). https://www.legco.gov.hk/yr03-04/english/panels/tp/papers/tp0423cb1-1413-1e.pdf.

Environmental Protection Department. "Information Note: Waste Reduction and Recycling Complementary Measures Launched by Environmental Protection Department and their Progress." LC Paper No. CB(1)187/20-21(01) (November 2020). https://www.legco.gov.hk/yr20-21/english/bc/bc01/papers/bc0120201116cb1-187-1-e.pdf.

- "Problems and Solutions." Last updated, May 12, 2020.https://www.epd.gov.hk/epd/english/environmentinhk/waste/prob_solutions/landfill.html.
- "Review and evaluation of the low-noise road surface programme for low-speed roads in Hong Kong, Final Report." Ulf Sandberg (March 13, 2008). https://www.epd.gov.hk/epd/sites/default/files/epd/english/environmentinhk/noise/studyrpts/files/LNRS-Mar08.pdf.

GovHK. "LCSD completes investigation of Tai Po tree pruning incident." December 1, 2017.https://www.info.gov.hk/gia/general/201712/01/P2017120100315.htm.

- "LCQ4: Public Lighting System." April 26, 2017. https://www.info.gov.hk/gia/general/201704/26/P2017042600277.htm.
- "Press Releases: AFCD rolls out wildlife-resistant refuse collection facilities (with photos)." October 24, 2019. https://www.info.gov.hk/gia/general/201910/24/P2019102300643.htm.
- "Press Releases: EPD to take over recycling bins," September 30, 2020.https://www.news.gov.hk/eng/2020/09/20200930/20200930_171427_696.html.

Gu, Mengyan. "Recycling to nowhere." *China Daily Hong Kong*, February 5, 2021. https://www.chinadailyhk.com/article/157039#Recycling-to-nowhere.

Highways Department. *Code of Practice for the Lighting, Signing and Guarding of Road Works*. Fifth Issue (2017). https://www.hyd.gov.hk/en/publications_and_publicity/publications/technical_document/code_of_practice/index.html.

- *Excavation Permit Administration Procedure*. Chap. 4, sect. 1, rev. 4.1.22: 4.1.1.https://www.hyd.gov.hk/en/publications_and_publicity/publications/technical_document/xppm/manual/.
- "HLDSDGE01-CL002J: Standard Dimensions for Public Lighting Columns." *Lighting Division Standard Drawings*, rev. June 2018.
- "HLDSDGE07-CL0053: Standard Dimensions for Smart Lamppost Column (Sheet 1 of 4)." *Lighting Division Standard Drawings*, rev. Feb. 2021.
- "HLDSDGE07-CL0057: Details of Type SL-A Bracket for Public Lighting Column." *Lighting Division Standard Drawings*, rev. Feb. 2021.
- "Hong Kong Road Network." Last updated, August 9, 2021. https://www.hyd.gov.hk/en/road_and_railway/existing/road_network/road.html.
- "H1118: Precast Concrete Kerbs (Sheet 1 of 2)." *Standard Drawings. Section 1: Roads*.
- "H1119: Precast Concrete Kerbs (Sheet 2 of 2)," *Standard Drawings. Section 1: Roads*.
- "H2104/1B: Standard Precast Profile Barrier." *Standard Drawings, Section 2: Street Furniture*, rev. Oct. 2019.
- "H2119E: Untensioned Beam Barriers with Concrete Footings for Post Spacing 4000mm (Sheet 2 of 3)." *Standard Drawings, Section 2: Street Furniture*, rev. November 2016.
- "H2130: Type 2 Railings – For Control Purposes." *Standard Drawing, Section 2: Street Furniture*, rev. June 2020.
- "H2131D: Type 2 and Type 4 Railings – Details," *Standard Drawing, Section 2: Street Furniture*, rev. June 2020.
- "H2163B: Details of Controller Plinth (Type C 2000 & C 3000 for Use on Hong Kong Island Only)." *Standard Drawings. Section 2: Street Furniture*, rev. March 2018.
- "H2186C: Fabricated Steel Recessed Cover And Frame For ATC/E&M Drawpit Opening From 400×400 To 600×600 (Sheet 2 Of 3)." *Standard Drawings, Section 2: Street Furniture*, rev. July 2010.
- "H2199C: Single Post Traffic Sign Support (Using Off-Centered Method) (Sheet 2 of 4)." *Standard Drawings. Section 2: Street Furniture,* rev. Feb. 2019.
- "H2206C: Street Name Plate With Building Numbers." *Standard Drawings. Section 2: Street Furniture*. rev. March 2018.
- "H2207: General Method of Assigning Building Number to Street Name Plates." *Standard Drawings. Section 2: Street Furniture*, rev. March 2004.
- "H2228E: Single Post Multi-Sign Support For Street Name Plates and Centre-Mounted Traffic Signs." *Standard Drawings. Section 2: Street Furniture*, rev. Feb. 2019.
- "H2300: Detachable Dome Shape Cap for Traffic Sign Post." *Standard Drawings. Section 2: Street Furniture*, rev. Feb. 2019.
- "H3158A: Mild Steel Gully Grating Type GA1-450." *Standard Drawings, Section 3: Drainage*, rev. Aug. 2016.
- "H4101: Granite Kerbs." *Standard Drawings. Section 4: Maintenance of Existing Installations Only*, rev. Jun. 1994.
- "H5118E: Tactile Pavers: Tactile Tiles / Slabs / Blocks," *Standard Drawings. Section 2: Street Furniture*, rev. May 2021.
- "H6112E: Temporary Tubulur Barrier." *Standard Drawings, Section 6: Miscellaneous*, rev. Jan. 2021.
- Research and Development Division. "Guidance Notes: Catalogue of Road Defects (CORD)." RD/GN/015B (January 2013).
- Research and Development Division. "Guidance Notes on Design and Construction of Pavements with Paving Units." RD/GN/044B (November 2020).
- Research and Development Division. "Guidance Notes on Installation of New Street Name Plates Inscribed with Building Numbers," RD/GN/031B, HKSARG (January 2006).
- Research and Development Division. "Guidance Notes on Low Noise Road Surfacing," RD/GN/011C (November 2016).
- Research and Development Division. "Guidance Notes on Road Markings," RD/GN/036A (January 2016).
- Research and Development Division. "Guidance Notes on Road Pavement Drainage Design," RD/GN/035A (February 2020).
- "Technical Circular No. 2/2017: Guidelines for the Provision and Design of Pedestrian Railings." HYD GR/1-50-1. July 10, 2017. https://www.hyd.gov.hk/en/technical_references/technical_document/hyd_technical_circulars/doc/2017/02/TC0217.pdf

Historical Laws of Hong Kong Online. "Emergency Regulations Ordinance, 1922." https://oelawhk.lib.hku.hk/items/show/1570.

- "Peak Reservation Ordinance, 1904." https://oelawhk.lib.hku.hk/items/show/942.

Hong Kong Construction Association. "Advocacy and Views." Accessed January 19, 2022. https://www.hkca.com.hk/advocacy-and-views

Hong Kong e-Legislation. "Prohibition on Face Covering Regulation." October 5, 2019. https://www.elegislation.gov.hk/hk/cap241K.

- "Road Traffic (Traffic Control) Regulations (Cap. 374 section 11)." July 2, 2021.https://www.elegislation.gov.hk/hk/cap374G.

International Standards Organization. "ISO 9001:2000." Accessed January 19, 2022. https://www.iso.org/standard/21823.html.

ISS. "Reopening Places: It's time to reopen—and rethink—your workplaces." Accessed January 19, 2022. https://www.hk.issworld.com/en.

Job Daily HK. "ISS Facility Services Limited: Senior Property Officer/ Property Officer (Job Ref: ADV/ 21/277)." December 9, 2021. https://www.jobdailyhk.com/job/issf.

Keegan, Matthew. "Hong Kong's 'cardboard grannies': the elderly box collectors living in poverty." *The Guardian*, April 24, 2018. https://www.theguardian.com/cities/2018/apr/24/hong-kong-cardboard-grannies-elderly-box-collectors-recycling-poverty.

Lands Department. "Survey and Mapping: Government Notices and Plans for Street Naming." Last update, July 30, 2021. https://www.landsd.gov.hk/en/survey-mapping/mapping/street-geographical-place-naming/street-naming.html.

Legislative Council. "Legislative Council, No. 11." March 27, 1888. Government of the Crown Colony of British Hong Kong. https://www.legco.gov.hk/1887-88/h880327.pdf.

- "Cap. 123, section 38. Building (Planning) Regulations." December 1, 2008. https://www.elegislation.gov.hk/hk/cap123F.
- "Cap. 123F. Building (Planning) Regulations." September 20, 1997. https://www.elegislation.gov.hk/hk/cap123F@1997-09-20T00:00:00.

Legislative Council Panel on Transport. "Staffing Proposal for the Walkability Project Management Office and the Regional Offices of the Highways Department." LC Paper No. CB(4)139/20-21(06). November 20, 2020. https://www.legco.gov.hk/yr2021/english/panels/tp/papers/tp20201120cb4-139-6-e.pdf.

Legislative Council Secretariat. "Report of the Bills Committee on Waste Disposal (Charging for Municipal Solid Waste) (Amendment) Bill 2018." LC Paper No. CB(1)849/19-20, Ref. CB1/BC/2/18. July 2020. https://www.legco.gov.hk/yr19-20/english/hc/papers/hc20200710cb1-849-e.pdf.

- "Updated background brief on construction manpower in Hong Kong." LC Paper No. CB(1)1086/18-19(04), Ref. CB1/PL/DEV. May 21, 2019. Panel on Development. https://www.legco.gov.hk/yr18-19/english/panels/dev/papers/dev20190528cb1-1086-4-e.pdf.

Lo, Clifford. "Hong Kong applies simple solution amid elaborate security plans for Xi Jinping's visit." *South China Morning Post*, June 28, 2017. https://www.scmp.com/news/hongkong/politics/article/2100347/hong-kong-applies-simple-solution-amid-elaborate-security.

Magramo, Kathleen. "Hong Kong waste charging scheme dumped as time runs out on long-delayed bill." *South China Morning Post*, June 22, 2020. https://www.scmp.com/news/hong-kong/health-environment/article/3090115/hong-kong-waste-charging-scheme-dumped-time-runs.

Nash, John. "Specification of the Patent granted to Mr. John Nash, of Dover Street, St. James's, Architect." In *Repertory of Arts and Manufactures*, vol VI, 361–67. London: Philosophical Societies of All Nations, 1797.

Ockenden, James. "Surprise Railing Deployment Ends Crossing Battle." *Transit Jam*, August 1, 2020. https://transitjam.com/2020/08/01/surprise-railing-deployment-ends-crossing-battle/.

- "Govt Gaslighting on Missing Soho Pedestrianisation Website, Deletes Records." *Transit Jam*. December 16, 2021. https://transitjam.com/2021/12/16/govt-gaslighting-on-missing-soho-pedestrianisation-website-deletes-records/.
- "Govt Tongue-Tied on Soho, San Po Kong Walkability Deaths." *Transit Jam*, January 6, 2022. https://transitjam.com/2022/01/06/govt-tongue-tied-on-soho-san-po-kong-walkability-deaths/.

Office of the Communications Authority. "Implementation Guidelines on Mitigating the Risk of Gas Explosion in Telecommunications Manholes." GN-14/2016. July 29, 2016. https://www.coms-auth.hk/filemanager/statement/en/upload/182/gn142016e.pdf.

Office of the Government Chief Information Officer. "Smart Lamppost 3D Model." Last updated, March 31, 2021. https://smartlamppost.ogcio.gov.hk/3DModel/index_en.html.

- "Report of the Technical Advisory Ad Hoc Committee on Multi-functional Smart Lampposts." (March 2020). https://www.ogcio.gov.hk/en/our_work/strategies/initiatives/smart_lampposts/committee/doc/CommitteeReport_en.pdf.
- "Update on Smart City Development." LC Paper No. CB (1)876/18-19(03). April 16, 2019. https://www.legco.gov.hk/yr18-19/english/panels/itb/papers/itb20190416cb1-876-3-e.pdf.

Oval Partnership. "Revitalizing Old Wanchai." Accessed January 19, 2022.https://www.ovalpartnership.com/en/work/project/Revitalizing-Old-Wanchai.

Research Office. "Food Safety and Environmental Hygiene: Statistical Highlights." Information Services Division, Legislative Council Secretariat. ISSH07/20-21. November 23, 2020.https://www.legco.gov.hk/research-publications/english/2021issh07-public-toilet-facilities-and-services-20201123-e.pdf.

Secretary of Development. "Landscape and Tree Management Work in Hong Kong." Legislative Council Panel on Development. LC Paper No. CB(1)776/17-18(01). April 4, 2018. https://www.legco.gov.hk/yr17-18/english/panels/dev/papers/dev20180227cb1-776-1-e.pdf.

Snøhetta. "Airside Hong Kong." Accessed January 19, 2022. https://snohetta.com/projects/525-airside-hong-kong.

Stanford's Geological Establishment London. "Plan of the City of Victory." 1889. In *Hong Kong Historic Maps*. Last updated, December 27, 2021. https://www.hkmaps.hk/mapviewer.html.

Sum, Lok-kei. "Hong Kong protests: government spent more than HK$66 million to repair damaged public facilities." *South China Morning Post*, June 10, 2020. https://www.scmp.com/news/hong-kong/politics/article/3088459/hong-kong-protests-government-spent-more-hk66-million.

SWARCO. "About Us." Accessed January 19, 2022. https://www.swarco.com/about-us.

The Guardian. "Hong Kong: anti-surveillance protesters tear down 'smart' lamp-post." Video. August 26, 2019. https://www.theguardian.com/world/video/2019/aug/26/hong-kong-anti-surveillance-protesters-tear-down-smart-lamp-post-video.

Tong, Elson. "Elderly woman faces up to HK$5k fine and jail after selling cardboard to domestic worker for HK$1." *Hong Kong Free Press*, June 15, 2017. https://hongkongfp.com/2017/06/15/elderly-woman-faces-hk5k-fine-jail-selling-cardboard-domestic-worker-hk1/.

The Museum of Modern Art. "Roads, New Exhibition at Museum of Modern Art." Press Release No. 91, August 15, 1961.https://www.moma.org/momaorg/shared/pdfs/docs/press_archives/2878/releases/MOMA_1961_0093_91.pdf.

Transit Jam (@Transit_Jam). "Remember those fancy new bolts Transport Department put on all the railings last year to stop people removing them with simple spanners?" *Twitter*. December 8, 2021, 7:48 a.m. https://twitter.com/Transit_Jam/status/1468472498975277056.

Transport Department. "Departmental Circular No. 2/2017: Guidelines for the Provision and Design of Pedestrian Railings." TD DS/6-5/1. July 10, 2017. https://www.hyd.gov.hk/en/technical_references/technical_document/hyd_technical_circulars/doc/2017/02/TC0217.pdf

- "Electronic Audible Traffic Signal." Last updated, April 13, 2021. https://www.td.gov.hk/en/transport_in_hong_kong/pedestrians/pedestrian_crossing_facilities/electronic_audible_traffic_signal/index.html.
- "Facilities for People with Disabilities." In *Transport Planning & Design Manual*, vol. 6, Chap. 8 (2001): 8.3.2.1.
- "Railings." In *Transport Planning and Design Manual: Highway Design Characteristics*, vol. 2, chap. 3 (2001): 3.9.2.
- "Smart Device for the Elderly and the Disabled." Last updated, April 15, 2021. https://www.td.gov.hk/en/transport_in_hong_kong/pedestrians/pedestrian_crossing_facilities/smart_device/index.html.
- *Transport Planning & Design Manual*. Hong Kong: Government Printer, 1984.

Transport for London. "Collisions Before and After the Removal of Pedestrian Railings at 70 Junctions and Crossings on the Transport for London Road Network." *Street Behavior*, Report No. SB257, Greater London Authority. July 2017. https://content.tfl.gov.uk/pedestrian-railings-removal-report.pdf.

Walk DVRC. "Railing over Railings." June 2020.https://walkdvrc.hk/upload/files/research/20200624120139_108.pdf.

Water Services Department. "Notes for the WSD Standard Drawings." Last updated, July 18, 2008. https://www.wsd.gov.hk/filemanager/en/content_1452/StdNotes.pdf.

- "WSD 1.17D: Typical Arrangement of DN150 Fire Hydrant (Sheet 1 of 2)." *Standard Drawings*, Vol. 1: Mainlaying, rev. Sept. 5, 2003.
- "WSD 1.17D: Typical Arrangement of DN150 Fire Hydrant (Sheet 2 of 2)." *Standard Drawings*, Vol. 1: Mainlaying, rev. Jun. 9, 1992.
- "WSD 1.34B: Painting on Fire Hydrant (Sheet 3 of 3)." *Standard Drawings*, Vol. 1: Mainlaying, rev. Nov. 20, 1995.
- "WSD 1.54: Details of Cast Iron Round Head Fire Hydrant." *Standard Drawings*, vol. 1: Mainlaying, rev. May 22, 2015.
- "WSD 1.55A: Swan Neck Fire Hydrant and Cap (Type II)." In Standard Drawings, Vol. 1: Mainlaying, rev. Feb. 3, 2021.

Wong, Natalie. "Hong Kong protests: security chief John Lee lays blame for water-barrier obstruction across city on 'rioters'." *South China Morning Post*, May 21, 2020. https://www.scmp.com/news/hong-kong/politics/article/3085348/hong-kong-protests-security-chief-john-lee-lays-blame-water.

Wong, Olga. "Transmission poles break rules, officials tell broadband firm." *South China Morning Post*, April 3, 2010. https://www.scmp.com/article/710435/transmission-poles-break-rules-officials-tell-broadband-firm.

World Integrated Trade Solution. "Hong Kong, China Glass microspheres; not exceeding 1mm in diameter imports by country in 2015 [-2019]." Last updated, August 14, 2021.https://wits.worldbank.org/trade/comtrade/en/country/HKG/year/2015/tradeflow/Imports/partner/ALL/product/701820.

Yuen, Chantal. "New rubbish bin design 'creating more work' for street cleaners." *Hong Kong Free Press*, June 14, 2016. https://hongkongfp.com/2016/06/14/street-cleaners-say-new-small-hole-rubbish-bins-are-creating-more-work/.

Zaha Hadid Architects. "The Henderson." Accessed January 19, 2022. https://www.zaha-hadid.com/architecture/2-murray-road/.

IMAGE CREDITS

Drawings and photographs may not be reproduced without the author's permission.

IMPRINT

Published by Applied Research and Design Publishing, an imprint of ORO Editions.
Gordon Goff: Publisher

www.appliedresearchanddesign.com
info@appliedresearchanddesign.com

Author
Sony Devabhaktuni

Lead Research Assistants
FAN Xinkai and
SOO Kwan Yau April

Research Assistants
Vernon CHANG, LEUNG Sin Tone Cynthia, SZE-TO Wai Ching Regina, SZE-TO Wai Lam Linda, and Alana TAM

Student Assistants
CHAN Shu Man Amanda, CHEN Chieh-Hsuan Jasmy, CHEUNG Hoi Ching Monia, CHOI Chung Hei Vincent, LAI Shu Fun Kevin, LI Xuechen Sigo, NG Tsing Yin Provides, and ZHU Jiqi Tod

Editorial Assistant
SOO Kwan Wo Ashley

Graphic Design
Studio Otamendi
(Manuela Dechamps Otamendi assisted by Yann Linguinou)

Copy-editing
Katherine Kinast

Proofreading
Phoebe Cowen

Project Manager
Jake Anderson

Color Separations and Printing
ORO Group Ltd.
Printed in Hong Kong SAR

Papers (Jacket)
Neobond Standard White 200g.

Font
TWK Everett
by Nolan Paparelli

AR+D Publishing makes a continuous effort to minimize the overall carbon footprint of its publications. As part of this goal, AR+D, in association with Global ReLeaf, arranges to plant trees to replace those used in the manufacturing of the paper produced for its books. Global ReLeaf is an international campaign run by American Forests, one of the world's oldest nonprofit conservation organizations. Global ReLeaf is American Forests' education and action program that helps individuals, organizations, agencies, and corporations improve the local and global environment by planting and caring for trees.

10 9 8 7 6 5 4 3 2 1
First Edition

ISBN: 978-1-954081-70-3